Progress in Rural Policy and Planning

Volume Three
1993

Progress in Rural Policy and Planning
General Editor: ANDREW W. GILG

Regional Editors:

Owen Furuseth (USA) Department of Geography, University of North Carolina, Charlotte 28223, North Carolina, USA

Andrew W. Gilg (UK) Department of Geography, University of Exeter, Exeter, EX4 4RJ, United Kingdom

Mark Blacksell and Andrew Gilg (Europe) Department of Geography, University of Exeter, Exeter, EX4 4RJ, United Kingdom

Robert S. Dilley (Canada) Department of Geography, Lakehead University, Thunder Bay, P7B 5El, Ontario, Canada

Geoff McDonald (Australasia) Institute of Applied Environment Research, Division of Environmental Sciences, Griffith University, Nathan Campus, Kessels Road, Brisbane, 4111, Australia

Progress in Rural Policy and Planning

Volume Three
1993

Edited by
Andrew W. Gilg
and
Mark Blacksell
Robert S. Dilley
Owen Furuseth
Geoff McDonald

 Belhaven Press
London and New York

*Co-published in the Americas with Halsted Press
an imprint of John Wiley & Sons, Inc.*

Belhaven Press
(a division of Pinter Publishers)
25 Floral Street, Covent Garden, London, WC2E 9DS, United Kingdom

First published in Great Britain in 1993

© The editor and contributors 1993

Co-published in the Americas by Halsted Press, an imprint of
John Wiley & Sons, Inc., 605 Third Avenue, New York, NY 10158–0012

British Library Cataloguing in Publication Data
A CIP catalogue record for this book is available from the British Library

ISBN 1 85293 1086
ISSN 0956–4187

Library of Congress Cataloging-in-Publication Data

ISBN 0 4702 1999 8 (in the Americas only)

Typeset by Acorn Bookwork, Salisbury, Wiltshire
Printed and bound in Great Britain by Biddles Ltd of Guildford and King's Lynn

Contents

List of figures   vii
List of tables   ix
List of contributors   xi
List of abbreviations and acronyms   xiii
Preface   xviii

Section I: United States of America
Introduction *Owen J. Furuseth*   3
 1 From conservation to preservation: New Deal land utilization
    projects revisited
    Michael E. Lewis   5
 2 The evolution of rural cultural resource management in the
    Boxley Valley of the Buffalo National River, 1972–92
    Kenneth Story   18
 3 Funding of disaster management and the changing structure
    of rural county budgets
    William D. Solecki   27
 4 1991–92, the year in review in US rural planning: riding
    the crest of conservation reaction?
    Mark B. Lapping and Eve Baron   45
 5 Current demographics and economic perspectives on rural
    America
    Owen J. Furuseth   57

Section II: United Kingdom
Introduction *Andrew W. Gilg*   61
 6 The Countryside Commission and the Thatcher years
    Adrian Phillips   63
 7 Progress in water management in the lowlands
    Hadrian F. Cook   91
 8 'Annual Review' of rural planning in the United Kingdom
    Andrew W. Gilg   104

Section III: Europe
Introduction: agriculture and the rural environment in Europe
Mark Blacksell   195
 9   Reforming the CAP: beyond MacSharry
    Guy M. Robinson and Brian W. Ilbery   197
10   The budgetary effects of the CAP reforms in the UK
    A.K. Copus and K.J. Thomson   208
11   Agriculture and rural areas: a 25-point declaration by the
    Permanent Assembly of the French Chambers of Agriculture
    Assemblée Permanente Chambres D'Agriculture translated by
    Mark Blacksell   219
12   The Community Structural Funds and Post-Maastricht
    cohesion
    Nelly Jazra Bandarra   221
13   Peripheral Labour Markets under pressure of change
    Lars Olaf Persson   243
14   Legislative developments in the European Community, July
    1991–June 1992
    Andrew W. Gilg   264

Section IV: Canada
Introduction *Robert S. Dilley*   285
15   Exclusive agricultural zoning in British Columbia and Quebec:
    problems and prospects
    John T. Pierce and Jacinthe Séguin   287
16   Providing post-secondary education in a remote rural area:
    the example of Northwestern Ontario
    E.R. Zimmermann and D.R. Pakulak   311
17   Canada: the rural scene
    Robert S. Dilley   319

Section V: Australasia
Introduction *Geoff McDonald*   335
18   Population resources and environment: contributions to the
    Australian debate
    K.D. Cocks   337
19   Recent developments in rural policy and planning in
    Australasia
    Geoff McDonald   361

List of figures

1.1 Land Utilization projects. Case study areas: (1) Great Plains; (2) Oregon High Desert; (3) North Carolina Piedmont   7

2.1 Buffalo National River and Boxley Valley, Arkansas   19

8.1 Percentage change in preliminary counts of population present 1981–91: districts of England and Wales   190

8.2 Percentage change in preliminary counts of population present 1981–91: districts and islands areas of Scotland   192

12.1 EAGGF Guidance Section: commitments by member in state in 1991   234

12.2 Agricultural income indicators 1, 2 and 3 for the Community from 1980 to 1991   235

13.1 The location of six clusters of labour market areas with declining population in Sweden   249

13.2 Age-group 25–44 per thousands of total population and *pro mille* females in the same age-group, 1990   251

13.3 Governmental transfers and resources for compensating regional problems   252

13.4 Population density inhabitants per square kilometre and percentage of all inhabitants in localities with more than 200 inhabitants, 1990   252

13.5 Annual population changes 1985–90, net migration and birth-death ratio, relative to total population   253

13.6 Change of employment in agriculture and forestry as a proportion of total employment, 1986–90   254

13.7 Change of employment in manufacturing industry as a proportion of total employment, 1986–90   255

13.8 Change of employment in health care and social services as a proportion of total employment, 1986–90   256

13.9 Married women with children 2–15 years   257

13.10 Females 25–50 years without post-secondary education working in public services   258

13.11 Technicians 25–34 years with university degree   259

15.1 Cities and regions within British Columbia's Agricultural Land Reserves   292

15.2 Relationship between housing starts and applications to the British Columbia Agricultural Land Commission for change of use and exclusion of land   295

15.3   The location of Saint-Constant and Saint-Philippe within the Montreal Urban Region   301

15.4   Change of use applications in agricultural zones for Saint-Constant   302

15.5   Change of use applications in agricultural zones for Saint-Philippe   303

16.1   Lakehead University off-campus centres   312

18.1   Schematic of the linkage between population growth and environmental quality   345

19.1   Area of the Mount Lofty Ranges Management Plan   379

19.2   Estimated extent and cost of land degradation problems in Western Australia   383

List of tables

3.1	County budget revenue and expenditure	33
3.2	Florida rural counties	34
3.3	County funding for disaster and hazards management	36
3.4	Selected services as percentage of total county expenditure	37
3.5	Comparison of counties with reduced and increased disaster management funding	38
3.6	Civil defense funding for counties with reduced and increased disaster management funding	39
8.1	Annual incentives under the FWPS	114
8.2	Specimen contents from First Year Report on *This Common Inheritance* on 'Countryside and Wildlife'	128
8.3	Specimen contents for 'Land Use and Planning'	130
8.4	Expenditure plans for rural planning	132
8.5	The May reforms to the CAP with subsequent details	143
8.6	List of new protected areas and designations	160
9.1	The MacSharry proposals	199
9.2	Reforms proposed by EC farm ministers, May 1992	201
10.1	Market support and direct subsidies to the UK arable sector in 1991 and after CAP reform	210
10.2	UK COPs and set-aside area, and compensation expenditure, after CAP reform	210
10.3	Market support for beef, 1991, and post-reform	211
10.4	Beef Special Premium payments in the UK, 1991, and post-reform	212
10.5	Suckler Cow Premium payments in the UK, 1991, and post-reform	213
10.6	Net change in expenditure on the UK beef sector	214
10.7	Overall EC budgetary impact of CAP reform in the UK	215
12.1	Structural Funds, breakdown by objective	222
12.2	Financial outlook 1987–97	222
12.3	Gross Domestic Product at current market prices per head of population	224
12.4	Disparities in GDP per inhabitant between the regions of the Community 1980–89	226
12.5	Community Structural Funds	227

12.6 EAGGF Guidance Section: breakdown of commitments by
scheme, 1987–91   236
12.7 EAGGF Guidance Section: breakdown of commitments by
member state, 1987–91   237
12.8 Indices of real net value added at factor cost, per AWU,
from 1973 to 1991   238
12.9 Relative macroeconomic importance of the CSFs and
Community Structural Funds (1989–93)   240
18.1 Two projections of Australia's population   338
19.1 Indicators of rural economic conditions in Australia, 1980–
92   362
19.2 The draft National Forest Policy—key elements   367
19.3 ESD priorities for agriculture   370
19.4 Some recent policy initiatives relevant to rural areas in
Queensland   387
19.5 Comparison of New Zealand's meat and dairy industries   391

List of contributors

Assemblée Permanente Chambres D'Agriculture, 9 Avenue Georges V, 75008, Paris, France.

Nelly Jazra Bandarra, Commission des Communautes Européennes, Rue de la Loi 120, b-1049, Brussels, Belgium.

Eve Baron, Department of Urban Planning, The Bloustein School of Planning and Public Policy, Rutgers, the State University of New Jersey, New Brunswick, NJ 08903, USA.

Mark Blacksell, Department of Geography, University of Exeter, EX4 4RJ, Exeter, United Kingdom.

K.D. Cocks, CSIRO Division of Wildlife and Ecology, Canberra, Australian Capital Territories, Australia.

Hadrian F. Cook, Wye College, Wye, Ashford, Kent, TN25 5AH.

Andrew Copus, Department of Economics, Scottish Agricultural College, Aberdeen, Scotland.

Robert S. Dilley, Department of Geography, Lakehead University, Thunder Bay, Ontario, P7B 5E1, Canada.

Andrew W. Gilg, Department of Geography, Department of Geography, University of Exeter, Exeter, EX4 4RJ, United Kingdom.

Brian W. Ilbery, Department of Geography, University of Coventry, CV1 5FB, United Kingdom.

Mark B. Lapping, Dean, The Bloustein School of Planning and Public Policy, Rutgers, the State University of New Jersey, New Brunswick, NJ 08903, USA.

Michael E. Lewis, Department of Geography, University of North Carolina at Greensboro, North Carolina, NC 27412, USA.

Geoff McDonald, Institute of Applied Environmental Research, Division of Environmental Sciences, Nathan Campus, Kessels Road, Brisbane, Queensland, 4111, Australia.

Lars Olaf Perrson, Research Group on Regional Analysis (FORA), Department of Regional Planning, The Royal Institute of Technology, S-10044, Stockholm.

Adrian Phillips, Department of Planning, University of Wales College of Cardiff.

D.R. Pakulak, Department of Continuing Education, Lakehead University, Thunder Bay, Ontario, P7B 5E1, Canada.

John T. Pierce, Department of Geography, Simon Fraser University, Burnaby, British Columbia, V5A 1S6, Canada.

Guy M. Robinson, Department of Geography, Drummond Street, University of Edinburgh, EH8 9XP, Scotland.

Jacinthe Séguin, Environment Canada, Solid Waste Management Division, Asticou Centre, 335–241 Cité des jeunes, Hull, Québec K1A 0H3, Canada.

William D. Solecki, Department of Geography, Florida State University, Tallahassee, FL 32306, USA.

Kenneth Story, Arkansas Historic Preservation Program, 225 E. Markham Street, Little Rock, Arkansas, AR 72201, USA.

Ken Thomson, Department of Agriculture, 581 King Street, University of Aberdeen, Aberdeen, AB9 1UD, Scotland.

E.R. Zimmermann, Department of History, Lakehead University, Thunder Bay Ontario, P7B 5E1, Canada.

Abbreviations and acronyms

Section I: USA

BLM	Bureau of Land Management
BNR	Buffalo National River
BVHD	Boxley Valley Historic District
CRP	Conservation Reserve Program
EPA	Environmental Protection Agency
EPPA	Farmland Protection Policy Act
ERS	Economic Research Service
FEMA	Federal Emergency Management Agency
LU	Land Utilization
NPS	National Park Service
OMB	Office of Management and Budget
PDR	Purchase of Development Rights
SCS	Soil Conservation Service
TDR	Transfer of Development Rights
USDA	United States Department of Agriculture
USFS	US Forest Service

Section II: UK

ADAS	Agricultural Development and Advisory Service
ALURE	Alternative Land Use and Rural Economy
AONB	Area of Outstanding Natural Beauty
BTA	British Tourist Authority
CAP	Common Agricultural Policy
CC	County Council
CCD	Countryside Commission Document
CCP	Countryside Commission Publication
CLA	Country Landowners Association
Cm.	Command
CMP	Catchment Management Plan
CPRE	Council for the Protection of Rural England
DNH	Department of National Heritage

DOE	Department of the Environment
EA	Environmental Assessment
ECU	European Currency Unit
EIA	Enviromental Impact Assessment
ERM	Exchange Rate Mechanism
ESA	Environmentally Sensitive Area
ESRC	Economic and Social Research Council
ETB	English Tourist Board
FWPS	Farm Woodland Premium Scheme
GATT	General Agreement on Tarrifs and Trade
GDO	General Development Order
GIS	Geographical Information Sytems
ha	Hectare
HC	House of Commons
HL	House of Lords
HLCA	Hill Livestock Compensatory Allowance
IDO	Interim Development Order
IMF	International Monetary Fund
LFA	Less Favoured Area
LGC	Local Government Commission
MAFF	Ministry of Agriculture, Fisheries and Food
MMB	Milk Marketing Board
MPG(N)	Mineral Policy Guidance (Note)
NCC	Nature Conservancy Council
NFU	National Farmers' Union
NNR	National Nature Reserve
NRA	National Rivers Authority
NPC	National Parks Commission
NSA	Nitrate Sensitive Areas
PAC	Public Accounts Committee
PIRPAP	Progress in Rural Policy and Planning
PPG(N)	Planning Policy Guidance (Note)
quango	quasi-autonomous non-governmental organisation
R&D	Research and Development
RSPB	Royal Society for the Protection of Birds
RTPI	Royal Town Planning Institute
RWA	Regional Water Authorities
SACTRA	Standing Advisory Committee on Trunk Road Assessment
SERPLAN	South East Regional Planning Conference
SI	Statutory Instrument
SOEND	Scottish Office Environment Department
SOS	Secretary of State
SPA	Special Protection Areas
SPZ	Source Protection Zones

SSSI	Site of Special Scientific Interest
WWF	World Wildlife Fund

Section III: Europe

ALURE	Alternative Land Use and Rural Economy
APCA	Assemblée Permanente Chambres d'Agriculture
AWU	Agricultural Work Unit
BSP	Beef Special Premium Scheme
CAP	Common Agricultural Policy
CFC	Chorofluorocarbons
CITES	Convention on the International Trade in Endangered Species
Cm.	Command
COPs	Cereals oilseeds and protein crops
CSF	Community Structural Funds
DDR	Deutsche Democratische Republik
DSP	De-seasonalisation Premium
EAGGF	European Agriculture Guidance and Guarantee Fund
ECU	European Currency Unit
EEA	European Economic Area
EIB	European Investment Bank
ERDF	European Regional Development Fund
ERM	Exchange Rate Mechanism
ERU	Expert Group on Regional and Urban Studies
ESA	Environmentally Sensitive Area
ESF	European Social Fund
FEOGA	see EAGGF
GATT	General Agreement on Tarrifs and Trade
GDP	Gross Domestic Product
GEF	Global Environment Fund
GNP	Gross National Product
ha	Hectare
HCFC	halegonated chlorofluorocarbons
IBAP	Intervention Board for Agricultural Produce
LEADER	Community Rural Development Initiative
LFA	Less Favoured Area
LIFE	Community Fund for the Environment
LMA	Labour Market Areas
MAFF	Ministry of Agriculture, Fisheries and Food
MLC	Meat and Livestock Commission
MGQ	Maximum Guaranteed Quantities
ODA	Overseas Development Administration

OECD	Organisation for Economic Co-operation and Development
SAC	Special Areas of Conservation
SCP	Suckler Cow Premium
SEK	Swedisk Krone
SPA	Special Protection Areas
t	tonnes
UNCED	United Nations Conference on Environment and Development

Section IV: Canada

ALR	Agricultural Land Reserve
BC	British Columbia
CORE	Commissioner on Resources and Environment Act
DAR	Designated Agricultural Regions
ELUC	Environment and Land Use Committee
FCC	Farm Credit Corporation
GATT	General Agreement on Tariffs and Trade
GRIP	Gross Revenue Insurance Plan
ha	hectare(s)
LU	Lakehead University
NAFTA	North American Free Trade Agreement
NDP	New Democratic Party
OECD	Organisation for Economic Co-operation and Development
PALC	Provincial Agricultural Land Commission
PI	Population Increase
PIRPAP I	Progress in Rural Policy and Planning Volume 1
PIRPAP II	Progress in Rural Policy and Planning Volume 2
RCM	Regional County Municipality
RDC	Rural Development Corporation
REDI	Rural Economic Development Initiative
UCR	Urban-Centred Region

Section V: Australasia

CALM	Conservation and Land Management (Department of)
CEPIP Act	Commonwealth Environmental Protection Impact of Proposals Act
CYPLUS	Cape York Peninsula Land Use Study
EEC	European Economic Community

EIA	Environmental Impact Assessment
EPA	Environmental Protection Agency
ESD	Ecologically Sustainable Development
GATT	General Agreement on Trade and Tariffs
MAF	Ministry of Agriculture and Fisheries (NZ)
NPWS	National Parks and Wildlife Service
NRC	Natural Resources Council
NSW	New South Wales
PPZ	Primary Production Zone
RAC	Resources Assessment Commission
SEQ2001	South East Queensland 2001
WSPZ	Water Supply Protection Zone

Preface

Progress in Rural Policy and Planning is a relatively new periodical which is published on an annual basis. Although PIRPAP, as it is known to its editors, is a new venture, rural planning afficianados will recognise that three of the editors worked on the former *International Yearbook of Rural Planning*, and one of the other two editors was a contributor. Going further back, Andrew W. Gilg, the general editor of PIRPAP, was of course the editor of the *Countryside Planning Yearbook* between 1980 and 1986, when it expanded from its UK base into the *International Yearbook*.

There is therefore some continuity between PIRPAP and its predecessors, notably in the UK section. This partly reflects the nature of the UK with its national legislature, which allows an attempt to be made to produce a comprehensive review. In the other sections, however, we are dealing either with federal systems as in Australia, Canada and the USA or with over 20 countries as in the case of Europe. The editors in these countries have therefore come up with a more flexible structure for their sections than the UK, which follows a slimmed down yearbook format.

The aims for PIRPAP are to provide a regular review of both the progress of rural policy development, and the implementation of these policies on the ground. These reviews can take three broad forms in either case: first, considered reviews of developments over a fairly long time-span, normally about 10 years; second, reviews of events over a much shorter time-span, normally two years or less, in order to provide a framework of information for those people working in one branch of rural planning who need access to information in other areas but do not have the time to research new ideas for themselves; and third, short topical articles or reviews of books or conferences which can either contribute to an ongoing debate or report on current research. PIRPAP is not meant to be a primary research journal, but rather an intermediate stage between such a journal and an abstract or yearbook type of publication. The emphasis is on 'Progress'.

The contents of the Periodical will be confined to the broad area of rural policy and planning. Rural policy is defined as legislation, government advice, government or judicial decisions involving case law or ministerial precedent, statements of policy by government organisations and the arguments of rural policy pressure groups. Rural planning is defined as the implementation of these policies on the ground via plans, land-use designations, controls, quotas, grant aid, loans, incentive schemes, capital provision and programmes of various kinds. Clearly both these activities overlap and the definitions are provided only as a guide and not as a complete or rigid list.

In a similar vein, the coverage of issues and topics is loosely defined to cover the planning of extensive land uses and social and economic provision in rural (non-urban low population density) areas on the following topics: agriculture; forestry; conservation; recreation; extractive industries; employment; transport; general land-use planning; and social issues. The areal coverage is confined to five regions of the world purely because they have a common rural structure and a set of rural planning systems which are broadly the same, thus allowing comparative work to be assessed and a broad sense of unity for papers from otherwise quite spatially far apart parts of the world.

In a reversal of normal alphabetical order, material from the five regions of the world included is presented in reverse order, namely: the USA; UK; Europe; Canada; and Australasia. The material is presented by region since it has been edited this way, rather than thematically. Comments and offers of papers can therefore be most effectively sent to the regional editors, rather than to me as general editor. In this role it remains only for me to thank all those who encouraged me to develop the *Yearbooks*, those who commented on draft proposals for PIRPAP and all those people who have worked so hard to bring the first three issues to fruition. It is now up to you, the reader, to tell us how we can improve PIRPAP and hopefully contribute to its development throughout the 1990s.

Andrew W. Gilg
Exeter
16 December 1992

Section I:
United States of America

edited by
Owen Furuseth

Introduction
Owen J. Furuseth

While no one can say with certainty what long-term impacts the 1992 Presidential Election will have on rural America, most professional observers are hopeful and optimistic that Washington will provide stronger, more positive leadership than has been evidenced over the past 12 years. The backgrounds and experience of Bill Clinton and Al Gore are unique in modern American political history, and bode well for rural America. Clinton is the long-term (12 years) governor of a disadvantaged rural state, who has struggled with a wide range of rural related afflictions. Few American political leaders have a better understanding and appreciation for rural issues like employment, health care, transportation, education and environment. While not all of Clinton's policy efforts in Arkansas have been successful, he is clearly a politician who can relate to the problems and needs of rural Americans.

Al Gore comes to the Vice-President's position with impressive credentials. He has been a US Senator from a predominantly rural Southern state. Gore's public record indicates an appreciation for rural issues. His strongest interests are in the environmental arena. During a period when 'environment' and environmental issues were not the most politically popular questions, Gore emerged as one of the most outspoken and eloquent champions of environmental causes. His book, *Earth in the Balance* (1992), presented a number of progressive solutions for global, as well as, national environmental problems. In a strategic move that apparecently backfired President Bush and Vice-President Quayle focussed vociferous attacks on Gore for his environmental positions. Bush disparagingly referred to him as 'ozone man' or 'ozone' and warned that concern over global warming would lead to economic ruin. In the aftermath of the Clinton-Gore election, federal policies emphasizing private profit at the expense of public environment are no longer the order of the day. I look forward to reporting on the Clinton-Gore rural policies over the next four years.

Appropriately, the focus of this year's Progress in Rural Policy and Planning (PIRPAP), USA section, is on rural environmental issues. The evolution and elaboration of environmental policies and plans is examined from several contexts. Michael Lewis provides a longitudinal persective on federal land management programs in marginal rural settings. The formulation of management strategies for rural cultural resources is the topic for Ken Story. Finally, Bill Solecki looks at the funding for disaster management programming in rural Florida. While each author has a separate research theme, they share the common thread of policy development and evaluation. Perhaps more importantly, each chapter raises issues and questions which challenge conventional or generally accepted principles.

Finally, Mark Lapping and Eve Barron have scoured the American legislation and planning scene and developed an insightful compendium of events and actions from the past year. Their paper is both comprehensive and thought provoking. The rebirth of growth management planning is balanced against the growing neo-conservative judicial activism of the Supreme Court. How these seemingly incompatible trends will eventually be resolved is a vexing issue. Lapping and Barron help elucidate the underlying issues.

Reference

Gore. A., 1992, *Earth in the balance, ecology and the human spirit*, Houghton Miflin, Boston

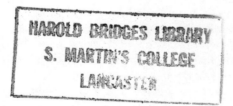

1 From conservation to preservation: New Deal land utilization projects revisited

Michael E. Lewis

US soil conservation programs launched during the 1930s provide an opportunity to examine some long-term outcomes of government planning for rural land use. Assessing long-term program outcomes can be more important than evaluating short-term intentions because of bias introduced by limited time frames, political and budgetary constraints and static considerations of place built into studies conducted soon after policy implementation. Outcomes that fail to appear until considerable time has elapsed are often left unexplored by such near-sightedness (Salamon, 1979).

New Deal soil conservation programs were themselves a long-term outcome of the early twentieth-century progressive conservation movement. Progressive conservationists believed sustainable development of natural resources was best accomplished through objective applications of scientific expertise rather than the economic interests of capitalist entrepreneurs. Between 1890 and 1910 those beliefs were translated into national policy. Large segments of public domain forest lands previously open to private acquisition were retained, so that comprehensive planning guided by the natural sciences could be implemented with the backing of federal dollars and administrative support (Pinchot, 1947; Hays, 1959).

Policy advisors to Franklin D. Roosevelt believed those same principles of faith in scientific expertise could be applied to the private agricultural land base. Their intent was to alleviate problems of accelerated soil erosion, flooding and the price depressing effects of overproduction. Such radical ideas would not have received political support and cooperation from farmers if not for farm income maintenance goals that were routinely added to conservation goals (Bennett, 1939; Kirkendall, 1966; Ervin and Ervin, 1982).

Contemporary evaluations of a wide range of New Deal soil conservation programs conclude that most did not stray far from their original goals of farm income maintenance, reducing commodity surpluses and controlling soil erosion, in that order of priority. Farmers vigorously opposed enforced regulation of private land use, preferring voluntary compliance to soil conservation practices through a mix of financial incentives (Steiner, 1990; Batie, 1985; Riebsame, 1983; Salutos, 1982; Held and Clawson, 1965).

Disregarded, or judged of little consequence, was the short-lived policy of demonstrating sustainable agricultural land use on lands acquired by the federal government from failed farmers. Evaluation of the initial intent and long-term outcomes of New Deal land utilization policy in three areas where demonstration projects were set up does however illustrate an evolving policy that has given the restoration and preservation of natural vegetation and wildlife new attention. In particular, shrinking numbers of farmers on land subject to severe erosion are being challenged at the federal level by increasing numbers of politically astute environmentalists, and environmental lobbies are demanding more environmental preservation from programs originally intended to augment farm incomes as an incentive for reducing accelerated soil erosion (Steiner, 1990; Batie, Shabman and Kramer, 1985; Crosson, 1984). Accordingly, this chapter examines the evolution of The New Deal land utilization policy, first generally, and then in three case study areas, before concluding with an evaluation of the project using the hindsight allowed by a 60-year time-space.

Origins and Intent

The Great Depression of the 1930s pushed many financially marginal farms and ranches to the brink of bankruptcy. Severe western drought following 20 years of expanding rain-fed grain farming led to accelerated wind erosion in West. Row cropped eastern hill farms, many worked by families living in chronic poverty, suffered from gully erosion, flooding and stream sedimentation (Bennett, 1939).

The deepening crisis elicited voter disillusionment with *laissez-faire* economic policies of the past. Newly elected Franklin D. Roosevelt responded with a New Deal, a policy of greater central government involvement in the general economy, aimed at correcting the past excesses of capitalism. Influenced by Webb's (1931) historical theme of adjusting to the constraints of the natural environment, *ad hoc* New Deal planning committees proposed a barrage of programs aimed at reforming rural land use and agricultural practices (Kirkendall, 1966; Clawson, 1981).

One of the most radical policy proposals called for federal acquisition, restoration and management of land suffering from severe erosion. Originally a crisis response to a temporary emergency, permanent program status came with passage of the Bankhead-Jones Farm Tenant Act in 1937. Title III of the act directed the Secretary of Agriculture to 'develop a program of land conservation and land utilization, including the retirement of lands which are submarginal or not primarily suitable for cultivation, in order thereby to correct maladjustments in land use' (Wooten, 1965, p.

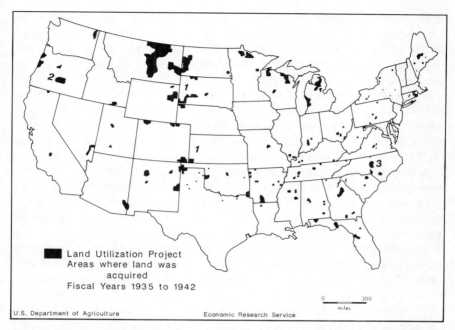

Figure 1.1   *Land Utilization projects. Case study areas: (1) Great Plains; (2) Oregon High Desert; (3) North Carolina Piedmont*

12). Responsibility for implementing the program was given to the Soil Conservation Service, itself created only two years previously.

Federal administrators purchased 11,652,062 acres between 1935 and 1942 (Wooten, 1965, p. 14). Acquired lands were grouped into patchworks of private and public tracts to form Land Utilization (LU) projects. The largest LU projects were on the Great Plains. Other areas of significant purchases included cutover forests of the Great Lakes states, semi-arid basins of the intermountain West and scattered hill farms cut from the forests stretching southeastward from New England to Oklahoma (as shown in Figure 1.1).

Project administrators intended to correct maladjustments in several ways. First private investment capital was in short supply, particularly among farmers, thus creating a market for otherwise unsalable property which would provide families on the worst land with funds to relocate elsewhere. Second a considerable number of purchases consisted of abandoned, tax delinquent tracts held by cash poor local counties. Federal acquisition thus provided a means for exchanging non-revenue generating land for cash, plus a promise that 25 per cent of any revenue accruing to the federal government from grazing leases or timber sales would be returned to its county of origin for construction and maintenance of roads and schools. Third, uneconomic farm sizes and the discontinuous patchwork of land ownership patterns had hindered farm enlargement and retirement of cultivated land to extensive grazing or timber production.

Federal intent in the West was to demonstrate appropriate land use, encourage farm diversification and reduce cash grain farming. LU purchases in those areas were consolidated into large blocks, restored to a grass or shrub cover, and made available for extensive livestock grazing (Gray, 1939; Hurt, 1985 and 1986; Lewis, 1989). East of the Mississippi River some LU land was retired from agricultural use altogether and turned over to the states for wildlife habitat restoration, public recreation, or watershed protection. Where timber production was possible federal planners retained control, intending to create jobs in forest products mills that would replace dependency on income from farming (Wooten, 1965).

The end of the US drought coincided with the onset of World War II. Normal rainfall and potential food shortages in Europe stimulated increased production of US agricultural commodities. As prospects for farm profits improved the Land Utilization projects came under increased fire from opponents of government involvement in private land use. Some Great Plains farmers particularly resented government claims that their earlier land-use decisions were maladjusted and unsustainable (Bonnifield, 1979; Worster, 1986). Acting on those feelings, Congress slashed funding for new land purchases. The fledgling Soil Conservation Service (SCS), aware of its tenuous status in the changed political and economic milieu, suspended additions to LU projects and focused on the less controversial work of reclaiming the soil and restoring a vegetative cover.

SCS control of LU projects ended in 1953 when the Eisenhower administration appraised the land reclamation work to be complete and transferred responsibility for them to either the Bureau of Land Management (BLM) or the US Forest Service (USFS). Great Plains LU projects came under USFS management and were renamed National Grasslands by the Multiple Use Act of 1961 (Argow, 1962). Eastern project lands became the foundation for new National Forests east of the Mississippi River. Western LU lands were integrated into BLM land resource management districts.

Historical summaries of LU projects on the Great Plains, Oregon High Desert and North Carolina Piedmont which illustrate successes and failures over the past half century are now presented, before The chapter concludes with an evaluation of the whole project.

Three case studies

Great Plains

News reports of an expanding Dust Bowl placed Great Plains agricultural land use in the forefront of the New Deal agenda. Dust storms had been reported on the plains before, but never of such magnitude and frequency. The *ad hoc* Great Plains committee estimated 24 million acres 'might well be acquired by the federal government . . . to protect the land and promote its best use . . .' (Great Plains Committee, 1936, p. 73). Actual implementation of the Land Utilization program on the Great Plains however fell far short of the committee's recommendations, and when purchases ended in 1942 only 4 million acres were in federal ownership in the Great Plains.

The Soil Conservation Service assumed a maternal attitude towards administering the LU lands. SCS contracted with local farmers for grassland restoration work, then leased the land to grazing associations or issued permits to individuals. Annual grazing levels were set after range conditions were evaluated by SCS personnel. Similar custodial control of grazing intensity on the National Grasslands continues under USFS management today.

The National Grasslands have achieved minor local successes in motivating a shift to fewer farmers managing larger, more diversified operations, including a mix of feed crops, livestock and cash grains (Hurt, 1986; Wallach, 1991). But shifts from cultivation to grazing on federal tracts has been offset by expanded cultivation of private land within the National Grasslands administrative districts, so that the intended overall reduction in cultivation was not achieved (Lewis, 1989).

Outside of local National Grassland districts the Great Plains remain dominated by dryland grain farms and extensive cattle ranches. As in local National Grasslands districts, widespread cropland retirement recommended by the Great Plains Committee in 1936 never materialized. The Conservation Reserve Program of the Food Security Act of 1985 has been far more successful in motivating farmers to remove land with a potential for severe erosion from cultivation. The 1985 program offers ten years of annual rental payments (averaging $48 per acre) in exchange for returning cultivated land to a natural vegetative cover (Hertz, 1988). Acreage enrolled in the CRP far exceeds that in National Grasslands. Farmers are clearly more responsive to cash payments than educational demonstrations when it comes to giving up cash grains for grass pasturage. Policy analysts are concerned, however, that much of the land idled under the Conservation Reserve will be returned to cultivated use in the late 1990s when most of the contracts expire (Steiner, 1990).

The most striking land-use change has occurred in areas where groundwater has become available for irrigation. Land formerly considered to be at the heart of a Dust Bowl has been transformed into an energy intensive center of crop irrigation, cattle feed lots and meat packing plants (Green, 1973). A suite of historical developments brought about the transformation. First, deep well turbine pumps introduced in the 1950s provided access to groundwater at depths approaching 50 metres. Second, drought resistance and other agronomic improvements have increased yields of grain sorghum (milo), corn and cotton. Third, refrigerated railcars and semi-truck trailers allow livestock fattening and processing to take place near the new feed sources, thus circumventing the need for inefficient shipments of live cattle to eastern corn belt stockyards. But despite the present prosperity, the horizon is clouded by questions of how long the non-recharging groundwater resource supporting the whole structure can be made to last (Kromm and White, 1992).

Oregon High Desert

Between 1908 and 1910 the Revised Homestead Act and rumors of a railroad crossing central Oregon's High Desert sparked one of the last land rushes in the American West. The focus of attention was some 282,000 acres of dry Pleistocene lakebed surrounding Fort Rock, a local volcanic landmark rising above the sage-covered desert plain. Hopeful dryland grain farmers, reasoning that advances into semi-arid portions of eastern Washington and central Montana could be repeated in central Oregon, eagerly grubbed out the sage brush and native grasses (Bowman, 1931). Unfortunately, the Weather Bureau did not begin recording local rainfall and temperature data until after cultivation began. After 15 years of records, annual precipitation had ranged from 6.73 to 11.22 inches, well below the requirements for good dryland yields. Cold night-time temperatures during the growing season retarded seedhead maturation and further reduced yields. When the rumored rail line failed to materialize by 1925, discouraged farmers began abandoning land in earnest. During a field reconnaissance in August 1930 Isaiah Bowman reported that all that remained of the hamlet of Fort Rock was 'two or three occupied houses besides the combined post office and general store' (Bowman, 1931, p. 108).

The Great Depression only deepened the malaise, and in 1937 the federal government assembled the High Desert Land Utilization project from land acquired from the tax delinquency rolls of Lake County or directly from bankrupt farmers. By 1942 the proportion of federal land in the Fort Rock basin had increased from 9 per cent to 65 per cent (Buckles, 1959). Within a few years the land was reclaimed by the sage and bunchgrasses. It remained the domain of range cattle until an incremental series of technological changes similar to those on the Great Plains motivated a re-evaluation of the desert's agricultural potential.

Geologists working near Fort Rock identified a large stock of groundwater beneath the ancient lakebed as early as 1925. But without a means of raising it to the surface the water was of little more than geologic interest. That situation changed when electric power lines financed under the Rural Electrification Act reached Fort Rock in 1956. The new energy source sparked interest in the potential for cash-crop cultivation using groundwater irrigation. Citing a highly variable growing season with temperatures often dipping below freezing on summer nights, the Oregon

State Agricultural Extension Service warned that dependence on cash-crops would be subject to considerable uncertainty (Castle and Dwyer, 1956).

Local ranchers generally heeded that advice until some 15 years later, when widespread application of centre pivot irrigation technology in semi-arid portions of Idaho and eastern Washington prompted a new generation of young farmers in search of cheap land to test the agricultural potential of the high desert (Lewis, 1985) Irrigated acreage in the Fort Rock Basin shot up from 6,000 acres to 74,000 acres between 1970 and 1984 as cash-crop alfalfa hay growers borrowed money to clear the sage and set up centre pivots (Lewis, 1985). Land speculators from all fifty states and several foreign countries bought up property in hopes of profiting from a modern-day land rush. The new owners demanded extended utility lines, schools, paved roads and other infrastructure from state and county agencies.

But past events began to be repeated before the anticipated new prosperity could be realized. Farmers still deeply in debt from the costs of setting up a centre pivot irrigation system were faced with rising energy costs, declining groundwater levels and irregular freezes throughout the summer months. Stagnation and decline set in as farmers tried to sell highly leveraged land to clear their debts. Many were unable to avoid bankruptcy. By 1984 a major portion of Lake County residents receiving public welfare assistance were living in the Fort Rock basin.

New Deal land utilization goals have clearly not thus attained any long-term influence on agricultural land use in the Oregon High Desert. The LU program was a short-term success at best, in that federal funds provided some immediate financial relief to Lake County government during the Great Depression. But public demonstrations of grazing use on acquired land did little to restrain motivations to experiment with cash-crop cultivation.

North Carolina Piedmont

During the 1930s, farms on the North Carolina Piedmont were made up of small tobacco, corn, or cotton fields scattered among hardwood forests and brushy pastures. Farms were small, tenancy rates high and poverty chronic. Many farms suffered from accelerated soil erosion and stream sedimentation because of row crop cultivation on the hilly slopes. Especially poor conditions were found within a small range of hills known as the Uwharrie Mountains.

New Deal planners took steps to reverse the effects of erosion and chronic poverty in the Uwharries with the combined help of the Soil Conservation Service and the US Forest Service. Federal foresters hired local work crews to replant trees, while the SCS employed local workers to curtail soil erosion by building sediment traps and field terraces on eroded fields, and by planting cover crops. In 1953 the former farm lands were combined with other forest land purchased by the Forest Service to form the Uwharrie National Forest.

Population declines and technological change have not been as dramatic in the Uwharrie National Forest as on the National Grasslands and Oregon High Desert. The principal difference is local availability of manufacturing employment. Many farmers retained their farmhouse and a plot of their best land before selling the remainder to the federal government. Those part-time farmers and their spouses, accustomed to 'fix it up, make it last' approaches to machinery, clothing and home furnishings were a ready labor pool for forest products, textile, or furniture manufacturing mills in nearby towns.

Remaining farm operations became more specialized after formation of the National Forest. Intensive chicken farming in specially designed barns replaced cultivated fields given over to the forest. Other farmers retired cultivated land to pastures for dairy operations serving the large urban population of the region. With its specialized hand labor requirements and high cash returns per acre, a strong tradition of tobacco farming remains a central feature of Piedmont agriculture. Raising tobacco remains viable largely because export markets have expanded, compensating for stagnant or declining demand in domestic markets.

Given the complex suite of variables at work it is difficult to evaluate how much of the contemporary agricultural landscape of the Uwharrie Mountains is a specific outcome of the Land Utilization program. Hart (1980) documented similar increases in forest land and shifts in manufacturing employment and agricultural operations in a Georgia Piedmont county without a land utilization project. He contended that such structural changes were typical throughout the rural Southern Piedmont since the New Deal era. If so, the changes within the former Uwharrie Land Utilization project reflect regional trends and not a local outcome of New Deal land-use planning.

Land Utilization revisited

The Land Utilization program succeeded in bringing emergency financial relief and land tenure stability to economically distressed local areas. But federal planning and land-use demonstrations clearly failed to bring about lasting regional reforms of private land use in three different areas. In that respect the former LU projects represent relics of a failed New Deal experiment in comprehensive environmental planning through public-private cooperation. Adoption and diffusion of land-use changes advocated by New Deal planners were compromised by unanticipated technological developments, cultural resistance to limiting property rights and expanding global markets for American agricultural products (White, 1986; Riebsame, 1983; Worster, 1986).

In spite of land-use reform failures, the most important contemporary outcome may prove to be unintended. When New Deal acquisitions began there were large areas of desert sage shrublands in the public domain, but most of the Great Plains and eastern hardwood forests were absent, having passed over to private ownership under various land disposal policies of the nineteenth century. Federal acquisitions returned small portions of those missing elements of America's natural landscapes to the public domain. As the end of the twentieth century approaches, federal land preservation has progressed from setting aside isolated wilderness remnants of the National Forests and National Parks to restoring functional examples of quasinatural landscapes, both public and private (Runte, 1987).

Since the New Deal era the United States has also become a highly mobile and mostly urban society. Urban and non-farm rural residents express increasing interest in the management of public lands once considered the exclusive concern of agricultural, mining, or timber industries. Current legislation directs the Bureau of Land Management and US Forest Service to develop policies that place recreation and preservation of endangered plants and animals on an equal footing with grazing, logging and mineral extraction from the public lands. Land resource management plans must be open and responsive to public comment. Environmental groups favor more low impact recreational uses and preservation of natural conditions on former LU projects, rather than emphasis on conserving soil to sustain farm incomes and stabilize agricultural land use.

The Uwharrie National Forest is the best example of increasing recreational demands. Forest Service records place the annual number of recreational visits at 100,000, but federal foresters estimate many casual visits go unrecorded. Hunting, fishing, hiking, camping and boating are major activities in the forest. Growth in manufacturing jobs has leveled off, prompting the local economic development commission to turn to promoting the recreational potential of the National Forest. Their goal is to double recreational visits by drawing from among three million urban and rural residents living within a one-hour drive to the forest. USFS is co-operating with the effort by providing $7,000,000 to purchase small privately owned lands within the National Forest, enlarge and improve campground facilities, lay out hiking trails and construct boat ramps. The Forest Service has also established a Research Natural Area within an area designated as the Birkhead Wilderness. The Natural Area protects a mature oak-hickory forest from future logging and permits basic research into forest ecosystem dynamics (Lewis, 1991).

Outcomes emphasizing natural restoration and low impact recreation, are also seen on the Great Plains National Grasslands and the Oregon High Desert. Recreational visits to those areas are below levels recorded in the Uwharrie National Forest because of physical isolation and a general lack of knowledge of their existence among the urban public. As a result, federal land managers receive less comment from non-agricultural land users in drafting management plans. In the past, the personal contact ranchers had with local federal land managers has kept livestock grazing at the top of the agenda. The pace of wildlife habitat and vegetation restoration, however, is beginning to increase as environmental groups and residents of Western towns and discover these overlooked lands. Those people value recreational uses and natural preservation over maintenance of grazing pasturage.

Fort Rock State Park and surrounding former LU lands in the Oregon High Desert are part of central Oregon's volcanic district. Amateur geologists and others are attracted to the peculiar landscape of lava flows, ice caves and cinder cones found in the geologically young volcanic area. The area also retains a number of secluded archeological sites dating back 13,000 years to a time when native people fished in the shallow waters of Fort Rock Lake. Land once purchased to create farms is now sold as recreational property to people seeking the cool desert relief from heat and humidity of the more populous valleys west of the Cascades Range. Native plants and animals are benefiting from habitat improvement efforts implemented with co-operation between the federal Bureau of Land Management and state wildlife agencies.

Recreational activity and wildlife habitat restoration efforts are also found on the National Grasslands. The Comanche National Grassland, in the southeast corner of Colorado, has set aside a lesser prairie chicken viewing area. Once on the verge of extinction because of habitat loss and overhunting, a small number of the birds have been re-established on the grassland. Their watering sites and nesting grounds have been fenced to exclude livestock. Limited numbers of visitors are permitted to observe the bird's mating rituals in their natural environment. Other native wildlife also benefit from the exclusion of livestock in limited areas of the grassland.

Similar efforts are seen to the north on South Dakota's Buffalo Gap National Grassland. There the black-footed ferret, a predator of prairie dogs, may be emerging from the brink of extinction. Under traditional grazing management prairie dogs were routinely shot or poisoned because of the animal's habit of clearing vegetation and digging burrows cattle were prone to step in and injure themselves. Other native plains wildlife, including American bison, pronghorn antelope and sharptail grouse, are increasing on the grassland and in the adjacent Badlands National Park.

One of the most visible signs of change in National Grassland management is seen in the Buffalo Gap National Grassland visitor center, scheduled for completion in early 1993. The visitor center symbolizes the move toward including outsiders in the life of the grasslands. It will be the first of its kind in the more than fifty years since New Deal planners began acquiring land on the Great Plains. Greater communication and co-operation between livestock owners and recreationists will be necessary if plans for restoring natural conditions on plains grasslands are to succeed. It is doubtful that service sector jobs in recreation or tourism can reverse population declines taking place in demographically aging National Grassland districts. But preservationists see propping up the economies of local communities as secondary to protecting and revitalizing natural environments of the public lands.

Plains ranchers and farmers particularly fear calls for a return to widespread federal acquisitions of land to create large African style wildlife preserves (Popper and Popper, 1987). Such proposals go far beyond the current size of National Grassland districts. Under present economic conditions federal offers to buy land would be in competition with private capital. In the extreme economic depression of the 1930s, with few private investors interested in buying drought blasted land, wholesale land abandonment was the only option for many plains farmers. The government stepped in and created a market where none existed. Prices paid were admittedly very low, averaging $3.65 per acre, but they did provide a small measure of financial relief until the drought broke (Wooten, 1965; Lewis, 1989). Given contemporary fiscal conservatism in Washington, however, and bipartisan efforts to reduce the federal budget deficit, a large-scale return to federal acquisitions appears doubtful in the near term.

A more modest solution would be to target federal acquisitions within the existing National Grassland administrative districts. The federal government might offer contracts to ranchers grazing livestock on the National Grasslands similar to the 10-year rental agreements now provided to farmers under the Conservation Reserve Program (Wallach, 1991). Ranchers would receive compensation in return for phasing out grazing on the National Grasslands. During the contract period landowners would have the option of selling their private holdings within the administrative district, either to the government or on the private market. The program would alleviate visitor-rancher conflicts over access to public parcels.

Most contemporary visitors know little of the origins and intent of Land Utilization projects, or current controversies over their use. Their interest in the natural qualities of the land are an outcome outside the narrow agricultural intentions of New Deal planners, who failed to see the intrinsic value in preserving these examples of the natural landscapes of North America. For millions of future non-agricultural visitors that may be their greatest contribution.

References

Argow, K.A., 1962, 'Our national grasslands: dustland to grassland', *American Forests*, **68** (January): 10–12, 48–50

Batie, S., 1985, 'Soil conservation in the 1980s: an historical perspective', *Agricultural History* **59** (2): 107–23

Batie, S., Shabman, L.A. and Kramer, R.A., 1985, 'US agriculture and natural resource policy' in K.A. Price (ed.), *The dilemmas of choice*, Resources for the Future, Washington, DC, pp. 127–46

Bennett, H.H., 1939, *Soil conservation*, McGraw-Hill, New York

Bonnifield, P., 1979, *The Dust Bowl*, University of New Mexico Press, Albuquerque

Bowman, I., 1931, *The pioneer fringe*, American Geographical Society, New York

Buckles, J.S., 1959, 'The historical geography of the Fort Rock Valley, 1900–1941', unpublished master's thesis, University of Oregon, Department of Geography, Eugene

Castle, E.M. and Dwyer, C., 1956, *Irrigation possibilities in the Fort Rock area*, circular of information no. 558, Oregon State College, Agricultural Experiment Station, Corvallis

Clawson, M., 1981, *New Deal Planning, the National Resources Planning Board*, The Johns Hopkins University Press, Baltimore

Crosson, P., 1984, 'New perspectives on soil conservation policy', *Journal of Soil and Water Conservation*, **39** (4): 222–5

Ervin, C.E. and Ervin D.E., 1982, 'Factors affecting the use of soil conservation practices: hypotheses, evidence, and policy implications', *Land Economics*, **58** (3): 277–92

Gray, L.C., 1939, 'Federal purchase and administration of submarginal lands in the Great Plains', *Journal of Farm Economics*, **21** (2): 123–31

Great Plains Committee, 1936, *The future of the Great Plains*, Government Printing Office, Washington, DC

Green, D.E., 1973, *Land of the underground rain: irrigation on the Texas High Plains, 1910–1970*, University of Texas Press, Austin

Hart, J.F., 1980, 'Land-use change in a piedmont county', *Annals of the Association of American Geographers*, **70** (4): 492–527

Hays, S.P., 1959, *Conservation and the gospel of efficiency: the progressive conservation movement, 1890–1920*, Harvard University Press, Cambridge

Held, R.B. and Clawson, M., 1965, *Soil conservation in perspective*, The Johns Hopkins Press, Baltimore

Hertz, M., 1988, 'Implementing CRP: progress and prospects', *Journal of Soil and Water Conservation*, **43** (1): 14–16

Hurt, R.D., 1985, 'The National Grasslands: origin and development in the Dust Bowl', *Agricultural History*, **59** (2): 246–59

Hurt, R.D., 1986, 'Federal land reclamation in the Dust Bowl', *Great Plains Quarterly*, **6** (2): 94–106

Kirkendall, R.S., 1966, *Social scientists and farm politics in the age of Roosevelt*, University of Missouri Press, Columbia

Kromm, D.E. and White, S.E. (eds), 1992, *Groundwater exploitation in the High Plains*, University of Kansas Press, Lawrence

Lewis, M.E., 1985, 'Agricultural evolution on secondary frontiers: an Oregon model', *Geographical Perspectives*, **55** (2): 46–52

Lewis, M.E., 1989, 'National Grasslands in the old Dust Bowl', *Geographical Review*, **79** (2): 161–71

Lewis, M.E., 1991, 'Windfall disturbance in a piedmont uplands forest', *Southeastern Geographer*, **31** (1): 1–14

Pinchot, G., 1947, *Breaking new ground*, Harcourt Brace Jovanovich, New York

Popper, D.E., and Popper, F.J., 1987, 'The Great Plains: from dust to dust', *Planning*, **53** (12): 12–18

Riebsame, W.E., 1983, 'Managing drought impacts on agriculture: the Great Plains experience' in R.H. Platt and G. Macinko (eds), *Beyond the urban fringe: land-use issues of nonmetropolitan America*, University of Minnesota Press, Minneapolis

Riebsame, W.E., 1986, 'The Dust Bowl: historical image, psychological anchor, and ecological taboo', *Great Plains Quarterly*, **6** (2): 127–36

Runte, A., 1987, *The National Parks: the American experience*, 2nd. rev. edn., University of Nebraska Press, Lincoln

Salamon, L.M., 1979, 'The time dimension in policy evaluation: the case of the New Deal land-reform experiments', *Public Policy*, **27** (2): 129–83

Salutos, T., 1982, *The American farmer and the New Deal*, Iowa State University Press, Ames

Steiner, F.R., 1990, *Soil conservation in the United States*, The Johns Hopkins University Press, Baltimore

Wallach, B., 1991, *At odds with progress*, University of Arizona Press, Tucson

Webb, W.P., 1931, *The Great Plains*, Ginn and Company, Boston

White, G.F., 1986, 'The future of the Great Plains revisited', *Great Plains Quarterly*, **6** (2): 84–93

Wooten, H.H., 1965, *The land utilization program, 1934–1964*, USDA, Economic Research Service, Agricultural Economic Report No. 85, Government Printing Office, Washington

Worster, D., 1986, 'The dirty thirties: a study in agricultural capitalism', *Great Plains Quarterly*, **6** (2): 107–16

2 The evolution of rural cultural resource management in the Boxley Valley of the Buffalo National River, 1972–92

Kenneth Story

Introduction

One of the most widespread criticisms of historic preservation as a profession is that even the best efforts of the practitioners accomplish little in the way of any genuine, physical preservation of anything, either through legal protection or broad financial incentives and assistance. Rural cultural resources, particularly historic farmsteads or other historic resources located on property currently under cultivation or pasturage, are especially vulnerable to destruction. This is largely due to the demands placed upon these properties by modern farming techniques and the pressure to maintain a profitable, working farm enterprise. Thus one would think that the legal protection afforded by the supervision and management of the entire length of the Buffalo River valley as a 'National River' in 1922 by the National Park Service (NPS) including the rich, agricultural bottomland at its western end known as the Boxley Valley, would have been a cause for celebration among preservationists. Yet the history of the Buffalo National River (BNR) and the evolution of its management policy over the past twenty years has left a legacy far more mixed than one might expect, particularly from the perspective of the valley's residents. More importantly, the lessons, learned have revealed a great deal, not only about the shortcomings of traditional NPS land acquisition and land-use policies, but also about the inadequacy of such trusted preservation tools as the National Register of Historic Places and the establishment of legally defined historic districts when applied to the peculiar character of rural historic cultural landscapes. This chapter presents a discussion of the events surrounding the development of policies for the Buffalo National River and an analysis of the policy-making process. Although this chapter is a case study, the events and circumstances of the BNR provide valuable insights and lessons for other rural cultural resource planners.

The Boxley Valley: background and setting

The Buffalo River is located in north central Arkansas, and entirely within the confines of the Ozark Mountains as shown in Figure 2.1. Beginning in western Newton County, the river runs roughly northeast, terminating at its confluence with the larger White River near the small community of Buffalo City in Baxter County. The Boxley Valley, which shelters the primary watershed of the Buffalo River, lies at the western end of the river and runs roughly southwest to northeast, before the river turns more easterly, running out of the valley. The valley itself is roughly seven-and-one-half miles in length and contains approximately 1,500 acres of arable

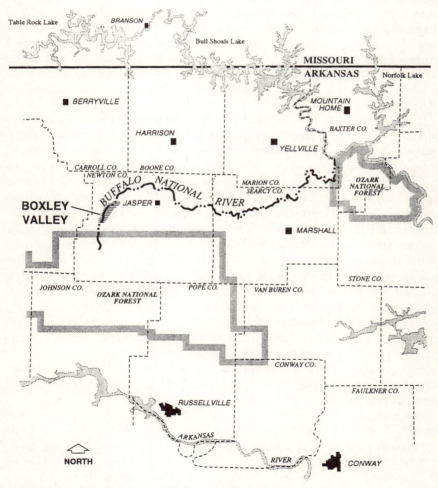

Figure 2.1 *Buffalo National River and Boxley Valley, Arkansas*

bottomland. The boundaries of the NPS-owned property within Boxley Valley include a total of roughly 8,000 acres, the balance of which is covered primarily in upland hardwood forest.

The historic significance of the Boxley Valley was noted early on by NPS officials largely due to the fact that it contains an overwhelming majority of the historic farms found within the Buffalo River valley. The arable plots of land typically cling to the river channel on alternating sides, and tend to extend narrowly along long stretches, seldom reaching more than two thousand feet in width. Due to the relatively poor quality of the soil, virtually all of the land under cultivation was historically put into the growing of hay and pasturage, along with small family subsistence plots. This cropping pattern continues today. Though the valley was inhabited by settlers of European descent as early as 1830, the bulk of its historic vernacular standing structures and landscape features date from 1870 to 1930. However, there are also within the valley a large number of non-historic resources of varied vintage, type, scale and visibility, creating a complex built environment. All these resources, considered within the surrounding landscape, form a pattern of relatively small, contiguous historic farmsteads that is both important and unique within the Buffalo River basin.

The first threat to the Buffalo River came during the Depression (1929–40) in the form of overzealous state and local elected officials who subscribed to the then popular view that one way out of the country's financial woes was the damming of its rivers for the purpose of producing hydroelectric power (Compton, 1992). At the time, this solution was thought to hold special appeal for rural residents, as they typically suffered the most from the effects of the Depression and they frequently lived adjacent to eligible rivers and streams and would thus fall within the proposed hydroelectric service area. As the Ozark Highlands of northern Arkansas and southern Missouri are essentially an ancient plateau that have not experienced the glacial activity seen elsewhere in North America—instead having been crossed and eroded over time by upland streams that gave it its steep, mountainous character—they not only offered a number of free-flowing rivers for the dam builders but also 'suffered' from an absence of lakes that could provide additional recreational opportunities. As one of the remotest and most undeveloped regions in Arkansas, Depression-era planners believed that the Buffalo River valley and its surrounding area could only stand to gain from the damming of the river and the abundant benefits that would result.

Around the same period, the national conservation movement was gaining broader support. The conservation ethic which emphasized the protection of natural resources struck a sympathetic chord among many northern Arkansas residents who valued the rugged, unspoiled beauty of the Buffalo River valley and could not accept the assertion that its effective destruction through the creation of a man-made lake was either beneficial or necessary. Effective but unco-ordinated resistance to the dam building effort grew over the years, eventually resulting in the formation in 1962 of the activist Ozark Society. The Society sought to tame the dam-building fervor by arguing for the preservation of the river, primarily from a natural conservation standpoint (Compton, 1992). The historic significance of the river's rich and varied past, and the protection of these values, escaped the notice of even the river's most impassioned defenders. Yet, at this early stage in America's historic preservation consciousness, no one could anticipate the need or desire also to protect the physical evidence of the Buffalo River valley's cultural heritage.

Buffalo National River: 1972–82

By 1972, the Ozark Society had been successful in fighting the hydroelectric interests and lobbying the US Congress to have the Buffalo River declared a 'National River'. Under the National River program the Buffalo River was thus included in the National Park system as a 'National River' in 1972. The language in the legislation creating the BNR reflected the 'conservation' bias of the river protection proponents. The legislative act mandated only the preservation of both the Buffalo as a free-flowing river and the protection of the natural character of its valley. There was no explicit reference to cultural resource preservation of any kind. None the less, the preservation of the rural character of the Buffalo River valley as a whole, and Boxley Valley in particular, was recognized in the legislative history of the act. The initial land-use recommendations contained in the legislation made explicit reference to a preference for leaving the land in the Boxley Valley and elsewhere within the proposed confines of the Buffalo National River in private hands. The purchase of scenic easements only was advocated whenever possible, with the understanding that such other options as purchase in-fee for either leaseback or sellback with deed restrictions could also be employed if necessary. Clearly, the tradition of agricultural usage of the land was respected and understood by the congressional authors of the legislation. The message from Congress was that agricultural traditions could best be upheld by keeping the individual farmsteads in private hands, if not in private ownership.

The congressional guides were not however followed by the NPS planners. Their approach was to acquire complete ownership (in-fee) to as much land as was possible. During the first ten years over 80 per cent of the land in the Boxley Valley was bought by the BNR (Liles, 1992). In light of the congressional guidance, why did the NPS pursue such an active land acquisition strategy? The answer has a great deal to do with the National Park Service's own tradition of purchasing property in-fee within the boundaries of proposed park property to insure total protection and control, along with their lack of familiarity and experience in sharing stewardship over rural agricultural property with private interests. The traditional and popular NPS management philosophy of the time held that National Parks were to come under the sole dominion and purview of the NPS. This gave the NPS full legal authority to exercise its greatest, and hopefully, most effective preservation and management control over all the included natural and cultural resources. Not only was purchase in-fee an ostensibly more comfortable and sensible method of management, but the potential conflicts posed by shared stewardship seemed both foolhardy and dangerous.

From a public relations perspective, the National Park Service's aggressive land acquisition efforts were a disaster. The first official contact received by the valley's residents came in the form of a letter from the NPS requesting that they sign an enclosed form giving NPS property appraisers the right to enter their property (Ferguson and Ferguson, 1992). The same letter went on to warn that if the property owner declined to grant such permission, the NPS would go to court and request a legal order allowing this access. Significantly, neither the letter nor any of the enclosures gave any hint as to the NPS's overall plans for the valley, nor did they request any input from the property owners in the planning process. Subsequent NPS correspondence exacerbated this officious and uncaring impression. As a result, many Boxley Valley families, some with roots on the land since the late nineteenth century, were left to feel as if they had no choice in the matter. Some residents, fearing that they would be forcibly removed from their property without adequate compensation, sold extensive timber harvesting rights to private lumbering companies (Ferguson and Ferguson, 1992). The results were the wholesale denuding of large tracts of forest. Those that insisted on remaining adopted a protective and defensive posture toward the NPS. As a result, a lingering cynicism and suspicion toward the NPS remains.

From a land-use and cultural resource preservation perspective, the results were equally bad, if not worse. No official action plan for historic .resource protection was prepared, and much of the property purchased outright by the BNR was initially left unattended. Consequently, historic and culturally significant buildings, structures and site features were allowed to deteriorate (Liles, 1992). Even in the six instances where scenic easements were sold by property owners to the BNR there was no specific language in the agreements surrounding the preservation of historic cultural resources. Instead the easements contained brief and vague language about the right of the landowner to maintain, repair, rehabilitate or replace existing structures 'so long as the general character of the buildings is not changed' (NPS Scenic Easement, 1979, p. 1).

Buffalo National River: 1982–92

Fortunately for the Buffalo National River the arrival of new park leadership set in motion a more responsible resource management direction. In 1982 Alec Gould was appointed park superintendent. Gould had both an academic background in history as well as historic park management experience. Previously, he had been park superintendent at the Lyndon B. Johnson Ranch in Texas, an NPS site significant for its associations with political history rather than its natural setting. Gould brought not only a far greater sensitivity to and interest in the historic cultural landscape of Boxley Valley but also signalled the beginning of a deeper understanding of the importance of preserving the valley's historic land use as well. For the first time since the establishment of the BNR, a series of public hearings was scheduled and announced so that valley residents could both ask questions directly of BNR/NPS staff and comment on proposed plans for the preservation of all of the valley's history, including both its historic cultural resources and its tradition of agricultural land use carried on by small, privately-owned farms. At the same time, Superintendent Gould also personally solicited the input of NPS field staff who had shown at least an intuitive sympathy toward such resources.

These hearings and discussions resulted in the *Land Use Plan/Cultural Landscape Report, Boxley Valley, Buffalo National River, Arkansas*, completed in the spring of 1985 (US Dept. of Interior, 1985). For the first time, the need to integrate the preservation of traditional land use and built historic resources was recognized and addressed in a considered and meaningful fashion. More importantly, there was a drastic turnaround in the BNR's policy for carrying out historic preservation and traditional land-use goals. Indeed, the plan contained some rather unorthodox proposals. Perhaps the most radical was the recommendation that as much property as possible within the valley be returned to private ownership. Private occupancy was also encouraged.

New more detailed comprehensive management agreements between the NPS and private property owners were thus outlined. These model agreements were intended to foster the implementation of BNR goals working in conjunction with private property owners. Clear and explicitly worded historic preservation easements, leaseback and sellback agreements were also developed. These agreements were written so that they could be specifically tailored to individual properties. They included more specific guidelines regarding what constituted acceptable maintenance and rehabilitation of historic structures. Also of note was the structure inventory included as an appendix to the report. This inventory included a significance ranking for each of the valley's known historic resources, with each of the categories keyed to assessments of eligibility for listing on the National Register of Historic Places. For non-US readers, the National Register is the nation's official list of historic properties worthy of physical preservation. This ranking system was created primarily as a necessary step toward the BNR's goal of nominating the Boxley Valley to the National Register as a rural agricultural district and not strictly as a preservation management mechanism.

In 1987, the Boxley Valley Historic District (BVHD), officially known as the Big Buffalo Valley Historic District, was added to the National Register. This action raised historic preservation awareness within the valley and among BNR and NPS staff. However, the problem of making hard decisions about economic preservation feasibility vs. agricultural usefulness and deterioration vs. private ownership remained. Certain private property owners questioned the BVHD determinations of relative historic significance, primarily out of concern for having to maintain historic agricultural structures that were either no longer usable or that were perceived as being less historically important than other structures within the valley. The National Register's relevance as a planning tool clearly left much to be desired, and by itself did little to resolve the resource management conflicts that remained between the BNR and private property owners. It soon became evident that more detailed cultural resource planning would need to be carried out.

The issues of land use and earlier professional judgment on the part of the BNR and NPS staff resulted in a 1991 re-survey of all approximately 250 standing structures in the Boxley Valley. This re-survey, and the resulting updated inventory, reflected a number of the lessons learned about integrating historic preservation and agricultural land-use concerns. The research process followed a two-tier preservation 'filtering' process for examining each structure (US Dept. of Interior, 1991). The first tier of screening criteria included three 'filters'—groups of structures with historical or architectural significance; groups of structures with significance to the cultural landscape pattern; and individual structures of historical or architectural significance. These categories directly related to traditional National Register eligibility. In contrast, the second set of 'filters' were practical and management-oriented. They considered the issues of safety; access; and interpretive value. Only after executing the two-stage process did the BNR and NPS staff consider themselves ready to make recommendations regarding resource management. This time the recommendations were well defined and specific. They included recommendations for preservation; stabilization; rehabilitation; adaptive use; and restoration, with each option accompanied by a clear definition of its practical and legal implications for the property owner. When these recommendations are considered in conjunction with the previously developed BNR/NPS guidelines for compatible new construction within Boxley Valley, what emerges is a more thorough, reasonable and sympathetic action plan for addressing the frequently conflicting goals of historic preservation and viable agricultural land use. The end result is the preservation of the historic and natural heritage of the valley in its fullest sense.

Lessons from the Boxley Valley

The experiences from the BNR provide insights for rural cultural resource planning efforts in other areas. Some of the more obvious lessons learned at Boxley Valley are the inadequacy of traditional NPS land acquisition procedures in the management of a living, historic agricultural valley and the need for active and continuous communication between BNR/NPS staff and valley residents. Fortunately the present posture of the BNR indicates that they have been learned well. Purchasing in-fee all the property within the boundaries of such a living, vital valley of historically-private agricultural farmsteads is simply not the best policy. When historic preservation is understood to include both the preservation of both traditional land usage and the historic built environment, private ownership and stewardship has been proven to be effective. Secondly, a more visible, regular and involved presence by BNR park rangers and staff in the field and improved written notification procedures and correspondence have resulted in a more casual and constant flow of information between the BNR and private property owners. This situation, in turn, has produced a far greater sympathy toward the goals of the BNR's cultural resource management policies from the residents, along with a far greater patience with their shortcomings. When considered in conjunction with the more explicit historic preservation management agreements that have gone into effect on many of these properties, this improved communication has also resulted in better on-site guidance for private property owners regarding their preservation responsibilities and how those were determined in the first place.

Perhaps the greatest lesson from the Boxley Valley is the need to integrate historic preservation with a concern for keeping the land in private hands. This model will produce an active, vital resource steward-ship. The National Park Service's experience with the successful management of a living, historic agricultural and cultural landscape is still in its early stages, and there certainly are more issues to be addressed. The federal stewardship of the valley includes policies and mandates that inevitably produce tension between public and private interests. This required NPS planners and staff to continue to forge informed NPS resource management objectives and policies that are both responsive to traditional usage concerns as well as being effective tools for the preservation of the historic cultural landscape.

In the mean time, one point on which all can agree is the belief that the presence of the BNR and its evolving attempts to draft an effective historic cultural landscape management policy has ultimately served the valley well. This is clearly evident when the Buffalo River Valley is viewed against the overdevelopment and commercial exploitation that have occurred within unprotected river valleys, in the Ozark region and other parts of the United States. Though, for now, land-use planners, historic preser-

vationists and valley residents may all have to settle for less, the rural
character of Boxley Valley has survived intact; hopefully this will prove to
be the legacy of the Buffalo National River.

References

Compton, N., 1992, *The battle for the Buffalo River*, University of Arkansas Press,
    Fayetteville
Ferguson, H. and Ferguson, M.V., 1992, *Interview*, Ferguson residence, Arkansas,
    28 July 1992
Liles, J., 1992, *Interview*, Buffalo National River office, Arkansas, 27 July 1992
National Park Service Scenic Easement, 1979, files of *Buffalo 'National River'*,
    Harrison, Arkansas
US Department of Interior, 1985, *Land-use plan/cultural landscape report, Boxley
    Valley, Buffalo National River, Arkansas*, Denver Service Center, National Park
    Service
US Department of Interior, 1991, *Land-use plan/cultural landscape report, Boxley
    Valley, Buffalo National river, Arkansas*, Appendix A, 1991 update, Hot Springs
    National Park, National Park Service

3 Funding of disaster management and the changing structure of rural county budgets
William D. Solecki

Introduction

During the 1980s, rural America experienced dramatic economic and social shifts (Luloff and Swanson, 1990; Marsden *et al.*, 1990; Robinson, 1990). While some areas remained stable, many others went through either rapid decline or rapid growth. Limited research is available on the impacts of these changes on the funding of public services in rural counties. However, there is enough information for this chapter to discuss: public service policy in rural communities in general; public service policy in declining rural communities; public service policy in high-growth rural communities; and impacts of the reduction of federal aid. This is followed by an investigation of changes in the county-level funding of a specific type of non-essential public service, disaster and hazards management.

The chapter then proceeds to report on attempts to investigate the status of disaster and hazards management within the rural counties of Florida in relation to local economic and social shifts and to the funding of other public services. Disaster and hazards management for the purposes of this project includes those activities which involve natural and technological disaster preparedness, response, recovery and mitigation. County expenditures for disaster management will be analyzed and compared in the 35 rural Florida counties. Information on funding for public services was gathered from county records for the fiscal years ending 1981, 1984, 1987 and 1990, including, for the purposes of this study, increases and/or decreases in the amount of money available for public disaster and hazards public service provision.

The chapter then examines three main hypotheses developed from the literature on rural restructuring and fiscal change. First, it is hypothesized that the absolute amount of county-level funding for disaster and hazards management will have declined from the period 1981 to 1990. Second, the funding of disaster management will have declined more than for other public services, particularly those defined as more critical such as police and fire fighting. Disaster management funding should decline in a way similar to other non-essential public services, such as county-level hospital, health and welfare programs. The third hypothesis is that differences in county-level funding will be driven by a set of changes in the economic and social character of the county. More specifically, disaster funding will have been cut the most in the poorer, less-populated counties; counties going through rapid population growth; and in the counties where federal funding was most dramatically cut back.

The rationale for the chapter is twofold. The first broad goal is to provide information about the status of disaster and hazards management in rural counties, since almost no information on the funding of this type of public service in rural communities is available. A second set of goals is to provide some general information on the impact of fiscal stress on the funding decisions of rural county governments.

Natural and technological disasters can devastate a community, as well illustrated by Hurricane Andrew which struck southern Florida on 24 August 1992 with 145 mph winds and caused billions of dollars of damage. The hurricane reaffirmed the fact that Florida counties, as well as others in hazard-prone areas, must maintain effective disaster management operations. This chapter will provide some information on how well these counties maintained this type of public service during the 1980s.

The funding of public services in rural counties

Public service policy in rural communities in general

Relatively little has been written about the way rural governments function and make budgetary decisions. Even less is known about the functioning of county governments in rural settings, even though these governments have become a more important source of public service provision in recent decades. What is known, however, is that the institutional structure and public service capacity of rural governments is quite varied (Streib and Waugh, 1991).

Moreover, it is also clear that rural governments faced a series of major challenges during the 1980s. One was the changing national economy and decentralized federalism, which placed new burdens on rural and small-town governments, particularly in terms of decline of revenue and increased service delivery responsibilities. There also has been an increased need for both policy coordination and expertise to operate a decentralized system, and these were balanced against demands for preserving local autonomy (Cigler, 1984). Rural communities continue to face the fact that they typically have higher service costs than their urban or suburban counterparts. These higher service costs are driven by high rates of poverty, long distances and low population densities (Browne and Reid, 1990; Camboni and Napier, 1985).

Seroka (1986) states that differing levels of service delivery in rural communities are a function of local governments' administrative needs, attitudes and capacity. He defines four types of administrative environments—decline, strain, preservation and dynamic—and concludes that population growth (or decline) and economic growth (for which income is presented as a surrogate) are the two community trends with the most impact on the administration, politics, policy choices and response capacity of rural governments.

Clark *et al.* (1986) propose and test three models of budgetary spending by rural governments. The first model claims that the amount of spending is dependent on the resource base of the government. The wealthier the government, the more it will spend on public and social services. The second model is that the budget decisions will be determined by the social needs of the community. For example, the greater the poverty of the community, the more the government will have to spend on welfare and other social programs. The third model is that budget decisions will be dependent on the political ideology of the community. More liberal communities will have larger, more progressive governments and will place greater emphasis on providing extensive public services, particularly social and welfare programs.

In their examination of county and local governments in New Mexico and Wyoming, Clark *et al.* (1986) found that no single hypothesis fully explained the observed budget decisions. Together, the resource base and social needs hypotheses explained the most amount of variation among the different government spending strategies. The political ideology hypothesis did not prove very useful. As with other studies, Clark *et al.* found that most rural governments typically have higher per capita spending levels than other governments and have to concentrate their spending largely on providing basic services.

Public service in declining rural communities

The 1980s brought particularly rapid economic growth or, in some cases, decline and social change to much of rural America. A concurrent shift was the decline in the amount of federal money being received by rural governments. Many rural communities, therefore, now face multiple forces of fiscal stress, notably the decline of local public revenues allied to the decline of federal and state money. Small governments are particularly vulnerable to local revenue loss because they lack the flexibility and diversity of revenue sources that larger governments maintain. This is coupled with the fact that rural communities typically provide only the most basic services such as fire protection and street maintenance, leaving only a few services to be cut back.

Some information is available on public service expenditure shifts during periods of fiscal retrenchment and economic decline. Typically, reductions in expenditures are not spread equally across all agencies or divisions.

Governments seem less likely to propose reductions in basic services, specifically the more 'visible' and direct service activities. Cut-backs are more likely to affect services related to long-term planning and research, training, equipment replacement and preventive maintenance (Downes, 1987; Cook and Poremba, 1985). New projects and programs, especially those with extensive start-up costs, are not likely to be funded (Walker and Chaiken, 1982; Downs and Larkey, 1981).

Lipset and Raad (1978) found that persons voting on California's Proposition 13 were strongly against the reduction in police protection but much less opposed to reductions in welfare programs. As a result of Proposition 13, health services were reduced most while fire and police services were little changed (Danziger and Ring, 1982). In a study of eight Washington state counties, Cook and Poremba (1985) found that agencies performing protective and court functions or those involved in administration and planning were less likely than social and health agencies to suffer fiscal cutbacks. Lassey *et al.* (1986) assessed the change in service provisions as seen by public officials in eight Washington state counties. Natural resources and pollution control were seen by these officials as the lowest priority issues. Overall, environmental programs absorbed the greatest reduction in budget support. MacManus and Pammer (1990) found that in rural Ohio communities, government officials faced with budget shortfalls would most likely choose to delay capital improvements and cut back all departments, rather than reduce or eliminate services or lay off personnel. Many rural communities had also become heavily dependent on federal and state grants for service provision, much more so than more urbanized communities. With 'shallow pockets,' rural communities had extremely limited capacity to respond to such changes.

Public Service in high-growth rural communities

Rapid rural community growth, typically related either to exurban growth or boomtown growth, also places tremendous pressure on local public service provision (Brown, Geertsen and Krannich, 1989; Bender and Zolty, 1986; Cortese, 1982). Rural communities do not have the ability to maintain services at a consistent level during periods of high population growth. In high-growth rural communities, the service demands can change substantially. Typically, long-term residents change their service demands as growth causes the disruption of existing services, and there are demands for efforts to lessen the impacts of growth. New residents, on the other hand, often put completely new demands on the local governments.

Halstead *et al.* (1984) defined several problems in financing public services during the rapid growth of a community. These included uncertainty surrounding the magnitude of the growth, temporal gaps between revenues and expenditures, jurisdictional mismatches, demand determination and fluctuating demand levels, maintaining existing service capacities and the delineation of responsibilities.

During periods of rapid growth, police, fire and education are seen as the primary public services to be maintained. Community adjustments to the change in service demands include selected decreases in services, increases in fees and taxes and occasional infusion of revenue from state and corporate sources, especially if a large single project is being built by a single company (Murray and Weber, 1982).

Rapid growth is particularly problematic in locales where a large facility is being built (Halstead *et al.* 1984). In these places, local governments are put in a dilemma because peak public service demand will come during the height of construction and is likely to trail off as the population declines with the completion of the project and the out-migration of workers and their families. Governments are caught between meeting the demands of the peak population and cutting back later, or between planning for short-term shortages which in the long term are eliminated.

Impacts of the reduction of federal aid

One of the significant changes during the 1980s was the cut-back and reorganization of federal and state-level aid programs for rural areas. The federal government and state governments have long funded projects in rural communities. Funding typically was allocated for development projects, basic local government operations, increasing the organizational capacity of local governments, the implementation of federal mandates and agricultural programs. The proportion of state and federal aid in rural community service budgets increased dramatically during the 1960s and 1970s (Camboni and Napier, 1985), and the amount of federal money received by small governments (those in communities with fewer than 25,000 residents) increased by more than 1,600 per cent between 1966–67 and 1976–77 (Sokolow, 1987). McKenna *et al.* (1990), in a review of literature, found that federal cut-backs have had three types of effects on local governments: fiscal impacts (change in the amount of money appropriated for services); programmatic impacts (change in the types of services provided) and institutional impacts (changes in the structure of governments).

The most significant single federal cut-back came with the expiration of General Revenue Sharing in 1986. Since its conception in 1972 as a program open to all governments to receive federal grants with limited obligations, General Revenue Sharing had become a major component of many rural government budget management plans. With its passing, 78 per cent of local governments with fewer than 25,000 people (n = 36,000) no longer receive any federal money (Moore, 1987).

Disaster and hazards management in rural communities

Local disaster and hazards management can be defined as efforts to plan for, respond to and recover from natural and technological hazards such as earthquakes, floods and acutely toxic chemical releases. Typically, disaster and hazards management is given only limited attention in most locales and is seen as peripheral to local government operations (Wolensky and Wolensky, 1991; May, 1988; Labadie, 1984; Rossi *et al.* 1982). Although disaster planning has become institutionalized in recent decades, its position within many local governments recently has become increasingly precarious (Wolensky and Wolensky, 1991). Its status in rural communities with extremely limited budgets and personnel has been widely accepted as chronically troubled (Faupel and Bailey, 1988; Garten and Russel, 1986).

Labadie (1984) cites the lack of general concern and interest in disaster management at the local level as a central problem. Often, disaster planning officials and operations lack equipment and are given limited funding and part-time personnel. For example, King and Harris (1989) observed that the planning boards of rapidly growing small rural northeast towns were quite sensitive to a broad range of environmental concerns during periods of rapid development but that disaster and hazards management was not, however, an explicit concern. Disaster management also has been affected by federal cut-backs. As seen recently in Oregon, federal funding cuts have affected the amount of money locally available for disaster planning (Downes, 1987).

More generally, the International City Management Association in 1982 carried out the most extensive survey of the structure of emergency management agencies so far undertaken (Hoetmer, 1983). Survey results from over fifteen hundred jurisdictions in the United States indicated that fewer than half of counties had full-time emergency preparedness coordinators. In conclusion, Wolensky and Wolensky (1991) go so far as to say that local governments consistently fail to present a clear agenda on emergency management largely because local managers do not really want to involve themselves with the issue.

The Florida study

Data collection

Data were gathered on rural county revenues and expenditures for the 35 rural counties of Florida. Counties identified as 'non-metropolitan' by the US Census Bureau in 1990 made up the sample of counties. Information on the county budgets was gathered from the state's annual surveys of county revenue and expenditure (Florida, 1981; 1984; 1987; and 1990).

Table 3.1 *County budget revenue and expenditure*

Revenue	1. total revenue
	2. intergovernmental revenue
	(a) federally-derived revenue
	(b) state-derived revenue
	3. disaster management revenue—civil defense (US FEMA)
Expenditure	1. total expenditure
	2. general government services
	(a) financial and administrative
	(b) judicial
	3. public safety
	(a) law enforcement
	(b) fire control
	(c) ambulance and rescue
	4. transportation—road and street facilities
	5. human services
	(a) hospitals
	(b) health
	(c) welfare
	6. culture and recreation
	(a) libraries
	(b) parks and recreation
	7. disaster management
	(a) personal services
	(b) operating expenses
	(c) capital outlay
Demographic and Social	1. population
	2. per capita income

Source: all data were derived from the Florida Department of Banking and Finance, 1981, 1984, 1987, 1990, except for the population and per capita income which were derived from the Bureau of Economic and Business Research, 1992

Four years were chosen for analysis: fiscal year (FY) 1981, FY 1984, FY 1987 and FY 1990. Each year included spending from 1 October of the previous year through to 30 September.

Data were gathered on several county-level sources of revenue and types of expenditure as shown Table 3.1. 'Revenue' included total revenue, money received from federal and state programs and money earmarked specifically for disaster management. Many of the counties received civil defense money from the US Federal Emergency Management Agency (FEMA), via the state of Florida, for increasing county nuclear attack preparedness. This money, although ostensibly allocated only for nuclear attack planning, typically is spent on projects which increase the county's preparedness for a much broader range of hazards. 'Expenditure' included information on total expenditure as well as expenditure for specific types of services, particularly general governmental services, public safety and human services.

Table 3.2 *Florida rural counties*—selected means (n = 35)[1]

	1981	1984	1987	1990
Population	25.4	28.0	31.3	33.8
Per Capita Income ($)	$10,926.00	$11,420.00	$12,429.00	$12,140.00[2]
Total State Expenditure ($)	$9,301,404.00	$10,542,980.00	$14,231,202.00	$18,170,812.00
State Expenditure—per capita ($)	$366.2	$376.5	$454.7	$537.6
State-derived revenue—per capita ($)	$114.4	$123.8	$137.3	$144.9
Federal-derived revenue—per capita ($)	$47.9	$31.4	$19.8	$23.3

Notes: 1. All dollars are in 1990 values
        2. 1989 per capita income

Source: all data were derived from the Florida Department of Banking and Finance, 1981, 1984, 1987, 1990, except for the population and per capita income which were derived from the Bureau of Economic and Business Research, 1992

Data on disaster management services expenditures originally were broken down into three categories: personnel services, operating expenses and capital outlay. For the purpose of this paper, the sum of all three disaster-related expenditures was used. Data on population and per capita income were gathered for each fiscal year.

Results

The data indicate that Florida's rural counties have changed significantly during the 1980s as shown in Table 3.2. The population, per capita income, total expenditures and per capita expenditures, on average, increased during the entire period of the 1980s. Average per capita income declined slightly, however, from 1987 to 1989. Changes in state-derived revenue and federal-derived revenue represent other important shifts. First, the amount of money received from the US federal government fell dramatically during the decade. The steepest decline occurred from 1981 to 1987, with a slight rise between 1987 and 1990. The 1990 amount of federal money available was non the less less than half the 1981 amount. Second, as the federal grants and programs faded, the contribution of state-derived revenue sources rose dramatically. Given these increases, one might expect significant shifts in the spending for public services in these counties.

The three main hypotheses

Spending on disaster management will have declined

The results show that disaster management funding in the counties in fact generally increased in constant dollars over the study period (as shown in Table 3.3). In FY 1981, a little under $37,000 (in 1990 dollars) was budgeted on average per county for disaster management. By FY 1990, rural Florida counties were budgeting, on average, just over $100,000. The spending per capita also steadily increased during the period, from $1.6 per capita in FY 1981 to $2.5 per capita in 1990, on average. The average percentage increase in funding per capita was 221.2 per cent.

A different pattern emerges, however, with a closer examination of the counties. The standard deviation of $1.7 for per capita spending indicates that there are large differences among the county funding strategies. Some counties were spending a lot more than other counties on disaster management. For almost a third of the counties, disaster management funding was less in FY 1990 than in FY 1981. Conversely, three counties had increased their funding by more than $4 per capita, an increase of more than several hundred per cent. Furthermore, the coefficient of variation of total disaster

Table 3.3 *County funding for disaster and hazards management*—means and (standard deviations)

	1981	1984 (in $)	1987	1990
Disaster management	$36,788.00 ($47,871.00)	$66,859.00 ($133,955.00)	$71,597.00 ($111,664.00)	$101,675.00 ($148,848.00)
Disaster management per capita	$1.6 ($1.3)	$2.0 ($2.2)	$2.6 ($2.6)	$2.5 ($1.7)

Notes: all dollars are in 1990 values

Source: all data were derived from the Florida Department of Banking and Finance 1981, 1984, 1987, 1990

management spending in FY 1981 was 130 per cent, and in FY 1990 it was 208 per cent, suggesting increased heterogeneity among county disaster funding strategies.

These differences are highlighted by a comparison of the quartile of counties with the greatest decreases and the quartile of counties with the greatest increases in disaster management budgets. The lowest quartile includes eight counties where disaster funding declined. In one of these counties, the decline was more than $6.0 per capita. All of the counties in the highest quartile had increases of at least $2.0 per capita. One county increased more than $5.0 per capita.

Funding for disaster management will have declined vis-à-vis *other public services*

Disaster management expenditure as a percent of total expenditure in fact remained fairly consistent throughout the period (as shown in Table 3.4). It was either 0.5 per cent or 0.6 per cent for the four fiscal years examined. Of twelve county-level public services, disaster management received the smallest percentage of the budget. It was hypothesized originally that disaster management would fare as well or as poorly as similar secondary services such as hospitals, health care and welfare programs. That, however, was not the case. All three of these other services faced reduced funding during the period from FY 1981 to FY 1990, falling, on average, by roughly 35 per cent.

Disaster management funding is related to county character

The role of population   It was hypothesized that different types of changes in disaster management funding could be related to demographic differ-

Table 3.4 *Selected services as percentage of total county expenditure*—means

	1981	1984	1987	1990
Disaster management	0.5	0.6	0.6	0.5
Administration	7.0	9.1	9.1	8.7
Judicial	3.4	3.9	4.0	4.0
Law enforcement	15.4	14.4	15.0	13.1
Fire protection	1.5	2.0	2.7	2.3
Ambulance and rescue	3.2	3.5	3.2	4.2
Roads and transportation	29.1	25.9	22.0	18.7
Hospitals	2.4	1.2	0.7	0.8
Health	2.9	2.4	2.4	2.4
Welfare	1.9	1.7	1.4	1.5
Libraries	1.0	1.0	1.5	1.6
Parks and recreation	1.0	1.0	1.6	1.1
Other expenditures	30.7	33.3	35.8	41.1

Source: all data were derived from the Florida Department of Banking and Finance, 1981, 1984, 1987, 1990

ences and shifts. The counties with declines in funding, on average, are slightly poorer and have considerably smaller populations (as shown in Table 3.5). The quartile with the greatest increases in disaster management funding have almost four times the population of the quartile of counties with the greatest decreases in such funding. Population size is suggestive of the tax base and overall amount of revenue available in the counties. As has been suggested earlier, counties with small populations typically have the least amount of fiscal flexibility.

During the increasingly tight budget periods of the 1980s, it seems that the counties with deeper pockets were able to make the decision to continue or to increase their funding of disaster management, while the other, more fiscally constrained counties could not. Fiscally constrained counties, in fact, had to focus on simply providing only basic public services. For example, proportional spending on primary services such as police enforcement and government administration grew twice as fast in fiscally constrained counties as in the counties with deeper pockets.

Rapid population growth seems to have come into play in the case of one county. Okeechobee county experienced very rapid population growth during the 1980s, with growth of almost 30 per cent in the decade. Per capita disaster funding, as well as funding for other services, did not keep up with the growth. Otherwise, rapid population growth did not seem to play a major role in the changing expenditures for disaster management.

The impact of other funding sources

It also was hypothesized that changes in external funding would play a critical role in the funding decisions of counties. This does not seem to be the case if one considers shifts in the total amount of federally-derived and state-derived revenue. Both sets of counties—those in the highest quartile, which increased disaster management spending, and those in the lowest quartile, which decreased such spending—experienced similar federal funding decreases and state funding increases (as shown in Table 3.5).

Money the counties might have received from the state through FEMA for civil defense planning also did not play a significant role. The amount of available money increased overall during the middle part of the decade, then declined by FY 1990. In the first three fiscal years examined, civil defense money made up roughly one-quarter of the total disaster management budget of the counties. In FY 1990, the proportion dropped to 14.1 per cent. There was no direct relationship between this shift and the pattern of overall county-level disaster funding, however.

Table 3.5 *Comparison of counties and reduced and increased disaster management fund*

	Lowest quartile (n = 8)	Highest quartile (n = 8)
Population 1990	14.8	57.3
Population change 1981–90	+3.0	+12.8
Income–per^2 capita	$11,437.00	$13,388.00
Income—per capita change 1981–89	+$1,173.00	+$1,341.00
Expenditure—per capita 1990	$494.00	$525.00
Expenditure—per capita —(1990–81)	−$120.00	−$147.00
State-derived revenue —per capita 1990	$147.00	$101.00
State-derived revenue —per capita—(1990–81)	+$39.00	+$34.00
Federal-derived revenue —per capita 1990	$20.00	$18.00
Federal-derived revenue —per capita—(1990–81)	−$33.00	−$19.00

Notes: 1. 1990 dollars
          2. 1989 per capita income

Source: all data were derived from the Florida Department of Banking and Finance, 1981, 1984, 1987, 1990, except for the population and per capita income which were derived from the Bureau of Economic and Business Research, 1992

Although in FY 1990 the highest quartile counties received more than one and a half times the amount of civil defense funding than the lowest quartile group, the highest-quartile counties, on average, lost funding during the period 1981–90 while the lowest-quartile counties gained funding. Furthermore, civil defense money for both groups in FY 1981 was comparable to about 23 per cent of the total disaster management budget. By 1990, the share of civil defense funding had declined to less than 10 per cent of the disaster funding in the upper quartile, while remaining constant in the lower quartile (as shown in Table 3.6).

Increased funding for hazardous materials incident planning during the later part of the 1980s did play a role in disaster management budget decisions at the county level. Since FY 1988, all facilities in Florida for which local emergency planning must take place (as designated under the Superfund Amendments Reauthorization Act of 1986) have paid a fee to the state government. This fee has been passed back to the counties to help in the development of chemical-emergency response plans. The amount a county receives is based on the population of the county, its percentage of the state population and the number of reported potentially hazardous facilities. Counties in the highest quartile received slightly more than $3,300 per year, while those in the lowest quartile received just under $800 per county per year.

Table 3.6 *Civil defense funding for counties with reduced* and increased disaster management funding*—means

	Lowest quartile (n = 8)	Highest quartile (n = 8)
Civil defense revenue —1990	$7,719.00	$12,554.00
Civil defense revenue —per capita—1990	$0.5	$0.2
Civil defense revenue —(1990–1981)	+$499.00	−$350.00
Civil defense revenue —as percent of disaster management 1981	23.3	23.2
Civil defense revenue —as percent of disaster management 1990	23.1	9.3

Notes: *—1990 dollars

Source: all data were derived from the Florida Department of Banking and Finance, 1981, 1984, 1987, 1990, except for the population and per capita income which were derived from the Bureau of Economic and Business Research, 1992

Grants and assistance from extremely large manufacturing facilities could also be a factor in why certain county disaster management programs fared better than others. Three of the eight counties in the highest quartile group have within their borders large (more than 500 employees) and potentially hazardous facilities, such as a nuclear power plant. Around the nation, facilities of this type have donated or given equipment and money to their local county governments to improve hazardous materials accident response capacity.

Local disaster management officials as policy advocates

One final factor in the differing funding decisions of counties which was not hypothesized at the outset is the character and interest level of the county director of disaster and hazards management. As many writers have argued, disaster management typically does not generate much concern at the local level. It is critical for the success of a local program that it have a strong director who can promote disaster planning and request increased funding. Much of the variation between the lowest-quartile and highest-quartile counties in the sample here can be explained with reference to local disaster-policy entrepreneurs (Koutnik, 1992). In the highest-quartile group of counties, most of the directors have been active and committed to disaster management. Many of them have consistently pressed for increased funding for disaster planning. In the other group of counties, many of the directors have been described as either unable or unwilling to commit much administrative attention to disaster and hazards planning (Koutnik, 1992).

Discussion and conclusions

The results generally refute the first and second main research hypotheses. First, total and per capita disaster management expenditures increased steadily during the 1980s, even as county per capita spending declined overall. Second, the status of disaster management spending relative to total expenditures remained steady, even as many other non-essential services declined in relative spending during the decade.

Although the overall growth of disaster management funding was positive, there was a considerable amount of variation within the sample of counties. Analysis of selected groups of counties within the sample helped to reveal some links contained in the third hypothesis between changing economic and social conditions and changing revenues and funding for disaster management. Variations in the sample could be explained by three sets of factors: population conditions, increased revenue for hazardous materials accident planning and the influence of county-level emergency management officials.

Several broad conclusions can be drawn from this research. Across all the rural counties of Florida, total per capita expenditures for public services declined by about 20 per cent during the 1980s. Budgets became increasingly tight. The results here seem to indicate that if a public service is to be maintained in this type of fiscal environment, at least two things must happen.

First, alternative funding sources for the services must appear. In practice, three new sources have appeared. First, county-level disaster management funding has greatly benefited from recent increased concern over hazardous materials accident response planning. Second, new state and local-level programs have been developed which have brought more money to county disaster management programs. Third, large local manufacturing or energy facilities have donated funds, equipment or expertise to county disaster planning operations.

A second thing that must happen is that county public services, particularly non-essential services, get local advocates. Most non-essential services have low political saliency, and without a strong local proponent they could easily become marginalized. This is particularly true for disaster management and planning, which typically generates wide general interest only just before or just after a disaster strikes. The importance of the disaster management director in pushing forward disaster planning has been cited in numerous cases (see Drabek and Hoetmer, 1991; Sylves and Waugh, 1990) and seems also to have played a role in the rural counties of Florida.

Although there always has been great variation in the extent and quality of services in rural counties, it seems that during the 1980s the differences became greater. Disaster management is an example of the wide range of county responses to the increased fiscal stress of the past decade. During the mid and late-1980s, many public administrators and researchers predicted that fiscal stress would cause increased heterogeneity among rural governments' abilities to provide and maintain public services (Stinson, 1987; Hite and Ulbrich, 1986). This study of disaster management funding offers evidence that this process is under way.

Acknowledgements

Earl J. Baker, Department of Geography, Florida State University, offered helpful comments on earlier drafts of this paper.

References

Bender, L.G. and Zolty, T.C., 1986, 'Rapid growth: impacts on the politics and administration of rural governments' in J. Seroka (ed.), *Rural public administration.*, Greenwood Press, New York, pp. 115–35

Brown, R.B., Geertsen, H.R. and Krannich, R.S., 1989, 'Community satisfaction and social integration in a boomtown: a longitudinal analysis', *Rural Sociology*, **54**(4): 568–86

Browne, W.P. and Reid, J.N., 1990, 'Misconceptions, institutional impediments, and the problems of rural government', *Public Administration Quarterly.*, **14**(3): 265–84

Bureau of Economic and Business Research, College of Business Administration, 1992, *1991 Florida statistical abstract*, The University Presses of Florida, Gainesville, FL

Camboni, S.M. and Napier, T.L., 1985, 'The perceived financial condition of small-scale jurisdications: the elected leaders' perspective', *Journal of the Community Development Society.* **16**(1): 16–40

Cigler, B.A., 1984, 'Small city and rural governance: the changing environment', *Public Administration Review.*, **44**(6): 540–5

Clark, C., Clark, J., Carruthers, G., Eastman, C., Hansen, K.R. and Jeffrey, T., 1986, 'Alternative models of the budgetary behavior of rural governments' in J. Seroka (ed.), *Rural public administration—problems and prospects*, Greenwood Press, New York, pp. 39–55

Cook, A.K. and Poremba, G.A., 1985, 'Budget changes in county organizations: who is affected and how do agencies cope?', *Journal of the Community Development Society*, **16**(2): 38–53

Cortese, C.F., 1982, 'The impacts of rapid growth on the provision and financing of local public services' in B.A. Weber and R.E. Howell (eds), *Coping with rapid growth in rural communities*, Westview Press, Boulder, CO, pp. 115–35

Danzinger, J.N. and Ring, P.S., 1982, 'Fiscal limitations: A selective review of recent research', *Public Administration Review.*, **42**(1): 47–55

Downes, B.T., 1987, 'The fiscal consequences of changing federal and state revenue policies: the case of small Oregon cities', *Publius: The Journal of Federalism*, **17**(4): 189–205

Downs, G.W. and Larkey, P.D., 1981, 'Fiscal reform and governmental efficiency: hanging tough', *Policy Sciences*, **13**(4): 381–96

Drabek, T.E. and Hoetmer, G.J. (eds), 1991, *Emergency management: principles and practice for local government.*, International City Management Association, Washington, DC

Faupel, C. and Bailey, C., 1988, 'Contingencies affecting emergency preparedness for hazardous wastes', *International Journal of Mass Emergencies and Disasters.*, **6**: 131–54

Florida, State Department of Banking and Finance, 1981, *State of Florida, local government financial report, fiscal year 1980–1981.*, Office of the State Comptroller, Tallahassee FL

Florida, State Department of Banking and Finance, 1984, *State of Florida, local government financial report, fiscal year 1983–1984.*, Office of the State Comptroller, Tallahassee, FL

Florida, State Department of Banking and Finance, 1987, *State of Florida, local government financial report, fiscal year 1986–1987*, Office of the State Comptroller, Tallahassee, FL

Florida, State Department of Banking and Finance, 1990, *State of Florida, local government financial report, fiscal year 1989–1990*, Office of the State Comptroller, Tallahassee, FL

Garten, R.H. and Russel, E.R., 1986, 'Integration of hazardous materials emergency planning into small-town planning; Recent advances in hazardous materials transportation research, an international exchange process', *Transportation Research Board*, National Research Council, Washington, DC, pp. 74–78

Halstead, J.M., Chase, R.A., Murdock, S.H. and Leistritz, F.L., 1984, *Socioeconomic impact management*, Westview Press, Boulder

Hite, J., and Ulbrich, H., 1986, 'Fiscal stress in rural America: some straws in the wind', *American Journal of Agricultural Economics*, **68**: 1188–93

Hoetmer, G.J., 1983, 'Emergency management: individual and county data', *Baseline Data Report*, **15**: 1–13

King, L. and Harris, G., 1989, 'Local response to rapid rural growth, New York and Vermont cases', *Journal of the American Planning Association*, **55**(2): 181–91

Koutnik, F., 1992, 'Personal interview', Bureau of Emergency Management, Florida Department of Community Affairs, October

Labadie, J.R., 1984, 'Problems in local emergency management', *Environmental Management* **8**(6): 489–94

Lassey, W.R., Butler, L.M. and Kullberg, V., 1986, 'Public service budget constraints: the perspective of rural officials in the USA', *Journal of Rural Studies*, **2**(4): 337–43

Lipset, S.M. and Raad, E., 1978, 'The message of Proposition 13, *Commentary*, **66**: 42–6

Luloff, A.E. and Swanson, L.E. (eds), 1990, *American rural communities*, Westview Press, Boulder, CO

McKenna, F. Jr., Russo, P.A., Jr., Hikbbeln, H.K. and Shumavon, D.H., 1990, 'National fiscal policy changes and the impact on rural governments: budget cuts and the loss of grants', *Public Administration Quarterly*, **14**(3): 324–52

Macmanus, S.A. and Pammer, W.J. Jr., 1990, 'Cutbacks in the country: retrenchment in rural villages, townships, and counties', *Public Administration Quarterly*, **14**(3): 302–23.

Marsden, T., Lowe, P. and Whatmore, S., 1990, *Rural restructuring, global processes and their responses*, David Fulton Publishers, London

May, P., 1988, 'Disaster recovery and reconstruction' in L. Comfort (ed.), *Managing disasters, strategies and policy perspectives*, Duke University Press, Durham, NC, pp. 236–51

Moore, J.W., 1987, 'Cutoff at town hall', *National Journal*, **19**(14): 862–67

Murray, J.A. and Weber, B.A., 1982, 'The impacts of rapid growth on the provision and financing of local public services' in B.A. Weber and R.E. Howell (eds), *Coping with rapid growth in rural communities*, Westview Press, Boulder, CO, pp. 97–113

Robinson, G.M., 1990, *Conflict and change in the countryside, rural society, economy and planning in the developed world*, Belhaven, New York

Rossi, P.H., Wright, J.D. and Weber-Burdin, E., 1982, *Natural hazards and public choice; the state and local politics of hazard mitigation*, Academic Press, New York

Seroka, J., 1986, 'A typology for rural administration' in J. Seroka (ed.), *Rural public administration—problems and prospects*, Greenwood Press, New York, pp. 21–37

Sokolow, A.D., 1987, 'Introduction: small governments as newcomers to American federalism', *Publius; The Journal of Federalism*, **17**(4): 1–13

Stinson, T.F., 1987, 'The farm crisis and the future of rural local governments', *Publius: The Journal of Federalism*, **17**(4): 175–88

Streib, G. and Waugh, W.L Jr., 1991, 'The changing responsibilities of county governments: data from a national survey of county leaders', *American Review of Public Administration*, **21**(2): 139–55

Sylves, R.T. and Waugh, W.L. Jr. (eds.), 1990, *Cities and disaster: North American studies in emergency management*, C.C. Thomas, Springfield, IL

Walker, W.E. and Chaiken, J.M., 1982, 'The effects of fiscal contraction on innovation in the public sector', *Policy Sciences*, **15**(2): 141–65

Wolensky, R.P. and Wolkensky, K.C., 1991, 'American local government and the disaster management problem', *Local Government Studies*, March/April: 15–32

4 1991–92, the year in review in US rural planning: riding the crest of conservative reaction?
Mark B. Lapping and Eve Baron

For rural planners, last year's Supreme Court decision in the case of *Lucas* v. *South Carolina Coastal Council* looms as one of the most significant rulings in recent years. The *New York Times* calls it one of the 'critical cases' signaling a shift or 'tilt in favor of the owner' against the state in land-use regulation (Dunlap, 1992). We will return to *Lucas*, but first we will attempt to analyze other events, cases and programs which may reflect more generally the nature and texture of US rural planning during the past year.

Wetlands

As in the past several years, wetland issues have again proven to be as important as they are contentious. Very little clarity has emerged over the year on wetland policy and planning. Problems persist over the definition of wetlands, the mapping of wetlands, programs to save and mitigate their destruction and the development of a cohesive federal policy to integrate these concerns.

The Bush Administration's efforts to redefine and to categorize wetlands met with substantial opposition both within the federal bureaucracy itself as well as outside of the government. Comments from the regional offices of the federal Environmental Protection Agency (EPA) indicated strong internal disagreement with a strategy which many saw as an attempt to remove millions of acres of wetlands from protection. The movement to redefine wetlands is headed by developers and farmers, each seeking to overturn 1989 EPA rules which put more land under the protection of the Clean Water Act, thus effectively removing them from development. The process has, if nothing less, spawned greater chaos and less coherence in federal policy.

EPA's new draft of the wetlands manual which, if accepted, would constitute federal policy, was leaked in May of 1991 to environmental groups and organizations. It generated substantial criticism. Essentially the draft rules would have required that to be classified as a wetland land would have met all three criteria for designation: hydrophytic vegetation, wetland hydrology and hydric soils. Yet, the draft itself recognized that any given site may not exhibit all of these characteristics at the very same time of the year. To compensate for this problem, certain types of land use, like potholes or vernal pools, would be classified as 'Difficult-to-Identify' wetland subject to further investigation (Land Use Planning Report, 1991a). Even so, the result of implementing these rules would be the withdrawal of millions of acres from protection, according to many environmental organizations.

If the proposed manual and rules garnered little support within the environmental community, they met with open hostility within other branches of the federal government, albeit for entirely different reasons. EPA's strategy ran into immediate opposition within the executive branch. The President's Office of Management and Budget (OMB) wanted more of the 'Difficult-to-Identify' lands deleted from the listing of potentially protected lands. Arguing for different vegetation criteria for identifying and inventorying wetlands, OMB's approach would have led to the withdrawal of even more acreage from protection, including a half million acres from the Florida Everglades region (Land Use Planning Report, 1991b).

In an effort to circumvent OMB's intransigence, EPA Administrator William K. Reilly released the proposed EPA wetland manual for public review in the partial hope of generating enough public support to derail executive branch opposition (Land Use Planning Report, 1991c). In testimony before Congress Reilly noted that the proposed new rules sought to address a number of outstanding issues and problems generated by the existing wetlands manual issued in 1989. These included, among others: (a) concern that wetlands determination did not reflect hydrologic, soils and plant life criteria; (b) the problem often voiced by developers and farmers that seven days of ground wetness should not constitute classification of land as a wetland—the OMB had pushed for a twenty-one day minimum while EPA endorsed study of a ten to twenty-day wetness rule; (c) that actual field conditions were often not reflected in the 1989 manual; and (d) that not enough public input was incorporated in the previous EPA rules (Land Use Planning Report, 1991d).

Reilly's gambit failed utterly, and a compromise approach much closer to OMB's aims and language emerged from Washington in August 1991. Brokered by the White House's Council on Competitiveness, headed by Vice President Quayle, the new language endorsed a twenty-one day minimum inundation requirement as well as vegetative classification criteria considered less restrictive.

Negative public reaction to the new language and proposed changes in EPA's wetlands manual was swift. Further, even from within the federal government criticism was intense. The Army Corps of Engineers, charged with enforcing Section 404 of the Clean Water Act which regulates wetland development permits, characterized the rules as 'ignoring the demonstrated interrelationships of soils, vegetation and hydrology' (Land Use Planning Report, 1991e). Criticism from the scientific community focused on the perceived unreasonableness of the twenty-one day inundation requirement for wetlands designation. Too much wetland acreage would have been lost, it was argued, under this rule.

By January 1992, EPA received over 40,000 public comments on its proposed revisions (Land Use Planning Report, 1992a). By mid-month Robert Wayland, Director of EPA's Office of Wetlands, Oceans and Watersheds, was forced to announce that final revisions to the rules were unlikely before the end of 1992, in part as a result of the number of public comments and the complexity of the issues involved (Land Use Planning Report, 1992b). By the summer of 1992, a further revision of the rules and manual were under development though this time spearheaded by the Corps of Engineers, the US Fish and Wildlife Service and the US Department of Agriculture. This new process is, as noted in one leading publication, 'an attempt to find some middle ground between the agencies' 1989 revision of the manual, criticized by the Bush administration as being an attempt to bring non-wetlands under Clean Water Act jurisdiction, and the administration's 1991 redefinition effort, criticized by environmental groups and biologists as removing too much wetlands from protection' (Land Use Planning Report, 1992c).

Although it is impossible to predict accurately the outcome of the wetlands debate in the United States, we can identify certain themes which seem to have emerged. First, definitions based on the validity of scientific criteria relative to wetlands delineation remain important matters for scientists and policy-makers, especially those within the federal government's environmental bureaucracies. Second, EPA Administrator Reilly does not appear to enjoy widespread support within the executive branch of the Bush administration. This was underscored, again, most recently by the absence of an endorsement of his proposed stand at the Rio Conference on the Environment. And third, Vice President Quayle's Council on Competitiveness has emerged as a new and powerful actor in the process of environmental and land-use decision-making—almost always on the side of those who seek to expand development activities. One can anticipate that it will play an increasingly more powerful role in future resource management debates.

Farmland preservation

In the effort to preserve farmland, increased local attention is being paid to the transfer of development rights (TDR) as a technique to retain critical agricultural lands. One of the reasons why TDR programs are growing is their relatively low cost when compared with purchase of development rights (PDR) techniques. The current economic recession has made it exceedingly difficult to generate the level of public funding necessary to purchase such rights in farmland, though public enthusiasm for such programs remains strong. Only a few states and localities have established permanent and dedicated funding sources for PDR and TDR programs. In the case of Maryland, for example, a land transfer tax is dedicated explicitly to fund its PDR program. As one expert has said of funding for PDRs, 'programs funded solely by state governments may become a thing of the past' (Farmland Preservation Report, 1991a). Within the past year new TDR programs have been initiated in Maryland, Pennsylvania, New Jersey, North Carolina, Michigan and Kentucky. Most of these programs are being carried out on the county level to augment state level programs, though in New Jersey and Pennsylvania the programs have been established on the township level, the most local of all types of jurisdictions in rural areas (Farmland Preservation Report, 1991c).

At the federal level, considerable debate has flared up over the long-standing issue of just how much agricultural land is being lost to urbanization and other factors. In early 1992 the Economic Research Service (ERS) of the USDA released a report seeking to quantify the nature and extent of farmland loss throughout the country (Farmland Preservation Report, 1992c). In essence this latest study comes to radically different conclusions from those stated in the National Agricultural Lands Study, issued in 1981. It argues that there is no legitimate cause for national concern over land loss given the amount of new lands being brought into production. However, even within the USDA the ERS study has had its critics, including Lloyd Wright, Director of the Soil Conservation Services' Division of Land Use, who stated that 'the land being converted is the very best land' whose impact is 'far more significant than the numbers would imply.' (Farmland Preservation Report, 1992c). Others have pointed out that the ERS study does not make adequate distinctions between types and quality of land lost or brought into production, the social and environmental costs generated when new and more erodible lands come into cultivation, nor the nature of local impacts of the loss of agricultural lands. In summing up his assessment of the study, noted farmland researcher and planner Robert Coughlin said that ERS was 'arguing a point of view rather than providing research here . . . the interpretation is misleading . . . it's certainly not an objective presentation of research' (Farmland Preservation Report, 1992c).

Disenchantment with the federal response to agricultural land loss runs deep. While the Farmland Protection Policy Act (FPPA) was passed as part of the 1981 Farm Bill, it now 'lies dormant on the shelves of the USDA' due to a lack of implementation, according to Ralph Grossi, President of the American Farmland Trust, a national farmland preservation organization (Farmland Preservation Report, 1991d). Ironically, as more states seek to meet the criteria for participation in the 'Farms for the

Future' program of the 1991 Farm Bill, whereby matching federal funds would be made available to states which establish 'trust funds' to create or maintain farmland preservation programs, the federal government's role in farmland preservation remains minimal, at best.

Indeed, it is precisely because few levels of government seem to have the capacity to arrest the erosion of agricultural resources, that private organizations, largely in the form of land trusts, have emerged to assume leadership positions throughout the country. Over 900 land trusts now exist in the United States. A significant increase in the number of such organizations, especially over the last decade, is 'partly a response to the lack of federal support for land conservation', according to one New York State environmental leader (Farmland Preservation Report, 1991h). By the end of 1991, land trusts were responsible for the protection of nearly three million acres nation-wide. While these lands do not constitute a large percentage of the total rural land base, many of these sites are of local importance. Trusts have directed their attention primarily to agricultural lands, river corridors, wetlands, forests and other natural areas. Perhaps the largest and best known trusts are the Nature Conservancy and the American Farmland Trust, though literally hundreds of organizations with a more local orientation toward their work have been created. As Jean Hocker, President of the Land Trust Alliance has noted, 'unlike global issues like tropical deforestation or ozone depletion, protecting lands in our own communities is something over which we can have a direct influence' (Farmland Preservation Report, 1991h). This local emphasis is perhaps the greatest strength of the land trust movement.

A good case in point is that of the Vermont Land Trust, which recently celebrated its fifteenth year in operation. While working closely with the Vermont Chapter of the Nature Conservancy and other organizations to protect important natural areas in its state, the Vermont Land Trust has focused much of its energy upon the preservation of farmland. Significantly, it believes that the most effective way to do this is by protecting and enhancing the economic viability of farming. Though it has purchased development rights, easements and entire farms throughout the state, one of its more interesting projects is the Mettowee Valley Conservation Project headquartered in Pawlett in the southern part of the state. Under the direction of Jacki Lappen, the Mettowee Valley project has sought to preserve a 'critical mass' of farms so that real farm economies and the necessary agribusiness infrastructure might be preserved and enhanced. Nearly 3,600 acres of prime agricultural land have been preserved either through Trust purchases of development rights—on eight farms to date— or by deed restriction purchases and donations on a number of other farms and properties. Long an important dairy region, the Mettowee Valley farms remain in active dairy production, while maple syrup products provide good supplementary incomes given the region's proximity to large tourist areas. Support for the Mettowee Valley Project throughout the region is strong and reflects something which land trusts have come to recognize as one of their great strengths; there is a reservoir of support for local land conservation efforts which preserve agricultural resources, so crucial to retaining a high 'quality of life'.

State growth control and planning

Rural land-use planning is increasingly becoming part and parcel of larger state-wide growth management programs. One journal has even asked if the 1990s will come to be known as the 'decade of growth management?' (Land Use Law Report, 1992a). In terms of trends in growth management policy this same assessment notes the following characteristics of the movement:

Top-down management imposed by the state is out, if in fact it was ever in. Bottom-up management is the watchword for the new wave. Will it work? Time will tell . . . the newer plans favor a building-block system; thoughtful local planning, integrated with other localities at the regional level, and regional planning that takes into account state-wide needs. At all levels, plenty of public input is encouraged. (Land Use Law Report, 1992a)

As noted in last year's annual review, Maryland is moving ahead with its program for state-wide growth management (Lapping and Moser, 1992). Its approach ran into significant opposition in the state legislature, led by counties and municipalities fearful of the loss of local power, and farmers who were, as one student of the process has remarked, 'more interested in land values than in land stewardship' (Bowers, 1991). What emerged in place of the previous initiative, known as the 2020 Plan, was a more modest and incremental approach. The new strategy would do several things, including: reconstituting the State Planning Commission as the Maryland Growth and Resource Committee; creating an interagency co-ordinating committee within state government to unify and clarify state-level decisions which hold the potential of generating new growth; requiring that local zoning and subdivision regulations be consistent with a comprehensive plan; and providing local governments with new growth control powers. The Director of State Planning Ronald Kreitner described the new proposal as—'not necessarily a bold initiative but a groundwork on which a consensus can be built' (Farmland Preservation Report, 1992a). None the less, the Economic Growth, Resource Protection and Planning Act was passed into law by the Maryland legislature after a year in which considerable energy was expended in numerous consensus-building public meetings and legislative sessions (Land Use Law Report, 1992b).

Other states are examining how different growth management techniques and approaches might be implemented. For example, Virginia is reviewing how growth management and a TDR program might be combined to offer greater protection to farmland, concentrate population into existing community centers rather than throughout the countryside and preserve the remaining open space amenities in the burgeoning northern Virginia region (Farmland Preservation Report, 1991f). California is also evaluating its growth management system. One of its most important goals is the preservation of agricultural land. Strong public support exists not only to secure the state's farmland for its own sake but also because, as one government official has noted of California, 'when people talk about preservation of farmland, yes, they're talking about open space and preventing sprawl' (Farmland Preservation Report, 1991e). Similarly, Massachusetts is beginning to review its options. A Special Commission on Growth and Change has held numerous public hearings throughout the state and completed a report which asks the rest of Massachusetts to follow the lead of its Cape Cod region in seeking to control unregulated growth and development before it is too late (Farmland Preservation Report, 1991g).

Turning to existing programs Washington State's growth management program, passed into law in 1990, has been subject to review by the state's new Growth Strategies Commission. Its primary new recommendation was required concurrence between local and county plans with state-wide goals (Farmland Preservation Report, 1991b). This requirement, together with other recommendations made by the Commission, was seen as leading to significant strengthening of the overall program. For example, before a community can place agricultural lands in an 'urban growth' boundary or zone, a TDR or PDR program must exist. This would not only provide equity for farmers but would, within the context of state-wide goals, frustrate the movement of large blocs of farmland into development. Other recommendations of the Commission were rejected, however, especially those calling for the acquisition by the state of more open space. Yet, the compromise reform legislation seems to have been well received. As one rural county planner put it, the new bill was 'our last best hope to preserve farmland at all. Not moving now would have lost it all in the next 10 years' (Farmland Preservation Report, 1991i). Further, a new private organization, 1,000 Friends of Washington, was founded to support the growth management program. Like similar groups elsewhere, most notably in Oregon where the concept of 1,000 Friends began, this citizen's group seeks to build a large public voice in support of growth controls to counteract other pressure groups opposed to controls.

After more than six years in the making, New Jersey's growth management strategy, its first state plan, was signed into law in June of 1992. While one of the primary goals of the plan is the concentration of development as part of a larger strategy to redevelop the state's cities—whose fortunes have been flagging since the early 1960s—the plan also seeks to preserve agricultural and forest lands, to maintain the integrity of existing rural villages and hamlets and to protect environmentally sensitive lands and critical areas. Opposition from a coalition of developers and farmers was largely nullified when the farming community, led by the New Jersey Farm Bureau, accepted a statement on the protection of farmer's equity in land as part of the final plan. The statement is vague and as one rural planner observed 'the State Planning Commission provided very little guidance on how [equity] should be interpreted—the equity policy could be the Achilles' heel of the state plan' (Farmland Preservation Report, 1992d). While that remains to be seen and will, in all likelihood, be determined by the courts, it is already clear that the state plan will bring about better coordination of capital facilities location with state-wide land-use goals. Further, the method of negotiating concurrence among the state, county, and local governments, known as the 'cross acceptance process', stands as a model for the resolution of land-use conflicts between different tiers of government.

It is perhaps significant that these discussions on growth management are taking place in the midst of very difficult economic times. While opponents of growth control often argue that strict policies will only retard development and thus push the economy into further decline, advocates counter with the assertion that the lack of growth management and land-use controls creates greater burdens upon taxpayers by promoting inefficient land-use patterns and expensive infrastructure costs.

Criticism of current growth management programs also exists. In Florida, for example, concern over the state's seven-year-old experiment in control has led Governor Lawton Chiles to appoint the Environmental Land Management Study Committee to review the Florida system with an eye toward addressing the problems many perceive it has created. Paramount among these, according to some, is the concurrency policy for roads wherein developers must finance road construction at the same time they are building developments which will be served by those roads. This requirement has been affixed to large-scale developments in Florida—between 750 to 3,000 units—and has led some developers to scale back on their projects. This often means that developers lose some of their profit margin. One critic has put it bluntly: 'Florida's growth management laws have strangled development' (McCloutier, 1992). While another, speaking about the approval process under Florida's law, says that 'The cost of time in that process is almost prohibitive' (McCloutier, 1992).

The Lucas decision and beyond

In 1986 David H. Lucas, a developer, purchased two oceanfront lots on the Isle of Palms, in South Carolina, for $4,975,000. It was his intent to build single-family homes on the land. In 1988 South Carolina passed its Beachfront Management Act which prohibited the building of such permanent structures on this property. The area in question was prone to flooding and in 1989, Hurricane Hugo devastated the area. It is quite possible that had any homes been built on the land, they would have been destroyed by the hurricane's intensity. Lucas sued the South Carolina Coastal Council, which enforces the Act and related plans, under the terms of the US Constitutions's Fifth Amendment, which requires 'just compensation' when a 'taking' of property has occurred. In a lower level trial court Lucas was awarded $1.2 million but the South Carolina State Supreme Court reversed that judgement, on appeal, accepting the argument that the regulation in question was necessary to protect public safety and thus compensation was not necessary. The logic of this argument appears to be consistent with the US Supreme Court's finding in the 1987 case of *Nollan* v. *California Coastal Commission* wherein it accepted the principle that a taking of private property by a public agency is acceptable when it is 'closely linked to a specific public policy that is in the interest of the state' (Farmland Preservation Report, 1992b).

Upon final appeal to the US Supreme Court, Lucas won. In a split decision, 6–3, the Supreme Court found that 'when the owner of real property has been called upon to sacrifice *all* economically beneficial uses in the name of the common good, that is, to leave his property economically idle, he has suffered a taking' (Dunlap, 1992). In dissent Justice Harry Blackmun wrote that 'the threshold inquiry for imposition of the court's new rule, "deprivation of all economically valuable use", itself cannot be determined objectively'. Further, 'as the court admits, whether the owner has been deprived of all economic value of his property will depend on how "property" is defined'. The decision in *Lucas* presents two potentially serious problems for planners and policy-makers. First, it would appear that compensation is required whenever there is a total destruction of economic value no matter the legitimacy and wisdom of the regulation in question, unless the law merely makes explicit an obvious and pre-existing limitation on the property. The Supreme Court decision takes us back to a period when land-use regulation was defined by the principles of nuisance law wherein some land uses were recognized as 'nuisance *per se*' as opposed to 'nuisance in fact'. Further, *Lucas* seems to limit the 'noxious uses' doctrine of law which has been used to justify total takings in many regulatory regimes (Payne, 1992).

Lucas has created great concern among planners and policy-makers alike. One analyst has said that the decision is likely to constitute 'a whole new battleground' (Dunlap, 1992). The real estate community, on the other hand, seems buoyed by the recent decision. As the President of the New Jersey Association of Realtors has commented, 'the decision by the US Supreme Court is a victory for private property owners', while another executive of the same organization said 'for too long, government has been cavalier concerning private property rights. This decision is tremendous' (Mosca, 1992).

Conservative activism

By itself *Lucas* will likely be an important case. More significantly, it is but part of a larger emerging pattern which challenges rural land-use planning and management throughout the country. In addition to the logic of *Lucas* there is the previously mentioned growing influence of Vice President Quayle's Competitiveness Council. The Council is working to undercut environmental standards in general and, more particularly, federal lands policy in the West, where so much of the land base is under the control of the government.

One example of this phenomenon is the Bureau of Land Management (BLM), the federal agency which controls the purchase and trade of some 270 million acres of public land (one-eighth of the total of the US land mass). It has emerged as one of those federal resource bureaucracies feeling the pressure to turn national treasures into ready cash. Critics claim that the BLM consistently underappraises the worth of public lands in order to sell them quickly and strategically to developers who share the Bureau's vision of efficient land use. Says Guy Martin, who monitored the Bureau for former President Jimmy Carter, 'all other values were subordinated to the goal of getting rid of lands . . . The signal came from on high, get that land off the public rolls. It was literally a mania' (Widener and Olney, 1992).

Finally, there is the growing power of the loosely organized 'wise use movement,' a successor to the Sage Brush Rebellion of the Reagan years. Funded and supported by the forest products and mining companies, the Rev. Moon's Unification Church, off-road vehicle manufacturers, like Honda and Kawasaki, and various conservative groups, the 'wise use movement' has mounted numerous local and national campaigns to defeat bond and tax increases for the purchase of additional public lands, worked for the elimination of restrictions on wetlands development, limitations on timber harvesting in national forests, proposed the further gutting of the Endangered Species Act, and other pro-environmental and public lands programs. Some of these efforts have been successful, as in the case of the defeat of New York State's 'Environmental Bond' in 1991.

This politicization of rural lands policy by conservative forces looms as a potentially significant issue for the future. Depending upon the decisions made in the current Presidential and Congressional elections, we could be witnessing only the proverbial 'tip of the iceberg' of a new conservative wave in rural land-use policy.

References

Bowers, D., 1991, 'Maryland state planning initiative sent back for more study', *Farmland Preservation Report*, **1** (7): 5

Dunlap, D.W., 1992, 'Resolving property "takings",: courts seem to tilt in favor of owners', *New York Times*, 8/23/92, p. 1

Farmland Preservation Report, 1991a, 'Budget cuts cripple easement programs in the northeast', **1** (4): 3

Farmland Preservation Report, 1991b, 'Legislative brief: Washington', **1** (4): 6–7

Farmland Preservation Report, 1991c, 'A dozen localities putting TDR on trial as preservation tool', **1** (6): 1–4, 8

Farmland Preservation Report, 1991d, 'AFT conference speakers sidestep federal role question', **1** (7): 3

Farmland Preservation Report, 1991e, 'New direction for growth management slated for California', **1** (8): 1, 4

Farmland Preservation Report, 1991f, 'Virginia legislators explore growth management options', **1** (9): 1, 3

Farmland Preservation Report, 1991g, 'Massachusetts could review statewide planning initiative', **1** (12): 1, 6–7

Farmland Preservation Report, 1991h, 'Land conservationists should seek to revitalize federal fund', **2** (1): 1

Farmland Preservation Report, 1991i, 'Washington planning law strengthened', **2** (2 and 3): 5–8

Farmland Preservation Report, 1992a, 'Maryland state plan tries "more incremental approach"', **2** (4): 2

Farmland Preservation Report, 1992b, 'Supreme court ruling could chill land conservation', **2** (4):6

Farmland Preservation Report, 1992c, 'Study heats up decade-long debate on farmland loss', **2** (7):1–3, 8

Farmland Preservation Report, 1992d, 'Equity issue puts pall of uncertainty over state plan', **2** (10 and 11): 3

Land Use Law Report, 1992a, 'The decade of growth management' **20** (9): 65

Land Use Law Report, 1992b, 'Maryland legislature passes growth management bill', **20** (9): 67

Land Use Planning Report, 1991a, 'Draft of revised EPA wetlands manual surface', **19** (11): 83

Land Use Planning Report, 1991b, 'EPA, OMB seemingly at impasse on wetlands issue;, **19** (14): 107

Land Use Planning Report, 1991c, 'EPA's proposed revision', **19** (15): 113

Land Use Planning Report, 1991d, 'Wetlands manual: EPA, OMB agree to disagree', **19** (15): 115

Land Use Planning Report, 1991e, 'Evaluations pan new wetlands definition', **19** (25): 1

Land Use Planning Report, 1992a, 'Wetland definition revisions published', **20** (1): 3

Land Use Planning Report, 1992b, 'Don't expect wetlands manual anytime soon, EPA official says', **20** (2): 12

Land Use Planning Report, 1992c, 'Wetland manual revision', revisited, **20** (16): 122

Lapping, M.B. and Moser, J., 1992, 'Contemporary issues in US rural planning and policy-making 1990–91', in *Progress in Rural Policy and Planning*, Belhaven Press, London pp. 34–43

McCloutier, M., 1992, 'Growth management act under review', *New York Times*, 10/23/92, p. D1

Mosca, P.J., 1992, 'NJAR supports supreme court opinion regarding private property rights', *New Jersey Realtor*, (August): 1

Payne, J.M., 1992, 'From the courts: takings and environmental regulations', unpublished manuscript, Rutgers University, School of Law, Newark, NJ

Widener, D. and Olney, W., 1992, 'This land was your land', *The Village Voice.*, 10/6/92, p. 25

5 Current demographics and economic perspectives on rural America
Owen J. Furuseth

Because of the dynamic character of rural population and economy, the basic data necessary to assess change on the rural landscape is often difficult to collect and can be problematic. Lacking sufficient information, it is hard to know what impacts large-scale social and economic events are having on rural America, or what form population and economic restructuring is taking in the countryside. Many fundamental questions surrounding rural populations, including farm residency; demographic structure; labor force participation; income; and poverty are addressed in a valuable (and inexpensive) new Federal publication, *Residents of Farms and Rural Areas: 1990*.

The report is a joint product of the Bureau of the Census and the Economic Research Service of the US Department of Agriculture. It presents a statistical portrait of US farm residents and rural area populations as of 1990. The current data are supplemented by historical information taken from past census products. In some instances, these data extend back as far as 1890. The text and multiple tables present numerous coarse grained examples of historical and geographical changes in rural populations.

As one would expect, the terminology and data definitions used in the report follow standard Census Bureau practice. Thus, farm residents consist of persons who reside on farms. The Census Bureau defines a farm as a place that sold agricultural products valued at $1,000 or more during the preceding year. Following Census Bureau practice, farms located in urban areas are not included in the data. The rural non-farm resident population includes persons living in rural areas but not on a farm. The term rural area is defined as all geographic areas outside of urban settlements. The Census Bureau classifies places with at least 2,500 residents as urban. Areas defined as rural and urban in the 1980 census were used as a basis for this report.

Perhaps the most valuable aspect of the report is that it provides an up-to-date composite 'snapshot' of rural America. Among some of the critical pieces of information included in the report are:

— The number of persons residing in rural areas was 66,964,000; or slightly more than 27 per cent of the total population. The population of rural America grew 12.6 per cent during the 1980s. However, the overwhelming majority of the increase (91.9 per cent) was within metropolitan settlements. Rural areas within metropolitan settlements grew by 28.6 per cent, while growth outside of metropolitan settlements was only 1.7 per cent. Consequently, much of this growth is probably more suburban rather than rural.

— The US farm population continues to shrink. Only 1.9 per cent (4,591,000 persons) of the population lives on farms. Over the past decade, the farm resident population dropped by 1.5 million people or 24.1 per cent. This decline paralleled the loss of the previous decade when farm population declined by 25.4 per cent. A majority of American farmers live in the Midwest, with the South following in second position. Together these two regions are home to nearly 80 per cent of the US farm population.

— Most farm residents do not work full time in farming. Fifty-five per cent worked in other occupations. A majority of men, nearly 60 per cent were employed primarily in farming, but only 22.1 per cent of the farm women worked primarily in farming. Farm workers were self-employed significantly more often than other workers; 38.2 per cent were self-employed whereas 8 per cent of non-farmers in the US are considered self-employed. Among male farmers working primarily in agriculture, the self-employment rate is 72.7 per cent.

— The median income for rural households was $28,906 (1989), with only slight differences between farm and non-farm households. Family incomes, however, showed some differences between farmers and non-farmers. Non-farm farmers had median incomes of $34,300 while farmers incomes were $30,809.

— Almost 13 per cent (12.8 per cent) of rural residents are living in poverty. The poverty rates between farm and non-farm persons and families are not significantly different.

— Racially, farm residents are overwhelmingly White. Moreover, the number of Black farmers continues to drop. In 1990 farm residents were 97.5 per cent White, 1.5 per cent Black, and 1 per cent other races. As recently as 1960, Blacks comprised 11.0 per cent of farm residents.

Readers wishing to order a copy of *Residents of Farms and Rural Areas, 1990* should contact the Superintendent of Documents, US Government Printing Office, Washington, DC 20402. The identifying code for the report is Current Population Reports, Series P-20, No. 457 (Stock No. 803–005–00057–5). The cost for a paper copy is $3.50.

Section II
United Kingdom

edited by
Andrew W. Gilg

Introduction

Andrew W. Gilg

This year the UK section is divided into two sections: first, two substantive articles; and second, an Annual Review for 1991/92. In the substantive articles section, Adrian Phillips, the former director of the Countryside Commission, reflects on his time as director and the influences of various Secretaries of State in the Thatcher and post-Thatcher era. This is a very interesting piece because it throws considerable light on the continuing debate in rural planning as to whether Britain is a pluralist democracy, a cosmetic democracy run by the Civil Service, or a cosmetic democracy tolerated by the financial classes. The reader is encouraged to read between the lines of Adrian's reflections, because Adrian has not been able for obvious reasons to make explicit some of the implicit observations he is making about the reality of power in Britain today. The article concludes by speculating that in reality there is no set pattern, only a random sequence of events, or even just a series of maverick cock-ups.

Another very interesting observation derived from editing and discussing the article with Adrian is that there is a stark division between those who theorize about rural planning and those who practice it. During this process it became clear that practitioners are almost entirely ignorant of the often heated debates that develop among academics about the nature and structure of power and about the development of theory. In the real world of policy-making and implementation there is no time for theory, only pragmatic decision-making, often under considerable pressure of time and as Adrian concludes 'what matters is what works'. Conversely, academics with long vacations for reflection are able to imagine up all sorts of complicated conspiracy theories. To these conspirators Adrians' article provides a badly needed draught of cold water to cool their fevered thoughts.

The final and saddest conclusion to be drawn from Adrian's article is that practitioners and academics are like ships that pass in the night in that they see but do not communicate with each other. To remedy this there should be a series of exchange schemes between the two groups.

The second article, by Hadrian Cook, focuses on water management in the lowlands and demonstrates how water has become and will continue to be perhaps the single biggest rural planning issue in the 1990s. For too long water has been assumed to be a free good. Now water pollution, droughts and water privatisation have shown that water is very much a scarce and costly good. Hadrian examines in depth some of the problems that have been revealed in recent years and some of the solutions tried or proposed. These include severe controls over land use around threatened groundwater areas, and indeed at the time of final editing (16/12/92) the NRA had just published proposals to put such controls into operation, with major implications for new housing and agriculture in the affected areas. These proposals will be covered in Volume Four.

The second part of the UK section is devoted to the Editor's Annual Review, which covers roughly the period from September 1991 to December 1992. Much of this review is taken up by the inauguration of powers under the Town and Country Planning Act 1990 and the Planning and Compensation Act 1991, emphasising the power of the executive arm of government to implement in detail the broad themes laid down by the legislative arm. In spite of the April election the year was a very busy one, and a mass of important changes were made. The changes as ever were of degree rather than kind, reflecting the essentially incremental nature of rural policy change, and even the much vaunted May 1992 reform of the CAP was incremental rather than radical, even though it did reflect a big shift away from subsidising production to subsidising farmers and the environment. In conclusion, the year was perhaps one of the most significant for change for several years, and this is reflected in the extra length of the UK section for this volume, and a bigger than usual overall volume.

6 The Countryside Commission and the Thatcher years

Adrian Phillips

Introduction

When the then Secretary of State for the Environment, Michael Heseltine, first looked at the Countryside Commission after the 1979 election, he asked his officials whether it should be done away with. Advised that this would require primary legislation and could cause some criticism, he settled instead for a cut in its approved staffing from 124 to 93, and pegged its budget at £7.62 million for 1980/1.

Twelve years later (and after five other Secretaries of State) Michael Heseltine was once more Secretary of State for the Environment. When he looked again at the Commission, he found a staff of around 250, and a budget due to rise from £30 to over £40 million over the next few years.

How had this turn around been achieved? How had the Commission, set up and later expanded by Labour administrations, survived and flourished as never before under 12 years of Conservative government? How had a quango, committed to intervention, promoting public expenditure by local authorities and generally arguing for more not less planning, become much more influential and grown more rapidly than the public sector as a whole during the period of Mrs Thatcher's Government?

This chapter seeks to explain this paradox. It is in two parts:

—Part I is a chronological, but selective, account of the Commission's work, focusing mainly on the period 1979–92;
—Part II is an analysis of the main factors which account for what the Commission achieved.

Inevitably, in telling the story from a sequential and then a analytical standpoint, there is some repetition between the first and second parts.

Though reference is made to the Commission's annual reports and other published material, this chapter also draws on the author's recollection, especially of the qualities of those people who played a central role in the story of the Commission in the Thatcher years.

Part 1: A short and subjective history of the Commission

The early days, 1968–79

The Countryside Commission replaced the National Parks Commission in 1968. The change of title reflected the bigger task given to the new body. In the language of the Countryside Act, the Commission was required to keep under review all matters relating to:

— the provision and improvement of facilities for the enjoyment of the countryside;
— the conservation and enhancement of the natural beauty and amenity of the countryside; and
— the need to secure public access to the countryside for the purposes of open-air recreation. (Countryside Commission, 1968, p. 1)

In current, less stilted language, the Commission now states its mission— still derived from the 1968 Act—as 'to care for the countryside and help people enjoy it'.

Like its predecessor, the Commission remained part of the central government departmental machinery, and was thus serviced by Civil Servants who were initially on the payroll of the Ministry of Housing and Local Government and then from 1970 the Department of the Environment. None the less, the new Commission took on a distinctive character. A team of mostly young professional staff were recruited to work for its dynamic and creative Director, Reg Hookway. The central challenge of the 1968 Act was to provide the newly mobile public of England and Wales with new opportunities to enjoy the countryside. The Commission's priorities, therefore, were to set up country parks and picnic sites, and to develop techniques for visitor management. But it also retained a commitment to the core of the work of the former National Parks Commission: national parks, areas of outstanding natural beauty (AONBs) and long-distance routes.

The Commission had limited powers. It could not direct or forbid anyone to do anything. Advice, persuasion and promotion were—and remain—its techniques of action. It owned no land; it employed no field staff. So working *through* others was a way of life for the Commission. Its success had to be judged not so much by what it did as by what it could get others to do.

There was an important exception to this. Section 4 of the 1968 Countryside Act enabled the Commission to undertake experiments. Though this power has invariably been used in partnership with others, it has enabled the Commission to test out the practicalities of new approaches to its task; to test, for example, methods of charging visitors for car parks—and, as we shall see, latterly far more ambitiously to seek new approaches to reconciling agriculture and conservation needs.

But, for the most part, the Commission achieved what it could through partnerships which it built with others, especially with local authorities. Here the changes brought about by the 1974 local government reorganisation were particularly important. These:

— created powerful new metro-counties and strengthened county councils, many of which were looking for a role in the countryside. The Commission found in Greater Manchester, Hampshire and Hertfordshire, for example, ambitious local authorities countryside teams who were more than ready to collaborate in innovative work which would give visibility to local authority efforts.
— strengthened the administration of the National Parks. Whereas previously only the Peak and Lake District had enjoyed a unified administration, all eight county council parks were henceforth to be run by a single committee. The work of each park was to be directed by one chief officer, subject to the guidance of a national park plan and funded with 75 per cent government funds. The Commission, which was given important roles in each of these arrangements, found in the National Parks a much strengthened group of potential partners.
— were accompanied by more flexible finance rules which enabled the Commission to grant aid to a wide range of activities provided by local authorities and others which fulfilled its aims.

During the 1970s, the Commission underwent two important organisational changes. In 1974, its headquarters were moved from London to Cheltenham. Here it took up residence in a former police station, renamed John Dower House after the author of the seminal, wartime report on National Parks. In 1977, as part of a misconceived attempt by the then Minister of Sport, Dennis Howell, to bring the Countryside Commission and the Sports Council together, the Commission was resourced to set up regional offices. These were in London and eight major English provincial cities (the Office in Wales had been set up after the 1968 Act to service its statutory Committee for Wales). For some staff, this meant three homes in as many years—say from London, to Cheltenham and then to Leeds. But the regional offices greatly increased the impact of the Commission's work with its partners.

However, working in Cheltenham—delightful a town as it is—has been a continuing handicap for senior staff and the Chairman. Fax and phone are no substitute for the kind of informal contacts with those in Whitehall, Parliament, the media and the non-governmental sector which are a necessary part of the job. Business over lunch, a drink after work, an evening lecture—none of these is easy to arrange from a base 100 miles away with a poor rail connection. How much better it would have been to regionalise the Commission but to have kept a small headquarters capacity in London!

As the 1970s drew to a close, the Commission's work focused more on the controversial issue of farming and conservation. The story and the figures have been told so often (Cripps, 1980) that they bear no repeating here. But it exposed the Commission's limitations in a painful way. Despite their statutory duties, the Commission—and, for that matter, allied bodies like the Nature Conservancy Council—were practically powerless before the forces of environmental destruction, brought about by a period of agricultural intensification which rivalled that of the wartime years. The title of Marion Shoard's influential book on the subject—*The Theft of the Countryside* (1980)—sums up the sense of anger and frustration to which this gave rise in conservation circles. Their criticisms in turn brought a hostile reaction from many of the farmers. Unable to do much more than point at the changes brought about by modern farming, for example in its *New Agricultural Landscapes* report of 1974, the Commission had to rely on underfunded programmes of tree planting and cosmetic conservation— modest gestures before a tide of destruction which it could not stem.

The years in the wilderness, 1979–83

When the Conservatives were elected in 1979, the Commission's Chairman was Lord Winstanley, who owed his position to the Lib-Lab pact. There is a photograph in the Commission's annual report for 1979/80 which shows him welcoming a smiling Michael Heseltine to the Cheltenham headquarters in May 1980. What, one wonders, was in the Secretary of State's mind on that occasion? His views about the Commission, after initial scepticism, had warmed. He told the National Parks Conference in the Broads in September 1981:

I was one of the first Ministers to be associated with the quango hunt exercise and I make no apologies for that. I think it is very easy for these semi-autonomous bodies to spawn, unchecked and unreviewed. . . . It was very important indeed that they should be subjected to the regular controls and the normal disciplines of accountability. Against that background and against the background of the very substantial number of quangos that have disappeared under my responsibility, I made a very positive decision that I wanted the Commission to remain. I believe in the Commission . . . I believe that with all the conflicting interests that affect the countryside . . . it is important to have a body where these things can be discussed and argued about outside the immediate environment of government and to give the government the best advice on the way forward. (Countryside Commission, 1981a, p. 20)

Nevertheless, the Secretary of State wanted to see changes made at the Commission. The key steps were:

1. the appointment, in January 1981, of Derek Barber as Chairman in Michael Winstanley's place;
2. the change in the Commission's status, brought about by the Wildlife and Countryside Act 1981; and
3. cuts in the Commission's staff numbers.

Together, these steps neatly underline the ways in which Ministers can exercise control over bodies such as the Commission: by the appointments which they make: through the legislation they promote; and through the resources they make available. In reality, therefore, the independent status of the Commission is heavily qualified and success is dependent on ministerial goodwill.

There can be little doubt that these changes helped to lay the foundations for the period of expansion and growing self-confidence of the Commission later in the decade. However, at the time, they appeared much more threatening. There were certainly some on the Commission's staff, and among its friends, who thought that the changes were motivated by a desire to cut the Commission down to size. They noted, too, the Prime Minister's lack of interest in countryside matters and her general views about the environment: 'when you have spent half your political life dealing with humdrum issues like the environment' she told Scottish Tories during the Falklands fighting, 'it's exciting to have a real crisis on your hands' (Young, 1991, p. 273). To some it seemed that the Commission was being sidelined at a time of indifference, if not hostility, to all it stood for.

The new chairman had a background in farming, land management and wildlife conservation. Derek Barber's immediate past position was as chairman of the Royal Society for the Protection of Birds (RSPB) and it was this which brought him to the attention of Michael Heseltine, himself a bird enthusiast. He took a conscientious approach to the job—but he also challenged much of the accepted wisdom of the Commission. He did not see the Commission as on one side of the countryside debate so much as an honest broker looking to build bridges between what he called 'the warring factions'. Recalling both his farming and conservation background, Derek Barber said: 'I am a compromiser since I have seen both sides of the argument. I am inevitably imprisoned in compromise and I do believe that we should be looking for a solution which is reasonably satisfactory to everybody' (Countryside Commission, 1981b, p. 94).

Several issues came quickly to the surface where Derek Barber imposed his own set of values on the Commission. He got the Commission to withdraw its opposition to the Bideford bypass on the grounds that the proposal for a high level bridge over the Torridge, though unwelcome, was not a matter of national concern in which the Commission ought to be involved (he had little time for gestures on the part of the Commission). He successfully challenged the staff position on the alignment of a section of the South Devon coastal path—a small, local issue but one where he felt that the Commission's staff were taking an arrogant view towards the concerns of local residents, who objected to the routing of the path between their gardens and the cliff top; Derek Barber thought it important to make the point that the Commission should respect the concerns of private individuals affected by its actions. And he persuaded the Commission to fund the work of the Farming and Wildlife Advisory Group, which he saw as helping to change farming attitudes towards the conservation of the countryside. He put his faith in this approach rather than a more regulatory one of the kind favoured by Marion Shoard and others. In all of this, the Chairman was close to the prevailing values of the new government, which was committed to the voluntary principle in the pursuit of nature conservation and countryside protection.

However it did not endear the Commission to the voluntary bodies, such as the Council for The Protection of Rural England CPRE and the Ramblers Association, which accused it of abandoning its principles. At the National Parks Conference in the Lake District, a few weeks before the 1983 election, the Commission's performance was bluntly criticised by the Chairman of the Ramblers Association, Lord Melchett. He was particularly scathing about the Commission's claim to be building bridges with the farmers and landowners; he argued that the Commission had been set up to pursue a cause, not to placate the landowning interests. About the same time, the Commission was taken to task in The New Statesman for its alleged subservience to the government. How the suspicions among the voluntary bodies came to be allayed, and their respect for the Commission rebuilt, forms a later part of this account.

Meanwhile the Commission had a set of domestic concerns to attend to which were more preoccupying for the staff. Reg Hookway had argued for many years that the status of the Commission as part of the Civil Service was a nonsense and sat uneasily beside the Commission's claim to independence. Most certainly it affected his ability to manage the organisation. Staff would tend to look to the Department of the Environment (DOE) for the settlement of grievances, for example, and his control over how the Commission's funds were spent was very limited. The 1981 Act changed all that by creating the Commission as a grant-in-aid body. Though still sponsored by the DOE, its chief officer became the Accounting Officer, ultimately responsible to Parliament for the way in which the resources of money and staff were managed. Under this arrangement, the Commission's staff were no longer to be Civil Servants but public servants and employees of the Commission itself.

Cynics said that the main purpose of the change was to reduce the size of the Civil Service by over 100 approved posts. But there were, in fact, real benefits for the Commission. While in *policy* terms grant-in-aid status may not have increased the Commission's independence, in *managerial* terms it was a revolution. The incoming Director General, who joined in

June 1981, was able to run the organisation as a discrete enterprise in a way which was never possible for his predecessor—though the DOE still held a number of irritating apron strings over the Commission's management. Independence extended, too, to the way in which the Commission presented itself: a new style annual report; revamped publications; an attractive newspaper, *Countryside Commission News*; and—after a false start with clumsy designs for which the author accepts responsibility—the emergence of a successful new house style.

But the Commission's statutory independence came with a parting shot from the Department. The Commission was told by Mr Heseltine that its approved staffing levels were to be cut by a quarter to 93, whilst at the same time it was made responsible for a bunch of new administrative tasks under its grant-in-aid status.

These cuts were, in fact, rather less drastic than they appeared because the actual number of staff in post had been run down by 1981 to about a hundred. Even so, the reduction was real and painful. It led to the closure of two of the Commission's regional offices, in Reading and Nottingham, and consequential regional reorganisation; it also meant a reduction in the number of staff at all levels at headquarters. Not surprisingly, staff morale was low and the negotiations about the new terms of employment protracted and difficult.

At the end of this painful period of readjustment, a handful of staff stayed on with DOE, either because they chose not to join the new Commission, or because they were not offered jobs with it. Some work was dropped entirely, and some work previously done in-house was contracted out. The Commission survived the slimming down with inconvenience but probably it increased efficiency. In particular, it was a stimulus to the adoption of a more programmed approach to the Commission's work. Some years before, other quangos were required to draw up a corporate plan the Commission already had such a plan in place. In later years its pioneering work in this area was held up, notably by the Treasury and the Civil Service College, as a model which others should emulate.

There was one other legacy of the Heseltine days: Groundwork. The Commission had pioneered the idea of countryside management during the 1970s. The climax of this was to be a major experiment in the management of the urban fringe in the St Helens and Knowsley area, run by the local authorities. The Secretary of State welcomed the idea but 'suggested that an environmental trust might be appropriate and stated that, in the event of an acceptable mechanism being found, the project would receive the full backing of the Department and his personal support' (Countryside Commission, 1981c, p. 19). Operation Groundwork was duly set up by the Commission as a trust, the first in what was soon to become a fast growing family of such trusts, which gradually moved away from the Commission's direct responsibility. The decision to proceed by the trust route was a clear indication that the tide was moving away from local government leadership in the countryside field; but also an example of how the Commission's experimental powers could be used to develop and test new approaches to tackling countryside issues.

The Waldegrave years 1983–87

William Waldegrave was appointed as Parliamentary Under-Secretary at DOE after the 1983 election, and went on to become the Minister for Environment, Countryside and Planning, a position he held until June 1987. During a period when Secretaries of State came and went, he was a constant; thus he worked for Patrick Jenkin, who came into office in 1983 after Tom King's short reign, Kenneth Baker and Nicholas Ridley. Waldegrave was an enthusiast for the Commission and an environmental politician before it became fashionable to be so. The Commission benefited greatly by his holding office.

After the difficult years of the early 1980s, things began to look up for the Commission. There were both external and internal reasons for this.

Externally, serious doubts were emerging about the direction of agricultural policy, both the inherent unsustainability of the Common Agricultural Policy (CAP), and the unacceptable impact of intensive agriculture on the rural environment. The sudden advent of milk quotas in 1984 was a significant portent. The message began to sink in: business as usual was no longer assured in farming. Increasingly henceforth the problem for policy-makers was not how to get farmers to grow more food, but less. Meanwhile, concern about the damage done by modern farming to wildlife and to the landscape had become a political issue, partly as a result of some particularly damning television programmes. William Waldegrave sensed this, and went as far as a Minister in one department can go in openly criticising those in another when he referred to the 'engine of destruction' (Pye-Smith and Hall, 1987, p. 102) to describe the environmental impacts of agricultural policy. These criticisms were reinforced in reports from committees of both the Commons and the Lords which were critical of MAFF's (Ministry of Agriculture, Fisheries and Food) lack of response to conservation concerns.

In policy terms, the need to cut production and the need to safeguard the countryside were, of course, potentially allies. The issues came together in the Halvergate Marshes saga, in which the Commission was centrally involved.

Conservationists, like soldiers, rarely have the luxury of choosing the ground upon which they have to fight. Halvergate was an improbable *cause célèbre*. Flat grazing marshes between the Yare and the Bure in Norfolk: the landscape appeal of Halvergate was somewhat esoteric. However, the rarity value of such places was undeniable and the marshes were important also for wildlife. Almost from the moment that the area was identified as critical to the conservation of the landscape of the Broads, it was under threat from drainage and conversion to cereal cropping: 'arabalisation' being the ugly word to describe an ugly process, but one which made economic sense for farmers, who could get grants for drainage and good prices for barley.

Various stop-gap palliatives were offered to persuade farmers not to convert the marshes, but some farmers went ahead undeterred. There were no sanctions and, with the government committed to the voluntary principle of conservation, there was no political mileage in advocating a compulsory approach. The solution that eventually emerged, after repeated crises—and more journeys from Cheltenham to Norwich than the author cares to remember—was the Broads Grazing Marshes Scheme, which paid incentives to farmers who were ready to continue to graze the marshes in the traditional way. The scheme was operated by the Commission, using its experimental powers and working closely with MAFF. It was entirely successful in its aim of checking the loss of marshland and was to become quite quickly the model for Environmentally Sensitive Areas as advocated by the UK in the negotiations in the mid-1980s on the CAP.

Internally, the Commission entered more peaceful waters after the stormy period at the time of change of status. The Chairman, knighted in 1984 for his services to the countryside and conservation, created a strong sense of loyalty among the Commissioners; a new management team was built up around the Director; and the Director and Chairman developed a productive relationship which exploited their complementary interests.

However, the steady build-up of morale was interrupted by a curious episode. Non-departmental public bodies (the Treasury's term to describe quangos quasi-antonomous non-governmental organisations) are subject to periodic staff inspections. These aim to check whether the organisation has the right number of staff for the job given to it, and that the staff are correctly graded. An inspection carried out in 1986 concluded that many of the Commission's professional staff were over-graded, especially those in the regions. In terms of staff morale, the impact of this report was deeply damaging. The senior management were confident that the staff inspectors' report was fundamentally flawed, but challenging a Treasury-backed review is no easy thing. It took a threat to engage outside consultants to undertake an independent review to convince the DOE Permanent Secretary that the Commission was adamant that the inspectors' conclusions had to be re-examined. With the help of two key DOE officials, Martin Holdgate and Timothy Hornsby, a way through was found. A further inspection was undertaken and the results tested before a panel set up by the Treasury. The Commission's case was entirely vindicated. Much rejoicing followed, but the hundreds of man-hours spent in combating the outcome of this superficial inspection could surely have been better spent.

However, this episode apart, the Commission's self-confidence grew over the period. In particular, a number of important policy initiatives were taken and generally well received. Thus the Waldegrave years saw the Commission undertake a comprehensive review of uplands policy; the establishment of the Groundwork Foundation to take forward the Commission's pioneer work with Groundwork; the launch of Recreation 2000, a wide-ranging review of the Commission's recreation and access policies; the setting up of the Common Land Forum; the re-establishment of a close working relationship between the Commission and the national parks; and the campaign to get the Broads a status equivalent to that of a national park.

Another success was recorded when an amendment to the Local Government Act of 1985 was moved and eventually adopted in the House of Lords following advice from the Commission. The amendment called on the Secretary of State to report to Parliament, before the date of abolition of the GLC and metropolitan counties, on the future of countryside services and facilities provided by them. A particular concern, pinpointed by consultants whom the Commission had engaged, was to get the successor districts to work together on countryside issues and to manage sites which cross administrative boundaries. The Secretary of State's report was duly laid before Parliament at the end of February 1986. At the same time he gave the Commission the extra staff and money to assist the successor authorities with advice and grants so as to safeguard the services and facilities at risk (the story is told in some detail in the Commission's *Annual Report 1985–6* on page 32).

All this, had the effect of requiring the government to put up additional moneys to safeguard the countryside services around the major cities of England after the planned abolition of the metro-counties.

From the outset, it had been Derek Barber's achievement to open a dialogue with the farmers: he could tell a farming audience that they had to come to terms with the demands of access, and he had good links to the top brass of the NFU (National Famers Union) and CLA (Country Landowners Association). He found it less easy, though, to establish quickly a trusting dialogue with the voluntary bodies. The setting up of Countryside Link, which brought together all the main countryside and access bodies, provided the much-needed bridge. Meetings took place three or four times a year, usually involving the chief officers of the voluntary bodies and a small Commission team led by the Director General, as well as annual meetings with the members of the Commission. At first, these events were rather reserved, but soon a more relaxed relationship developed. Confidence and understanding—if not 100 per cent agreement—were once again built between the Commission and those upon whose support it is so dependent. Countryside Link was an excellent investment of time for all concerned.

Of course there were setbacks too. The uplands report failed to dent the vested interests of government departments and its call for an integrated approach to the conservation of the uplands was one for which the government was not ready. Having invested so much time and effort in the uplands review, the Commission's standing was not enhanced by the cool response given to its recommendations in Whitehall (it is an interesting comment though, on how times change, that many of the recommendations have now become official policy).

The government's insistence on building the Okehampton bypass through the northern edge of Dartmoor was as bad a defeat for the Commission as any it had sustained: the disregard of the government's own policies in building the bypass was demoralising to all who cared about the parks. The measured language of the Commission's *Annual Report* of 1985/6, which comments that 'it is an outcome which we regret' (Countryside Commission, 1986, p. 17) disguises the anger which the decision caused among many at John Dower House.

Much of this period was spent reviewing the Commission's established policies. Committed to wide consultation and seeking to offer solutions which would appeal to government, the Commission put considerable member and staff time into the preparation of influential policy statements. The results began to emerge during 1987. In that year, the Commission issued the report of The Countryside Review Panel, which highlighted the dramatic policy options facing the countryside at a time of rapid change, especially in the area of farming. Also in 1987 its statement on recreation and access, *Enjoying the Countryside*, was published: it contained the bold policy aim of having all the rights of way properly recorded, available for use and effectively publicised by the end of the century. Finally, in 1989 the Commission set out its support for a strong and effective planning system in its report *Planning for a Greener Countryside*.

The Commission had learnt that influencing the political process required that it put should put its ideas into the public arena. Much thought, and some expenditure, went into the presentation of these policy statements so that they had the maximum impact. Timing was important too; it was no accident that there was a flurry of Commission activity in the run-up to the general election. A characteristic of these policy statements was that they placed the Commission a few years ahead of current government thinking; in other words, they offered a way forward for the government, but were not so radical that they would be dismissed out of hand. Even so, there were signs that the flood of proposals from Cheltenham was thought to be a little bit too much of a good thing by the DOE officials who had to brief Ministers for a response: they pleaded for a pause in the flow.

On balance, the Waldegrave years were good ones for the Commission. It established itself as an authoritative voice on countryside topics at a time when public opinion was becoming increasingly interested in the subject. A sympathetic Minister helped to give the Commission the confidence to pursue its agenda. His influence was apparent, too, in the drafting of the 1987 election manifesto for the Conservatives which contained promises to introduce Landscape Conservation Orders and legislation for Commons as recommended by the Common Land Forum.

The Ridley years, 1987–9

The new Secretary of State was appointed a year before the election, but initially, at any rate, his attentions were focused elsewhere—on the poll tax. Although Nicholas Ridley was a lover of the countryside, it was as a self-styled 'countryman'. He had no time for conservation experts, EC officials, pressure groups and other Greens. He dismissed all of these contemptuously in his autobiography, claiming that 'the countryman in Britain knows more about preserving wildlife than the lot of them put together' (Ridley, 1992, p. 114). This idiosyncratic view of the world was hardly likely to make the Commission's task easier.

None the less, 'it is an ill wind . . .'—and the storm of 16 October 1987 brought the Commission to the Secretary of State's attention in a rather dramatic way. On that fateful Thursday night, the members of the Commission and senior staff were housed in a somewhat fragile hotel on the edge of Maidstone. The purpose of their visit to Kent was to examine the effectiveness of tree preservation orders in withstanding the assaults of a local farmer, a Mr Batchelor, who delighted in felling mature trees in the Kent Downs AONB. Having picked their way out of the mayhem on the following morning—and in the process discovered that the Almighty's influence over the Kentish landscape was greater even than that of Mr Batchelor—the Chairman and Director General were summoned to London to see Mr Ridley. They found there a Minister who was understandably anxious to respond to the public mood of environmental despair.

The Commission has so far been described principally as a body advising on public policy as it affects the countryside, but most of its staff and even more of its money was—and is—committed to the promotion of practical work through thousands of schemes which it supports in the public, private and voluntary sectors. The Commission's reputation for acting speedily and getting a job done made it the obvious candidate for the tree planting and landscape recovery programme which the Secretary of State wished to see undertaken in the wake of the storm. Task Force Trees, as the Commission's unit to spearhead this programme was known, was in action within two weeks: its remit extended to the towns, including central London, as well as the countryside. Its budget was to exceed £12 million pounds over the next few years—a larger sum than originally planned because of the damage wrought by further storms in January 1990.

The next two years were full of contradictions. On the down side, Task Force Trees apart, the Commission's funding fell behind inflation. The Commission was greatly disappointed, too, that the government did not honour either of its countryside pledges in the manifesto. The rejection of work done by the Common Land Forum, under pressure from the grouse moor owners, was particularly galling. The Commission was openly alarmed at proposals to relax planning controls in the countryside, especially over farm diversification schemes like farm shops and livery enterprises. And the decision to split the Commission's Welsh responsibilities away from it in order to form the new Countryside Council for Wales was not to everyone's liking, especially as it was taken without any consultation in the best traditions of closed government. However, the Commission took the view that, as the decision had been made, the need was to assure the success of the new body in Wales.

On the other hand, the government fulfilled its promise to complete the legislation to set up the new Broads Authority as a national park in all but name. In 1988, it confirmed the North Pennines as an AONB after a record 10-year delay since the Commission's designation and a protracted and hard-fought public enquiry which upheld the Commission's views about the quality of the area. The Commission's 1987 policy statement on forestry was well received by the Secretary of State, whose own strong views about the need to reshape forestry policy were widely known and no doubt influenced the decision in the 1988 budget to withdraw all tax support for forestry. A more skilfully-won success was the Commission's achievement in getting safeguards over the future of water authority land which has conservation and recreation value written into the 1989 Water Act. Against the government's wishes, but briefed by the Commission working closely with several statutory and voluntary bodies, the House of Lords successfully introduced protection clauses over the management and disposal of most of the half million acres in the water authorities' ownership. The information which the Commission made available on the distribution and status of this land was effective ammunition for the opponents of the bill.

In the agricultural field, the Commission needed to influence both DOE and MAFF. Its success was variable. It was able to persuade the DOE to back it in setting up the Countryside Premium scheme in Eastern England to show how set-aside land could be used for conservation and access. This was a most constructive response to the Commission's criticism of set-aside that it did nothing positive for the countryside. However, when the Commission launched its proposals for a reshaping of agricultural support, with a nation-wide system of incentives for conservation and access, the MAFF response was frosty. While the Commission's ideas were imaginative, its policy document had some holes in it. On this occasion, the Commission had not done its homework as it should.

The real significance of this period, however, was that environmental issues pushed themselves to the top of the political agenda. Despite— or was it partly because of?—the Secretary of State's evident lack of enthusiasm for planning and many other aspects of the environmental agenda, these were the days when 'green' entered the political vocabulary. The

Prime Minister's Royal Society speech in 1988, the green vote in the European elections of 1989, the criticisms which Ministers encountered over road schemes in particular—and so on. All these helped to create a climate in which a body like the Commission was bound to be a significant beneficiary.

This Common Inheritance, 1989–92

The appointment in July 1989 of the new Ministerial team of Chris Patten as Secretary of State and David Trippier as Environment and Countryside Minister was political recognition at the highest level that environmental concerns and the conservation of the countryside mattered.

There were some quick signs of progress. At the Conservative Party Conference, Mr Patten announced that he would not be going ahead with his predecessor's proposals to remove planning controls over farm diversification schemes, and singled out advice from the Commission as the chief reason he had changed his mind. In December, at a Conference to mark the fortieth anniversary of the passing of the 1949 National Parks and Access to the Countryside Act, the Secretary of State gave a warm welcome to the Commission's announcement that it was intending to undertake a review of the national parks—and enjoined it to be 'bold' (Patten, 1990, pp. 60–7). A month later, the Junior Minister, David Heathcoat Amory, gave government support to the Commission's target of having the rights of way in shape by the end of the century.

Early on in his time as Secretary of State, Mr Patten had promised an environmental White Paper. It was plainly tough going working out agreed positions with the Treasury and Departments like Transport and Energy. What the Minister wanted was some areas where the DOE could make progress without too much difficulty. The Countryside Commission offered three: the New National Forest project in the English Midlands; twelve Community Forests around many of the major cities of England; and 'Countryside Stewardship', a large-scale pilot project which would test the incentives approach to conservation and access on farmland advocated by the Commission since 1989 in *Incentives for New Direction in Farming*. All three projects figured in the white paper, *This Common Inheritance*, launched in September 1990. Although the White Paper was greeted generally with cries of disappointment (the victim of its own hype, perhaps?), from the far narrower perspective of the Commission's interests, it was a launching pad for a much expanded programme.

A few months later, hands were put where mouths had been. The Commission's grant-in-aid was boosted from a 1990/1 level of £24.539 million to £30.227 million for the following year—allowing for the loss of the Commission's Welsh responsibilities in April 1991, this amounted to an unprecedented increase of 30 per cent in its funds. This was matched by approval to recruit more staff, needed especially to run the Countryside Stewardship programme. However, while staff numbers had more than doubled since the 93 figure was imposed, the Commission held staff and associated running costs at or below 25 per cent of the total budget.

The pace of change continued undiminished despite the departure of the two principal architects of the memorable 1991/2 settlement. Chris Patten was moved in the aftermath of John Major's election as Prime Minister, to be replaced by Michael Heseltine in his second incarnation as Secretary of State for the Environment. Sir Derek Barber's term as Chairman ended in March 1991. His successor was Sir John Johnson, a distinguished former diplomat who had come to Ministers' attention through his work as the UK Representative to the United Nations Environment Programme in Nairobi—but who brought to the job of Chairman of the Commission not only well-honed diplomatic skills but an enthusiasm for walking and an encyclopaedic knowledge of upland Britain.

Sir John inherited an organisation in the throes of expansion and highly regarded by the Minister, David Trippier. In his first year, the government backed several of the key proposals in the national parks review, notably that to establish independent authorities to run all the parks, an aim long cherished by the Commission; and to put the New Forest on a par with the national parks and the Broads. The Commission's budget was further enlarged to £35.4 million in 1992/3 and £38.23 million in 1993/4. In January 1992, a few weeks before the announcement of the election, a group of new initiatives were unveiled in which the Commission was to play a central role. These involved the expansion of the stewardship programme, a hedgerow protection scheme, a project to help parish councils care for rights of way and another to encourage community groups in a range of local environmental action in the countryside (Department of the Environment, 1992). These activities, in the words of the Commission's new Director General, Michael Dower, brought the Commission 'into yet closer partnership, at local level, with those who live and work in the countryside of England' (Dower, 1992, p. 3).

Where next?

The Countryside Commission in the early 1990s faces very different challenges from those ten years ago. The development of Countryside Stewardship may force the Commission to rethink its traditional view of itself as a small, non-executive, promotional body working through others to achieve its ends. The full implications of the recent CAP reforms will make demands upon the Commission, as well as creating exciting opportunities. A new environmental agenda, concerned with the impact of water, energy, minerals and road space on the countryside seems set to dominate debate in the next few years. And there remains a suspicion that further changes in the structure of conservation and countryside agencies may appeal to politicians. In the immortal words of the Chinese philosopher, the Commission seems destined to continue to live in 'interesting' times.

Part 2: a short and subjective analysis

Introduction—and a health warning

The above account of the Commission during the Thatcher years may suggest a story of success. But there is a far less flattering conclusion that can be drawn. Throughout the '80s, the values which the Commission was established to defend were in retreat. Despite the move within the farming industry away from production at all costs, and despite an environmental awakening on the part of many farmers, destruction on the farm continued. The Commission's own research, doubted by MAFF but later confirmed by DOE's surveys, showed hedgerows in decline during the period and further landscape losses in the uplands. Despite public concern about the quality of the built environment in the countryside, the prevailing political philosophy of deregulation and poor design standards among builders have done violence to many a village scene: 'the Government's impact on villages during the 1980s was almost universally harmful as controls were removed to encourage new housing regardless of the visual qualities' (Worsley, 1992). Even in the area of access to the countryside, where real progress was made in the condition of rights of way, the Commission was unable to break the political log-jam over access to common land. Moreover, the need to spend substantial sums on the management of visitors to the countryside, e.g. on the repair of eroded footpaths, was not readily grasped by many authorities. Nor were many of them ready to face up to the need to introduce controls over traffic and inappropriate tourism so as to protect sensitive areas. In consequence, too many popular parts of the countryside bore greater marks of over-use at the end of the '80s than ten years earlier.

The countryside of the 1990s had begun to show more worrying signs of general environmental degradation: falling water-tables and dwindling streams resulting from over-abstraction; continued declines in the number of many rare (and some recently common) species of flowers, birds and reptiles; and the near universal impact of cars on the countryside—even the refuge of darkness is denied to those living within sight of sodium lights; and total escape from traffic noise seems ever harder to find in the English countryside. In all these respects, the countryside of the early 1990s is a poorer place than that of the late '70s.

In brief, the environmental values of the countryside have been eroded over the past dozen years, despite the efforts of the Countryside Commission and all its partners. Therefore, the claim that these were on the whole successful years for the Commission can be only a modest and relative assertion albeit offset by the fact that the Commission's own standing and influence grew appreciably over the period, and that things would have been worse without it. The reasons for this modest achievement are the subject of the second part of this chapter.

Six main factors can be adduced which account for such progress as was made by the Commission in the Thatcher years. The Commission benefited from:

—having the right kind of *modus operandi*;
—a successful combination of ideas and practicality;
—a reputation for good housekeeping;
—public opinion and political support;
—success in handling its relationships with Ministers; and
—the qualities of the Chairman, Commissioners and staff.

These are now considered in turn and the threads drawn together in some concluding reflections.

The Commission's modus operandi

When the establishment of the Countryside Commission's predecessor, the National Parks Commission, was under discussion in the late 1940s, enthusiasts for national parks wanted to see a strong Commission with executive powers. They were frustrated by the combined influence of the Civil Servants of the Ministry of Town and Country Planning (who warned the Minister at the time that the Commission might threaten the future existence of their Ministry), of the Treasury (who feared the Commission's capacity to spend) and of the local authorities (who feared for their planning powers if the Commission were too powerful) (Blunden and Curry, 1990, pp. 67–75). In consequence, the body which emerged lacked the powers to hold land, and those to direct, or prohibit, others. It was permitted to employ a mere handful of staff and they were to be civil servants, not employees of an independent Commission. It was to be an advisory body. At the time, and for many years later, these seemed to be fatal weaknesses. The National Parks Commission (NPC) and the Countryside Commission after it were often compared unfavourably to the Nature Conservancy (later the Nature Conservancy Council (NCC)). In contrast to the Commission, the NCC owned land and had powers of last resort to protect nature. Its budget was roughly twice the size, though that included responsibilities in Scotland where the Commission did not operate. Moreover, while the NCC's staff numbers grew quickly, those of the NPC were tightly constrained. Understaffed, underfunded and underpowered, the National Parks Commission was very much the junior partner in the early years. Whereas the Nature Conservancy was described as 'a quite remarkable success story' (Stamp, 1969, p. 48), the Commission was dismissed as a 'weak and ineffective body' (MacEwen and MacEwen, 1982, p. 18).

Yet, paradoxically, the seeds of the Commission's future success were contained in the kind of organisation which the crabby bureaucrats of the 1940s had created, and which was largely carried forward into the new Countryside Commission in 1968 (just as it can be argued that the very characteristics which Stamp and others admired in the NCC in the past were to contribute to its downfall in 1989). In the absence of executive powers, the Commission had *force majeure* to develop the art of working in partnership with others to achieve its aims. It formed alliances with those in the public sector (and especially the local authorities), in the voluntary sector (the National Trust, the British Trust for Conservation Volunteers and many others) and with private owners and managers of land. On average, some two-thirds of the funds which it received from government went to such organisations in the form of grant-aided projects and programmes. It thus built relationships with influential organisations which saw the Commission as a supporter, not a rival.

A great advantage of the approach of working through others in the conservation and enjoyment of the countryside was the flexibility which it gave the Commission. It was able to redeploy funds from one subject area (e.g. country parks) to another (e.g. rights of way work), when its studies showed this was needed. And it could move resources from one part of the country to another to meet changing needs. There were limits to such flexibility, of course, because the Commission could not afford to abandon its partners overnight nor offend major actors in the countryside, but with a proper lead time and diplomatic explanations, it was able to achieve changes in policy and practice which an executive body would have found much more difficult.

Moreover, lacking a large executive staff or a substantial estate, the Commission was never seriously in the target line for being required to put many of its operations out to tender—tenderisation—nor was it possible to consider it as a candidate for privatisation. Yet tenderisation and privatisation were fates which threatened, or befell, the work of other heritage and conservation quangos in the Thatcher years. On the other hand, it was able to generate income through sponsorship for a number of initiatives; indeed, it set up several arm's length mechanisms, e.g. the Groundwork Foundation and the Countryside Trust, for this purpose.

Flexibility, the capacity to be fleet of foot, the relative shortness of the administrative tail, a wide range of partners and a reputation for minimal bureaucracy made the Commission more acceptable to the government of the 1980s as a public body than many. One might speculate whether this would have been the case had the Commission entered the 1980s with significant land holdings (compare the fate of the Forestry Commission under continual pressure to sell off part of its estate). Or if it had employed a field staff of several thousand (compare the fate of local authority direct labour teams, broken up and their work put out to tender). And would a Countryside Commission with executive powers not have been faced with the same kind of anguished dilemmas that dogged the NCC for much of the period and led to its eventual demise in the Environmental Protection Act?

So one can conclude that the Commission was required by circumstances to develop a particular approach to countryside issues of the 1980s which fitted well with the needs of the time. It put emphasis on working through others rather than doing the task itself because it owned no land and had a small staff. It offered financial incentives to land managers rather than imposing restraints upon them because it had no powers to coerce or compel. And it was able to respond quickly to new public and political concerns because its *modus operandi* gave it considerable freedom of manoeuvre.

Ideas and practicality

During the 1970s, the Commission had developed an approach to its work which served it well. It researched problems; it developed solutions to these, which it tested through experiments; it promoted the solutions through advice to the government and others; and, on the basis of a positive response, encouraged implementation through technical advice and grant-aided projects undertaken by others. Public information and training were developed in support of these initiatives. Implicit in this entire approach was that the Commission's work should be ideas-driven and based in practicality.

By 'ideas driven' is meant the capacity to develop bold concepts that capture public and political imagination. The new National Forest, the Community Forests and the Thames Path are obvious examples. So was the idea of a national target for the rights of way—and more recently the nation-wide parish paths partnership, which will give parish councils around England the opportunity of bidding to look after the paths in their area. It is interesting, though, that several of these ideas were greeted cautiously by the government at first (the Forestry Commission's initial reaction to the Countryside Commission's forestry proposals was particularly sceptical), and is only became supportive once public support had crystallised around the ideas.

'Practicality' in this context means a realistic appreciation of what actually works on the ground. It is here that the limitations of the promotional, non-executive style of the Commission are most apparent—and the experimental powers so valuable. Experimentation and demonstration have indeed been essential to the Commission's success in promoting such concepts as countryside management in upland, coastal and edge-of-town settings; or in the management of countryside under heavy recreation pressure. During the second half of the 1980s, the Commission's experimental powers were used to test and develop government policy towards agriculture and conservation. Thus the Broads Grazing Marshes Scheme became the model for ESAs (Environmentally Sensitive Areas); the Countryside Premium scheme was regarded by MAFF as a model for an environmentally-sound form of set-aside; and the Countryside Stewardship scheme seems likely to be important in developing the new 'agri-environmental programmes' of the CAP (from where else but Brussels would such a clumsy title come?).

'Practicality' has a political meaning too. The Commission was clear that it was not a lobby—not the government-funded version of the CPRE as some commentators seemed to think—but a source of independent advice to government on countryside matters. As such, it was ready to criticise government practice, but thought it more important to offer practical and credible ways forward. Indeed, in a whole range of policy areas—agriculture and conservation, forestry, planning, rights of way, the future of the Broads and the New Forest, for example—its advice to government was (in the advertisers' phrase) 'just slightly ahead of our time'. Even if Ministers did not immediately and publicly rejoice over the Commission's advice, they came in fact to adopt a remarkably large part of it within a relatively short time.

Good housekeeping

The Commission remained part of the public sector when it left the Civil Service. It was therefore obliged to maintain the same standards as any other public body in terms of accounting for the expenditure of money and of keeping records, in achieving value for money, and in securing economy, efficiency and effectiveness.

The Commission's performance in this respect is hard to compare with others, although DOE officials were generally complimentary about the running of the Commission. Of course, complaints arrived from time to time about alleged delays in processing grant claims; some people asserted that the Commission was too bureaucratic—but more often the Commission was complimented for being refreshingly free of too much bureaucracy. Although these are subjective impressions, and one is always in danger of hearing what one wants to hear, there are a couple of objective performance measures.

In the world of quangos there is one unforgivable offence, and one unmitigated terror. The offence is to return to the Treasury a large sum of money unspent at the end of the financial year without good reason; to do so not only throws doubt on the effectiveness of financial management, it also undermines the case for more funds in future years. The terror is to be called before the Public Accounts Committee (PAC) because the government's auditors do not like what they find. An appearance before the PAC could make even Sir Humphrey tremble; and however good the answers may be, the suspicion that there can be no smoke without fire can hang over the organisation for years afterwards. The offence did not occur, nor was the terror realised. The Commission maintained intact its reputation as a tightly-run ship, a source of reassurance to the DOE as the Commission's sponsoring department. The stock of goodwill which was built up in DOE was drawn upon successfully during the staff inspection episode described above. It also made it easier for the Commission's friends in the DOE—Ministers and officials—to respond positively to its ambitious bids for funding and staffing in recent years; indeed, on occasion they went as far as to encourage the Commission to bid high in the annual round.

But there were difficulties too. The Commission's initial experience with computerisation was, to put it mildly, a bit trying. That other bodies in the public and private sectors had gone through the same traumas was little consolation to frustrated staff trying to make the books (or the spread sheet) balance. The installation of the second generation of Commission computers drew on the ample experience of what to avoid. Negotiations towards a freeing of DOE controls over the Commission were painfully slow—although eventually successful. The implications of the Citizen's Charter for the Commission were just beginning to be taken on board as the new Director General took up the reins; they could in fact be quite far-reaching in requiring high standards of staff when replying to correspondence or answering telephone enquiries.

Public opinion and political support

However good the Commission's programme, however well run it may be, it will achieve little without the backing of public opinion and political support, principally from Ministers in DOE, but also from politicians in Parliament and local government.

The relationship between public opinion and political action is a complex one; the sudden burst of interest in environmental issues following Mrs Thatcher's green speech in 1988 suggests that politicians lead opinion. But there is also evidence that tides in public opinion can emerge from below, in response to widely held if poorly articulated concerns: did not the *political* origins of that same speech lie in part at least in the impact of Chernobyl on British public opinion?

Whatever the nature of this relationship, there can be little doubt that the growing concern about the state of the environment generally in the 1980s was to the Commission's benefit. Environmental campaigners often made the point that the government's green credentials could be assessed by the position which it adopted on countryside issues. Some, such as the Ramblers' Association or the CPRE, argued indeed that a good test of green-ness was the funding given to the Commission. So when Chris Patten's environment White Paper heralded a major boost in the Commission's funding, Ministers were surely giving a signal whose significance went beyond the immediate tasks for which the funds were allocated.

The Commission was also the beneficiary of the changed outlook for agriculture. The dethroning of what Professor Gerald Wibberley used to call 'agricultural fundamentalism' as the CAP moved into surplus with one item after another created a very different situation from that of 10 years earlier. For the Commission it meant that a close dialogue developed with MAFF; indeed, along with the NCC, the Commission was given a statutory role to advise MAFF on ESAs in the 1986 Agriculture Act, the first piece of agricultural legislation which made specific mention of the Commission. As has been seen, the Commission played a significant part in the development of agricultural policy in the second half of the 1980s in respect of ESAs, environmentally-sound set-aside and the agri-environmental programmes of the CAP. More generally, it meant that the values which the Commission embodied—the protection of the landscape and its enjoyment by the public—at last received serious attention from farmers (as they looked for new sources of income) and from the government (as it looked for more acceptable reasons to subsidise the occupiers of agricultural land than to add to the height of the grain mountain).

And finally the Commission has benefited from the general election cycle. If one plots the grant-in-aid settlements over the past twelve years, there is a rise ahead of each election, a step up to a higher plateau, so to speak. The increase ahead of the most recent election was the most marked (and, because it is projected to continue rising over the next few years, may represent a break from the trend). Of course, in this the Commission's budget may just mirror the pattern of public expenditure generally; and the subsequent levelling off has meant in some years a real decline when inflation is taken into account. None the less, the Commission can draw some comfort from this cynical analysis: it suggests that politicians recognise that the Commission has political value.

Relationships with Ministers

In the Thatcher years, the Commission had six Secretaries of State for the Environment, Messrs Heseltine (twice), King, Jenkin, Ridley and Patten. As long as it had Welsh responsibilities, it also reported to the Secretary of State for Wales. It also had the attentions of numerous junior Ministers, of which Mr Waldegrave and Mr Trippier were the most influential and longest serving.

The above account of the Commission's varying fortunes over the years is in part a commentary on the role which individual Ministers played. Some took an active interest in the work of the Commission; some did not. But even the enthusiast had little time to devote to the Commission's affairs. What stands out is that when a Minister decided that a Commission initiative was worth backing—for example, Task Force Trees or Countryside Stewardship—the funds were readily found (after all, in the astronomical scale of public expenditure, the Commission's budget is lost in the rounding of the figures). The challenge to the Commission in such circumstances was to come up quickly with viable ideas that both attracted public attention and were compatible with the Commission's way of working.

On the other hand, the Commission stood for little when greater policy considerations were at stake. The decision to sever the Commission's Welsh operations in July 1989 in the wake of the NCC break-up was one such example. Another was the disregard of the Commission's advice over the Okehampton bypass and the M3 Motorway at Twyford Down. Nor was the Commission more successful in its dealings with the Ministry of Defence: in particular it lost in disputes over existing training land in Dartmoor, new training land in the North Pennines and the rebuilding of the early warning station at Fylingdales in the North York Moors. It is interesting to contrast this string of policy set-backs when confronted with the power of government departments with the relative success of the Commission in opposing quarrying schemes in the Peak District and the Yorkshire Dales promoted by aggregates companies, a new village in the Metropolitan Green Belt proposed by developers and a local bypass to Lyndhurst in the New Forest promoted by Hampshire County Council. While the evidence is not conclusive, it appears to suggest that the Department of the Environment has more success in backing the Commission's views when these concern the operations of private developers or local government than when it means confronting other departments of state.

The Commission took an active part in influencing several important pieces of legislation promoted by the government over the 1980s. As noted above, p. 72 and p. 75 on two occasions the Commission was successful in defeating the government in the House of Lords. In both cases, the Commission first argued its corner with Ministers and officials. Only when that failed did it contemplate carefully a course of action in Parliament. But the arguments were so compelling that the Commission decided to proceed by way of advice to MPs and Peers on certain clauses which caused it most concern. To do this authoritatively, it first collected and published detailed factual information—in one case on the value of countryside services run by the metro-counties which would be put at risk by their abolition, and in the other on the details of the conservation and recreation value of the land held by water authorities which might be developed, or disposed of, after privatisation. The Commission sought safeguards in the

legislation in both cases and helped draft alternative clauses to those in the
Bill which would achieve this. It built alliances with other interest groups—
with the NFU over the abolition bill, and with the National Trust, RSPB,
the Ramblers and others over the water privatisation Bill. Throughout, it
kept the lines of communication open with Ministers and officials so that
at no time would the Commission's public views come as a surprise. In
both cases the government got their clauses through the Commons but
were forced into amending the Bills after defeat in the Lords.

So the record confirms that in public enquiries, in comments on government policy and even in Parliament, the Commission took up a critical
position towards the government on a number of issues in the 1980s
(overseas visitors often express wonder at the Commission being able to
operate this watchdog role on the public stage, a most curious thing they
consider for a government-funded body). How did it do so without
incurring the hostility of Ministers in a government not always noted for
its tolerance of criticism from official quarters?

The answer lay in the tactics which the Commission employed. First, it
was essential that Ministers knew in advance if the Commission was
planning a public statement that was critical of government conduct. Next,
the choice of language used in any statement: firm but not offensive. And
third, the Commission was clear that it was not a lobbyist; its job was to
advise government, and if—as a last resort—it was necessary to go to
Parliament or carry an objection to a public enquiry, this was only after
all the other channels had been exhausted. All this may seem obvious, but
in the heightened emotions which surround controversial issues, and given
the interest of the media, it was always a challenge to get the *style* of the
Commission's objections to government in the most effective form possible. The test was not what would grab the headlines, but what would most
likely secure the Commission's immediate and longer-term aims.

Officials figure little in this account—which is proper, for they are there
to serve their Ministers and give their advice in confidence. And yet their
attitude is absolutely critical to the success of the relationship between the
Minister and the Commission. For example, a briefing to the effect that
the Commission's housekeeping is suspect will be damning; a positive one
will create a constructive climate. The officials in DOE with the responsibility to 'sponsor' the Commission have generally played a most helpful
role. An atmosphere of trust is essential between senior DOE staff and
those of the Commission if the Commission is to succeed in its objectives.
That in turn derives from a willingness on both sides to communicate
information in the knowledge that confidentiality will be respected—and
a mutual understanding of the right (indeed the necessity) of the Commission to take a different line from government on occasion. Such a subtle
relationship depends on the character of the individuals concerned and the
willingness of both parties to keep the channels of communication constantly open. All in all, this relationship was a good one in the 1980s.

The qualities of the Chairman, Commissioners and staff

One of Derek Barber's claims to fame must be that he got on with all the Ministers, and thus maintained that essential link of trust at the political level. But he had other distinguished skills. Too patrician for some perhaps, he was none the less a remarkable chairman, who made Commission meetings both enjoyable and businesslike. He had a style of writing, and a turn of phrase, that made the reader sit up—or the listener wake up. And he had great gifts as a persuader: he rarely lost an argument, but he had the charm needed to make his adversary almost enjoy being routed.

This chapter is neither a biography nor a tribute, but no analysis of the Commission's achievements of the 1980s would be complete without a recognition that Derek Barber was at the centre of the organisation's success.

If the Chairman was a constant throughout most of the period, the cast of Commissioners changed a good deal. Only Mark Schreiber, now Lord Marlesford, was a Commissioner throughout Derek Barber's and the author's terms; his political insights and eternal enthusiasm for the Commission were immensely valuable qualities.

Meeting once every other month, and with two three-day visits a year, the Commission established for itself a clear role as a policy board, leaving the day-to-day running of the organisation to the Director General and his staff. Commission meetings were lively and at times amusing. Often issues were hard fought, but differences of view were never aired in public; Commissioners' loyalty to the Commission saw to that.

And finally the staff. The author could not complete this account without expressing his admiration for the dedication of the Commission's staff at all levels, and for the quality of their contribution to its work. Naming individuals would be invidious and misleading. In all parts of the Commission there was a commitment to high standards and a belief in the value of the mission.

Concluding thoughts

This account of the Commission during the Thatcher years provides some modest clues to the exercise of power in Britain today. Certainly it suggests what is the potential of a body like the Commission—and what are its limits.

The conclusions are pragmatic ones, which do not sit comfortably alongside some of the theories about models of power and politics in Britain put forward by Cloke *et al.* which have been critically discussed by Gilg (1991 and 1992). In essence these models suggest that—in the countryside arena at any rate—though ultimate power may rest with those whom we elect, the way that power is exercised is triggered by preordained structural factors based on class divisions and capital; and that to understand the politics of the countryside is no less complex an intellectual task than to understand the workings of the countryside itself. Alternatively, Gilg (1992) has argued that the process is more random and shaped by powerful individuals and chance events.

Five similar conclusions can be drawn from my experience:

1. In the countryside, politics change and action takes place when there is a coincidence of favourable circumstances. For example, the solution to Halvergate was found because the environmental arguments, to protect the grazing marshes, coincided with the agricultural ones, to cut back cereal production, and also with the presence of an Organization—the Commission—which had the experimental powers to test a new relationship between farming and conservation. Another case, the forestry changes introduced by the 1988 budget happened because the Treasury's interests and those of a number of conservation groups also coincided. Although quite different reasons were advanced both wanted an end to tax reliefs for forestry, and both found sympathetic ears in cabinet, in Chancellor Lawson and Secretary of State Ridley. Finally, the Commission's target of putting the rights of way into shape by the end of the century became practical politics when both *Telegraph* and *Guardian* readers complained over the state of footpaths and bridle-ways, and when landowners and farmers decided the bad press from blocked paths more than outweighed the perceived advantage to the farming community of discouraging people from walking or riding across farmland.

2. The influence of exceptional individuals is important. The Commission worked for a number of Ministers who made little impact on it—or it on them. But Michael Heseltine, Nicholas Ridley, Chris Patten, William Waldegrave and David Trippier all in different ways imposed their own enthusiasms, interests and prejudices in ways which were felt at Cheltenham. There can, for example, be no doubt that Chris Patten's battle with Treasury to fund the Commission's initiatives in *This Common Inheritance* gave an immense impetus to its work at the start of the 1990s. On the other side, the role of Derek Barber as bridge-builder able to maintain ministerial support for the Commission, even during bouts of ideological hostility, is clear. Other chairmen of quangos, for example those who had their effigies burnt by angry farmers or who became caught up in public rows with Cabinet Ministers, were notably less successful.

3. Government, whatever it may wish to appear, is not seamless. Thus, the Department of the Environment's countryside record, though hardly without fault, contrasted sharply with the depressing record of the Departments of Defence, Energy and Transport. Whilst there were during the 1980s some far-reaching changes in the practice and policies

of the Ministry of Agriculture towards the countryside (more than the voluntary bodies have given credit for), it was hard to find many vigorous strands of greenery in other parts of Whitehall. Accordingly, when the balance sheet of successes and failures is drawn up by the Commission for its efforts in the 1980s, many of the setbacks can be traced to the lack of sympathy for conservation objectives in certain departments. The greening of Whitehall has a long way to go.

4. There is an element of maverick chance at work. The Liverpool riots in the early 1980s convinced Michael Heseltine that Groundwork should be rapidly expanded to demonstrate government concern about the quality of the rural environment in the run-down parts of North-West England. The 1987 storm brought chaos to South-East England, but a fillip to the Commission. The criticism of the NCC's role in Scotland led by a chain of events which had nothing to do with any criticism of the Commission's performance in Wales, to the loss of its role in the Principality.

5. And finally, there are some enduring lessons which can be drawn from the Countryside Commission's experience in the 1980s about how a quango like the Commission should play its hand in an area of increasing political sensitivity. It must be clear about what it wants to achieve, but subtle about how it gets there. It must adhere to principle as to ends, but be opportunistic and flexible as to means. It needs to understand the limits of its independence and the reality of its role as part of government machinery. It should cultivate its allies, especially those in the voluntary sector. It needs to keep open the channels to Ministers and officials at all times, most of all when publicly in dispute with the government. Above all, it should be guided by the principle that what matters is what works.

References

Blunden, J. and Curry, N., 1990, *A people's charter?*, HMSO, London

Countryside Commission, 1968, *First annual report*, HMSO, London

Countryside Commission, 1981a, *Conference of national park authorities, 1981: report of proceedings*, Countryside Commission, Cheltenham

Countryside Commission, 1981b, *Conference of national park authorities, 1981, report of proceedings*, Countryside Commission, Cheltenham

Countryside Commission, 1981c, *Thirteenth report, 1979–80*, HMSO, London

Countryside Commission, 1986, *Annual report 1985–86*, Countryside Commission, Cheltenham

Cripps, J., 1980, 'The Countryside Commission: its first decade', *Countryside Planning Yearbook*, **1**, 38–48

Dower, M., 1992, 'Comment', *Countryside*, **54**

Department of the Environment, 1992, *Action for the countryside*, DOE, London

Gilg, A., 1991 *Countryside planning policies for the 1990s*, CAB International, Wallingford, pp. 4–15

Gilg, A., 1992, 'Restructuring the countryside: an introductory essay' in A. Gilg (ed.) *Restructuring the countryside: environmental policy in practice*, Avebury, Aldershot, pp. 3–18

MacEwen, A. and MacEwen, M., 1982, *National parks: conservation or cosmetics?*, George Allen and Unwin, London

Patten, C., 1990, in *Report of the national parks 40th anniversary conference*, CCD 57, Countryside Commission, Cheltenham

Pye-Smith, C. and Hall, C. 1987, *The Countryside we want*, Green Books, Bideford

Ridley, N., 1992, *My kind of government*, Fontana Books, London

Shoard, M., 1980, *The theft of the countryside*, Maurice Temple Smith, London

Stamp, D., 1969, *Nature conservation in Britain*, Collins, London

Worsley, G., 1992, 'Rural housing design: the search for a middle way', Paper for the RTPI National Planning Conference, Birmingham (unpublished). See *The Planner*

Young, H., 1991, *One of us*, Macmillan, Basingstoke

7 Progress in water management in the lowlands

Hadrian F. Cook

Growing demands and problems

Demands upon water resources in lowland Britain (by which is meant England south and east of roughly the Tees-Exe line) are increasing in terms of both quantity and quality. Policy responses to these growing demands need to be matched by technical and land-use change responses if real progress is to be made. In the 1990s legislation derived from European Community directives is now the prime mover in the drive to improve or maintain drinking water standards. Currently the implementation of recent directives is being achieved by the development of appropriate land management and land-use controls.

In terms of quantity, estimated total abstraction increased throughout the 1980s in all the National Rivers Authority (NRA) regions of lowland Britain (DOE, 1990). With a rising projected demand (NRA, 1992a), aggravated by a drought in recent years, increased demand by itself is causing severe problems, for example, dried-up river beds, reduced supplies for farmers and subsidence of buildings caused by subsoil shrinkage and lowered water-tables. A number of solutions have been offered including water meters and a crackdown on the 25 per cent of water estimated to be wasted from leaks in the supply system.

In terms of quality, the normal approach in recent years has been to use 'standards' set at levels considered not harmful to human health or to the environment; water undertakers must then endeavour to meet these standards. In the UK, surface and groundwaters are prone to contamination from many sources of point and diffuse pollution.

Point pollution is in theory controlled by setting consents to discharge. One example is provided by farms which contribute around 12 per cent of *reported* pollution incidents (NRA, 1992b). This figure is however misleading, not only against a (suspected) larger proportion of unreported incidents, but also against the diffuse pollution from intensive arable land. In many ways it is *diffuse* sources which provide the most problems, precisely because of the manner in which these pollutants enter the hydrological cycle. Accordingly, this chapter concentrates on diffuse pollution from agriculture.

Diffuse pollution from nitrates rises indirectly from both organic and inorganic fertiliser applications (DOE, 1986) to arable and horticultural land, as well as intensively managed grass. Nitrates may contribute to eutrophication of surface waters; while concentrations in aquifers frequently exceed EC limits (Foster, 1992). The practice of sewage sludge disposal to fields also presents problems of nitrate pollution of waters, and it may also cause problems of heavy metal contamination of land, in spite of EC directives to limit sludge application.

Diffuse pollution from pesticides, for example, in surface waters may cause problems, and Stansfield *et al.* (1989) have implicated them as a major contributor to the breakdown of aquatic ecosystems in the Norfolk Broadland. Pesticides are now also to be found in groundwaters (NRA, 1992b), and measures will have to be taken if concentrations are to be maintained in all waters below EC limits. Soil erosion, which can be locally serious in Britain, has immediate repercussions with respect to the sediment loading of watercourses (Boardman and Favis-Mortlock, 1992). Because both pesticides and phosphate (a major contributor to eutrophication) form complexes with soil particles, soil erosion also contributes chemical pollutants, and moved-on soil particles, to watercourses.

Moving towards solutions

Catchment definition is an essential precursor to source protection. Defining a catchment when only surface waters are under consideration is straightforward, and planning for protection need not be difficult. Establishing the location of groundwater divides creates problems for subsurface catchment definition, however, especially since divides tend to move if patterns of aquifer recharge or discharge (especially borehole abstraction) alter. Furthermore, groundwater quality, due to problems with understanding residence times and travel times in aquifers for both water and pollutants, is more difficult to protect, and once polluted, groundwater is less easy to rehabilitate (NRA, 1992c). Despite these difficulties, because groundwater supplies around one-third of total abstractions in England and Wales, rising well above 50 per cent in parts of eastern England (DOE, 1990), pollution of aquifers needs to be taken seriously. Accordingly, groundwater protection should definitely be within the scope of land-use controls, and indeed has been the subject of recent EC Directives.

The development of solutions

The solutions offered can be divided into three areas: *administrative measures*, *land-use measures* and *standard setting*. These are considered in turn.

Administrative measures

Measures have long been taken to protect water resources with water 'catchment' areas comprising the logical unit of management. From this concept the idea of 'integrated catchment management' was developed whereby all aspects of water resources, including regulation, piped supply and sewerage, were managed by the same authority. This strategy formed the philosophy behind the establishment of Regional Water Authorities (RWA) in England and Wales after 1973. However, criticisms surrounding the supposed 'poacher and gamekeeper' role of the former RWAs led to a split in functions by the early 1990s. The National Rivers Authority (NRA) came into being on the first of September 1989 under the Water Act of that year, and is a public body created as 'guardian of the water environment', with a wide range of regulatory powers. It is geographically based upon the ten former RWA regions. The supply side of the RWAs, together with the sewage disposal functions, were privatised into ten private limited companies, thereby joining the 29 former water supply companies which were private companies before and since 1973.

There are two very different sides to this restructuring of the water industry. One is the functional split and creation of the NRA, an important development for regulation; the other is the wholesale privatisation of sewerage and supply functions. Many see the latter as more ideological and less concerned with meeting the need for water resource management. None the less it is the NRA which has to address problems of water quality regulation and develop strategies for meeting demand within the now powerful framework of EC—and UK—legislation.

Arising from the 1989 Water Act, catchment management is moving towards land-use control through the planning process (Newson, 1992), with the NRA developing Catchment Management Plans (CMPs) aimed at balancing the needs of all water users (NRA, 1991). CMPs are action plans which state objectives for both water and associated land use including potential conflicts, and will enable the NRA to manage catchments proactively rather than reactively.

Land-use measures

Land-use control to benefit water resources is not new. On the eve of privatisation, the water industry owned around 150,000 hectares of England and Wales, mostly in upland areas and serving the purpose of protecting catchments and reservoirs. However it is the likely switch to large-scale land-use controls in lowland Britain, and especially in the agriculturally productive east of England, that represents a departure in water protection policy. It should also be remembered that options other than land-use controls, such as blending and treatment at source of waters, are available to the industry.

The most overt type of land-use control are the ten pilot Nitrate Sensitive Areas (NSAs) which will operate initially between 1990 and 1995 (NRA, 1992b). Farmers are compensated for losses incurred from restrictions on the use of nitrate fertiliser. The take-up rate so far has been encouraging (Foster, 1992). More recently a plan to establish groundwater Protection Zones (SPZs) has been published Source (NRA, 1992c). Under the Water Resources Act (1991) the NRA has powers to prevent discharges, prosecute polluters and designate water protection zones (NRA, 1992b). Within SPZs, a wide range of activities including discharges above and below the water-table, landfills and mineral extraction likely to damage the aquifer, are to be controlled. This approach permits not only the division of entire land areas on the basis of the vulnerability of the underlying aquifers to pollution, but also the definition of special protection areas for individual sources (Adams and Foster, 1992). A criticism of such SPZs is that they are not pollutant specific. However they are defensible because the potential for generating pollutant-specific maps is enormous, especially since the advent of Geographical Information Systems (GIS). In practice the implementation of pollutant specific land-targeting would be very complicated.

These two land-use control schemes are accompanied by a growing array of policy options aimed at conserving the countryside, protecting the wider environment or reducing agricultural surplus. Many of these will also benefit water quality, even where this is not a stated aim. There are three main examples, *Environmentally Sensitive Areas, Set-Aside* and the *Farm Woodland Scheme*.

The Environmentally Sensitive Areas (ESA) Scheme seeks to conserve and recreate habitats by compensating farmers, for example, by not ploughing pasture or by re-establishing grass on former ploughland. The restoration of pasture at low stocking densities and zero fertiliser regimes will reduce the risks of pollution of waters and of soil erosion. A development of the ESA scheme, the Countryside Stewardship scheme, offers farmers contracts to manage, restore and recreate natural features in the wider countryside. Enrolment is for a ten-year agreement (ESA is five) and target landscapes include chalk and limestone landscapes, and waterside landscapes.

The Set-Aside scheme, whereby farmers are paid an annual amount per unit area of land effectively not to produce anything, has the objective of reducing EC cereal surpluses. In its original form this scheme is not considered by some as either successful, or indeed desirable. Apart from being negative in its approach to land use, it arguably leads to intensification of agriculture on land not enrolled. Any environmental benefits, such as a reduction of agrochemical pollution, may be viewed as accidental.

The CAP price reforms in May 1992 could potentially lead to 15 per cent of all arable land being set-aside. The details of schemes to manage this land more environmentally, such as the adoption of 'agri-environmental' farming methods (EC, 1991), have yet to emerge. These could be crucial if water quality is to be improved.

The Farm Woodland Scheme encourages the planting of broadleaved woods as an alternative crop. Farmers are encouraged to plant a minimum of three hectares with the objectives of reducing agricultural surpluses by diverting land from agriculture, enhancing the landscape, supporting farm incomes and encouraging timber production. Looking to the longer term, the Community Forest scheme aims at extensive tree planting adjacent to cities. Here the objective is primarily amenity, but timber production is proposed for suitable areas. In these schemes MAFF and the Countryside Commission are working with the Forestry Commission.

Water yield is however affected by tree planting. For example, conifer-isation of upland catchments has long been known to reduce yield (Calder, 1990), and coniferous afforestation of an aquifer in eastern England has been shown to reduce recharge compared with grass cover (Cooper, 1980). In contrast, Hall and Roberts (1989) suggest that annual water use by both coniferous and broadleaved plantations in eastern England may not be very different when compared with grass. However maximum water use by broadleaves is more concentrated in the summer months when con-sumer demand upon water resources is highest. Rainfall regimes, species composition, losses from understories and edge effects on small plantations may also be important. Where management is by coppicing, stool density and the age since cutting have been shown to affect soil water status, and hence local water balances in drier years (Cummings and Cook, 1992). In spite of these uncertainties, the planting of trees on former intensively managed land to prevent agrochemical pollution has long been considered to be a serious option (DOE, 1986).

Standard setting

The Water Act of 1989 allows (for the first time under UK legislation) a series of water quality objectives to be introduced. Statutory Water Qual-ity Objectives (SWQOs) are to be set and implemented through the publication of Statutory Instruments (NRA, 1991). The first three to be introduced following the Act concern: the classification of surface fresh waters with respect to their abstraction (SI 1989/1148); the listing of permitted concentrations of certain 'dangerous' substances in order to implement EC directives (SI 1989/2286); and bathing water quality (SI 1991/1597). 'Controlled waters' under these instruments comprise all groundwaters, lakes, reservoirs, rivers, canals and the first three miles out to sea. It is proposed that statutory application will be met by means of 'Use Classes' (defined according to the uses of the waters such as fisheries or potable supplies), and a 'General Classification Scheme' incorporating standards for key chemical parameters and biological measurements.

Land-use changes for the 1990s and beyond

Clearly we face a changing landscape in lowland Britain. It has long been realised that the European Community is facing an agricultural land surplus which could mean 500,000 to 800,000 hectares of cereal land in the United Kingdom being removed from production (Potter *et al.*, 1991). The Set-Aside scheme is one attempt to come to terms with the consequences of overproduction by the use of this option. However reducing the intensity of production is also available, and indeed fertiliser use may already have declined since the mid-1980s (Chalmers *et al.*, 1990). Perhaps more 'low-input' or organic farming will result from changing market demands, restrictions on agrochemical use or further policy directives from the EC. Many farmers in a range of landscapes will be subsidised to farm in 'traditional' ways for reasons of conservation and countryside. Away from agriculture there is likely to be a steady land-take for urban uses.

Elsewhere, Forestry Commission statistics show a decrease in the area of scrub and a slight increase in broadleaved woodland in England and Wales since the 1950s (Locke, 1987). The implication is that some scrub is growing to mature secondary woodland, and the effect of this change on water yield and quality would be the same as that of plantations, only less predictable. In future, woodland areas may increase either actively through policy implementation (such as farm woodlands) or through the abandonment of marginal land.

If the proponents of global warming prove correct, then the effects on land use and water resources represent another important variable. A recent report (DOE, 1991) summarises current thinking on the likely effects for the United Kingdom including increased winter precipitation. This may partly alleviate greater summer demand brought on by increased overall evapotranspirational demand, and a higher frequency of hot summers. None the less, it is probable that the water industry will have to adjust to increased pressures on resources in southern and eastern Britain in whatever form annual rainfall is distributed. In terms of water quality, changes in soil structure may cause increased leaching of agrochemicals with adverse effects. Meanwhile the agricultural economy could change considerably in response to changing cropping patterns. In coastal areas, following a rise in sea level, increased vulnerability to flooding, saline intrusion of aquifers and increased salinisation of soils could result. The net result would be a loss of agricultural land.

Perhaps the most fundamental problem is that, should rainfall decline over the long term in hitherto agriculturally productive regions of the world, then northern and western Europe may increase in importance as a global 'bread basket'. Pressure to increase the production of foodstuffs may return to Britain, creating severe difficulties for future environmental protection against an intensifying and changing agriculture.

Possible technical responses

These can broadly be divided into *better use of information and modelling*, and *physical controls*.

Better use of information and modelling

In the drive to maintain water quality, laying aside water industry based measures such as source blending and water treatment there remains the option of source protection. Variation in the natural environment, coupled with elements of predictive uncertainty with respect to source protection, give rise to GIS-based spatial models. These rank land areas over an aquifer, in a surface catchment or around a source according to vulnerability to pollution of waters. Available input data is derived from survey information on soils, geology, hydrology etc. which varies in terms of availability and spatial resolution (Norman *et al.*, 1992; McCallister *et al.*, 1992).

Models which aim to map the vulnerability of groundwaters to nitrate pollution include factors such as soil type, aquifer drift cover, effective rainfall, unsaturated zone geometry, depth to water-table and proximity to abstraction points (Cook, 1992). The flexibility provided by GIS makes it possible to locate and examine the most vulnerable areas in greater detail, provided the input data is of sufficient spatial resolution. This approach permits sophisticated targeting, with the most vulnerable areas being enrolled in the most stringent land-use controls. To control nitrate pollution, the NRA currently favours a two-tier approach with fertiliser application at recommended rates over large areas with specific sources being protected as NSAs (NRA, 1992b).

The general purpose SPZs proposed by the NRA are designed to control both potential point and diffuse sources of pollution. They further refine the spatial hydrogeological components by identifying zones with boundaries based upon supposed groundwater 'travel times' to an abstraction point from any point below the water-table (NRA, 1992c).

Zone One (inner source protection) boundaries are defined at 50 days, but not less than 50 metres radius from the source, these criteria being based upon the decay period for biological contaminants. Zone Two (outer source protection) is defined at 400 days, and is designed to provide delay and attenuation of slowly degrading pollutants. It is likely to be far larger in area than Zone One, and will anyhow not be less than 25 per cent of the source catchment. Zone Three (source catchment) comprises the complete catchment area of a groundwater source, defined as an area required to support abstraction on a long-term basis. Its outer edge could be a few kilometres from an average source in Triassic sandstone, and considerably larger for chalk boreholes in eastern England. The size and shape of protection zones is a function of aquifer characteristics and recharge conditions. Hitherto the travel times selected in order to define protection zones have varied greatly (Adams and Foster, 1992); the criteria selected by the NRA are based upon experience throughout Europe.

Pollution risk assessment maps may also be produced as part of CMPs to display the vulnerability of surface waters. For example, a map showing pollution vulnerability arising from soil slurry acceptance has been produced for a catchment in west Wales (Scofield *et al.*, 1989). Another example is a map showing the vulnerability of surface waters to sheep dip pollution at a national scale (NRA, 1992b), and the practice of mapping land areas for soil erosion liability in UK and USA has been discussed by Potter *et al.* (1991).

A model has been described by Hollis (1991) which permits the vulnerability of land to pesticides leaching from soils to ground and surface waters. Pesticides are complicated chemicals, their behaviour in the environment uncertain, and mapping for vulnerability difficult. There are as yet no pesticide protection zones, but it may be that any measures aimed at extensifying agriculture or removing land altogether from production will reduce pollution as a by-product, *provided* the pesticides are agricultural in origin.

It is also important to consider the effects upon the draught of the aquifer itself. Speculatively we can imagine any extensification measures, such as a loss of cropland or a lowering of irrigation inputs, to cause lower water consumption by agriculture. In regions such as East Anglia where total abstraction of water for the agricultural industry amounted to some seven per cent of the total in 1989 (DOE, 1990), the saving may be considerable.

Physical controls

The more efficient channelling of water to the sea as a flood control measure in recent years may have contributed to problems of rivers running dry in the summer and thus higher concentrations of pollutants. Such flood control is increasingly being moved away from urban areas, generally to upstream flood alleviation schemes, for example near Ashford, Kent (Gibbs and Lindley, 1990). Although such schemes cannot be described *senso stricto* as protecting water resources, they represent an example of water resource planning affecting land use.

One partial solution to agrochemical runoff and sediment loading from soil erosion may be the designation of protection zones set parallel to vulnerable watercourses. In the USA the Conservation Reserve Program targets land alongside rivers for diversion out of crops (Potter *et al.*, 1991) or the maintenance of riparian forest. Strips of varying width designed to operate as filters to reduce pollution of watercourses from forestry and agriculture are frequently recommended in UK (Newson, 1992). Although the efficacy of differing widths and soil types has yet to be fully evaluated, fertiliser-free grass strips as narrow as five metres may be effective in reducing nitrate pollution in some situations (Moorby and Cook, 1992).

Whilst consumer demand rises, and there is a probable largest need for additional resources in the Anglian, Southern, Thames, Wessex and South-West NRA regions, there is potential for conflict with conservation needs in some areas (NRA, 1992a). Abstractions in eastern England in recent (dry) years have caused concern over the maintenance of aquatic habitats and loss of flows in chalk streams. Options for meeting imbalances include leakage control, further groundwater or surface abstraction (limited potential), new reservoir or groundwater storage developments, inter-regional transfers, setting up a national water grid (which would be costly), reusing effluent (which has operational problems and attendant health risks), desalination and the importation of water to the UK (NRA, 1992a). Clearly we have a situation demanding collaboration between the appropriate statutory bodies, and fortunately this is emerging.

Concluding comments

Three main issues have emerged from this chapter, the problem of the *integration of organisational policies*, the issue of *land use* and the use of *targeting and zoning* as a policy and technical response.

Integration of organisational policies

Frequently the objectives of UK public bodies (such as MAFF, DOE, NRA, Countryside Commission, English Nature etc.) are not incompatible with respect to land use, conservation goals or environmental enhancement, although closer integration regarding the targeting of land-use policies is desirable. The proposed creation of an umbrella 'Environment Agency' including the NRA, along with air and land pollution control functions should encourage policy integration.

Future policies aimed at water resource protection will need to be brought in line with schemes arising from policies aimed at farmer income support, diversifying agriculture or at other aspects of countryside or environmental enhancement. The NRA already works with MAFF in NSAs and benefit could accrue from it working with other bodies connected with farming. MAFF might be encouraged to extend its grant-aid system to further 'incorporate aspects of pollution control' (NRA, 1992b), and it has been suggested that set-aside land should be targeted as buffer zones to reduce soil erosion and agro-chemical inputs to watercourses. Furthermore reinstated wetlands, strategically placed, may intercept agrochemical pollutants.

Land use

In Britain land-use controls to protect catchments are not new, and much research has been directed at the effects of land management on waters. From now on, in agriculturally productive areas, controls of diffuse sources of pollution are being introduced with the primary aim of protecting water resources. The introduction of grassland is probably the least obstrusive and most straightforward land-use change either in local protection zones or as a wider land diversification measure. In order to maintain the grassland, management by low-stocking density grazing or mowing is required. Broadleaved afforestation is likely to be more visible but requires relatively little maintenance, whereas restrictions on fertilisers while arable production continues is difficult to 'police' after implementation.

Targeting and zoning

The liability of land areas to transmit pollution to waters can be expressed in maps displaying zones of different vulnerability. This provides a framework for land targeting where source protection is the chosen method to maintain water quality. Measures specifically designed to protect-water resources could provide a suitable framework for wider-scale countryside planning, especially land targeting, because the legislative back-up is so powerful. The efficient targeting of land diversion into zones located to protect water resources is not only liable to be more successful because it is affirmative in its approach, but also avoids any risk of duplication of effort by public bodies, and would thus be more efficient in the use of public funds.

Zoning such as in the proposed SPZ scheme is immediately attractive for the targeting of land uses because it provides a concrete basis for planning. For example in Zone One (close to water sources) land uses as well as consents to discharge might be severely restricted. Only broadleaved woodland, low intensity grazing, or set-aside might be permitted. Zone Two may have low input or organic farming targeted so that pesticide input is reduced. Properly managed, organic farms should leach little nitrogen throughout a complete rotation (Stopes and Phillips, 1992), although effective management cannot always be assured. Only in Zone Three might more conventional farming remain, but with agro-chemical application according to recommended rates. Such a practice would be in keeping with the two-tier approach favoured for NSAs, but in SPZs the zonation is not pollutant specific.

NSAs and SPZs are the first major initiatives aimed specifically at water protection, and are implemented despite problems of groundwater catchment definition. This move reflects the relative severity of the problem of groundwater contamination and the legislative drive from the EC. It is now appropriate to further develop surface water protection policies, and the vehicle for such schemes would be the CMPs. Indeed because surface water is both visible and accessible, the task of protection zone definition is simpler.

The background against which rural changes occur is an ever-shifting one, not only of agri-environmental policy, but also of conservation goals and possible long-term climatic change. It may be unwise to be too specific about the future land-use pattern of lowland Britain in, say, fifty years time. Whereas we can be cautiously optimistic that appropriate measures are now being taken to commence the task of water source protection, evaluation of measures through long-term monitoring of water quality has yet to be undertaken. The first such results should come from those pilot NSAs established on low residence time aquifers. The policing of land-use controls and monitoring water quality will depend upon appropriate resources being allocated to environmental agencies.

Acknowledgements

Peter Buckley, Ian Cummings, Howard Lee and Geoff Mason are thanked for discussions during the preparation of this article. Clive Potter and the *Progress in Rural Policy and Planning* referees and editor are thanked for their comments on the manuscript. Opinions expressed are entirely those of the author.

References

Adams, B. and Foster, S.S.D., 1992, 'Land surface zoning for groundwater protection', *Journal of the Institution of Water and Environmental Management* **6** (3): 312–20

Boardman, J. and Favis-Mortlock, D., 1992, 'Soil erosion and sediment loading of watercourse', *SEESOIL*, **7**: 5–29

Calder, I.R., 1990, *Evaporation in the uplands*, John Wiley, Chichester

Chalmers, A., Kershaw, C. and Leech P., 1990, 'Fertiliser use on farm crops in Great Britain: results from the survey of fertiliser practice, 1969 to 1988', *Outlook on Agriculture*, **18** (4): 269–78

Cook, H.F., 1992, 'A spatial model for identifying nitrate protection zones over an aquifer', *SEESOIL*, **7**: 49–63

Cooper, J.D. 1980, *Measurement of moisture fluxes in unsaturated soil in Thetford Forest*, Institute of Hydrology Report 66, Wallingford, Oxon

Cummings, I. and Cook, H.F., 1992, 'Soil-water relations in an ancient coppiced woodland' in G.P. Buckley (ed.), *Ecology and Management of Coppice Woodland*, Chapman and Hall, London, pp. 57–75

Department of the Environment (DOE), 1986, *Nitrate in Water*, Pollution Paper no. 26, HMSO, London

Department of the Environment (DOE), 1990, *Digest of Environmental and Water Statistics*, **13**, HMSO, London

Department of the Environment (DOE), 1991, *The potential effects of climate change in the United Kingdom*, HMSO, London

European Commission (EC), 1991, *The development and future of the common agricultural policy* com(91)258, HMSO, London

Foster, I., 1992, 'Protection of water quality from agricultural pollution: some observations on recent developments', in A. Gilg (ed.), *Progress in Rural Policy and Planning*, Volume II, Belhaven Press, London, pp 136–9

Gibbs, G.M. and Lindley, M., 1990, 'Flood alleviation works for Ashford, Kent', Proceedings of the Institution of Water and Environmental Management Annual Symposium held at the Scottish Exhibition centre, Glasgow, 4–6 September 1990, Paper 30, 10pp

Hall, R.L. and Roberts, J.M., 1989, 'Hydrological aspects of new broad-leaf plantations', *SEESOIL*, **6**: 2–38

Hollis, J.M., 1991, 'Mapping the vulnerability of aquifers and surface waters to pesticide contamination at the National/Regional scale' in A. Walker (ed.), *Pesticides in soils and water*, Monograph 47, British Crop Protection Council, Symposium held at the University of Warwick, Coventry, 25–26 March 1991, pp. 165–74

Locke, G.M., 1987, *Census of woodlands and trees 1979–82*, Forestry Commission Bulletin No. 63, HMSO, London

McCallister, R., Shelley, K.B. and Thum, P.G., 1992, 'The use of GIS for nitrogen management planning in Wisconsin' in A. Gilg (ed.), *Progress in Rural Policy and Planning*, Volume II, Belhaven Press, London, pp. 5–16

Moorby, H. and Cook, H.F., 1992, 'Use of fertiliser-free grass strips to protect dyke water from nitrate pollution', *Aspects of Applied Biology*, **30**: 231–4

National Rivers Authority, 1991, *Proposals for statutory water quality objectives report of the National Rivers Authority*, Water Quality Series no. 5, NRA, Bristol

National Rivers Authority, 1992a, *Water resources development strategy: a discussion document*, NRA, Bristol

National Rivers Authority, 1992b, *The influence of agriculture on the quality of natural waters in England and Wales*, Report of the National Rivers Authority, Water Quality Series no. 6, NRA, Bristol

National Rivers Authority, 1992c, *Policy and practice for the protection of groundwater*, NRA, Bristol

Newson, M., 1992, 'Land and water: convergence, divergence and progress in UK policy', *Land Use Policy*, **9** (2): 111–21

Norman, C., Cook, H.F. and Potter, C.A., 1992, 'Targeting environmental policy—developing a GIS methodology' in T.W. Rideout (ed.) *GIS and Urban and Rural Planning*, Institute of British Geographers, London, pp. 116–28

Potter, C.A., Burnham, C.P., Edwards, A., Gasson R. and Green, B., 1991, *The diversion of land: conservation in a period of farming contraction*, Routledge, London

Scofield, K., Seager, J. and Merriman, R.P., 1989, 'The impact of intensive dairy farming activities on river quality: the eastern Cleddau catchment study', Proceedings of the Institution of Water and Environmental Management Annual Symposium held 21–22 March 1989 at the University of York, Paper 3, pp. 14–16

Stansfield, J., Moss, B. and Irvine, K., 1989, 'The loss of submerged plants with eutrophication III: potential role of organochlorine pesticides, a palaeoecological study', *Freshwater Biology* **22**: 109–32

Stopes, C.E. and Phillips, L., 1992, 'Organic farming and nitrate leaching', *SEESOIL*, **7**: 37–48

8 'Annual Review' of rural planning in the United Kingdom

Andrew W. Gilg

The purpose of this Annual Review is to provide a survey of the following items: legislative changes; changes in grant aid and other support for rural areas (e.g. farm support prices, forestry grants); major policy statements, policy advice and consultations; land-use designations (eg. new National Parks, Nature Reserves etc.); and an annotated list of major books, reports, articles and statistical sources, published in the year. The style is intended to be mainly factual, short and snappy, to give coverage in breadth but not in depth or detail: its main purpose is to provide a check-list, for all those academics/planners/pressure group personnel and other people employed in rural organisations, who feel that the world is passing them by as they are submerged under the weight of new material which day-to-day demands of the job prevent them from reading. The Review is thus an *aide mémoire* rather than a discursive piece. Where possible, further reading is listed so that the reader can follow up a topic.

In order to clasify matters the Review is broken up into three major sections: Legislative review; Review of events and news stories; and Literature list. This follows the previous pattern of the *Countryside Planning Yearbook* (1980–6) and the *International Yearbook of Rural Planning* (1987–8). In order thus to provide continuity with the Yearbook, Volume One of Progress in Rural Policy and Planning PIRPAP, covered the period from 1 September 1987–31 August 1989, Volume Two covered the period from 1 September 1989–31 August 1991 and Volume Three resumes the annual period by covering the period 1 September 1992–31 August 1992 (with extensions to October and November for news items).

In more detail the review is divided up as shown below:

1. Legislative review, 1 September 1991 to 31 August 1992
     Acts of Parliament
     Bills in progress or not proceeding to Acts
     Statutory Instruments
     Advice from central government: DOE and Department of Transport
     Circulars, DOE Planning Policy Guidance Notes, DOE Mineral
     Policy Guidance Notes, Scottish Office Environment Department
     Circulars and Planning Advice Notes
     Command Papers (Statements of policy)
     Review of Policy in House of Commons, (HC) and Command
     (Cm.) papers.
     House of Lords Papers

2. Reviews of events and news stories in rural planning, 1 September 1991
   to 31 October 1992
     Three major issues
       Changes to agricultural policy
       Schemes and initiatives
       International, national and local political economy
     Consultation papers (not already discussed)
     List of new protected areas and designations (see Table 8.6)

3. Literature list
     Selected publications
     Selected articles
     Annual reports and accounts
     Statistics

The division is meant to devolve down from formal legislation to implementation via advice and consultation. It is based on the type of document involved but increasingly some sections are not mutually exclusive; for example, HC and Cm. papers where policy is being evaluated are grouped together. Also considerable cross-referencing is made between Statutory Instruments (SIs) Circulars, Planning Policy Guidance (PPGs) and Consultation Papers.

Legislative review

Most of the attention in the year was focused on implementing those Acts passed in previous years, notably the Planning and Compensation Act 1991. Much time was also spent reformulating advice in the light of this Act. The year also saw a substantial move back towards planning as a good thing following the return of Michael Heseltine as Secretary of State—and then his replacement by Michael Howard in April 1992—and the publication of the 1990 White Paper on the Environment. Most of the action is thus to be found in the SI section, the Circular section and the Planning Policy Guidance Section.

Acts of Parliament

In a year split by the April election there were not surprisingly only a few Acts. The most significant of these was the Local Government Act 1992 (Chapter 19, £6.10) which contained two main provisions. First, it provides a system of performance standards for local government including more provisions for privatising or subcontracting council services (but not including planning), and second, a new review system for local government boundaries, structures and electoral arrangements. It is this latter provision which will have the main impact on planning, but only in England, since, as the Review of events section shows, Wales and Scotland are following a different model.

In England the Act set up under Section 12 a Local Government Commission (LGC) with 5–15 members (Schedule 2). Under Section 13 (1) the Secretary of State (SOS) for the Environment can direct the LGC to conduct a review of areas to recommend whether the SOS should make such structural, boundary, or electoral changes as they recommend or to make their own independent review but only with respect to electoral changes. The main thrust of the recommendations are expected to be to substitute two-tier authority areas with one-tier authority areas, but in making their recommendations the LGC should have regard to the need (15)(5)(a): 'to reflect the identities and interests of local communities'; and (15)(5)(b): 'to secure effective and convenient local government'.

It is also the task of the LGC to recommend which type of plans should be prepared by the new authority (Section 14 (5)(d) namely, unitary, structure, local, mineral and waste plans and in which combination, depending for example on whether a district council(s) is (are) becoming a county council or a county council is becoming a district council.

Ironically, the Act received the Royal Assent in March 1992 only one month after the revised two-tier plan-making system came into force (see SI2794/91 on p. 110 and PPG 12 on p. 121).

Finally, the recommendations of the LGC must be made public in a report, and the SOS must consult before making an Order which sets out the new boundaries and duties of any new authority.

In conclusion, the Act, in common with its predecessors in the early 1970s, once again made the mistake of divorcing legislation for local government from legislation for planning. This time, however, there will be no big bang as on 1 April 1974 but a series of small explosions, as the LGC proceeds on an erratic progress around England in the mid-years of the 1990s, as the Review of events section shows in more detail on p. 151.

Further commentary can be found in *Planning* 8/11/91, p. 1; 17/1/92, p. 20; and 13/3/92, p. 3; and in *The Planner* 15/11/91, p. 4.

The Act was originally published as HC 7 (91–92) followed by HL 22 (91–92), and HL 32(91–92) before moving to the Commons as HC 49 (91–92) which was examined by Standing Committee D before emerging as HC 65(91–92).

Local government powers over transport developments were the subject of the Transport and Works Act 1992 (Chapter 42, £7.40) which implemented, with modifications, the 1991 proposals for giving permission for either new railways and harbours or modifications to existing facilities (See Volume II, p. 88 (Cm. 1110) and p. 106 for details). Under the Act schemes of 'national significance' (Section 9) now have to be approved in principle by Parliament before being debated at a public inquiry. Parliament will receive detailed information on proposed schemes, including environmental assessment. This reversed the procedure proposed in 1991 which would have placed the parliamentary process after the public inquiry, a schedule preferred by the CPRE. Other schemes will be the subject of an Order made by the Secretary of State which will now be decided outside Parliament by him or by the public local inquiry process if objections are made to the scheme. For further commentary see *Planning* 8/11/92, p. 1; 29/11/92, p. 14; and 20/3/92, p. 1.

Turning to agriculture, the Finance (No. 2) Act 1992 (Chapter 48, £14.50) made a minor but significant change to Inheritance Tax when in Section 73 and Schedule 14 it raised relief from the tax on owner-occupied agricultural land from 50 to 100 per cent and on tenanted land from 30 to 50 per cent. At a stroke this removed the incentive for landowners to claim tax relief by registering it as part of the nation's heritage and providing reasonable public access. The Countryside Commission estimates that over 750,000 hectares have been protected, and English Nature that 25,000 hectares of SSSI and ancient woodland have also been protected under these provisions. In spite of their pleas to make 100 per cent relief conditional on maintaining wildlife, geological, scenic or historical features, and public access, the Act did not include such a provision. In the future, any attempts to preserve such land will need extra public funding, claimed the Commission and English Nature, as reported in *Planning* 26/6/92, p. 3.

One of the Bills to straddle the election was the Consolidation Bill for the Protection of Badgers which was given the Royal Assent in July as the Protection of Badgers Act 1992 (Chapter 51, £3.20). This consolidated the Badgers Act 1973, the Badgers Act 1991 and the Badgers (Further Protection) Act 1991 (see Volume II, pp. 77–8, for further details). The Act began life as HC 33(91–92), was modified by the Consolidation Committee in HC 40(91–92) and became HC 96(91–92). After the election it reappeared as HL 8(92–93) before its penultimate form as HC 34(92–93).

In Wales the Tourism (Overseas Promotion) (Wales) Act 1992 (Chapter 26, £0.65) enabled the Wales Tourist Board to carry on abroad activities to promote tourism to and within Wales, and the Welsh Development Agency Act 1991 (Chapter 69, £0.60) increased the financial limit for the Agency from £700 to £950 million.

Bills in progress or failing to proceed to Acts

The Hedgerows Bill 1992 was introduced as a private member's Bill in June. Details of the Bill were due to be set out in the second reading on 22 January 1993 and it was expected that these would include: (1) notification to be required of any intention to destroy a hedgerow, and power for local authorities to prevent destruction subject to appeal; (2) power for local authorities to register hedgerows following notification and to protect them from destruction for a subsequent period of years; (3) make it an offence to destroy a hedgerow without prior authorisation; (4) introduce a system of fines for offenders; and (5) enforce the replanting of hedgerows which have been illegally removed or destroyed. The Bill, which was believed to have DOE support, was intended to complement the hedgerow incentive scheme introduced in the summer of 1992 (see p. 146 for details), and followed a 1990 report and 1991 consultations as outlined in Volume II, pp. 104–5. For further commentary see *Farmers Weekly* 3/7/92, p. 14.

While the Hedgerow Bill was expected to proceed, the Wild Mammals (Protection) Bill 1991 (HC 20(91–92) was 'negatived' after its second reading. The Bill would have made it a criminal offence to inflict unnecessary suffering upon wild mammals in line with the law on domestic and captive animals.

Statutory Instruments

The Year saw a good deal of detailed change in the provisions of the Town and Country Planning Act 1990 and related Acts, and the Planning and Compensation Act 1991 (referred to in the commentary as the 1990 and

1991 Acts respectively). These changes were mainly implemented in a series of Commencement and other Orders.

Begining with the Planning and Compensation Act 1991 the following provisions were commenced by: (a) 2067/91 and 2092/91 which brought into force on 25 September 1991 *inter alia* assessment of environmental effects, power of local authority to decline to determine applications, old mining permissions, status of development plans and functions of Historic Buildings and Monuments Commission; (b) 2272/91 which brought into force on 13 October 1991 fees for deemed applications for planning permission, and planning obligations in Scotland; (c) 2728/91 which brought into force on 25 November 1991 costs when a public inquiry or hearing does not take place (also see 2698/91 which brought the power to award costs under other legislation as from 2 January 1992); (d) 2905/91 which brought into force on 2 January 1992 planning contravention notices, injunctions restraining breaches of planning control, other provisions to tighten up enforcement, controls over fish farming and further streamlining of the development plan system; (e) 71/92 which brought into force as from 24 January 1992 provisions dealing with old mining permissions and other matters relating to mining in Scotland; (f) 334/92 brought into force as from 24 February 1992 the provisions for planning contravention notices, interdicts relating to breaches of planning control and other provisions relating to enforcement and listed buildings in Scotland; (g) in England and Wales, 665/91 brought the advertisement provisions of the Act into force as from 6 April 1992 (see also 666/92 which updated the 1989 Advertisement Regulations); (h) 1279/92 brought the demolition of houses under planning control in tandem with 1280/92 as from 27 January 1992; (i) 1630/92 brought into force the provisions relating to certificates of lawful use or development and other provisions on enforcement as from 27 July 1992; (j) and in Scotland 1937/92 brought into force as from 10 August 1992 provisions of the Act relating to certificates of lawful use and development, fish farming, advertisement control and various enforcement provisions.

Enforcement controls were also re-enacted and amended by 2804/91 in terms of the contents of notices and procedures to be followed as from 2 January 1992.

Enforcement in Scotland was also the subject of 477 and 478/92 which replaced the 1984 enforcement and special enforcement regulations in the light of the 1991 Act above. 477/92 also made some other changes to procedures. In England and Wales the special enforcement regulations 1992 (1562/92) empowered local authorities to issue special enforcement notices in respect of development carried out on Crown Land, for example by trespassers (new age travellers, rave festivals etc.)

The rules for appeals against enforcement and refusal or non-determination of a new certificate of lawful use for development were set out in 1903/92 which replaced the 1981 rules in light of changes made in the 1990 Town and Country Planning Act, while some detailed regulations were set out in 1904/92.

A new system of plan making was brought into operation on 10 February 1992 by 2794/91. In addition to the provisions of the 1990 and 1991 Acts the Regulations 9 (1)(a) ask planning authorities to have regard to environmental considerations. The Regulations also add English Nature, the Countryside Commission and other environmental bodies, including the NRA, into the bodies to be consulted during plan preparation, 10(1)(e)(f)(g). Finally, planning authorities will have to deposit a statement of publicity and consultation undertaken when plans are deposited. Advice on the new regulations was provided by PPG12.

In February 1992 the DOE and Welsh Office issued directions requiring local authorities to notify the Secretary of State of any major applications which would be a departure from the development plan in light of the new plan-led development control system which came into force on 10 February 1992. The directions also required local authorities to advertise such departures in the local press. In an accompanying letter major applications were listed as

a. more than 150 houses or flats;
b. more than 10,000 square metres of retail floor space;
c. any other development which by reason of its scale or nature or the location of the land would significantly prejudice the implementation of the development plan's policies and proposals; in more detail:

    i. proposals for major development having more than local significance;
    ii. proposals giving rise to significant public controversy;
    iii. proposals which raise important or novel issues of development control;
    iv. proposals which would normally be inappropriate in an approved Green Belt;
    v. major proposals involving the mining and working of minerals, or waste disposal, treatment and processing facilities;
    vi. proposals which raise significant legal difficulties;
    vii. proposals which while not significant in themselves might affect the plan because of their likely impact, setting or location, especially in national parks, AONBs, SSSIs and conservation areas.

In development control, conditions as to the siting, design and external appearance of agricultural and forestry buildings and operations given permitted rights by the General Development Order (GDO) could be imposed as from 2 January 1992 under the amendments made to the GDO by 2268/91. In essence, developers have to apply for a determination as to whether prior approval is needed and if it is to seek permission relating to the siting, design and external appearance of a building before development commences.

Further controls which also came into force on 2 January 1992 were brought in by 2805/91. These included the extension of full planning controls to farm and forest buildings and operations to all holdings below 5 ha in size. Elsewhere the order restricted development rights in Sites of Special Specific Interest (SSSIs) where the land would be used for certain motoring activities, clay pigeon shooting or war games, and extended consultation requirements for SSSIs to a radius of two kilometres around them. This followed a consultation exercise in March 1991 (see Volume II, p. 104). Consultation over applications for fish farming was extended to include the NRA and fish farms were brought under full control or prior approval control over siting, design and appearance depending on the nature of the proposal. Finally applications to be decided by county councils should be sent to them and not to the district council. (See PPG7 for further advice on how to implement the new controls.)

Demolition of houses was brought under control on 27 July 1992 by 1280/92 and also by 1279/91. Advice on the exceptions to the control was contained in DOE Circular 16/92.

Provisions to make the GDO comply with new concept of 'lawful use' under the 1991 Act were contained in 1563/92.

Provisions amending the requirement to publicise applications were made by 1493/92 which included the need for farmers and foresters to display notices where it is determined that prior approval over sites, design etc. is needed.

In Scotland, the 1981 GDO and its numerous amendments were replaced by two new orders 223 and 224/92 which came into operation on 13 March 1992, following consultation in 1990. The main change is a restructuring of the Order to make it more user-friendly which has been a success (Scottish Planning—Law and Practice 36, 1992, pp. 46–7). The main policy changes to the Order are discussed in Scottish Office Environment Department (SOEND) Circular 5/1992, on p. 124; these include the provision of prior approval for farm and forestry buildings and operations, a 400 m cordon sanitaire around agricultural permitted development, the need for planning permission for any buildings for intensive livestock within 400 metres of existing buildings, tighter controls over developments in conservation areas and in the curtilage of listed buildings, and new procedures for neighbourhood notification. Some amendments to the detail of the Orders were made in 1078/92, notably with regard to National Scenic Areas. Finally, 1763/92 amended the GDO with regard to advertisements.

Fees for planning applications were increased by around 20 per cent as from 2 January 1992 by 2735/91. Other changes included a £20 fee for applications relating to prior approval for farm and forest buildings and operations (see 2268/91 and 2805/91), and removal of the 75 per cent reduction for so-called twin-tracking applications—those submitted within 28 days of a previous application. 2765/91 made similar changes in Scotland.

Fees for certificates of lawful use or development under the 1991 Act were brought in as from 27 July 1992 by 1817/92 for England and Wales and by 1951/92 for Scotland. Fees for prior approval of agricultural buildings and operations were also brought in for England and Wales by 1817/92 and in Scotland for agricultural and forestry buildings and operations by 1951/92.

General provisions relating to planning were set out in 1492/1992, The Town and Country Planning General Regulations 1992, which dealt *inter alia* with land owned by planning authorities and the need to submit planning applications for the possible development of such land; compensation for planning blight; and rights of way provisions under compulsory purchase.

Detailed changes to the procedures with regard to Environmental Assessment (EA) set out in the 1988 Regulations were made in 1494/92, including the new procedures for planning authorities to submit planning applications set out in the regulations (1492/92) above, and an EA if necessary with the application.

Finally, Regulations requiring most local authorities to publish information about unused and underused land in their ownership, according to paragraph 8 of the Code of Recommended Practice as set out in the Annex to DOE Circular 18/89, came into force on 12 February 1992 under 73/92.

Payments to farmers were amended in several cases. For example, the Suckler Cow Premium Regulations 1991 (2632/91) amended and revoked some previous regulations but kept the rate at £51.69 per cow in Less

Favoured Areas (LFAs) and £47.43 elsewhere. Over 70 per cent of the suckler beef herd are in the LFAs. The total cost of the scheme for 1991/92 was estimated to be £74 million. On 18 February 1992 the rates were increased to £59.64 and £55.38 by 270/92, bringing the total cost of the scheme to an expected £85 million, but the extra premium was restricted to applications made between 15 June 1991 and 31 January 1992 by 1210/92.

Hill Livestock Compensatory Allowances were modified as from 17 February 1992 as follows: a definition of overgrazing was introduced, and references to the stocking limits contained in EC Regulation 2328/91 were introduced. The rates of payment remained the same, although the total amount payable per hectare was increased from £62.48 per ha to £81.13 in Severely Disadvantaged Areas and from £46.86 to £60.85 in Disadvantaged Areas, costing an estimated £2.5 million and bringing the total cost of payments to an estimated £148.5 million.

In dairying, the Dairy Produce Quotas Regulations of 1989 were consolidated and amended by 2232/91. The principal change was provision for the award of quota to producers making sales of dairy produce other than milk, butter, cream or cheese (for example yogurt and ice cream).

In Set-Aside, 1847/91 set out the procedures for a temporary set-aside scheme for 1847/91 while 1993/91 modified the existing 1988 scheme by extending the LFA areas in which lower rates of payment for set-aside are made.

For those seeking to set aside land more permanently, the Farm Woodland Premium Scheme (FWPS) was brought into force on 1 April 1992 by 905/92. The scheme, which applies to Great Britain, provides for the payment of annual grants to abate financial losses incurred in consequence of the conversion of agricultural land (and in Scotland rough grazing) to woodland. The scheme complies with EC regulation 2328/91 and replaces the Farm Woodland Scheme 1988, by increasing the rate of grant and making the scheme easier to understand and operate, as a result of consultations in 1991. Under the scheme, which is intended to lead to an improved environment, farmers apply first to the Forestry Commission for grants for establishing trees under the Woodland Grant Scheme (£615 to £1575 per hectare) including the Better Land Supplement (£400 to £600 per hectare) and the Community Woodland Supplement (£950 per hectare) where appropriate and then apply to the agricultural departments for the annual incentives under the FWPS, which are as follows:

Table 8.1   *Annual incentives under the FWPS*

	£/ha	No. of years
Converted land formerly arable land or improved grassland		
if severely disadvantaged	130	
if disadvantaged	190	
if neither	250	
Converted land formerly improved land which was either		
severely disadvantaged or disadvantaged	60	
Maximum number of payments:		
Converted land consisting of more than 50% by area of		
broadleaved trees		15
Converted land consisting of less than 50% by area of		
broadleaved trees		10

Another scheme allowing farmland to be forested, the Crofter Forestry (Scotland) Act 1991 (see Volume II p. 78), was brought into force on 1 April 1992 by 504/92.

Elsewhere, in the Highlands and Islands of Scotland, 772/92 extended the definition of persons eligible to make applications for aid to members of the immediate family of the occupier of agricultural land, and extended the diversification measures for which assistance may be given to include *inter alia* certain horticultural enterprises and the provision of horses and ponies for pony trekking and fish for managed waters. 1764/92 dissolved the Highlands and Islands Development Board as from 20 July 1992 to make way finally for its successor—Highlands and Islands Enterprise.

Also in Scotland, the provisions of the Act which dealt with the establisment of Scottish Natural Heritage which came fully into operation on 1 April 1992 were contained in 2633/91. Other provisions of the Natural Heritage (Scotland) Act 1991 were brought into force by 2187/91 which from 1 October 1991 introduced new powers to control the abstraction of water for irrigation and to control water use in times of drought.

In England, the Code of Good Agricultural Practice for the Protection of Water was approved by 2285/91. In another area of pollution control the provisions of the Environmental Protection Act 1990, which deal with controlled wastes, by imposing a duty of care and making it a criminal offence to cause pollution of the environment with them, were brought into operation on 1 April 1992 by 2829/91 and 2839/91. Farmers moving hard core and waste on to farms could face a fine of £2,000 if they do not have a licence to do so. The move was meant to crack down on illegal fly tipping on farm land.

However, local authority bye-laws relating to the burning of straw and other crop residues were repealed by 693/92 as a consequence of the 1991 regulations banning the burning of such residues coming into force (see Volume II, p. 82) in 1993.

More positively, changes to several Environmentally Sensitive Areas were made as follows: (a) in West Penwith new opportunities to maintain field systems (51/92); (b) in the South Downs more incentives to return arable land to chalk downland (52/92); (c) in the Somerset Levels and Moors new encouragement to raise water-table levels (53/92); (d) in the Broads the area was extended and more attractive payments made to revert arable land to grassland (54/92); (e) in the Pennine Dales the area was trebled (55/92) and rates of payment increased (301/92); (f) in the Cambrian Mountains changes were made to the definition of heather, new rates of payment were set and new provisions for heather and woodland attracting higher rates of payment were introduced (1359/92); and (g) in the Loch Lomond and Breadalbane areas orders were replaced and amended with regard to grazing plans intended to conserve, enhance or extend areas of wetland, woodland and other desirable features (1919 and 1920/92).

On a broader front, seven species of animal, eight species of plant and one group of species of plant not to be released or planted in the wild under the 1981 Wildlife and Countryside Act were added to the existing list by 320/92, but the Nature Conservancy Council was finally dissolved on 21 December 1991 by 2923/91.

Finally in the social field, the tenant's right to buy provisions from a public sector landlord used to be lost if a public sector landlord disposed the house to a private sector landlord, but under 325/92 the right is now maintained as from 13 March 1992.

Advice from central government

DOE and Department of Transport Circulars   (All DOE unless stated) 12/91, Redundant hospital sites in Green Belts: planning guidelines. This circular closely follows the policy proposed in a March 1991 consultation paper (Volume II, p. 105) in that the policy set out in paragraphs 17 and 18 of PPG2 on Green Belts is now extended to sites that are only partly redundant. The basic policy remains the same, namely, keeping any new building to the same volume as before and respecting the amenity value of the site within the Green Belt.

16/91, Planning Obligations. Draws attention to Section 12(1) of the Planning and Compensation Act 1991 which substitutes a new Section 106 for Section 106 of the Town and Country Planning Act 1990, and was brought into effect on 25 October 1991. This section introduces the concepts of planning obligations which are *either* a planning agreement between a developer and the local planning authority *or* by the developer making a unilateral undertaking to use land in a certain way. Obligations run with the land and thus carry on from owner to owner. Annex A and B of the Circular explain the legal use of the new section and alter the advice on the concept of planning gain as set out in Circular 22/83 which is now cancelled. The advice is more relaxed than in 1983 and also more relaxed than the draft advice published in March 1989, but it is advised that conditions are to be preferred to obligations. If an obligation is necessary, the Circular sets out a series of five tests of 'reasonableness'. *Planning* 1/11/91, pp. 16–17.

17/91, Water Industry Investment: planning considerations. Provides advice about the planning implications of the investment programmes being undertaken by the water industry in the wake of privatisation and the need to improve water quality. Some of these proposals will need an environmental assessment and special care will need to be exercised in protected areas, but everywhere planning authorities should work to ensure that such developments as far as possible are 'good neighbours'.

18/91, New Development Plans System. The new system came into force on 10 February 1992 and advice was provided in PPG 12 published on the same day. This Circular dealt with the transition period between December 1991 and February 1992 in terms of plans already in preparation or submitted for inquiry, and defined those plans that could continue after February 1992 because they complied with the new law under the Planning and Compensation Act 1991, e.g. a district-wide local plan.

20/91, Fees for applications. Draws attention to and sets out the revised fees payable as from 2 January 1992 (SI 2735/91), and also to three substantive amendments to the regulations, notably in introducing a fee of £20 for seeking to find out if prior approval is needed for the detailed design of farm development required as from 2 January 1992 by the 1991 amendment to the GDO (SI 2268/91).

21/91, Planning and Compensation Act 1991: implementation of the main enforcement provisions. This Circular explained how the provisions of Sections 1–11 of the Act and other related enforcement provisions in the Act were to be brought into force during 1992. The 6 Annexes to the Circular provided detailed guidance about the use of the new and revised powers (see PPG 18), notably the new 'planning contravention notice', enforcement notices, stop notices, and injunctions to restrain a breach of control. (Also see Circular 17/92).

22/91, Travelling Show People. Provides advice as how best to provide sites for such business people, notably in the winter months when permanent sites are needed. Local Plans should address this issue, rather than treat it as a one-off.

23/91, Awards of Costs in Planning Proceedings. This Circular is concerned with two issues: first, the award of costs on late cancellation of an inquiry or hearing and second, the introduction of costs in 'hearing' cases. The idea is to foster a sense of discipline in the development control process. Annex 3 also reprints Circular 2/87 on the general awards of costs, in which paragraph 23 is now cancelled.

1/92, Planning Controls over Sites of Special Scientific Interest. Provides guidance on two changes to the GDO (SI 2805/91). The first change specifies that planning permission is now required for all proposals for war games, motorsports and clay pidgeon shooting in SSSIs. The second change requires local planning authorities to consult English Nature or the Countryside Council for Wales before deciding planning applications likely to affect land in an SSSI. This extends the previous requirement from inside the SSSI to any area around the SSSI where a land-use development might affect the SSSI itself, e.g. water abstraction some distance away, lowering the water-table of a wetland. The conservation bodies listed above can define a consultation area and the government has asked them to give priority to this task.

5/92, Town and Country Planning (Control of Advertisement) Regulations 1992. This Circular provides an outline of the new system set up by SI 666/92 and guidance about how to operate the system in addition to the guidance also set out in PPG 19. The main changes from the previous 1989 and 1990 Regulations are set out in the Circular.

15/92, Publicity for planning applications. Draws attention to changes to the GDO in the summer of 1992 as a result of the Planning and Compensation Act 1991 which made provision for compulsory publicity for all planning applications. The Circular discusses which of the three basic types of publicity—newspaper adverts, site notices or neighbour notification—are most appropriate for different types of development, in addition to the four categories of 'major' developments for which the type of publicity is specified by the GDO. An unofficial list is also included, since the February 1992 Direction (see p. 112) revoked the list of developments formerly classified as 'bad neighbour'.

16/92, Planning controls over demolition. Draws attention and provides advice on SI 1280/92 which brought Section 13 of the Planning and Compensation Act 1991 into force. Under the SI certain types of demolition are now controlled via the planning system. There are, however, three exceptions: first, listed buildings and buildings in conservation areas and scheduled monuments (these are already protected by other legislation); second, demolition of buildings less than 50 cubic metres; and third, most buildings that are not used as dwellings, e.g. factories, warehouses, offices, churches, theatres and shops.

17/92, Planning and Compensation Act 1991—implementation of the remaining enforcement provisions. This Circular explains how the remaining provisions not implemented in January 1992 (see 21/91) but instead in July 1992 are to be brought into force. The big change is the concept of 'lawfulness' under Section 10 for those developments which have become immune from planning by virtue of being in existence for at least ten years. This replaced the concept of 'established use' and 'Established Use Certificates' which had a broad test of four years before immunity was assumed.

19/92, The Town and Country Planning Regulations 1992 and the Town and Country Planning (Development Plans and Consultation) Directions 1992. This Circular refers to two quite separate issues. First, the 1992 Regulations (SI 1492/92) introduced a general principle that local planning authorities have to make planning applications and follow the same procedures as everybody else, as from July 1992. Second, the 1992 Directions require local planning authorities to notify the DOE of all local planning authority development proposals which are not in accordance with the development plan as from July 1992, rather than only material departures as before.

20/92, Responsibilities for conservation policy and casework. Following the creation of the Department of National Heritage (DNH) after the 1992 general election this Circular sets out the new departmental responsibilities as follows.

Policy responsibility for archaeology and the conservation of the built heritage was tranferred to the DNH and the DNH also assumed responsibility for English Heritage, the National Heritage Memorial Fund, the Royal Commission on the Historical Monuments of England and other heritage public bodies. DNH will however liaise with the DOE.

Casework transferred to DNH includes: the listing of historic buildings; scheduling of monuments; repairs and other notices; and grants to heritage bodies. However the DOE retained casework control over decisions over call-ins of listed buildings or conservation area consent applications; appeals; all related enforcement work; and Article 4 Direction matters.

Other existing arrangements with regard to consultations over development plan proposals, listing building consents, or the designation of conservation areas were unaltered.

23/92, Motorway Service Areas. Following the decision to deregulate the control of activities within these Areas, in spite of appeals not to do so by the Countryside Commission in response to a consultation paper, this Circular provides advice on how to consider applications for new Areas. Attention is drawn to PPG 7 under which new Areas in the Countryside are not ruled out, but should be strictly controlled, unobtrusive and sensitive to the landscape. In designated areas, however, Areas should not be permitted. A proven national interest and a lack of alternative sites may, justify an exception. Critics, however, feared that such Areas would be a back door to major developments under the guise of a Service Area.

Department of Transport Circular 3/92, Transport Policies and Programme Submissions for 1993/94, HMSO, 1992, £4.00.

DOE Planning Policy Guidance Notes (PPGs)   These documents, which began their life in 1988, have now become very useful statements and justifications of policy, especially since most of them have been revised in the early 1990s.

PPG1: *General Policy and Principles*, HMSO, 1992, £2.75. This Note is a revision of the note first issued in 1988 and now cancelled. The revision takes account of the changes of law and policy set out in the Planning and Compensation Act 1991 and the 1990 White Paper *This Common Inheritance*. The Note begins with a re-endorsement of planning as a system for balancing growth with conservation, and argues that planning if properly used can secure economy, efficiency and amenity in the use of land.

In making decisions, planners should follow the new policy as set out in Section 26 of the 1991 Act which 'introduces a presumption in favour of development proposals which are in accordance with the development plan' (para. 25), unless material considerations indicate otherwise.

Proposals in accordance with the plan should thus be allowed unless they would cause 'demonstrable harm to interests of acknowledged importance' (para.5). Similarly, proposals 'clearly in conflict with the plan would need to produce convincing reasons why the plan should not prevail' (para.25). The rest of the Note discusses which considerations should be regarded as material and how they might be ranked *vis à vis* other material or policy statements.

The Note, which was the result of a consultation exercise in the autumn of 1991, was warmly welcomed by the Royal Town Planning Institute (RTPI) president and the editor of *The Planner*, 20/3/92, p. 4 and p. 3, but the draft had been criticised by the CPRE *Planning*, 13/12/91, p. 1 for its advocacy of development as contained in the advice in Paragraph 5 (reproduced above) advocating approval for conforming proposals unless they would cause 'demonstrable harm'.

PPG3: *Housing*, HMSO, 1992, £3.45. This Note replaces the 1988 version, and also cancels Circulars 24/75, 72/77, 76/77, 15/84, 7/91, Development Control Policy Note 2, and certain parts of Circulars 12/78, 22/80 and other advice documents.

The main changes are:

— to put increased emphasis on reusing urban land as a means of relieving pressure on the countryside;
— to stress the importance of local choice via the local plan;
— to encourage local authorities to take account of planning guidance in preparing area housing strategies; and
— to withdraw the special presumption in favour of releasing land for housing (formerly in Circular 22/84).

In more detail, the Note provides bland advice on housing in rural areas (paras 18–19), but more specific advice on 'affordable housing' in paragraphs 38–44 and Annex A. If such housing is desirable, its continuation can be provided by using conditions or the new system of 'obligations' (see Circular 16/91), but more commonly by involving housing associations or other social bodies. Annex A discusses the issue of 'affordable housing for local needs in rural areas' and considers that the need for such housing could lead to the release of small sites on which housing would not normally be allowed. Any provision for such housing should be regarded as additional to the provision in the development plan for general housing demand, since it is not practical for plans to be able to predict how much housing would be needed in a plan period or where.

The Note also discusses the issue of 'New Settlements' in paragraphs 32–7 and argues that they normally should only be contemplated where: the alternative of expanding existing settlements is less satisfactory; the proposal is a clear expression of local preference supported by local planning authorities; there would be no risk of coalescence with existing settlements; there would be significant environmental improvements, e.g. land reclamation; the proposal would deflect pressure from an area under restraint; or the proposal is not within a designated/protected area or on the best and most versatile agricultural land.

The Note, the result of a consultation exercise which began in 1989 (see Volume I, p. 87), was criticised by planners as being too timid both in regard to minimal releases of land for affordable rural housing, and in its negative attitude to new settlements. Many planners would like to see a more relaxed policy on infilling, village expansion and new settlements, especially in the light of the changed economy and society of the 1990s; see for example *Town and Country Planning*, May 1992, pp.128–9, and *The Planner*, 20/3/92, p. 3.

PPG7: *The Countryside and the Rural Economy*, HMSO, 1992, £5.20. This Note, which replaces the 1988 Note entitled *Rural enterprise and develop-*

ment and follows a 1989 draft (Volume II, pp.103–4), sets out the general policy for the countryside, followed by specific advice on different aspects, and then advice for special countryside designations, eg. National Parks. One of the 6 Annexes, E, sets out advice on the operation of the new design controls over agricultural buildings which took effect on 2 January 1992 (see p. 111 for details), and which were the result of a consultation exercise began in September 1991. Most of the other Annexes provide detailed evidence on other agricultural issues.

In general, the Note argues that the guiding principle should be that development should benefit the rural economy and maintain or enhance the environment. Building in the open countryside should be strictly controlled. When preparing development plans and exercising development control local planning authorities should weigh the following factors:

— the need to encourage rural enterprise
— the need to protect landscape, wildlife habitats and historic features
— the quality and versatility of the land for use in agriculture, forestry and other rural enterprises
— the need to protect other non-renewable resources.

The Note received mixed reviews. Most concern (*Planning*, 24/1/92, pp. 20–1) centred over a perceived reduction in support for the protection of agricultural land, notably grade 3b and below and for the countryside as a whole, although the note in paragraph 2.1 does argue that the 'countryside should be safeguarded for its own sake'. The CPRE warned that it could bring huge environmental conflict and cause irretreivable damage to our precious countryside. *Farmers Weekly*, 31/1/92, p. 18, interpreted the Note as a relaxation of planning rules, and reported that it was welcomed by both the NFU and CLA.

Finally, the Note cancelled Circulars 24/73 and 16/87 and Development Control Policy Note 4 (1969), as well as its 1988 forerunner.

PPG 12: *Development Plans and Regional Planning Guidance*, HMSO, 1992, £8.00. This Note introduces the new plan-led system set up by the Town and Country Planning Acts 1990 and the Planning and Compensation Acts 1991 (Volume II, pp. 74–6). It follows a long saga of consultaion and discussion papers (Volume II, p. 100) and is based on a September 1991 draft, which also discussed the proposed Regulations which provide the legislative clout for the Note (see SIs 2794/91 and 2905/91). The final Note introduces new advice on sustainable development and moves advice on 'Plans and the Environment' to the main body of the Note from an Annex.

The Note argues that the planning system provides *guidance*, *incentive* and *control* which was welcomed in an editorial in *The Planner* (21/2/92, p. 3) as being as good a rationale for planning as is likely to be devised. The Note stresses that the development plan provides the main component in the plan-led planning system now being promoted by the DOE. It then outlines the new system and considers that each region should have up-to-date regional planning guidance by the end of 1993.

The Note then advises that Structure Plans should: provide the strategic policy framework for planning and development control locally; ensure that the provision for development is realistic and consistent with national and regional policy; and secure consistency between local plans for neighbouring areas.

Local Plans should set out detailed policies, should guide most day-to-day planning decisions and as well as being in general conformity to the structure plan should set out the authority's policies for the control of development and make proposals for the development and use of land and allocate land for specific purposes. Local plans can be supplemented by 'supplementary planning guidance'.

The Note also provides advice about Minerals Local Plans and Waste Local Plans. This is followed by a detailed section on plan preparation procedures, which strongly follows the Geddes model of survey-plan monitoring. The next section examines the type of topics to be considered and some of the considerations to be examined, before another section provides advice on 'plans and the environment'.

The Note also contains 6 Annexes, including a Code of Practice and advice on the format of Local Plan Inquiries and the Examination in Public.

Finally, the Note cancels the two previous Notes on Plan preparation, PPG 12 and PPG 15, and also cancels Circulars 22/84, 30/85, 24/87 and 3/88. Annex F, however, provides a cross-reference guide by topic to those Circulars, Notes and other advice that remains extant. All in all, a very comprehensive piece of advice that will cause the textbooks to be re-written, largely one suspects from some of the refreshingly clear and logical paragraphs of the Note.

PPG 17: *Sport and Recreation*, HMSO, 1991, £3.50. This new Note is a substantially modified version of a draft issued for consultation in 1990 (Volume II, p. 106). It advocates that facilities for sport and recreation are part of a civilised society and that provision for them should be set out within the development plan framework laid out in PPG 12. In the countryside the aim should be to balance and reconcile conservation and leisure interests through appropriate management measures, but in designated areas where the conflicts are irreconcilable the conservation interest should prevail. In more detail, sympathetic consideration should be given to the relocation of football stadia following the Taylor Report's recommendation that such stadia should be all seat, but it would be most unusual for such stadia to be welcome in a Green Belt.

Golf courses are more welcome in Green Belts, but special care would be needed in such areas as well as other designated areas. Elsewhere they should be located and designed to ensure harmony with the surrounding countryside. Finally, the Note cancels Circular 33/70.

PPG 18: *Enforcing planning control*, HMSO, 1991, £1.80. New and substantially improved powers to enforce planning control were provided by the Planning and Compensation Act 1991 (Volume II, p. 74) and the Carnwath Report (1989) on which these provisions were based recommended that policy guidance should also be revised. This Note provides revised guidance about enforcement generally and about the new provisions in particular.

In detail, 5 new and improved powers are provided. First, the power to serve a 'planning contravention notice' when planners require information where there is an apparent breach of control. Second, the power to serve a 'breach of condition notice'. Third, the ability to seek an injunction to restrain an actual or expected breach of control. Fourth, the power to serve a stop notice on people using a caravan as a main residence, and fifth, improved powers of entry onto land. The Note also outlines various enforcement scenarios and discusses how planners should react.

Critics of the Note, however (*Planning*, 20/12/91, p. 12, and 7/2/92, p. 19), argued that it did little to improve the main problem which is not the law itself, but institutional practice within local authorities, and that the Note or its accompanying Circular (21/91) failed to provide a stimulus to a 'best practice' system.

PPG 19: *Outdoor advertisement control*, HMSO, 1992, £1.95. In spite of requests for a tightening of control made during the consultation process, the Note confirms that outdoor advertising is essential to commercial activity and should be allowed even in sensitive locations. Applications for consent can, however, be blocked on amenity and public safety grounds.

DOE Mineral Policy Guidance Notes (MPGs) MPG 8 and MPG 9: *Interim Development Order Permissions*, HMSO, 1991, £4.50, and 1992, £3.45. The Planning and Compensation Act 1991 introduced new provisions for dealing with permissions for mineral working granted under Interim Development Orders (IDOs) between 1943 and 1948. The Act required such permissions to be registered with mineral planning authorities by 25 March 1992 and subsequently to apply for determination of the conditions with which the permission is to be subject. These conditions should secure improved operating and environmental standards. Accordingly, MPG 8 sets out the procedures to be followed in applying for registration and determination of conditions and MPG 9 gives advice on the considerations to be taken into account in determining the conditions to which registered applicants should be subject. These new procedures should both tighten up control over sites working under lax conditions and also prevent new sites being worked with the benefit of 40-year-old permissions that have never been exercised.

MPG 10: *Provision of raw material for the cement industry*, HMSO, 1991, £4.25. Provides a mass of background information on the industry and the establishment of a system of 'quarry plans' for each quarry to provide a framework for both current operational practices and longer-term strategies for restoration and after use.

Scottish Office Environment Department Circulars and Planning Advice Notes

26/91, Environmental Assessment and Private Legislation Procedures. As from 1992 development proposals approved by private legislation needed either an Environmental Assessment or a direction by the Scottish Office that such a statement is not needed. This Circular provides guidance on the new procedures introduced by General Order 27A as from 27 March 1992.

27/91, Fees for applications. Draws attention to the general 20 per cent rise in fees for planning applications brought in by SI 563/90 on 31 December 1991, and sets out the main scales.

1/92, Agreements relating to Crown Land. Draws attention to a change in the Planning and Compensation Act 1991 (Section 49) which allows, as from January 1992, for Crown Land to be subject to planning agreements restricting or regulating the development or use of land.

2/92, Planning and Compensation Act 1991: Commencement of Minerals Provisions. Draws attention to the provisions brought into force by a Commencement Order (SI 71/92) in January 1992. These include bringing up to date the provisions relating to the creation and enlargement of mineral workings, including aftercare. Most of the Circular, and its substantial annex, however, refer to the requirements for registering Interim Development Order Permissions from the 1940s by 24 July 1992, and then guidance as to how to deal with such registrations, depending on whether the sites are active or not. See also 26/92.

5/92, General Permitted Development (Scotland) Order 1992. Provides advice on the 1992 Order (SI 223/92) which consolidates and amends changes to the 1981 Order and which came into force on 13 March 1992. The main changes were rescheduling the 28 'Classes' of permitted development into 22 new 'Parts'. Within agriculture, previous exemptions are tightened up, both with regard to the size of unit allowed (either over 465 square metres or over 12 metres high), and in relationship to neighbouring buildings, notably where intensive livestock or slurry are involved. For permitted developments, the Order also brought in a prior notification scheme for farm and forest developments which gives planners 28 days to decide whether to ask for a formal submission of details for approval where a significant impact on the surroundings are likely.

6/92, General Development Procedure (Scotland) Order 1992. Provides advice on the Order which accompanies the Order discussed in the previous Circular. This Circular provides advice on the Order, which sets out the procedures to be followed under the 1992 GDO(SI 224/92). It deals with the notification of neighbours and provides a list of statutory consultees, which have been extended for example in the case of fish farming and historic gardens or designated landscapes. For areas of special interest for nature conservation, the requirement to consult NCC was extended to proposals outside the area which may affect it, not just to proposals within the area.

8/92, Enforcing planning control. Provides advice on the new enforcement provisions which came into force under the 1991 Planning and Compensation Act in March 1992 (see SI 334/92). These add to existing powers and notices: 'planning contravention notices'; 'breach of condition notices'; and 'interdicts' to restrain breaches of planning control. The Circular gives advice on when to use the full weaponry available or when to use a softer approach, but reminds planners that the integrity of the development control process depends upon the readiness to take effective enforcement action when necessary. (Historic Scotland also issued a Circular (11/92) which drew attention to the listed buildings and conservation area aspect of the changes.)

9/92, Enforcement of Tree Preservation Orders. Provides guidance on substantially increased fines under the 1991 Planning and Compensation Act, and also new powers over rights of entry to land to enforce the law.

26/92, Interim Development Order Permissions. Following the advice contained in 2/92, this Circular sets out advice on the considerations to be taken into account in determining the conditions to which registered permissions for mining development granted between 1943 and 1946 should be subject. These should be: necessary; relevant to planning; relevant to development; enforceable; precise and reasonable in all other respects.

31/92, Control over fish farming. Draws attention to new sections under the Planning and Compensation Act 1991 which makes it clear that placing a cage or other structure in inland waters for fish farming requires planning permission. A consultation paper on a National Planning Policy Guideline for fish farming was promised for later in 1992.

Planning Advice Note 37: This Note published in 1992 replaced PAN 27 published in 1981. It lists six achievements of Structure Plans in Scotland, as well as some weaknesses. The achievements are however stressed and the impression is given that the structure planning process will survive any changes in local government. With regard to eliminating weaknesses the Note places stress on clearly differentiating between policies and proposals, and the need to concentrate on physical land-use development (this does however include traffic management and environmental conservation). Finally, Structure Plans should incorporate a long-term (10-year) vision and settlement strategy, *Scottish Planning Law and Practice*, 36, 1992, p. 52.

Command Papers (Cm.)

As last year, the most important white paper was entitled *This Common Inheritance*. But this time the paper dealt with progress between September 1990 and September 1991, in *This Common Inheritance: The First Year Report* (Cm. 1655, £21.00). The report is set out in two main sections, the first section containing 70 pages in which the 400 or so commitments are listed in a left-hand column, followed by a middle and right-hand column in which 'Action to Date 1990–91' and 'Commitments to Further Action' respectively are set out, as shown in Tables 8.2 and 8.3 which give sample pages from the sections on 'Countryside and Wildlife' and 'Land Use and Planning' respectively.

The second section provides a commentary on the progress made in 18 short chapters divided by sectoral activity and by county, covering 100 pages. The document is topped and tailed by a 10-page introduction, and a series of annexes which, summarise new controls and publications, tell one how to find the names of the 'green' Ministers charged with implementing green policies in each department; and give a list of environmental organisations.

While the White Paper provides a useful *aide memoire* and a companion to this publication it is still, however, too cosy a view, and a reader from Mars would readily believe that there are few environmental issues in the UK. Most readers of the documents would, however agree with O'Riordan's review in *Ecos*, 12 (4), 1991, pp. 5–7, that the White Papers, while deserving a half cheer each, are still too cosmetic and token. However, in the sense that environmental accountability is now subject to an annual audit, they do represent a considerable step forward in attitude if not yet in really radical action. The Secretary of State for the Environment was cross-examined by the House of Commons Environment Committee about the Papers on 14 November 1991 (HC 56-i (91–92), £2.75).

As part of the increasing accountability and openness of govenment, the annual expenditure White Papers have undergone a radical transformation in recent years, to become a very valuable source of data and other information. The crop published in February 1992 continued this trend, but as Table 8.4 shows the increased devolution of spending to the various countries of the UK means that the information is now more scattered than before. UK data are available in Cm. 1920 (1992, £17.20) but for more detailed data, recourse must be made for MAFF expenditure to Cm. 1903 (1992, £13.90); for the Department of Transport to Cm. 1907 (1992, £14.60); for the DOE to Cm. 1908 (1992, £17.35); for the Scottish Office, including forestry, to Cm. 1915 (1992, £19.50); and for the Welsh Office to Cm. 1916 (1992, £13.60). For the nearly £80 that these documents cost, much information can be garnered not only of a statistical and financial nature but also of the work of the organisations, since these documents now double up as annual reports or reasoned justifications of the organisation's work.

The Royal Commission on Environmental Pollution, which published its first report in 1971, has been a long-standing example of the great and the good prodding the government into environmental action throughout its history, via its production of 15 reports, including its Sixth Report on 'Agriculture and Pollution' in 1979. Now in its sixteenth report, Cm. 1966, published in 1992 at an amazing £57.00, it has turned its attention to 'freshwater quality'. In its 300 pages (100 of them Appendixes) the Report devotes some 30 pages to agriculture and forestry, and makes 108 recommendations. In Agriculture it notes that farm pollution incidents peaked at over 4,100 in 1988 after rising from 1,500 in 1979, and now stand at 3,147 in 1990. The Report hopes that the new regulations which came into force in 1991 (See Volume II, pp. 81–2) with regard to control over farm wastes and Nitrate Sensitive Areas will cut these incidents further as will the revised Code of Good Agricultural Practice.

The 108 recommendations, can be divided into six subgroups for the purposes of rural planning. First, the Report recommends a new general scheme to assess water quality based on a wider set of determinants. Second, water policy plans should be drawn up, notably with regard to improving the quality of the worst rivers. Third, afforestation may need to be restructured in sensitive areas and other measures taken to reduce acidification of water in the uplands and elsewhere. Fourth, more research and in certain cases controls and restrictions should be carried out into agriculture as a source of pollution, notably on intensive livestock units, fish farms, farms in Less Favoured Areas, the disposal of veterinary medicines and the impact of pesticides. Fifth, economic instruments should be used alongside regulation notably with regard to the adoption of a charging scheme for point discharges to replace the cost-recovery scheme currently in operation. Finally, planning authorities should work more closely with water authorities and companies to prevent further pollution and to draw up lists of areas worthy of specific protection by zoning or other devices.

Other Command Papers are considered in the House of Commons section where they contain the Government's response to reports of Committees.

Table 8.2 *Specimen contents from First Year Report on This Common Inheritance from the 'Countryside and Wildlife' section*

Summary of white paper commitments	Action to date	Commitments to further action
S.28 The Government is working towards the integration of environmental considerations with economic activity in the countryside. It has taken a number of steps to build environmental protection into the following agricultural policies:	The Government has continued to encourage farmers to take care of the countryside and its living resources through specific environmental schemes and has taken the lead in seeking to incorporate environmental conditions into the Common Agricultural Policy. Action to date includes:	The Government will continue, where appropriate, to improve the environmental benefits associated with specific environmental schemes and to press for environmental conditions to be taken properly into account in the Community's agricultural policy. It will:
● Set-aside (7.17); *MAFF*	– specific environmental provisions agreed as part of a new one-year EC Set-aside scheme;	– press to ensure that environmental measures are part of any Set-aside scheme introduced under Common Agricultural Policy reform;
● Nitrate Sensitive Areas (7.15, 12.20); *MAFF*	– establishment of a NSA pilot scheme with applications to join now made in respect of 87% of the agricultural area;	– monitor and evaluate data to guide decisions on the implementation of the Nitrates Directive;

● Extensification Schemes for Beef and Sheep (7.14); *MAFF*

– operation of the pilot extensification schemes;

– evaluate the pilot schemes. Wider application of the extensification schemes for beef and sheep is under consideration in the context of the Common Agricultural Policy reform proposals; and

– continue to help farmers tackle pollution and conserve the countryside.

● Farm and Conservation Grant Scheme (7.16); *MAFF*

– payment of £58m (to the end of June 1991) under the Farm and Conservation Grant scheme since 1989, mainly to reduce water pollution risks; and

– further help for farmers under scheme changes introduced in July 1991.

It will:
● review the operation of the Countryside Premium Scheme which offers farmers extra conservation payments for Set-aside land (7.18);

It has:
– begun reviewing the operation of the Countryside Premium Scheme with a view to it being taken over by the Agriculture Departments when legal powers are available;

– agreed in principle that the scheme (or similar) will extend to all England and Wales;

It will:
– consider extending the Countryside Premium Scheme to other parts of Britain;

Table 8.3 *Specimen contents from the 'Land Use and Planning' section*

Summary of white paper commitments	Action to date	Commitments to further action
S.25 In development control, the Government will:	In development control, the Government has:	In development control, the Government will:
● seek to speed up decision taking, for the benefit of the environment and the economy, and ask the Audit Commission to examine local authorities' performance (6.12);	– taken powers in the Planning and Compensation Act 1991 to turn away repetitive planning applications and delayed appeals. The Audit Commission is conducting a study of local authority performance;	– keep under review measures for speeding up the system in the light of the Audit Commission report;
● consider extensions of planning control over satellite dishes and the demolition of houses (6.14);	– taken powers in the Planning and Compensation Act 1991 to require permission for housing demolition and introduced new controls over the number, size and siting of satellite dishes;	– implement new controls over housing demolition; introduce further controls over Telecommunications Code Operator equipment and issue planning guidance on telecommunications;

• consult on whether to require prior notification of new farm and forestry buildings and to increase the size of holding to which ordinary development controls apply (6.15–6.16);	– announced new controls over the construction of farm and forestry development, stricter than those originally proposed; – consulted on new planning controls over fish farms;	– introduce the new controls over farm and forestry buildings and roads by the end of 1991; – implement new controls over fish farms in the light of consultation by the end of 1991;
• extend the tree preservation order system to cover hedgerows of importance (6.17); and	– issued a consultation paper in December 1990, with proposals to give local planning authorities powers to protect key hedgerows; – announced revised proposals in July 1991 based on prior notice to local authorities of proposed removal of hedgerows, and a new scheme to promote environmentally beneficial management; and	– work up proposals for the early introduction of a 'hedgerows incentive scheme'. Legislation on the notification scheme is to be introduced when Parliamentary time allows; and
• improve the enforcement of planning control (6.18).	– included the promised measures in the Planning and Compensation Act 1991; and issued a draft Planning Policy Guidance note.	– implement new enforcement measures and publish new Planning Policy Guidance note.

Table 8.4 *Expenditure plans for rural planning* (£ million)

Agriculture UK (Cm. 1920)	1988–9	1990–1	1992–3	1994–5
Market regulation and production support	1,134	1,715	1,644	1,650
Structural measures	209	294	327	354
Other services including R&D	173	251	306	330
Department research and admin.	313	394	382	429
Forestry	58	91	107	102
National Rivers Authority	—	204	244	295
Total agriculture including expenditure not shown	1,965	3,057	3,113	3,250
Other spending by country				
England				
Countryside Commission (Cm. 1908)	21	24	38	46
NCC/English Nature (Cm. 1908)	39/	48/	/36	n.a
Rural Development Commission (Cm. 1908)	29	23	11	18
Scotland				
Countryside Commission (Cm. 1915)	5	6	—	—
NCC for Scotland (Cm. 1915)	—	19	—	—
Scottish Natural Heritage (Cm. 1915)	—	—	34	n.a.
Highlands and Island Enterprise/ HIDB (Cm. 1920)	32	33	48	51
Wales				
Countryside Council for Wales (Cm. 1916)	—	—	17	—
Development Board for Rural Wales (Cm. 1916)	11	12	16	16

Reviews of policy in HC and Cm. Papers.

This year, as part of a general attempt to make the Review more analytical, this section not only combines House of Commons Papers and Command Papers where they are related, for example, the government's response to a House of Commons Committee report, but also presents the material by topic rather than by Committee. It is to be hoped that this will be more useful to readers, but those preferring the list format either by Committee or House of Commons Number are asked to appraise the editor of their views.

The House of Commons Select Committee on European Legislation produced as in previous years an excellent set of commentaries on documents produced by the European Commission, mainly draft regulations. All published in 1992, under HC 24-nn (91–92) they are now outlined by topic rather than seriatim.

The MacSharry proposals for CAP reform continued to produce a number of draft regulations from the Commission including: (a) three draft regulations on (i) agricultural production methods compatible with the protection of the environment and the maintenance of the countryside; (ii) a community aid scheme for forestry measures in agriculture; and (iii) a community aid scheme for early retirement from farming (24-iii £9.75); (b) Eight draft regulations including details of a proposed support system for arable areas linked to compulsory set-aside, and amendments to the schemes for beef and veal including the proposed introduction of a suckler cow premium (24-ii, £8.75); (c) proposals to introduce new administrative arrangements for switching aid to farmers related to land area totals, e.g. set-aside, the introduction of one claim form for many schemes and monitoring schemes to check for fraud and seeing what land is being used for (24-x, £6.20 and 24-xi, £7.90); and (d) a MAFF estimate that the reforms would cost the UK a net increase of £350 million by 1997 (24-iii, £9.75). However, all these documents predate the May 1992 reforms and so reflect the development of thought prior to that date.

The Committee also examined other aspects of farming: six draft regulations on milk including the introduction of a dairy cow premium scheme for up to 40 cows at 25 European Currency Units (ECU) per cow rising to 75 ECU per cow by 1996 (24-iii, £9.75); draft regulations on wholesale milk marketing (24-vii, £9.75); and reviewed a report on how the £280 million ECU raised by the milk co-responsibility levy is spent (24-xv, £12.95).

Elsewhere the Committee examined: the use made of the Structural Funds in 1990 (24-xi, £5,35); a proposal to add five species to the 1979 Birds Directive (24-xv, £12.95); the Land Use and Physical Planning implications of the Commission report on 'Europe 2000' (24-viii, £8.75); and a draft regulation on protecting forestry from air pollution (24-vii, £9.75). In conclusion, this is a useful set of summaries, but paying around £10 for a document that includes many other items to the ones shown above is not recommended: these are definitely library reading.

Most of the European legislation was concerned with agriculture and one aspect of this, overproduction by farmers, continues to be a major problem for rural planners. The 35-million-tonne EC surplus in cereals formed the focus of a House of Commons Agriculture Committee report into 'Commodity Markets in the 1990s—Cereals' (HC 98-I, and II (91–92), 1991, £7.15 and £22.00). The surplus will not disappear because, according to the report, world trade will not mop it up and biofuels are uncompetitive unless petrol prices are to double. So far attempts to cut the surplus have failed but farm incomes have been cut by two-thirds. Accordingly, the witnesses and the Committee agree that four objectives are needed for the 1990s:

i. reducing the supply of cereals, and with it the level and cost of intervention buying to the CAP;

ii. bringing EC prices closer to world prices, and eliminating the distortions caused by artificially low prices;

iii. providing protection for farmers against the effects of these changes; and

iv. promoting environmentally friendly farming.

The Committee then examined 8 options including: cutting prices, set-aside, quotas, input controls and export refunds, before focusing in detail on the MacSharry proposals (see Volume II, p. 96–8). The Committee agreed with the principle of major price cuts proposed by MacSharry, and the related payment of compensation based on the area of land under cereals, but disagreed strongly against the principle of weighting this compensation towards smaller farmers, and argued that the detailed proposals for set-aside needed significant changes.

In their response, the government (HC 278 (91–92) 1992, £1.45) broadly agreed with the need to reform policy by focusing on price reductions but disagreed with the Committee that aid for environmentally friendly farming should take place outside the CAP. They concluded, however, in agreement with the Committee that 'In the longer term, farmers' best chance of survival lies not in extensive protectionism, but in achieving maximum efficiency within a new economic order in agricultural trade'.

These statements made in November 1991 and February 1992 of course predated the May 1992 reforms which went some way towards meeting the criticisms of the MacSharry proposals but not all the way, as pp. 141–6 show.

In spite of EC food surpluses and increased productivity in the UK farm sector, Britain remains a major food importer, and in recent years, 1985–90, the gap between food exports and imports has been widening, so that by 1990 it stood at £6 billion, or 42 per cent of the UK trade deficit. More worrying, according to the House of Commons Agriculture Committee in their report on 'The Trade Gap in Food and Drink' (HC 112-I and II (91–92), 1992, £6.20 and £32.50) are the facts that 63 per cent of the gap is made up of food that could be grown in the UK and that an increasing amount of the gap is caused by imports of food from similar farming systems on the near continent.

Accordingly, the Committee in their report called for the elimination of unfair competition, better promotion of exports, and more import substitution.

In their reply, however, the government (Cm. 1982, 1992, £1.95) noted that the gap, although growing recently, is significantly smaller than in the 1970s, and that there are no inherent reasons why the gap could not be narrowed further. Accordingly the reply did not offer any extra help, for example more cash for Food from Britain as advocated by the Committee, or signal any policy change, but concluded that the principal responsibility for action lies with the agricultural food industry. The government's role is thus limited to trying to identify what has to be done, bringing the interests concerned together and facilitating the changes needed, rather than changing legislation.

One of the groups involved, The Agricultural Development and Advisory Service (ADAS), was the subject of a Committee of Public Accounts of the House of Commons investigation into 'Advisory Services to Agriculture' which developed an earlier report by the Agriculture Committee as reported in Volume II, pp. 90–1, by taking evidence from the Agricultural Departments. They concluded (HC 465 (90–91), 1991, £9.00) that the 'public good' advice aspect of the Service had lagged behind the commercial work since the division between commercial and 'public good' (Free) advice in 1987. The Committee recommended that the precise nature of 'public good' advice should be spelt out by the time ADAS became an agency in 1992, and that MAFF should provide Parliament with a full report of ADAS's achievements against its objectives and targets across the whole range of its activities. Other conclusions and recommendations referred to the percentages of costs to be recovered, and ways of improving the management information system which oversees ADAS's work as an agency which does both 'commercial' and 'public good' work, so that the costs of these different types of work can be appropriately divided.

Turning to the wider environment, in October 1991, the DOE issued a consultation paper on a proposed Environment Agency as a result of a pledge in the 1990 White Paper '*This Common Heritage*'. The Environment Committee of the House of Commons produced a report (HC 55 (91–92), 1992, £23.80) on the proposals as part of the consultation exercise which had to be completed by the end of January 1992. The committee examined the four options proposed by the consultation paper for setting up an agency responsible for pollution control, and concluded that in the long term a single Agency for Great Britain should be set up. In the short term the first priority however must be to implement the system of Integrated Pollution Control established by the Environmental Protection Act 1990 (see Volume II, pp. 75–6). Returning to the longer term, the single agency when set up should not in any way be a comprehensive environment agency, but instead should restrict itself to its core activity of pollution control and in due course might mean that agricultural pollution control is taken away from MAFF and into the new Agency. Indeed, the Committee argued that English Nature and the Countryside Commission should keep their status and that the National Rivers Authority should largely be retained, only losing its pollution control powers to the new agency. None the less, the Agency should be expected to play a vigorous and active role in co-ordinating consultation, over pollution control and waste management, in the preparation of land-use plans.

Some 88 per cent of solid waste in the UK is disposed of by landfill, so an EC draft directive on 'the landfill of waste' was of concern to the House of Commons Environment Committee. In their report (HC 263-I and II (90–91), 1991, £12.85 and £22.00) the Committee welcomed the directive because it would harmonise Community practice and also act as a catalyst for improving UK standards which in some areas, for example the collection of data, were appalling. The Committee had, however, no objection to the principle of landfill, believing it to be a safe and efficient method of waste disposal. This was a view with which the government concurred in their reply to the report (Cm. 1821, 1992, £3.85). Although the government disagreed with a number of the Committee's detailed findings and recommendations, both parties did agree that the EC draft directive required further amendment if it were to benefit both the environment and the waste management industry.

'Renewable energy' also promises many other environmental gains including the disposal of waste by turning it into energy, and a 1992 report from the Energy Committee of the House of Commons (HC 43-I, II, III, £10.75, £22.20 and £23.80) has proposed that the energy created this way should increase to 3,000–4,000 MW by 2000, or 10 per cent of all electricity generated, instead of the 1,000 MW target proposed by the 1990 White Paper *This Common Inheritance*. However, there are significant environmental problems, and the Committee argued that a draft Planning Policy Guidance Note issued by the DOE in December 1991 during their deliberations is too weak, since the Note suggested that it may be desirable to give permission for renewable energy developments even in designated areas. In contrast the Committee argued

landscape protection should be an important factor in reaching planning decisions relating to renewable energy projects. We recommend that there should be a presumption against renewable energy developments within National Parks. We consider that this would strengthen the welcome presumption in favour of renewable energy development outside designated areas.

In this regard the Committee concluded that on-shore wind energy offers the most immediate potential, especially in small sites, and that wave energy offers plenty of long-term potential but again in small sites, rather than the massive barrage proposals presently under discussion. Also see CCP 357 on p. 171.

Coastal planning, except for barrage proposals, has been a neglected topic for many years and so the House of Commons Environment Committee on 'Coastal Zone Protection and Planning' (HC 17-I and II (91–92), 1992, £11.85 and £33.60) is a very welcome source of new information and ideas. Indeed, the report comes out with some radical solutions. The main thrust of the report is that although the coast should be seen as an integrated unit, current legislation is too diffuse and administrative arrangements too complex for an integrated or efficient framework. Accordingly, the report recommends that coastal zone policy should be reviewed in order to reduce unnecessary duplication of responsibilities and to improve co-ordination. To help this process a National Coastal Zone Unit should be set up, and a National Coastal Strategy formulated, with a hierarchical nesting of policies devolving down through the regional to the local levels, via the mechanism of Coastal Zone Management Plans.

In more detail the report recommends the extension of planning controls to beyond the low-water mark and the transfer of the planning functions of the Crown Estate Commissioners to a more appropriate authority, and that the government should consider the desirability of extending planning controls over fish farming below the low-water mark. The report met with a widely enthusiastic response including that from the RTPI, English Nature and the World Wildlife Fund (WWF).

The government in their reply (Cm. 2011, 1992, £5.30) were more cautious. They divided their response into four broad headings and 17 detailed topics. Among the four broad headings the government encouraged the preparation of management plans but within the context of development plans, and they rejected the idea of a major reformulation of legislation for the coastal zone. Similarly, a National Coastal Zone Unit was rejected in favour of the continuation of a group within the DOE which already oversees coastal policy.

Turning to some of the 17 detailed points, notably planning control, the government promised to issue a discussion paper on whether planning authorities should extend their powers out to sea, and was even more cautious with regard to fish farming, noting that they were committed to an evolutionary approach. The response ended with a list of 19 commitments which the government will be including in future annual updates of the *This Common Inheritance* White Paper (see p. 126.). These included maintaining national co-ordination arrangements for coastal policy.

In summary, the three documents provide a wealth of ideas, debate and evidence about one of the most important, but also one of the most neglected parts of the countryside, the coast. It is to be hoped that it will be the forerunner to a new interest in this vital resource and will introduce further efforts to co-ordinate and streamline our over-complex planning system which has grown, like Topsy, over the last 40 years. To some extent this is already happening as shown on pp. 152. (DOE Consultation Papers) and in the 'Diary' for March 1992.

The physical protection of the coast and flood protection is also a complex administrative matter, although in 1985 things were simplified when MAFF took over from DOE the responsibility for coast protection to add to its responsibilities for sea defence. The National Audit Office has carried out an examination of the work of MAFF since 1985 and the subsequent report on this work has been published in a report on 'Coastal Defences in England' (HC 9(92–93), 1992, £7.80). This report concludes that the complex interrelationships between the organisations involved, including district and county councils, are working albeit with significant gaps, notably a lack of information on the adequacy of coastal defences, but that the development of a national strategy for the coast (see also HC 17(91–92) above) would provide a further opportunity to discuss the important issues involved, notably the need to deal with rising sea levels and the increasing significance of environmental protection in all policy areas. MAFF officials were cross-examined by the Committee of Public Accounts Committee in June 1992 (HC 85-i (92–93), 1992, £10.25).

Finally four unrelated reports dealt with heritage, defence, Welsh housing and public spending. These are now considered in turn. The DOE spends £120 million a year on grants to the five main heritage bodies. The way in which this money is spent has been the subject of a National Audit Office examination and a Comptroller and Auditor General report (HC 132 (92–93), 1992, £8.75). The report notes that the listing of buildings has been a success, but that three problems remain. First, the need to computerise the list; second, the poor state of repair of around 73,000 of the 500,000 such buildings; and third, poor monitoring of the advice given to local authorities on listing building applications for change or demolition. Scheduling of monuments is very poor with only 13,000 scheduled against an estimated potential 60,000 monuments. Financial assistance to privately owned properties is thought to be well spent, but the properties owned and managed by the heritage organisations are thought to be subject to a big backlog of repairs and are marketed and presented to the public in a dreary fashion, notably Stonehenge, where 'a lot needs to be done'.

Defence land has always been a controversial subject, and the peace dividend offers the possibility that much of this land, notably in National Parks, could be returned to another use. However, a national Audit Office investigation reported by the Comptroller and Auditor General (HC 218 (91–92) 1992, £7.10.) notes that the lack of accurate data makes it difficult to assess the Ministry of Defence's claim that they actually needed more land. The report thus calls for a more rigorous audit of defence land use. In the mean time, it acknowledges that current arragements to limit environmental damage are satisfactory but that the conflict between military training and public use was the largest issue that still needed to be addressed once the facts of the matter were better known.

The subject of 'Affordable Housing' was addressed by the Welsh Affairs Committee in HC 281-I and II (90–91), 1991, £8.90 and £22.00. Three of the report's 39 pages were devoted to rural housing, and as part of a solution the Committee recommended the creation of a Welsh Rural Housing Trust as an equivalent of the English Rural Housing Trust. More generally, the Committee examined various ways of providing affordable housing including expanding the Welsh Office Scheme which enables local authorities to purchase houses that would otherwise become second homes. In all, the Committee made 17 recommendations along the lines that have been generally agreed by housing experts as being sensible palliatives rather than radical solutions to the housing problem.

In their reply to the report the government (Cm. 1793, 1992, £2.90) responded to each of the 17 recommendations, but rejected the two recommendations outlined above. First, the proposal to set up a Welsh Rural Housing Trust was rejected because it would not have a significant additional role to play since 27 per cent of the resources of Housing for Wales are already directed to rural needs. Second, the expansion of the Welsh Office Scheme to buy up potential second homes was rejected since the scheme is in fact being changed partly as a result of a new series of bids in 1991.

Finally, the Appropriation Accounts provide a mass of detailed data on how rural planning money is actually spent; see, for example, HC 655 (90–91), notably Volume III, 1991, £5.20, dealing with MAFF, the Intervention Board Executive Agency and the Forestry Commission. Similarly, the Supply Estimates for 1992–3 are found in HC 273(91–92), 1992, notably Volume III (£9.85), dealing with MAFF, the Intervention Board Executive Agency and the Forestry Commission; Volume VII (£7.95) dealing with the Department of Transport; Volume VIII (£15.70) dealing with the DOE; Volume XV (£20.20) dealing with Scotland; and Volume XVI (£14.40) dealing with Wales.

House of Lords Papers

European Community environmental law now contains over 200 pieces of legislation and will become even more important in the future, yet very few people are aware of its influence or requirements, let alone its implementation. The Select Committee on the European Community has therefore carried out a study of 'Implementation and Enforcement of Environmental Legislation' (HL 53-I, II (91–92), £11.85 and £25.50).

In their report they conclude that such legislation is being widely ignored and that the EC has paid insufficient attention to how its policies can be given effect, enforced or evaluated. The Committee argue that unless member states can show via subsidiarity that they can implement the legislation that the pressure will grow for the EC to be given more competence in this area. A substantial change of attitude is thus needed by member states.

However, the Commission too needs to make more effort in drafting the legislation in the first place, with more consultation. It also needs to provide better supporting data and clearer indications of the technicalities and costs of implementation and enforcement. Directives should remain the favoured form of legislation, since they allow flexibility for member states.

The European Environment Agency will have an important role to play, notably in spot checks on the data collected by national authorities, and the Committee deeply regretted the delay in setting it up. However the Committee do not believe that the EC should direct powers of enforcement in the member states but that convergence of enforcement policies should be effected through co-operation between enforcement authorities, and the use of the Cohesion Fund to soften the economic costs of implementation.

Cohesion, namely the convergence of regional economies, is one of the aims of 'EEC Regional Development Policy' as reviewed by 4219/91 (COM (90) 609 final), 'Fourth Periodic Report from the EC on the Social and Economic Situation and Development of the Regions of the Community'. This review formed the basis of a report by the Select Committee on the European Communities (HL 20 (91–92) £27.20). In general, the Committee urged the government to redouble their efforts to satisfy the Commission that 'additionality' of grants from the Structural Funds is being undertaken by the UK. With regard to rural areas, the Committee argued that Objective 5b regions (rural areas in need of help) receive comparatively small sums of money for a disproportionaly large bureaucratic effort, and that the rules for these areas should be made less stringent than for Objective 1 (lagging) regions. Finally, the decision to move the Highlands and Islands of Scotland from Objective 1 to Objective 5b status should be reviewed in 1993, in view of the sparcity of the population and the peripherality of the region.

Turning to responses to earlier reports by the Select Committee on the European Communities namely, 'the Development and Future of the CAP' (HL 79 (90–91), Volume II, pp. 94–5), the government (HL 21 (91–92))agreed with most of the conclusions and recommendations made by the Committee, notably the need to achieve *effective* reform of the CAP, mainly via broad reductions in the level of price support.

In another reply to a Select Committee on the European Communities report, this time on the 'Non-Food Uses of Agricultural Products' (Volume II, p. 95.), the government (HL 21 (91–92)) agreed with the Committee that the economics of such uses are at present unfavourable and that they would be opposed to any proposals to stimulate the *large-scale* use of agricultural products in industrial processes via adjustments to the CAP. The government will therefore limit its expenditure to research and development.

Finally, a letter to the Minister of Agriculture criticising aspects of the draft regulation on establishing a support system for producers of certain arable crops (EC 7022/92) written by Lord Boston, Chairman of the European Community Committee is reproduced in HL 18 (92–93).

Fans of the House of Lords Select Committee reports over the years will thus find 1991–2 a disappointing year at least in volume terms, since few reports were produced.

**Review of events and news stories in rural planning, 1
September 1991 to 31 October 1992**

This review is structured into four sections. The first section contains a set
of reviews of three major issues: changes to agricultural policy; schemes
and initiatives; and international, national and local political economy.
This is followed by a summary of consultation papers, a diary of news
stories and a list of new designated places (see Table 8.6 on p. 160).

Three major issues

Changes to agricultural policy   Agriculture again dominated the rural
policy year as it has done for many years. Much progress was however
made when the MacSharry proposals (see Volume II, pp. 96–9) were
accepted in a modified form in May 1992. The details and implications of
the reforms are also discussed at length in the mainland Europe section.
The purpose of this review is to provide an historical account, and to
emphasise the UK perspective.

In September the need for reform was confirmed by a harvest of around
22.7 million tonnes, similar to 1991, in spite of a reduced crop area. The
UK continued throughout September and October to argue against those
elements of the MacSharry proposals that discriminated against Britain's
above average farm size. These negotiations were conducted against a
background of falling farm incomes, down 22 per cent in 1990, and
according to the NFU the worst financial position for farming since the
war.

Some progress was made in November with a new oilseeds regime. This
involved a price cut from the world price of £225 per tonne to £130, but
was offset by an area payment of £385 for each hectare under oilseed rape.
This model of cutting support prices, but compensating by an area payment, was a forerunner to the May 1992 reforms, as was the subsequent
revision of the regime in February 1992 to take account of General
Agreement on Tarrifs and Trade (GATT) rules.

Elsewhere MAFF announced a new £5.4 million package aimed to help
farmers with food marketing. Critics pointed out that this was merely a
reinstatement of a scheme dropped in 1990.

Aside from price negotiations, the European Commission produced a
draft regulation to extensify production, provide grants for afforestation
and for improving woodland, and aid for early retirement. At the same
time the Countryside Commission sent a letter to MAFF with a six-point
plan which included proposals for an agri-environment programme and a
Conservation Lands Programme aimed at using set-aside land to restore
valued landscapes and habitats, and to create new woodland.

Further pressure on MAFF came in December when *The Sunday Times*
published details of how much money wealthy individuals were making

from set-aside, and how easy it was to defraud the system by making bogus claims. The CPRE also joined the chorus when it made a formal complaint to the EC over the implementation of set-aside in the UK.

Meanwhile, the scheme continued to grow slowly and MAFF published figures showing that after 4 years of set-aside, some 4,478 farmers had set-aside 154,579 ha. The majority was in permanent fallow, and in the five-year, rather than the one-year scheme.

Further pressure to reach a CAP deal came in January 1992 when the Director-General of GATT, Mr Dunkel, proposed a 36 per cent cut in expenditure on export subsidies, and a 20 per cent cut in internal support, in order to move the deadlocked GATT talks forward.

In Britain, the Milk Marketing Board (MMB) announced plans to reform itself and to separate off from its manufacturing arm, Dairy Crest, to become a producer co-operative only.

The 1980 Variable Sheep Premium was ended and replaced by ewe headage payments which were limited to various maxima numbers of ewes.

More doom and gloom emerged in February when a survey for the National Westminster Bank showed that about half of the farms surveyed had no successor either in the form of an heir, or a relative wishing to take the farm on. Ironically the percentage of non-successor farms was highest in the more prosperous areas, and least in the remote uplands.

In March the European Commission announced price proposals for 1992–3 centred around price cuts for cereals as a consequence of the 160 million tonne threshold being exceeded by the previous harvest. For the longer term farm Ministers reached agreement on the base levels to be used for calculating set-aside and stocking levels for livestock under the MacSharry reforms.

Within Britain the Budget reduced the Inheritance Tax burden on farmers (see the Finance Act 1992 on p. 107 for details), but plans to expand the pilot UK extensification scheme were shelved for lack of public funds.

In April further reforms to milk marketing were announced with the introduction of four new types of contract for dairy farmers. The guaranteed price for potatoes was kept at £53 per tonne, but the price for wool fell from 120p to 117 pence per kilogramme.

These changes were only interim, since the Queen's Speech for the 1992–3 session, following the April election, announced that a Bill would end the Annual Review of agriculture, guaranteed prices for wool and potatoes, and abolish marketing boards, including the MMB. The Bill was in fact published in November 1992.

The big news in May, however, was the agreement on 22 May 1992 to make substantial changes to the CAP. In essence, the so-called May reforms involved cutting support prices for cereals by 29 per cent between 1993 and 1996, cutting beef support prices by 15 per cent, but offsetting these by paying direct payments to farmers in the form of area payments for arable farmers and headage payments for livestock farmers. For details see Table 8.5.

In spite of much euphoria in some circles, *The Sunday Times* called the changes a 'sham reform', and pointed out the proposals would actually increase CAP expenditure from £26 to £39 billion a year. Even John Gummer, the Agricultural Minister, admitted that he did not like set-aside, and that given time he favoured different ways of bringing supply and demand into line. However, most farmers were relieved that set-aside would not be limited as under the initial proposals. In June in a speech to the House of Commons, the Minister emphasised that the reforms were

Table 8.5   *The May reforms to the CAP with subsequent details*

Cereals
1. 1992–3 prices cut by 3% due to threshold being exceeded but offset by abolition of co-responsibility levy of 5%.
2. Cut of 29% in intervention prices for cereals in stages between 1993 and 1996 to bring intervention price down to around £80 per tonne in 1996.
3. In August it was announced that only one price would apply as from 1993, and that quality standards would exclude most British cereals. However, a safety net for lower quality cereals was promised if prices collapsed.
4. Area compensation payments to be introduced for those setting aside 15% of their arable land.
5. In September, five rates were set for different regions of the UK calculated on the basis of average yields in the region and dependent on regional plantings not exceeding the base area for that region. The rates were set at September 1992 exchange rates and were to be recalculated on the exchange rate prevailing on 1 July 1993. The rates in September were as follows: in £ per hectare for cereals, oilseeds, proteins and set-aside for each region:
(a) England—£121; £383; £315; £218 (b) Wales—£95; £390; £247; £171 (c) Scotland, LFA—£98; £353; £256; £177 (d) N. Ireland—£96; £363; £250; £173 (e) Scotland, non-LFA—£115; £434; £300; £208.

In other words, a farmer setting aside arable land in England would expect to be paid £218 per hectare for each ha set-aside and then would receive a direct payment on the crops growing on the other 85% depending on where he farms, and whether he fulfils all the requirements (see text for details), e.g. £98 per ha for cereals in Scotland LFA.

Milk
Co-responsibility levy of 0.33p. per litre to end after the 1992/93 milk year. Intervention butter price cut by 2.5%. No change in milk quotas but this will be reviewed in 1993 and 1994.

Beef
Intervention prices cut by 5% a year as from 1993/94, and limited to 750,000 tonnes in 1993 falling to 350,000 in 1997. Safety net available at 60% of intervention price. Special beef premium of £72 per head paid twice at 10 and 22 months for up to 90 male cattle. Where stocking rates fall below 1.4 LU/ha the special beef premium and suckler cow premium rises by £24 a head. Standard Suckler Cow premium will rise from £56 in 1993 to £96 per head in 1995.

Sheep
Sheep annual premiums will be paid on up to 500 ewes on lowland farms and 1,000 ewes on LFA farms. Ewes above the limit will be paid half premium.

far more in line with UK ideas than the original 1991 proposals. He also emphasised that the reforms marked two significant shifts in agricultural and food policy:

1. Moving away from support paid by consumers in the form of higher food prices, to support by taxpayers; and as a corollary,
2. Moving away from production support to direct support to farmers.

Such support is of course very susceptible to fraud and so the Commission also began work on monitoring schemes to prevent abuse.

Also in June, proposals were made for a green package to accompany the price reforms. These included aid for the upkeep of woodland; long-term set-aside for 20 years or more; aid for land management involving access or leisure; help to cut inputs or reduce stocking rates; and training in environmentally friendly farming. Once approved, these were expected to be implemented by member states in 1993.

In the UK, Mr Gummer gave a speech in July setting out his views on the agri-environment action plan. He noted that it required all member states to draw up programmes with a range of options, depending on localities, to encourage farmers to take care of the countryside, including: crop or livestock extensification; environmentally friendly management; protection of water; organic farming; set-aside for at least 20 years for environmental purposes; and management of land for public access and recreation. However, Mr Gummer then argued that although this was an important step in the right direction he did not simply want to replace a regime of dependency on production subsidies with a regime of unlimited state support for environmental measures. Nor did he want to see environ-mental policy as just an added-on extra to the main body of the CAP. He remained committed to making environmental concerns a more integrated part of the CAP.

However, in September the CPRE claimed that MAFF merely intended to repackage existing schemes. Instead, they called on MAFF to: make sure that environmental support funds were made available to all farmers; make a commitment to moving towards less-intensive farming rather using than set-aside as a weapon for combating surpluses; and to restrict arable compensation payments to those farmers willing to agree to maintain environmental features. Earlier in the year, in March, the NFU had taken a similar line when it advocated the introduction of a Farm and Horticul-ture Conservation Scheme under which farmers would commit land for 5–10 years to a flexible range of measures. The scheme would be available to all farmers, not just those at present eligible for limited schemes, like ESAs.

Meanwhile, back in July, the new pricing scheme for milk was forecast to give an average boost of £4,000 to dairy farmers, offset by £1,700 over two years which would have to be raised from dairy farms to fund rationalisation. In October the milk price rose by 0.5 p. per litre to just under 20p per litre.

In August a *Farmers Weekly* poll of 200 growers showed that 90 per cent. would set aside land, but mainly by setting aside the poorest land, and cutting back on barley and oilseeds.

Many farmers were, however, unsure of the exact nature of the scheme, even when the MAFF produced a set of rules, which included a green cover to minimise nitrate leaching, minimal use of chemicals and some planting of crops for industrial uses. However, the rules for tree planting were postponed till 1993. Farmers did not have to decide whether to rotate their set-aside land or not. The rules forecast that non-rotational set-aside land—that is, using the same land year after year for set-aside—would need to meet a higher percentage commitment and be subject to different management rules, when these rules were made in 1993. The NFU argued that the rules were tough and complex, but manageable.

In September, a 44-page booklet on the Area Payment Scheme was issued to farmers. 120,000 copies were printed. However, like the set-aside rules, this left grey areas of uncertainty and many farmers had to make snap decisions over their autumn plantings. In a silver lining to a wet harvest, some were physically forced to delay this decision till the 14 per cent devaluation of the pound in mid-September, which provided two boosts to farmers. First the CAP prices were lifted; for example common wheat intervention prices rose from £122.24 on 16 September 1992 to £139.28 by 26 November as both the pound was devalued and the Exchange Rate Mechanism (ERM) was realigned twice. Second, interest rates were cut from 10 per cent in September to 7 per cent in November.

The need for the reforms was emphasised again when the harvest was estimated at 22.2 million tonnes, down only 0.4 per cent from 1991, in spite of a wet harvest. Earlier in August provisional results from the June Census showed a slight rise in the cereals area up to 3.5 m ha, but still down by 0.4 m ha, from 1987. Beef and sheep numbers rose by around 1.6 per cent, but the dairy herd recorded a 3.1 per cent fall.

By October, the fraud detection and monitoring scheme was estimated to cost £340 million to set up, and £40 million a year to run. It was based on the need to identify land use in 10 million land parcels (fields) and to cross-reference these to farmer's claims for set-aside and area payments.

However, October ended with the reforms still cloaked in uncertainty as the GATT talks foundered yet again. This time the issue was oilseed production. The USA demanded a big cut in EC production and when an agreement reached by MacSharry (the EC farm Commissioner) was vetoed by the French in the form of Jacques Delors, he resigned. After much pressure, he was reinstated after the USA threatened a trade war beginning with the imposition of steep tariffs on mainly French products—200 per cent on French wines. On the evening of writing (17 November 1992), MacSharry was touching down in Washington to resume talks. NFU experts forecast that the US demands would lead to set-aside rising from 15 to 18–20 per cent and large cuts in oilseeds area, and in milk and sugar beet quotas. The French made it clear they would not accept such cuts and so the potential for a full-scale collapse in one or both of the CAP and GATT threatened.

Stop press: On the evening of Friday 20 November 1992 the negotiators announced a deal based on cutting back oilseed production to around 9 million tonnes, using set-aside. It was also forecast (at the time of editing on 2 December 1992) that in Britain the deal could lead to set-aside rates rising to 21 per cent and to milk quota cuts of 8 per cent (or a price cut of 20 per cent). Immediately, French farmers began to riot and the French Government announced that they would fight this deal both within the EC and GATT. Watch this space.

Schemes and initiatives   In February 1992 the Countryside Commission, DOE and MAFF jointly launched a £45 million package to open up the countryside, conserve historic and ancient landscapes, halt the loss of hedgerows and encourage environmental action by local communities, under the umbrella title of 'Action for the Countryside'. This contained four initiatives to be run by the Commission.

First, there was a Parish Paths Partnership, under which £1 million will be paid in the first year for councils or groups to undertake surveys and clear paths as part of the Commission's target of having all 120,000 miles of public rights of way open by 2000. A leaflet (Countryside Commission Publication 370) (CCP) was issued to explain the scheme.

Second, there was to be an extension to the Countryside Stewardship Scheme (see CCP 346 on p. 166), with an extra £3 million available over three years, and including two new landscape categories, historic parkland and old meadows/pastures. The inclusion of historic landscapes will attract English Heritage survey grants to help applicants identify suitable land. The addition of meadows and pasture will in the first instance be aimed at conserving Culm grasslands in Devon and Cornwall, and the species-rich grasslands of Hereford and Worcester. A leaflet (CCP 373) was issued to explain the scheme. Under the existing scheme launched in June 1991, 1,200 applications had been made, and the first-year budget had been heavily oversubscribed, the Commission reported in January 1992. An extra £1 million had thus been allocated by the government and £3.6. million approved for expenditure. In August 1992, the Commission reported that 900 agreements had been signed in the first year, covering some 30,000 hectares, and involving some 7,000 hectares of new or improved access. A similar scheme was launched in Wales in July 1992, and in England applications for the second year of the scheme were made during the summer.

Third, a Hegerow Incentive Scheme was to be brought in to restore and improve the management of important hedgerows, for their amenity, wildlife and historic value. £3.5 million will be allocated over three years, which will normally apply to the whole farm to achieve the best results. The scheme will complement hedgerow grants offered by MAFF. A leaflet (CCP374) was issued to explain the scheme. See also CCP 383 on p. 166.

Fourth, 'Rural Action' was to be launched to support local communities in caring for their local countryside, by taking direct action. Over the first three years £3.2 million will be allocated to the scheme. Rural Action will be formed by a partnership between the Commission, English Nature and six other organisations. A leaflet (CCP 369) was issued to explain the scheme.

Expenditure under these schemes only amounted to *c*. £15 million, but with other schemes (outlined below) it represented £22.5 million of new money, or an increase of 0.2 per cent of government spending on agriculture and the environment.

Other schemes involved a £4.25 'Countryside Employment Programme' for the Rural Development Commission to launch three new pilot areas for countryside employment in areas where the local economy could find it difficult to absorb jobs lost from agriculture, by providing small workshops, training, advice, grants and loans.

The Rural Development Commission's Redundant Buildings Grant Scheme was also relaunched and extended to all the national parks, and to the pilot areas in the Countryside Employment Programme. Maximum grants were raised from 25 to 30 per cent or up to £75,000, at a cost of £6 million over three years.

The Rural Development Commission also relaunched its Accord programme, which provides initial funding for large-scale schemes usually costing more than £250,000 in the Rural Development Areas, at a cost of £5 million.

The Rural Development Commission's social programmes were set to receive £4.8 million under the package to help local organisations improve amenities like village halls and shops, parking, access and planting schemes.

Finally, English Nature will spend an extra £1.25 million over three years to save six endangered species, including the red squirrel and the dormouse. Additional funding would also be provided to pay for English Nature's Wildlife Enhancement Scheme, which was launched in November 1991.

Under this scheme, intended to promote the positive management of SSIs, two pilot areas—the Culm Measures in Devon, and the Pevensey Levels in Sussex—have been set up to test this completely new way of working with SSSI landowners and occupiers. Landowners are receiving payments for carrying out work specifically to encourage wildlife. These payments include annual management payments to cover the additional cost of managing land for nature and fixed-cost payments to cover the costs of labour and materials for any work needed to improve the site under a simple management agreement and plan. However, the pilot scheme only involved around 30 of the UK's 5,700 SSSIs.

Earlier in September 1991, the Forestry Commission launched a Community Woodland Scheme under which £950 per hectare can be paid in addition to grants under the Woodland Grant Scheme, but only where a community woodland plan had been agreed by the Commission. The Commission also announced that as from October 1991 local authorities would be able to enter into legal agreement to secure access to woodlands sold by the Commission to the private sector.

Turning to Environmentally Sensitive Areas (ESAs), MAFF announced in July 1992 that the five ESAs that were modified in November 1991 (see SI section) had attracted 2,272 applications over 57,872 hectares compared to 2,190 agreements over 46,744 hectares under the pre-November 1991 arrangements. In August 1992, MAFF announced proposals for revisions to five more ESAs: the Breckland; North Peak; Shropshire Borders(Clun); Suffolk River Valleys; and the Test Valley. Six further ESAs were also being considered: the Avon Valley; Exmoor; Lake District; North Kent Marshes; South Wessex Downs; and South-West Peak. In Scotland, five new ESAs were being considered: the Argyll Islands; Cairngorm Straths; the Central Southern Uplands; the Shetland Islands; and the Western Southern Uplands. However, after a bullish announcement which followed pleas for further ESAs by both English Nature and the Countryside Commission in November 1991, involving not only the above schemes but also the Blackdown Hills, the Cotswolds, Dartmoor, the Essex coast, Shropshire Hills and upper Thames tributaries, progress during the year was slow. The autumn statement of 1992, however, gave the financial go-ahead for further designations in 1993 and 1994.

Research into four ESAs at Wye College reported by *Farmers Weekly* (13/3/92, p. 29) found that ESAs made farmers better by sums ranging from between £1,050 and £1,750, but that Farm Woodland Schemes made farmers worse off by around £210/ha. In terms of 'environmental gain' defined by Wye as the net cost to the exchequer and the increase or decrease of farm income, the cheapest was the Somerset Levels ESA, but the most expensive was the Farm Woodland Scheme.

Finally, in October, *Farmers Weekly* (9/10/92, pp. 66–8) published a most useful summary of all the schemes available to farmers; in essence these are as follows:

1. Agricultural production—Arable Support Regime, Sheep Annual Premium, Beef Special Premium, Suckler Cow Premium, Hill Livestock Compensatory Allowance, Farm and Conservation Grant Scheme;
2. Extensive farming/Landscape and nature conservation—Countryside Stewardship Scheme, Environmentally Sensitive Area Scheme, Landscape Conservation Grants, Nature Conservation Grants, Hedgerow Incentive Scheme, Farm and Conservation Grant Scheme;
3. Woodland establishment and maintenance—Woodland Grant Scheme, Farm Woodland Premium Scheme;
4. Diversification—Farm and Conservation Grant Scheme;

5. Housing and building maintenance—House Renovation Grant, Listed Building Grant, Redundant Building Grant, Farm and Conservation Grant Scheme.

International, national and local political economy   Internationally, the Earth Summit (United Nations Conference on the Environment and Development), held in Rio in June 1992, promised much but delivered little. The vested interests of the rich nations, notably the USA, prevented any real shift of resources from rich to poor. However some progress was made as detailed below.

A biodiversity agreement was reached on protecting plants and species. The implementation of this weak agreement depends however on how far developing countries are paid to protect their resources.

A legally binding treaty on avoiding global warming was signed by 110 countries, but was weakened by the USA which refused to allow timetables and targets.

Agenda 21, a 800-page blueprint for action to lead development into environmentally sound areas, was agreed. The guidelines within the agenda are to be implemented by nations at their own pace. In the UK this means that Britain is committed to reviewing and developing policies to support the best possible use of land and the sustainable management of land resources by 1996. By the end of the century, it also agreed to improve and strengthen planning, management and evaluation systems for land and land resources. Specifically, this means that Britain should integrate land-use and transportation planning to encourage development patterns that reduce transport demand, with all that this implies for rural settlement planning.

Agenda 21 also includes a number of checklists which stress that countries should: develop integrated goal-setting and policy formulation at the national, regional and local levels that takes into account environmental, social, demographic and economic issues; develop policies that encourage sustainable land use; review the regulatory framework for controlling land uses; restrict the transfer of productive arable land; and encourage the principle of delegated policy-making to the lowest level public authority consistent with effective action.

The verdict on the summit was one of cosmetic progress, but little power to monitor implementation. However, most agreed that the environment was now a political matter to be considered at the highest level.

Nationally, the year was dominated by the April re-election of a Conservative Government. The three manifestos differed widely on their attention to both the countryside and the environment. The Liberal Democrats gave the most attention, but gained the least votes. They proposed *inter alia*: improving countryside protection policies; introducing countryside management agreements; a reform of land-use planning; creating a new Department of Natural Resources and an Environmental Protection

Agency; more investment in public transport; new incentive payments for environmental objectives; extension of Rural Development Agencies; and doubling the forested area.

The Conservatives paid the second amount of attention (as judged by manifesto space), and under the heading of a 'Brighter Britain' they promised in addition to existing commitments: to press for EC help for organic agriculture; a review of forestry incentive schemes; guidance on the preparation of local Indicative Forestry Strategies; and to establish an Environment Agency which will publish an annual State of the Environment report.

The Labour Party in three brief sections promised: a cleaner and safer environment; a transformation of transport policy; and a better life in the country. The manifesto was strong on commitment but weak in detail, although the manifesto was backed up by more detailed publications. In the event, Labour were to some people surprisingly beaten (but not by Gilg, who in a 1991 book—see review on p. 162—had predicted a Conservative victory, although personally he wanted a hung parliament). The conservatism of John Major is, however, a more pragmatic one than that of Mrs Thatcher, and the rest of the year saw policies remorsely sweep. back towards interventionism and a re-espousal of the ideas of Keynes and Roosevelt. Whether the CAP reforms and 'Action for the Countryside' will ever amount to a 'New Deal' for the countryside remains unlikely, although the autumn statement did increase spending after months of rumours that a Thatcherite cut-back was due. Indeed, public borrowing was set to rise to levels unprecedented in post-war Britain, even well above the International Monetary Fund (IMF) crisis years of the late 1970s. This perhaps was the truest measure of the U-turn in government policy that began with the withdrawal from the ERM in September 1992 and the immediate devaluation of the pound. Planning is back on the agenda.

Locally, in England the long process of local government reform began with a consultation paper being issued by the DOE in November to coincide with the publication of the Local Government Bill (see p. 106 for the subsequent Act). This stressed that a strong community identity for the revised area should be a key factor, and expressed a preference for unitary authorities to replace the 1974 two-tier system. This could mean a reinstatement of some of the Counties lost in 1974.

In June and July 1992, the DOE issued Policy Guidance to the newly formed Local Government Commission, which reaffirmed the desirability for authorities to respect topography, geography and people's expressed preferences. Where possible, existing areas should not be divided, but unitary authorities were deemed to be desirable. The Guidance did concede, however, that two-tiers could be acceptable.

The Commission began work in July 1992, and was expected to complete its work by 1998. Areas are to be considered in five tranches as follows:

First tranche—Avon, Gloucestershire, Somerset;
     Cleveland, Durham;
     Derbyshire;
     Humberside, Lincolnshire, North Yorkshire;
     Isle of Wight;
Second tranche—Cambridgeshire;
     Cumbria, Lancashire;
     Devon;
     Hampshire;
     Leicestershire;
     Nottinghamshire;
     Staffordshire;
Third tranche—Bedfordshire;
     Berkshire, Oxfordshire;
     Buckinghamshire;
     Cheshire;
     East Sussex, West Sussex;
     Kent;
     Northamptonshire;
Fourth tranche—Dorset;
     Essex;
     Hereford and Worcester;
     Norfolk;
     Suffolk;
     Wiltshire;
Fifth tranche—Cornwall;
     Hertfordshire;
     Northumberland;
     Shropshire;
     Surrey;
     Warwickshire.

In Scotland, a consultation paper, 'Shaping the new Councils', which was issued in October 1992 floated four models, ranging from 15 councils mainly based on current health board areas, up to 24, 35 and 51, the latter based largely on the existing lower-tier structure of 54 districts. According to auditors, the 15-council structure would save £192 million, but the 51-council set-up would increase spending by £58 million. None the less, the Secretary of State for Scotland said he had an open mind.

Finally, in Wales the Secretary of State for Wales announced in March 1992 that 23 unitary authorities would be put in place, probably by 1995. This followed a June 1991 consultation paper which had floated a choice of 13,20 and 24 all-purpose authorities. The 1992 announcement predicted the rebirth of many of the pre-1974 rural Welsh counties, and thus a radical change.

Consultation papers (not already discussed)

By issuing organisation and by date.

Department of the Environment

1. In September 1991 the DOE issued proposals to relax controls over telecommunications installations. In July 1992 a draft review of PPG 8 made it clear the relaxation would not extend to protected areas.
2. In October 1991 the DOE issued a consultation paper on four options for creating an Environment Agency, centred on the NRA (see p. 135 for Environment Committee response). Definite proposals were made in July 1992 (see the Diary section on p. 158).
3. In December 1991 the DOE issued draft planning policy advice on renewable energy which argued that, by their very nature, such developments, notably wind farms, would be in the countryside. To the wrath of most countryside organisations, the draft did not rule out national parks for such developments. See Environment Committee report on p. 136 for a wider discussion.
4. In January 1992 the DOE issued a draft Planning Policy Guidance Note on planning and noise to replace Circular 10/73. It proposed categories of noise which would largely determine the planning response.
5. In February 1992 the DOE issued a draft Planning Policy Guidance Note on nature conservation. Apart from emphasising the importance of conservation, it proposed more consultation over SSSI developments in zones around them, but did not propose a presumption against development within them, much to the opprobium of countryside pressure groups and the RTPI. See Circular 1/92 on SSSIs and SI 2805/91.
6. In February 1992 the DOE issued a consultation paper proposing controls over alterations to ecclesiastical buildings unless the religious groups involved could demonstrate an independent vetting process was in place. The RTPI argued for normal controls to apply.
7. In February 1992 the DOE published consultation proposals which would allow local authorities to reclaim derelict land not in their ownership and then recoup the cost as a financial contribution from the owner.
8. In March 1992 the DOE issued a consultation paper on updating mineral permissions granted in the 1950s and 1960s to modern standards. The mineral industry reacted with predictable outrage.
9. In March 1992 the DOE issued a draft Planning Policy Guidance Note on the coast. This proposed more stringent controls, including a partial ban on development along undeveloped stretches of coast. However,

it rejected the idea of elevating Heritage Coasts to a separate statutory designation.

10. In March 1992 the DOE issued a draft Planning Policy Guidance Note on tourism which emphasised the need for tourism to be included in development plans. However, tourism should not be treated as a special case, although major new developments, like tourist villages, could be acceptable in the countryside if suitable sites could be found.

11. In March 1992 the DOE issued a consultation paper outlining proposals for the methods to be used in identifying polluted waters under the Nitrates Directive.

12. In May 1992 the DOE issued a draft Circular on development in flood risk areas, which should be identified in local plans, and for which specific policies should be formulated. Coastal protection schemes could also be subjected to environmental assessment.

13. In May 1992 the DOE issued a consultation paper on planning obligations (see DOE Circular on p. 115) which proposed that anyone bound by an obligation could seek a modification after five years.

14. In June 1992 the DOE announced that a consultation paper would be issued proposing the end of Crown exemption from the planning system.

15. In June 1992 the DOE issued a consultation paper proposing an extension of Environmental Assessment to: trout farms; water treatment plants; wind generators; motorway and similar service areas; coast protection works; and golf courses.

16. In June 1992 the DOE issued draft guidance on planning and pollution control, which emphasised the need for planners not to duplicate the work of other agencies, but called on planners to identify sites where potential polluters could be directed and sites where it would be wrong to allow say housing because of the presence of a polluter.

17. In July 1992 the DOE issued a consultation paper on the use of water which stressed the need to make the most efficient use of existing resources.

18. In August 1992 the DOE issued a consultation paper on the frequency with which certain temporary uses like clay pigeon shooting, car boot sales and war games could operate without permission. These varied from no days for war games in SSSIs to 28 days for war games elsewhere, or 14 days for motor sports. The aim was to bring the situation into line with Scotland.

19. In August 1992 the DOE issued a consultation paper on illegal camping by gypsies and travellers. This proposed substantial new powers to prevent such use, and proposed a shift in policy away from providing sites for such people, and encouraging them to move into permanent accommodation, by reforming the Caravan Sites Act 1968.

20. In August 1992 the DOE issued a consultation paper on the future

role of parish councils which ruled out any increases in their rights or powers.
21. In September 1992 the DOE launched a consultation paper about the future of the New Forest. This involved setting up a new body to co-ordinate management of the area. However, this was a long way short of full National Park status, since although the new body would draw up a strategic plan, it would not have any day-to-day powers.

Department of Trade and Industry   In June 1992 the Department announced a review of the regional aid, the first major review since 1984. Under the proposals North-West Scotland, including the Hebrides, would lose assisted area status and thus also EC aid status. Other rural areas would have the size of their areas reduced.

Maff

1. In November 1991 MAFF issued a consultation paper on the Environmental Aspects of Hill Farming. This included proposals for more ESAs (see p. 148), a new code of Good Upland Management (see p. 158) and changes to the Hill Livestock Compensatory Allowance (HLCA) scheme to prevent overgrazing (see p. 113).
2. In December 1991 MAFF issued a consultation paper on the criteria for licensing badger sets under the Badgers Act 1991; see Diary for further developments.
3. In July 1992 MAFF announced proposals to change the Agricultural Training Board into an independent non-statutory organisation.
4. In October 1992 MAFF issued a second consultation paper on farm tenancies which reiterated the suggestion made 18 months earlier (see Volume II, p. 107) that there should be no minimum term for a tenancy.

Scottish Office Environment Department

1. In September 1991 the Department issued a consultation paper on the demolition of houses under Section 44 of the Planning and Compensation Act.
2. In September 1991 the Department issued a draft circular on guidance as to how the enforcement procedures under the Planning and Compensation Act 1991 should be implemented; see SOEND Circulars for subsequent advice.
3. In October 1991 the Department sought views on a draft National Planning Policy Guideline on Land for Business and Industry.
4. In December 1991 the Department sought views on draft guidance on the location of marine fish farms. This identified 44 very sensitive areas, mainly major sea lochs on the west coast, where severe constraint

should be placed on further development, and added on to the list 25 sites identified in 1989.

5. In January 1992 the Department published a consultation paper proposing the establishment of a Scottish Environment Protection Agency by 1995. The proposal hoped to create a strong and independent body with an overview across a wide range of environmental issues, capable of taking a strong line with the public and private sectors.

6. In March 1992 the Department issued a consultation paper on planning controls over agriculture and forestry roads. This looked beyond the 1992 GDO which introduced a notification regime (see p. 111) and set out options ranging from the *status quo* to full planning control.

7. In June 1992 the Department issued a consultation paper as to how the process of reviewing post-1948 mineral permissions under the 1981 Minerals Act could be improved. It set out four main options.

8. In July 1992 the Department sought views on a draft National Planning Policy Guideline on Land for Mineral Working.

9. In August 1992 the Department sought views on a draft National Planning Policy Guideline and a draft Planning Advice Note on Archaeology and Planning.

Welsh Office   In September 1991 the Office sought views on draft policy guidance concerning the operation of the new development plan system as from 1992.

Countryside Commission   In 1992 the Commission sought views on a proposed Pennine Bridle-way (CCP 377) which followed a submission they had made in 1991 to the DOE in CCP 349. They also published a consultation document in July 1992 over the proposed National Trail along Hadrian's Wall Path in CCP 391.

National Rivers Authority   In November 1991 the NRA announced proposals to create as many as 750 vulnerability zones in which a great variety of activities and developments would be banned to curb groundwater pollution. In December 1991 the NRA issued another consultation paper, this time on Statutory Water Quality Objectives, which proposed setting legal standards for water quality in order to control pollution from farming.

National Farmers Union   In October 1992 the NFU submitted a discussion document to the government on Water Resources to ensure that farms had adequate supplies in the light of forcast increases in demand of up to 45 per cent by 2021.

Audit Commission   In September 1992 the Commission issued a consultation paper on Citizen's Charter Performance Indicators which included five indicators for land-use planning including the percentage of decisions which are materially different from the local plan.

A Diary of events 1 September 1991 to 31 October 1992

September 1991
Scottish Office rejects Countryside Commission for Scotland proposal for National Parks; see Volume II, p. 118.

October 1991
English Nature's refusal to confirm designation of a peatland SSSI in Cumbria annoys Peat Consortium of amenity groups.

November 1991
English Nature fights back over peat by releasing a statement on 'Lowland Peat Policy'.
DOE admits in written answer to Commons that 21 per cent of English hedges were lost between 1984 and 1990.
It is announced that Michael Dower will succeed Adrian Phillips as Director of Countryside Commission (see pp. 63), and Fiona Reynolds will take over from Andrew Purkis at CPRE.

December 1991
European Environment Council agrees Habitat's Directive which aims to establish a network of special areas for conservation by the year 2000.
English Nature and National Trust sign Statement of Intent concerning nature conservation of Trust property.
Countryside Commission decides on boundary of new National Forest.

January 1992
DOE responds to 1991 report on National Parks, *Fit for the Future* (see volume II, p. 117) by agreeing to create independent national park authorities, after consultation. The DOE also promised a new statutory statement of national park purposes and a restatement of the Silkin test which only allows major developments in the parks if there is an overriding national interest. The DOE also announced that the New Forest would be designated a landscape of national significance. *Planning*, 7/2/92, pp. 14–17; 24/1/92, p. 1; and 31/1/92, p. 4; and *Ecos*, 131, 1992, pp. 61–2.
English Nature signs agreement with Fisons to save key peat areas from extraction.
MAFF announce pilot study to help farmers dispose of organic waste in a less polluting way.

February 1992

Law Lords weaken the so-called Steinberg doctrine which in 1988 declared that a new building should do more than avoiding harm to a conservation area's character but should actively enhance it. The new decision, which arose from an appeal against refusal of a vicarage in the Lake District, returned to the pre-1988 definition of a new building being neutral in its effect.

Peat Consortium attack previous month's agreement as a sell-out which allows Fisons to continue existing peat diggings.

English Nature and Ministry of Defence agree to continue an agreement first made in 1988 to enhance the conservation value of the Ministry's land holdings, which have been described as the first wildlife estate in England. New development plan system comes into operation (see PPG. 12 and SI 2794/91).

March 1992

DOE announces successful schemes under the Rural Housing Programme. The allocations should support the creation of 1,016 new units from 138 schemes in 112 local authorities, at a cost of £30 million.

DOE rejects 8 new settlement schemes along the A45 corridor in Cambridgeshire in the same week as revised PPG3 advises against such new villages.

DOE welcomes and broadly endorses Countryside Commission's policy statement on heritage coasts and publishes draft PPG note on coastal planning; see p. 152.

Sports Council issues statement on countryside and water recreation taking PPG17 as its starting-point. It advocates the preparation of strategic plans at national, regional and local levels.

April 1992

Forestry Commission further formalises the division of its work into the Forest Enterprise and the Forest Authority.

Planning Inspectorate becomes an Executive Agency under the Next Steps Initiative with six main performance measures.

Scottish Natural Heritage takes over the work of the Countryside Commission for Scotland and the Nature Conservancy Council, and inherits a funding crisis arising from expenditure on management agreements and other compensation payments under the 1981 Wildlife and Countryside Act. One of its first tasks will be to examine the desirability of creating natural heritage areas, if not national parks, which remain on the agenda in spite of the September 1991 rejection.

After the election, Michael Howard, a legal planner, becomes Secretary of State at the DOE.

May 1992

Creation of Department of Natural Heritage forces a reallocation of listed building and conservation area functions; see DOE Circular 20/92. The new Department is also given responsibility for tourism and sport.

English Nature announces new schemes to safeguard estuaries and to fund County Wildlife Trusts' work in SSSIs.

The International Centre for Protected Landscapes at Aberystwyth University promotes itself via a new newsletter, *Protected Landscapes*.

June 1992

Prime Minister reveals 26 committees of the Cabinet which exist to take Cabinet-level decisions and to co-ordinate work between Ministries. These include an Environment Committee on which the DOE and MAFF have equal status.

Scottish Natural Heritage launch detailed agenda for investment in Scotland's natural heritage for replenishing the natural capital depleted in living memory and then to use it in a sustainable way in the future.

Rural Development Commission launches a Rural Social Partnership Fund under the 'Action for the Countryside Package' (see p. 146), and a scheme to allow options to be held on sites for affordable rural housing while the details are being worked out.

MAFF launches a 'Code of Good Upland Management' in the form of a booklet sent to all farmers claiming payments for sheep and cattle in the uplands.

CPRE calls for a new direction for forestry policy centred on environmental principles and society's needs.

Three Welsh regions receive £26 million from EC structural funds to combat rural decline in Dyfed, Gwynedd and Powys.

July 1992

DOE announces structure of new Environment Agency. It will bring together the functions of the NRA, Her Majesty's Inspectorate of Pollution and the waste regulation work of local authorities. This followed an October 1991 consultation paper (see p. 152). The government promised legislation at the earliest opportunity for this substantial new public body.

Southern Water Authority acquitted from causing 'ecological vandalism' by House of Lords under a technicality. Under a loophole in the 1981 Wildlife and Countryside Act those causing damage to SSSIs can only be prosecuted if they are 'occupiers'. In this case the Authority were not occupiers.

English Nature announce new grant aid of £60,000 to aid farmers in managing land around SSSIs.

MAFF publish 'Code of Good Agricultural Practice for the Protection of Air'.

August 1992

Rumours abound about plans to privatise the Forestry Commission.

Scottish Office commission consultants to examine the future of Scottish water management, including a privatisation option, in light of possible reorganisation of the regional councils currently in charge.

EC drops five charges against Britain for failing to conduct Environmental Assessments for five major developments, including the Twyford Down extension of the M3, scene of major demonstrations in the spring. Two further charges remained, however, over Oxleas Wood due to be bulldozed for the East London River Crossing and an extension to an oil refinery at Grangemouth on the Firth of Forth.

Meanwhile, the Institute of Environmental Assessment proposed a professional registration scheme for environmental auditors.

September 1992

DOE survey reveals that 90 per cent of local authorities expect to complete district-wide local plans by target date of 1996.

Earl of Selborne takes over from Sir Frederick Holliday as Chairman of the Joint Nature Conservation Committee.

MAFF launch an updated 'Heather and Grass Burning Code of Practice'.

Highlands and Islands Enterprise issue first edition of a new bulletin on their work entitled *The Brief*.

Peak National Park welcome Strategy Report for Trans-Pennine transport which rules out substantial road building through the Park.

October 1992

English Nature launch 'Campaign for a Living Coast' to encourage the adoption of good conservation practices. At the same time their funding was increased by £1.04 million to enhance lowland peatland sites, to boost work for Special Protection Areas and to increase the rate of concluding management agreements. English Nature also launched a new newsletter for owners and managers of SSSIs entitled *SITE LINES*.

MAFF announced the arrangements for licensing interference with badger sets under the Badgers Act 1991; see p. 108.

It is reported that the EC will prosecute Britain for neglecting to set up enough protected areas for wild birds, and for failing to regulate shooting of certain birds.

Hampshire threatens to leave SERPLAN in showdown over row between Hampshire's policy for 73,000 new houses and SERPLAN's target of 92,000 between 1991 and 2006.

Table 8.6   *List of new protected areas and designations*

In September 1991 the Peak National Park completed two new access agreements to bring the total to 81 square miles or nearly 15 per cent of the Park.

In October 1991 the DOE designated Rutland Water as a Special Protection Area (SPA) under the EC Birds Directive, and as a Wetland of International Importance under the Ramsar Convention. It was the first such designation in England since January 1989.

In November 1991 the DOE designated three further sites as Ramsar Wetlands. They were Llyn Tegid and Llyn Idwal in North Wales, and Esthwaite Water in the Lake District.

In December 1991 the DOE announced the designation of two more sites as SPAs and Ramsar Wetlands. They were Walmore Common in Gloucestershire and Abberton Reservoir in Essex. In the same month English Nature declared an extension to the Ribble Estuary National Nature Reserve (NNR) making it, at over 4,000 ha, England's largest.

In March 1992 three wetlands were classified by the DOE as SPAs and as Ramsar Wetlands. They were the Exe Estuary, Old Hall Marshes on the Blackwater Estuary and part of Lindisfarne. Chippenham Fen in East Anglia was also listed as a Ramsar site. These additions brought the total number of Ramsar sites to 54, covering 216,000 ha.

In June 1992 the Caerlaverlock NNR on the shores of the Solway was extended by 2,200 ha. In the same month Scottish Natural Heritage announced an increase in the Glencripesdale NNR by Loch Sunart from 93 to 609 ha. The ancient native woodlands around Loch Sunart are amongst the most important sites for nature conservation in Britain.

In July 1992 the DOE designated Porton Down on the Wiltshire-Hampshire border as an SPA, bringing the total to 53, covering over 150,000 ha.

Literature list, 1991–2

184 Selected publications

Format: Author, *Title*, Publisher, Date. If title is unclear a subtitle is provided in parentheses. Brief review, or source where a review may be found, or quotation from a review, may then follow.

General publications

Aslet, C. and Heath, M., *Countryblast: how your countryside needs you*, John Murray, 1991, £11.95. Popular polemic illustrated by Heath cartoons

Civic Trust, *Audit of the environment: final report*, the Trust, 1992, £4.50. A survey of 650 local amenity societies and their views on planning. Recommends a ban on new village developments in the absence of public transport, and more financial support for affordable housing in rural areas. *Planning*, 7/2/92, p. 8

Cloke, P. (ed.), *Policy and change in Thatcher's Britain*, Pergamon, 1992, £35.00 or £11.95. Contains a chapter by Paul Cloke on the countryside which argues that the need to appease conflicting interests in rural areas led to a series of pragmatic rather than ideological policy changes in the 1980s. The only consistent theme was a deteriorating situation for the disadvantaged as the countryside became an ever increasingly popular site for middle-class life-styles and environments, e.g. golf courses

Coker, A. and Richards, C., *Valuing the environment: economic approaches to environmental evaluation*, Belhaven, 1992, £32.00

Council for the Protection of Rural England, *Putting our own house in order—the UK's responsibilities to the Earth Summit*, CPRE, 1992, £2.50. Exhorted the government to examine its own backyard, where road and house building are causing massive landscape loss, and hedgerows and woodlands are being mismanaged, before they take a high moral tone at the Earth Summit in Rio in June 1992. See Annual Review, p. 149 and *Planning*, 6/3/92, p. 5

——*65 years of achievement*, CPRE, 1991. A brief year-by-year account of achievement, e.g. 1973: 'CPRE attacked Government plans for release of green-belt land and dropping of presumption against development of white land'

Countryside Commission, *At work in the countryside*, CCP 348, 1991, and CCP 386, 1992, free leaflets, outlining Commission's programme for 1991–3

——*Caring for the countryside: a policy agenda for England in the nineties*, CCP 351, 1991, £2.00. This is a revised form of the consultation document CCP 336 issued by the Commission in April 1991 (see Volume II, p. 103). The vision of an environmentally healthy, beautiful, diverse, accessible and thriving countryside is maintained, as is the big new idea of a 'green dividend' to be potentially paid from the 15 per cent of land thought to be surplus to farming needs. The agenda calls for this land to be put into a 'Conservation Lands Programme', in which Countryside Stewardship, long-term set-aside, new woodlands and Environmentally Sensitive Areas would be used to create land for conservation and public access. Remaining farmland would also be the subject of conservation grants, especially in the uplands and National Parks. Elsewhere, the agenda proposed forestry strategies for England, and an integrated strategy for the countryside to co-ordinate the detailed agenda for recreation, traffic, etc. The heavy emphasis on landscape and paying farmers to manage land was, however, criticised as not being radical enough, and not being social enough, by Curry in *Ecos*, **12** (4), 1991, pp. 63–4, and Fyson in *The Planner*, 1/11/91, p. 3

——*Countryside Education and Training Directory 1992*, CCP 363, 1992, £2.50. Lists with brief details several hundred courses

——*Your countryside our concern*, CCP 384, 1992, free. 18-page booklet about the Commission

—— *A commitment to quality*, CCP 400, 1992, free. Leaflet setting out the service standards set by the Commission as a contribution to the Citizen's Charter

Countryside Recreation Research Advisory Group, *Our priceless countryside— should it be priced?*, School of Advanced Urban Studies, Bristol, 1992, £10.00. Proceedings of the Group's 1991 conference on the application of environmental economics to the countryside

Dargie, T. and Briggs, D., *State of the Scottish environment*, Scottish Wildlife and Countryside Link, Perth, 1992, £5.00. A broad-ranging yet concise report which represents a solid contribution to the debates about the Scottish environment, *Scottish Geographical Magazine*, **108**, (2), 1992, p. 132

Department of Environment, *Policy appraisal and the environment*, HMSO, 1991, £6.75. Produced as one of the pledges in the 1990 White Paper on *This Common Inheritance* (see Volume II, pp. 86–7), this document tells middle-ranking civil servants how environmental factors can be added to other factors when making a decision. *Planning*, 27/9/91, p. 1

Dickens, P., *Society and nature: towards a green social theory*, Simon and Schuster, 1992

Duncan of Jordanstone College of Art and University of Dundee, *Occasional Papers 30 and 31*, the College, 1989. Contains a numerous and diverse set of articles on rural planning matters

Eckersley, R., *Environmentalism and political theory*, UCL Press, 1992, £30.00 and £10.95. According to O'Riordan in a prepublication review for the publishers, this text synthesises a vast range of ideas into a simple, powerful vision, which replaces fear of catastrophe with the hope of emancipation.

Ellis, A. and Brennan, A., *Ethics for environmentalists* and *Environmental philosophy*, Centre for Philosophy and Public Affairs, University of St Andrews, 1990, £8.00. Three booklets—the third is a bibliography—which provide a user-friendly guide to attempts to evolve a theory to back up our intuitive beliefs about nature. *Ecos*, **12** (3), pp. 60–1

Flynn, A., *The English ideology: party politics and rural policy-making*, Avebury, 1994, £35.00. Studies the role that the major political parties have played in actively shaping countryside issues from agricultural policy to the environment

Friends of the Earth, *Off the treadmill*: a way forward for farmers and the countryside, Friends, 1991, £4.95. Maps out a complete agricultural policy aimed at achieving five broad objectives: landscape and nature quality; satisfying work; animal welfare; and sustainability. This is to be attained by a less-intensive agriculture using three mechanisms: nitrogen quotas; farm management plans under regionalised ESA schemes; and increased tariff protection. *Ecos*, **13** (1), 1992, pp. 66–8, and *Farmers Weekly*, 15/11/91 p. 21

Gilg, A., *Countryside planning policies for the 1990s*, CAB International, 1991, £40.00. A survey of 1,500 publications outlining policy options for the countryside at both the holistic and sectoral level. 'An extremely useful guide to recent policy developments', *Land Use Policy*, October 1992, pp. 306–7; 'a massive effort of both analysis and compilation', *Scottish Geographical Magazine*, 1992, pp. 60–1

—— (ed.), *Restructuring the countryside: environmental policy in practice*, Avebury, 1992, £35.00. A set of substantially revised conference papers and specially commissioned papers which are divided into underlying issues and concepts, and case studies. Main themes are the food system, the restructing of agriculture, set-aside and nitrates.

Green Alliance, *The failure of the departmental Annual Reports to reflect integrated policy-making*, the Alliance, 99 Wellington St, London, WC2E 7BN. A review of the annual reports of 19 government departments has revealed that they have failed to set out their green credentials à la the 1990 White Paper, see p. 126, and *Ecos*, **13** (1), 1992, p. 70

Harper, S., *The greening of rural planning*, Belhaven, 1992, £35.00

Hogwood, B.W., *Trends in British public policy: do governments make any difference?* Open University Press, 1992, £32.50 and £10.99. Encourages the reader to develop a healthy scepticism

Institute for European Environmental Policy, *Green or mean?*, Council for the Protection of Rural England, 1992, £6.00. Argues that the £316 million allocated to the agri-environment section of the May 1992 CAP reforms represents only 1 per cent of the CAP budget or only £1 per acre. Instead it advocates that 10 per cent should be allocated by 1997. *Planning*, 5/11/92 p. 4

International Union for Nature Conservation, Worldwide Fund for Nature and United Nations Environment Programme, *Caring for the Earth*, Earthscan, 1991, £9.95. An update of the 1980 World Conservation Strategy, which develops more clearly the concept of sustainable development and what this means for political economy. *Ecos*, **12** (4), 1991, pp. 3–4

McCormick, J., *British politics and the environment*, Earthscan, 1991, £7.95. A worthy attempt to fill a gap in the literature, but fails because it concentrates on the views of pressure groups outside power, rather than those within the corridors of power who prefer sectoral division rather than the integration that green policies need. *Ecos*, **12** (4), 1991, pp. 59–60

Marsh, D. and Rhodes, R. (eds), *Implementing Thatcherite policies: audit of an era*, Open University Press, 1992, £35.00 and £13.99. Includes chapters on 'Environmental Policy' and the 'CAP and agricultural policy'

Natural Environment Research Council, *The land of Britain: land-use research for the future*, the Council, 1992. Contains the Councils' mission statement, which aims to ensure that comprehensive land-use information and predictions are available to policy-makers; this document examines the issues involved

Norton, B., *Toward unity among environmentalists*, Oxford University Press, 1991, £25.00

Organisation for Economic Co-operation and Development (OECD), *Environmental policy: how to apply economic instruments*, HMSO, 1991, £15.00

O'Riordan, T. and Weale, A., *Greening the machinery of government*, Friends of the Earth, 1990, £2.50. According to the authors the major inadequacy at present is the lack of any process to integrate environmental policies between sectors; this however would go counter to the long established tradition of establishing agencies for individual problems. *Ecos*, **12** (3), 1991, pp. 54–6

Pearce, D., Turner, K. and Bateman, I., *Environmental economics*. Harvester Wheatsheaf, 1992, £16.99. An introduction for students with no economics background

Porritt, J. *et al.*, *Save the Earth* Dorling Kindersley, 1991, £14.99. Doom and gloom facts are used to argue for sustainable development. *Ecos*, **13** (1), 1992, pp. 68–9

Royal Society for the Protection of Birds, *Our countryside our future*, the Society,

1992, £5.00. Because intensive farming is still destroying wildlife the RSPB calls for 30 per cent of farmland to be put into ESA schemes by 2000, for one million hectares of land to be put into wildlife set-aside by 2000, and for national rural land-use policies. *Planning*, 18/9/92, p. 3, and *Farmers Weekly*, 11/11/92, p. 21

Selman, P., *Environmental planning*, Paul Chapman, 1992, £13.95. This is a book that should be read by all students of rural planning. It takes an ecological approach and could perhaps be subtitled 'Countryside planning in practice'. It is divided into five chapters. Chapter One sets the scene by examining the context in which planning operates. This is followed by three lengthy chapters which form the core of the book: 'Productive uses of land, namely agriculture and forestry'; 'Amenity uses of land; and 'Industry's use of the environment'* which concentrates on (EIA*). The final chapter on integration reiterates Selman's views that the three C's, Collaboration, Consultation and Consensus, can be used by all sorts of rural planning organisations to achieve *ad hoc* integrated management ahead of legislation. In the longer term legislation could introduce the idea of integrated environmental management backed up by state of the environment Reports. This would replace the present nature of government which is over-based on vertical divisions of power with a horizontal integration. In the mean time the vertical nature of current power forces Selman into at times a bitty and repetitious presentation. This is only a minor criticism of a very readable account of planning from the field rather than the office, or the political economist's couch (the Editor)

*EIA = Environmental Impact Assessment

Taylor, A., *Choosing our future: a practical politics for the environment*, Routledge, 1992, £30.00 and £8.99. A personal but rigorous analysis from a leading Labour politician

Turner, R.K. (ed.), *Sustainable environmental economics and management: principles and practice*, Belhaven, 1992, £36.00 and £10.95. Completely rewritten 2nd edition

Agriculture

Agriculture, Fisheries and Food, Ministry of, *Our farming future*, the Ministry, 1991, free. A policy statement (i.e. negotiating stance at Brussels) from MAFF which calls for further reforms to the CAP, more emphasis on marketing by farmers and extensions to environmental programmes, notably more ESAs and more research into organic farming. Overriding all this is an endorsement of cross-compliance, but according to Crabtree, writing in *Ecos*, **13** (1), 1992, pp. 67–68, there is' nothing very new' here

Arkleton Trust, *Rural change in Europe, Second review meeting, July 1989*, the Trust, 1991. 447 A4 pages which record the data and papers presented to the meeting by 29 researchers involved in the project. A massive source of very useful information on the nitty gritty of farm level change

—— *European pluriactivity programme funded by EC and ESRC*:

    a. *Use made of structures policy by farm households*, 1990, 2 Vols, £40.00

b. *Proceedings of the Braemar Colloquium*, 1991, £13.00

c. *Farm family pluriactivity in Europe* 1991, £12.00. A series of maps detailing pluriactivity in 24 case study areas across the EC, backed up by text, written by A. Brun and A.M. Fuller

d. *Rural poverty and deprivation in Europe: report of 1990 symposium*
—— *Rural policy issues. Papers from recipients of the Europe-North America exchange programme*, edited by M. Tracy, the Trust, 1991

Centre for Management in Agriculture, *Food: its production, marketing and consumption*, complied by H.F. Marks, the Centre, University of Reading, 1992, £10.00. 113 pages of very useful tables and graphics about agriculture, with accompanying text. It concludes that no one anywhere in the food chain is benefiting from current policies

Errington, A. and Tranter, R., *Getting out of farming? Part Two: the farmers*, Department of Agriculture, Reading University, 1991, £7.50. A resurvey of an 1986 survey of 1,269 farmers which reveals that 70 per cent were still planning to increase output and that few were planning to leave farming. *Journal of Agricultural Economics*, **43** (2), 1992, pp. 297–8

Marsden, T., Lowe, P. and Whatmore, S. (eds), *Regulating agriculture*: Volume 5 in 'Critical perspectives in rural change' Series, David Fulton, 1992, £30.00

Marsh, J. (ed), *The changing role of Common Agricultural Policy*, Belhaven, 1991, £27.50. A set of essays written by a brainstorming group which is intellectually stimulating but does not provide a textbook list of changes

Murphy, M., *The economics of organic farming*, Land Economy Unit, University of Cambridge, 1992. A study of 238 organic farms which showed that they were making very small profits or quite often losses. In reply, the organic farm lobby argued that conventional farms would also do as badly if CAP help was cut. *Farmers Weekly*, 10/7/92, p. 37 and 17/7/92, p. 29

Royal Agricultural Society of England, *The state of agriculture in the UK*, the Society, 1991, £10.00. A 77-page report of a study group chaired by Sir Derek Barber, former chairman of the Countryside Commission. Two core issues were targeted, the sustainability of modern farming, and reform of the CAP. In the first case the report finds that much of the concern over the damaging effects of farming is misconceived and that new technologies will reduce any damage even further. In the second case the report argues for progressive price reductions with support for farmers over a 7–20 year period to cushion the blow. This support should not however be channelled via environmental programmes, since these fudge the two separate issues of farm profits and environmental management. In a review of the report, Crabtree, in *Ecos*, **13** (1), 1992, pp. 66–8, concludes that few farmers will support the policy and that the 'lack of environmental concern is provocative in the extreme'

World-Wide Fund for Nature, *Reforming the EC agricultural policy*, the Fund, 1991. A discussion paper which argues that environmental concerns should be fully integrated into farm policy, and agricultural policy should not be the only means of supporting the rural economy. *Farmers Weekly*, 6/12/91, p 16

Agriculture and the environment

Addiscott, T.M., Whitmore, A.P. and Poulson, D.S., *Farming, fertilisers and the nitrate problem*, CAB International, 1991, £13.50. Argues that limiting fertiliser use is an over-simplistic solution, and that changing crop production to mop up excess nitrate may be a better solution

Agriculture, Fisheries and Food, Ministry of, *MAFF environment research strategy and requirements document 1992–94*, the Ministry, 1992. Sets out the strategy for research within MAFF. Some £8.4 million is to be spent in 1992/3 on research into the control of agricultural pollution from nitrates, other nutrients and from farm wastes. Conservation in farmland management, farm woodlands, soil protection, environmentally sensitive disposal of crop residues and soil erosion will take a further £6 million
—— *Environmental aspects of hill farming*, the Ministry, 1991
Countryside Commission, *Handbook for the Hedgerow Incentive Scheme*, the Commission, CCP 383, 1992. A handbook for farmers explaining how a new scheme launched in July 1992 will work. Under the scheme farmers enter a 10-year agreement aimed at restoring declining hedges, maintaining them as historic parts of the landscape and conserving them as important wildlife habitats. To this end grants are available at various rates, for example: gapping-up £1.75 per metre; hedge laying £2 per metre; and coppicing £1.50 per metre
—— *Countryside Stewardship: an outline*, the Commission CCP 346, revised 1992 edition, 1992. A booklet to accompany the 1992 scheme which expanded the 1991 pilot scheme (see Volume II, p. 99) by targeting two new landscape types and providing new access agreements. In the first year 30,000 ha had been comitted to the scheme
—— *Hedgerow Incentive Scheme Leaflet*, CCP 393, 1992. See above
Friends of the Earth, *Environmentally Sensitive Areas—assessment and recommendations*, the Friends, 1992, £7.00. Argues that current policies are too weak and diffuse. If ESAs are to work, they need to be larger, compulsory, be better funded and payments should be linked to a farm conservation plan. *Farmers Weekly*, 1/11/92, p. 16 and *Planning*, 1/11/92, p. 20
Howarth, W. and Rodgers, C. (eds), *Agriculture, conservation and land use: law and policy issues for rural areas*, University of Wales Press, 1992, £35.00
Miller, F.A. (ed.), *Agricultural policy and the environment*, Centre for Agricultural Strategy, 1991, £13.50. 6 conference papers from 1991, including those by John Gummer, Howard Newby and Bryn Green

Conservation and designated areas

Appleton. J., *The funny thing about landscape: cautionary tales for environmentalists*, Book Guild, 1991, £9.50. In spite of the title a profoundly serious book from a well-informed author. *Ecos*, **12** (3), 1991, p. 57
Association of County Councils, *National Parks: the new partnership*, the Association, 1992, £5.00. Withdraws earlier objections to the idea of independent National Park Authorities in the light of the goverment's decision to accept the recommendation by the *Fit for the Future* report to set up such authorities; see pp. 156. Most of the document deals with how these new authorities should relate to the County Councils (CC), for example, in Structure Planning the Lake District model, where Cumbria CC does most of the leg work but the Park makes the policy, is proposed
Council of Europe, *The Berne Convention on nature conservation*, HMSO, 1991, £3.35
Countryside Commission, *National Parks in England and Wales*, the Commission, CCP208, rev. edn., 1992, free. Publicity leaflet about the Parks, both generally and individually

—— *Landscape change in the National Parks*, the Commission, 1991, £15.00. A study for the Commission by Silsoe College using air photos from the 1970s and late-1980s to show that coniferous forest had increased by 11 per cent, cultivated land by 13 per cent and developed land by 5 per cent. In contrast, rough pasture had decreased by 11 per cent and moor and heath by 2 per cent. It is argued that though these changes are relatively small, they could be serious in either small areas, or could mask a loss in landscape quality. Most of the document deals with the changes in each park; for those wishing more detail a volume for each park is available from the College at £50.00

—— *National Parks marketing and conservation survey*, the Commission, CCP 354, 1991, £4.50. A consultant's report which records that £26 million was spent by businesses and £2 million by public bodies on promoting visits to the Parks. Recommends that the Parks should attempt to influence this promotion more closely and should increase funds for conservation from those businesses which benefit from the Parks

—— *Action for National Parks*, the Commission, CCP 394, 1992, free. Following the government's endorsement of the *Fit for the Future* report the Commission in this 8-page document calls on it to put its proposals into legislative form, particularly the restatement of National Park purposes, the creation of independent authorities and strengthening the presumption against major new developments in the Parks. The document also contains advice on how to implement detailed proposals in the report

—— *Areas of Outstanding Natural Beauty: a policy statement*, the Commission, CCP 356, 1991, £2.00. Second edition of 1990 statement (CCP 302 reported in Volume II, p. 117) which includes a 1991 endorsement of the policy by the Secretary of State for the Environment, and his hope that more AONB officers will be added to the four already in post

—— *AONB management plans: advice on their format and content*, the Commission, CCP 352, 1992, £4.00. A 38-page users' guide to the preparation of plans which are meant to promote awareness of the AONB, to agree a set of common aims, and to co-ordinate the activities of land users

—— *Directory of Areas of Outstanding Natural Beauty*, the Commission, CCP 379, 1992, £17.50. A second edition of a 1989 directory (CCD54) which provides information about pressures on and policies for all the 39 AONBs

—— *The East Hampshire landscape*, the Commission, CCP 358, 1991, £7.00. An assessment of the AONB's landscape produced jointly by consultants and local councils

—— *The Tamar Valley landscape*, the Commission, CCP 364, 1991, £6.00. An assessment of the AONB's landscape by consultants, the eighth in the series

—— *The Chilterns landscape*, the Commission, CCP 392 1992, £7.50. Another AONB assessment produced by consultants

—— *The Chichester Harbour landscape*, the Commission, CCP381, 1992, £7.00

—— *Protected landscapes in the United Kingdom*, the Commission, CCP 362, 1992, £12.50. An update of the first edition written by Duncan and Judy Poore. It has two aims, to illustrate the variety of scenery, and to show how protection is achieved in practice. It does this by some excellent pen portraits and photographs of designated areas, notably National Parks

English Nature, *Erosion and vegetation change on the saltmarshes of Essex and North Kent between 1972 and 1988*, Nature, 1992, £20.00. Records an alarming loss of saltmarsh, up to 49 per cent in some areas

Evans, D., *A history of nature conservation in Britain*, Routledge, 1991, £45.00 and £14.99. A readable and thorough book which not only recounts the story but throws light on the wider issues and politics of conservation, most interestingly perhaps not from an academic's or practitioner's view but from the view of a working policeman. *Ecos*, **13**(1), 1992, p. 64, and *Countryside Commission News*, **53**, 1992, p. 7

Fladmark, J.M., Mulvagh, G. and Evans. B., *Tomorrows architectural heritage— landscape and buildings in the countryside*, Mainstream Publishing, 1991, £14.99. Takes vernacular architecture as a starting-point and shows how its principles can be put into practice. *Planning*, 27/3/91, p. 7

Spellerberg, I.F., *Evaluation and assessment for conservation*, Chapman and Hall, 1992, £29. 95. Substantial expansion of previous book *Ecological Evaluation for Conservation*

Wildlife Link, *SSSI's—a health check*, Link, 1991. A report by T. Rowell which shows that up to 40 per cent of SSSIs have experienced damage, and that 21 per cent are threatened. The proposed solution is more positive management agreements, and better monitoring and review. *Planning*, 17/11/92, pp. 6–7

Extractive industries including water

British Coal, *Opencast goal mining in Great Britain*, British Coal, 1991. Six sites are refused planning permission for ten that are given permission. *Planning*, 25/10/91, p. 2

Council for the Protection of Rural England, *Water on demand? The case for demand management in water charging policy*, the Council, 1991, £6.00. More efficiency in water use is urgent and so the CPRE advocates more recycling by industry, more on-farm storage of water and more efficient irrigation, water metering for houses, and better leakage control

Department of Environment, *Environmental effects of surface mineral working: report by Roy Waller Associates*, HMSO, 192, £16.00

Liberal Democrats, *Coming clean on the water we drink*, Democrats, 1992. More than 10 million people are drinking water that breaks EC limits on nitrates and pesticides, and so the Liberals advocate stricter controls, better management of water and the establishment of an Environment Protection Agency. *Farmers Weekly*, 10/1/92, p. 14

National Rivers Authority, *Water resources development strategy*, NRA, 1992, free. In spite of plans for major water transfers (but not a water grid) and better use of existing supplies, the NRA forecasts the need for more reservoirs in the south in the next 20 years. *Planning*, 20/3/92, p. 24

—— *The influence of agriculture on the quality of natural waters*, NRA, 1991, £10.00. A survey of 10,400 farms which shows that 42 per cent of farmers were polluting rivers or at high risk of doing so, and that between 1979 and 1990 the number of pollution incidents doubled to 3,000 a year. *Guardian*, January 1992, and *Farmers Weekly*, 24/1/92, p. 15

—— *Water pollution incidents in England and Wales 1990*, NRA, 1992. A record 28,143 incidents were recorded. *Farmers Weekly*, 7/2/92, p. 23

Royal Society for Nature Conservation, *Losing ground—leaving the stone age*, the Society, 1992. Highlights the need to control the aggregates industry more closely, by devising a new sustainable minerals policy. *Planning*, 15/11/92, p. 7

Walsh, F., Lee, N. and Wood, C., *The environmental assessment of opencast coal mines*, Department of Planning and Landscape, University of Manchester, 1991, £5.00

Warren. L., *Marine fish farming and the Crown Estate*, World Wide Fund for Nature, 1991. A report endorsed by WWF which would give planners power to control fish farming, in the context of national policy and compulsory environmental assessments. *Planning*, 1/11/91, p. 6

Forestry

Adam Smith Institute, *Wood for the trees*, written by D. Mason, the Institute, 1991. Calls for the Forestry Commission's activities to be exposed to the full discipline of the market place. *Ecos*, **13**(1), 1992, p. 71

Benson, J.F. and Willis, K.G., *Valuing informal recreation on the Forestry Commission Estate*, HMSO, 1992, £7.50. Visitors to 14 Forestry Districts were surveyed between 1987 and 1988 and the Clawson-Knetsch method was used to produce an annual consumer surplus per visit of £2 at 1988 prices. The total surplus was estimated at £53 million, five times more than the £10 million estimated by a National Audit Office study. Areally, the average surplus is £47 per hectare, varying from £424 in the New Forest to only £1 per hectare in Loch Awe

Council for the Protection of Rural England, *Community Forest Charter*, CPRE, 1991. Proposes a 12-point charter to prevent Community Forests being used as a back-door for damaging developments. These include environmental assessments and the approval of forest plans through the development plan process. *Ecos*, **12**(4), 1991, pp. 64–5

Countryside Commission, *After the Great Storm: an assessment of two landscape rehabilitation schemes programmes supported by Task Force Trees*, CCP 355, the Commission, 1991, £6.50. Consultant's report which concludes that the majority of planting is making a positive contribution to the landscape, and argues that real benefits have been gained from preparing a Landscape Rehabilitation Strategy in each area

—— *Silvanus: the first four years*, CCP 360, the Commission, 1991, £4.50. Sponsors report on a six-year experiment, 1986–92, to restore farm woods in south-west. Progress on the project's four aims has been patchy. Woods have begun to be restored but much remains to be done. Employment has, however, been provided. In the short term income is low, and will not grow until 20–30 years' time, and likewise the market for timber from neglected farm woods remains gloomy

Forestry Authority, *Forest Recreation: Guidelines*, HMSO, 1992, £7.00. One of a series of six guidelines designed to pass on 70 years of Commission experience to all managers of woodland in both the private and public sector. All forms of recreation are examined in a colourful 36 pages

—— *Lowland Landscape Guidelines*, HMSO, 1992, £9.95. Same series as above and provides lots of 'how to' sketches in 56 pages of advice from the Authority's Senior Landscape Architect, Simon Bell

Forestry Commission, *Community Woodland Design: Guidelines*, HMSO, 1992, £9.75. Provides 49 pages of advice for those about to plan for community woodlands. It suggests that much can be learnt from older urban fringe projects in Germany and the Netherlands. Similar design advice to that outlined in *Lowland Landscape Guidelines* but with more emphasis on public access

—— *Forests and Water Guidelines*, HMSO, 1991, £5.25. Second edition of an 1988 booklet which shows how to avoid erosion and to prevent or ameliorate acidification of watercourses in 24 pages

—— *Establishing farm woodlands*, by D.R. Williamson, HMSO, 1992, £6.75. Technical guide to planting and after-care. Only one of the 42 pages deals with establishing woods for conservation

—— *Forestry practice*, edited by B.G. Hibberd, HMSO, 1991, £14.95. Eleventh edition of industry standard

—— *Continued public access to Forestry Commission woodlands after sale: guidelines*, the Commission, 1991. Gives local authorities the right to negotiate access agreements when forests are sold

Harris, E. and Harris, J., *Wildlife conservation in managed woodlands and forests*, Basil Blackwell, 1991, £55.00. A practical book which emphasises the opportunities offered by Britain's maturing first-generation forests

Pryor, S., *Future forestry*, Wildlife Link, 1992, £4.50. Argues that the first priority is to apply environmental imperatives to form the core of forestry policy. Once this is done detailed policies flow naturally, for example, grant-aid being linked to public benefits. *Planning*, 8/5/92, p. 7

Rickman, R., *What's good for the woods—promoting the industry, protecting the environment*, Centre for Policy Studies, 1991, £6.95. Forestry Commission forests should be sold by tender, with holdings of importance for wildlife, landscape and recreation handed to public and voluntary bodies. *Ecos*, **13**(1), 1992, p. 71

Royal Society for the Protection of Birds, *Forests for the future: integrating forestry and the environment*, the Society, 1991. Proposes replacing five forestry/woodland grants with one, and reducing the basic grant so that extra environmental grants could be provided on a menu basis. *Farmers Weekly*, 1/11/91, p. 18

Whitbread, T., *County woodland strategies*, Royal Society for Nature Conservation, 1991, £4.50. Calls on the private sector to get together with local authorities and produce a woodland strategy for each county. *Planning*, 13/9/91, p. 5

Land-use-planning

Audit Commission, *Building in quality: a study of development control*, HMSO, 1992, £8.50. A report on the quality of service offered by development control departments in local authorities. It recommends that the crude target of 80 per cent of decisions being reached in 8 weeks should be replaced by more precise performance targets. Planners welcomed the proposed shift away from speed to quality, but were worried about how quality could be measured. *Planning*, 15/5/92, pp. 1, 8, 9; and 5/6/92, pp. 6–7; *The Planner*, 15/5/92, pp. 3, 5; and 5/6/92, p. 6; and *Town and Country Planning*, June 1992, pp. 162–3. Also see consultation paper section p. 156

Ball, S and Bell. S., *Environmental law*, Blackstone Press, 1991, £21.95. An excellent book which includes a guide to planning law. *Scottish Planning Law and Practice*, **36**, 1992, pp. 63–4

Bate, R., *A campaigner's guide to local plans*, Council for the Protection of Rural England, 1992, £9.00. A tool kit or menu rather than a blueprint designed to put the power of real influence into the hands of citizens

BDP Planning-Oxford Institute of Retail Management, *The effects of major out-of-town retail development*, HMSO, 1992, £16.00. Criticises central and local government for failing to identify a regional strategy for such developments, and for being too lax in giving permission compared to growing strictness in Europe. *Planning*, 20/3/92, p. 3

Brotherton, I., *Towards a theory of development control*, Department of Landscape Architecture, University of Sheffield, 1992, £6.00. Not a theory but a new methodology for analysing development control data, based on the idea that central government could classify appeals into 'strong' or 'weak' refusals, depending on the strength of the case against the application. Once this classification is made inconsistencies, and irrationalities between authorities could be discerned. *Planning*, 10/4/92, pp. 20–1

Churchill, R., Gibson. J. and Warren, L. (eds), *Law, policy and the environment*, Basil Blackwell, 1991, £11.95

Carter, N., Brown, T. and Abbott, T., *The relationship between expenditure-based plans and development plans*, School of the Built Environment, De Montfort University, 1992. A study of the devaluation of both types of plan in the 1980s, and one which attempts to sever the crucial links between them, for example between structure plans and housing and transport programmes. *Planning*, 10/7/92, p. 7

Council for the Protection of Rural England, *Mock EA Directive*, the Council, 1992, £4.00. Proposes the creation of an Environmental Assessment Authority in each member state of the EC and the extension of the EA to all plans, policies and programmes, at all levels of government

Countryside Commission, *Wind energy development and the landscape*, CCP 357, the Commission, 1991, £3.00. A consultants report which points out that wind energy structures are large and extensive features likely to have a major landscape impact. Achieving the potential 10 per cent of Britain's energy needs from wind power could take between 1,500 and 3,250 sq. km. The Commission believes that wind farms should normally be excluded from protected areas, and that there should be a presumption against them elsewhere when they would have a significant adverse impact. Applications should normally include a landscape assessment and environmental statement. Also see Energy Committee report on pp. 136

—— *The Countryside Commission and Development Control*, CCP378, the Commission, 1992, free. One-page statement pending a review of the Commission's role due to be completed in 1993. In the interim, to reduce the severe demands on staff resources, the Commission decided to limit its involvement in development control to those cases setting a national precedent or where a new form of development was involved

Department of Environment, *Planning pollution and waste management*, written by Environmental Resources Ltd. in association with Oxford Polytechnic, 1992, £12.50. Reports that planners are wary of treading on other organisation's toes following bitter experience in the past when trying to impose controls on pollution via the planning system. *Planning*, 19/6/92, pp. 18–19

—— *The strategic approach to derelict land reclamation*, By D. Johnson, HMSO, 1992, £8.00

—— *Evaluating the effectiveness of land-use planning*, by D. Diamond, PIEDA, and Leeds Polytechnic, HMSO, 1992, £7.75. Building on the lessons of Lichfield's Planning Balance Sheet, the report develops the Adapted Balance Sheet approach which is then tested in three areas. According to the methodology, planning has been effective in accommodating new development but house buyers have borne the extra costs in areas of pressure. *The Planner*, 17/7/92, p. 4

—— *The use of planning agreements*, by Grimley Eve, Thames Polytechnic and Alsop Wilkinson, HMSO, 1992, £10.40. According to a survey of 25 local authorities only about one-half of one per cent of permissions were subject to agreements between 1987 and 1990, and most of these were concerned with land-use matters rather than wider community interests. *Planning*, 5/6/92, p. 1; and 3/7/92, pp. 6–7

—— *Land-use planning and climate change*, by S. Owens and D. Cope, HMSO, 1992, £12.50. The main conclusions of this report are that threats to the coast caused by potential climate change, and the need to reduce the emission of greenhouse gases from transport, are matters for land-use planners to consider. Indeed, in an early response the government indicated that land-use policies should take a precautionary approach. The report warned, however, that planning policies could only work if accompanied by measures in other areas, e.g. fuel taxes. *Planning*, 1/5/92, pp. 18–19

—— *The relationship between house prices and land supply*, by Grimley Eve and Department of Land Economy, University of Cambridge, 1992, HMSO, £10.60. The impact of restrictive planning policies on the south-east may have increased house prices by as much as 40 per cent, but there would have to be significant relaxations of policy for there to be any effect on house prices, and even then other factors may offset the relaxation. *Planning*, 20/3/92, p. 24

Department of Planning and Housing, *Index to Local Authority Green Plans*, Edinburgh College of Art, 1991, £5.00. A survey of Britain's 514 local authorities which found—via a 79 per cent response rate—that 67 per cent had produced at least one of the four types of 'green plan' identified by the surveyors: an environmental charter; an environmental action plan; an internal environmemtal audit; or state of the environment reports. *Planning*, 20/11/91, p. 9

Garner, J.F. and Jones, B.L., *Countryside law*, Shaw and Sons, 1991, £16.95. New edition of excellent book which includes 1989 and 1990 legislation. *Countryside Commission News*, **52**, 1991, p. 7

Jones, C, Lee. N. and Wood, C., *UK environmental statements 1988–90: an analysis*, Department of Planning and Landscape, University of Manchester, 1991, £5.00

Macrory, R., *A campaigner's guide to using European Community Environmental Law*, Council for the Protection of Rural England, 1992, £9.00. Describes key EC legal instruments, and then how citizens can use these, for example, the Canford Down case in which campaigners showed that a proposal to build houses on an SSSI had not followed EC law, leading to the proposal being defeated

Owen, S., *Planning settlements naturally*, Packard Publishing, 1991, £19.95. Sets out to re-establish the lost link between nature, settlements and planning, both philosophically and practically. *Countryside Commission News*, **49**, 1991, p. 7

Planning Inspectorate Executive Agency, *Agency Business Plan 1992–93*, the Agency, Bristol, 1992. Sets out performance targets for the cost and time to be taken in deciding planning appeals or reporting on development plans. 20 more inspectors will be needed to deal with the surge in local plan inquiries. *Planning*, 3/7/92, p. 1

Royal Institution of Chartered Surveyors, *Shaping Britain for the 21st century—a land-use and transport policy*, RICS, 1992, £13.95. Argues that a national strategy is necessary, with stress placed on the need to minimise car journeys and maximise the scope for public transport, and to build higher density self-contained communities. *Planning*, 16/10/92, p. 20

Sidaway, R., *A review of marina developments in southern England*, Royal Society for the Protection of Birds, 1991, £10.00. A 60 per cent rise in new sites in the last 10 years points to disaster for birds and other wildlife. Accordingly the report calls for a system of regional coastal management to ward off the threat to further damage. *Planning*, 1/11/91, p. 6

Sinclair, G., *The lost land: land-use change in England 1945–1990*, Council for the Protection of Rural England, 1992, £10.00. This 80-page report is one that all rural planners should read closely since it blows apart some comforting myths about land loss. Its main finding is that MAFF data which have been used to show falling rates of land loss were no longer collected after 1986 since they could no longer be underwritten statistically. This means that policy documents like ALURE, and PPG7, were based on faulty data which the government knew about. Sinclair, by combining several data sources, produces consensus data which shows that though land lost to urbanisation between 1985–90, at 11,000 ha/year, was less than the post-war average of 15,700 ha/year, it was none the less twice the official figure of 5,000 ha/year.

More worryingly, this high rate of land loss was recorded at a time of static population growth, and when planning policy was no longer centred around the need to protect farmland. Accordingly, the report recommends a fundamental review of planning policy and the formulation of a policy to minimise the loss of rural land. As part of this process, PPG7 should be withdrawn, and a systematic land-use survey should be set up to provide accurate data

Spencer, D., *Towards a firmer understanding of counterurbanisation*, Department of Geography, University of Reading, 1992, £2.50

Thomas, P., Aisbett, A., O'Keeffe, J., Snaith, J. and Perry, A., *The planning factbook*, Professional Publishing, 1992, £65.00 and annual update, £50.00. A loose-leaf information service which concentrates on the nuts and bolts of planning

Recreation and Tourism

Central Council of Physical Recreation, *Sport and recreation in the countryside*, the Council, 1992, £2.00. Booklet attempting to persuade government at all levels to take proper account of rural recreation

Countryside Commission, *Pennine Way survey 1990: use and economic impact*, CCP361, the Commission, 1991, £20.00. A survey by consultants which reveals that the Way was used by 10,000 long-distance walkers and 153,000 day walkers between April and October. They spent just under £2million, which generated £400,000 for the area, and 100 full-time equivalent jobs. Long-distance walkers generate three times the jobs and income of day walkers

——— *The Pennine Way: trail leaflet*, CCP366, the Commission, 1992, free

——— *North Downs Way: publicity leaflet*, CCP 367, the Commission, 1992, free

——— *Wolds Way: publicity leaflet*, CCP 388, the Commission, 1992, free

——— *South-West Coast Path: publicity leaflet*, CCP 389, the Commission, 1992, free

——— *Thames Path design guide*, CCP 342, the Commission, 1992, £10.00

——— *Rights of Way: an action pack*, CCP 375, and *an action guide*, CCP 375P, the Commission, 1992, £6.50 for the pack, £5.00 for the Guide by itself. The Action

Pack contains a set of previously published booklets and leaflets, plus the Action Guide which is 37 pages that tell citizens how they can get together to provide rights-of-way networks. The aim is to enthuse enough volunteers to open up England's 120,000 miles of public rights of way

—— *Parish Paths Partnership: an outline*, CCP 380, the Commission, 1992, free. A 4-page booklet outlining a scheme to boost the process outlined above, by paying for the necessary skills and resources to be acquired. It is funded for three years in the first instance with £3.7 million. The scheme works through local authorities and was limited to 15 of these in its first year

—— *Golf courses: a position statement*, CCP 365, the Commission, 1991, free. Recommends a presumption against new courses in protected landscapes. Elsewhere they should contribute to and enhance the landscape, and they would be welcome in restoring derelict landscapes or in the new community forests

—— *Enjoying the countryside: policies for people*, CCP 371, the Commission, 1992, £2.00. Develops the approach set out in policy documents since 1987, notably in CCPs 234, 235, 266 and 273, and in a 1991 consultation paper (see Volume II, p. 106). The new policy sets an agenda for widening access to the countryside for hitherto under-represented groups. This can be done by improving awareness, developing an understanding of the countryside and making people feel more confident about their rights

—— *National Park visitor centres: study of good practice*, CCP 390, the Commission, 1992, free. Consultants' report which sets out performance indicators and makes 30 recommendations. Visitor centres should *inter alia* increase awareness and understanding, influence visitor movements, stimulate business for the local economy and establish a 'direct sales' opportunity

—— *Training for countryside managers, staff and volunteers*, CCP 372, the Commission, 1992. Details of Commission sponsored training courses in 1992–3

Countryside Commission, Countryside Council for Wales, English and Welsh Tourist Boards, Rural Development Commission, *Tourism in National Parks: guide to good practice*, the Commission *et al.*, 1991, free. A guide for people who have a tourist enterprise urging them to take a sensitive approach to development, to support local labour and produce, to extend quiet recreation facilities, to support practical conservation and to improve information and marketing

Countryside Commission, Rural Development Commission and English Tourist Board, *The green light: a guide to sustainable tourism*, Joint Publication, 1992, £10.00. Aimed at the tourist industry it provides advice on developing sites environmentally, and encourages businesses to carry out environmental audits

Departure of Environment, *Tourism in the UK: realising the potential*, HMSO, 1992, £5.00

Harrison, C., *Countryside recreation in a changing society*, TMS Partnership, 182 Upper Richmond Road, London, 1991, £18.00. Unlike Glyptis' descriptive account (see Volume II, p. 121), Harrison's excellent book is informed by a central theory, namely, that private property rights have created a 'countryside aesthetic' which has been used to perpetuate the ideology of quiet countryside recreation. In the short term, the rise of the 'service class' and the appearance of surplus farmland are leading to new types of rural recreation, but these are still dependent on private property or clubs. For the longer term, Harrison would

like to see the development of genuine public demand and fun-based access to
the countryside as a right not a privilege

National Economic Development Office, *The planning system and large-scale
tourism and leisure developments*, NEDO Books, 1991, £81.20. A commissioned
report for the Office which recommends that the large-scale leisure industry
(schemes costing £20 million plus) should be more proactive in influencing the
content of development plans. Large projects should, however, be kept away
from protected landscapes, but may be suitable for Green Belts. Elsewhere there
should be a presumption for them. *The Planner*, 13/12/91, p. iii; and 15/5/92, p.
12; and *Planning*, 13/12/91, p. 16

Office of Population Censuses and Surveys, *Leisure day visits in GB 1988/89*,
HMSO, 1991, £40.00. A study for BTA, ETB *et al.* by T. Dodd

Sports Council, *A countryside for sport*, the Council, 1992. The aim of this report
is healthy people in a healthy environment and it wants to promote a more
welcoming attitude by recreation managers towards active sports

Socio-economic

Agricola Conference, *Rural society—issues for the nineties*, Wye College, 1992,
£4.00. Collection of papers from March 1991

Audit Commission, *Developing local authority housing strategies*, HMSO, 1992,
£12.00. The Commission identifies a shortfall of 12,000 affordable houses a year
out of an estimated demand for 74,000. The gap is unbridgeable given present
policies. *Planning*, 29/5/92, pp. 2–3

Barlow, J., *Planning agreements and affordable housing provision*, Centre for
Urban and Regional Research, University of Brighton and Joseph Rowntree
Foundation, 1992. A survey which found that the number of affordable houses
being built as a result of agreements was low and would remain so given existing
policies. *The Planner*, 3/7/92, p. 6; and *Planning*, 28/2/92, pp. 4–5

Blacksell, M., Economides, K. and Watkins, C., *Justice outside the city: access to
legal services in rural Britain*, Longmans, 1991, £11.99

Clark, D., *Rural housing supply and trends—a 1992 survey of affordable homes*,
ACRE, 1992, £10.00. Reports on a survey which shows an increase in affordable
housing provision, but not enough to meet demand. *Planning*, 14/8/92, p. 8; and
The Planner, 4/9/92 p. 6

Council for the Protection of Rural England, *Where motor car is master*, the
Council, 1992. A critique of the growing importance of the Department of
Transport and its ethos of road construction. Calls for an environment-centred
policy which is fair to all modes of travel

——*Concrete and tyres*, by P. Headicar and B. Bixby, the Council, 1992, £9.00.
A study of the M40 corridor which shows that new roads become magnets for
new developments and thus threaten the countryside twice. A more integrated
policy is needed. *Planning*, 4/9/92, pp. 4–5

——*Wheeling out of control*, the Council, 1992, leaflet. The roads programme
threatens 160 SSSIs, 800 ancient monuments, 12 AONBs, 2 National Parks and
30 National Trust properties

Countryside Commission, *Trends in transport and recreation*, CCP 382, the Commission, 1992, £5.00. Consultant's report which discusses the implications of the

Department of Transport's 1989 forecasts that traffic will grow between 83 and 142 per cent by 2025, and proportionately more in rural areas

—— *Road traffic and the countryside*, CCP 387, the Commission, 1992, free. Position statement by the Commission related to CCP 382 above. It argues that the construction of new roads and improvements to existing roads are already spoiling the countryside, and that the car will need to be used more selectively in the future. To this end the Commission will raise awareness of traffic, advocate close links between transport and land-use policy and propose that new developments are accessible by other means than cars alone

Department of Environment, *Business success in the countryside: the performance of rural enterprise*, by D. Keeble, HMSO, 1992, £8.00. A survey of over 1,100 enterprises which discovered that most rural enterprises are relatively new, small, independent and locally formed. However, most rural entrepreneurs are in-migrants strongly influenced in their migration decision by the attractive residential environment of rural areas. Firms in remote rural areas offset this disadvantage by specialising in market niche products

District Planning Officers Society, *Affordable housing*, the Society, 1992. A survey of planning authorities which shows that not enough landowners are coming forward to make 'exceptions' policies effective in rural areas. *The Planner*, 2/10/92, p. 3

European Communities Commission, *Community support frameworks 1992–93 for the development of rural areas (Objective 5b)*, HMSO, 1991, £5.00

Fielding, S., *Confronting rural deprivation*, Department of Geography, St Davids University College, Lampeter, 1992. A discursive essay on the merits of humanist and structural approaches to deprivation, which favours the Marxist view

Institute of Housing, *A radical consensus—new ideas for housing in the 1990s*, the Institute, 1992. A discussion paper which argues that the 100,000 affordable houses needed a year will not be produced by present policies. Advocates a new social housing-use class and specific programmes for rural areas. *Planning*, 17/1/92, p. 5

Institute of Housing and House Builders Federation, *Planning for affordable housing—a practical guide*, IoH and HBF, 1992, £10.00

John Richards Associates, *Kit houses in the countryside*, Scottish Office, 1992. Report cum discussion paper. *Planning*, 3/7/92, p. 8

Marsden, T., Lowe, P. and Whatmore, S., *Labour and locality: uneven development and the rural labour process*, Volume 4 in *Critical Perspectives in Rural Change* Series, David Fulton, 1992, £30.00

Newby, H., *The future of rural society: strategic planning or muddling through?*, ESRC, 1991. Dartington lecture which calls for more emphasis on people, and a farm policy that would divide farms into: agribusiness; community sustaining farms; and environmental farms. *The Planner*, 1/11/91, p. 3

Royal Agricultural Society of England, *Women and employment in rural areas*, Rural Development Commission, 1991. A survey which found that women are a deprived section of the work-force, in virtually every respect, with a chief constraint being poor access to childcare. *Journal of Rural Studies*, 1992, pp. 125–6

Royal Society for Nature Conservation, *Ever increasing circles—the impact and effectiveness of the M25 and the new M25 plan*, the Society, 1992. Plans for widening the M25 are an expensive and destructive white elephant, which could lead to a net increase in congestion and directly damage 81 wildlife sites. *Planning*, 21/2/92, p. 6

Rural Development Commission, *A decade in Ashford*, the Commission, 1992, £10.00. A survey which shows a significant loss of employment sites between 1980 and 1990 as a result of redevelopment or allocation for other uses in local plans. *Planning*, 17/4/92, p. 12

—— *Survey into traffic generated by conversion of rural buildings into commercial purposes*, the Commission, 1992, £10.00. A study which found that such businesses generate less traffic than planners had allowed for, namely 9 movements/1,000 sq. foot compared to the 11–14 forecast. *Planning*, 17/4/92, p. 12

Royal Town Planning Institute, *Planning policy and social housing*, the Institute, 1992, £3.00

School for Advanced Urban Studies, *Homelessness in rural areas*, Rural Developement Commission, 1992, £12.95. A report which finds that homelessness has tripled in the last 4 years, and that attempts to solve the problem are slow and piecemeal. More social housing is needed, and ways to provide this by amending right to buy provisions are suggested. *Planning*, 5/6/92, p. 5

SERPLAN, *The provision of affordable housing in the South-East*, SERPLAN, 50–64, Broadway, London, SW1H ODB, 1992, £15.00. Although the supply of affordable housing is rising there is still a large gap between it and demand and this is being exacerbated by council house sales. Structure plan reviews are, however, including affordable housing policies. *Planning*, 14/8/92, p. 8

Standing Advisory Committee on Trunk Road Assessment (SACTRA), *Assessing the environmental impact of road schemes*, HMSO, 1992, £15.00. A workmanlike review of the system which recommends that environmental assessment should be related to explicitly stated environmental policy objectives. *Ecos*, **13** (1), 1992, pp. 58–9

Transport, Department of *Government response to the SACTRA report on assessing the environmental impact of road schemes*, HMSO, 1992, £6.50. A response to the report outlined in the previous entry. It is generally in agreement, but detailed implementation of any changes were delayed till the forecast revision of the *Manual of Environmental Appraisal* first published in 1983. *Planning*, 20/3/92, p. 6

Williams, G., *Evaluating the low-cost rural housing initiative*, HMSO, 1991, £12.50. Reports that 75 per cent of the 185 responding districts had formulated an 'exceptions' policy, and that between 1989 and 1991 about 3,000 potential houses had been approved under the initiative. Much progress has been made in fine-tuning the scheme, but it is still a long and complex process, over-reliant on a buoyant market for more expensive housing. *Planning*, 22/11/91, pp. 16–17; and 15/11/91, p. 17

Woodward, R. *Deprivation and marginalization in rural areas*, Department of Geography, St Davids University College, Lampeter, 1992. Conventional models of deprivation rely on normative standards but real people falling below these norms do not see themselves as 'deprived'. Accordingly, Woodward argues for a new concept based on life-styles and the idea of marginalisation as measured by traditional measures like transport and income

Bibliography

Countryside Commission, *Agricultural landscapes (Bibliography)*, CC376, the Commission, 1992, free. Fourth revised edition

152 selected articles

Format: Author, 'Title', *Journal*, Vol. no. (if one) Issue no. (if use), Year, Pages. If a title is unclear, a subtitle is provided in parentheses.

The subdivisions below are not mutually exclusive, thus as article on forest recreation in National Parks may be found in any one of the three subdivisions. Hopefully, the articles are listed where the lead topic occurs.

General articles

Clarke, R., 'The English countryside: challenge and opportunity', *Journal of Royal Agricultural Society of England*, 151, 1990, pp. 44–50

Cloke, P., 'Community development and political leadership in rural Britain', *Sociologia Ruralis*, 30, 3–4, pp. 305–22

Errington, A., 'Modelling the seamless web: economic linkages and rural policy', *Sociologia Ruralis*, 31, 1 1991, pp. 17–22

Green, R. and Holliday, J., 'Country planning: a time for action', *The Planner*, 77, 36, 1991, pp. 6–9

Hague, C., 'A review of planning theory in Britain', *Town Planning Review*, 62, 3, 1991, pp. 295–310

Herbert, M., 'Environmental foundation for a new kind of town and country planning', *Town and Country Planning*, 61, 6, pp. 166–8

Ilbery, B.W., 'From Scott to Alure and back again?', *Land Use Policy*, 9, 2, 1992, pp. 131–42

Jacobs, H.M., 'Planning the use of land for the 21st century', *Journal of Soil and Water Conservation*, 47, 1, 1992, pp. 32–4

Kayser, B., 'Country planning, development policies and the future of rural areas', *Sociologia Ruralis*, 31, 4, 1991, pp. 262–8

Lee-Wright, M., 'Country estate action for rural areas?' *Planning*, 983, 28 August 1992, pp. 14–15

Luttrell, B. *et al.*, 'Special feature: regional England?' *Town and Country Planning*, 61, 4, 1992 pp. 101–8

Moon, G. and Parnell, R., 'The changing role of local government: a political geographic perspective', *Geographica Polonica*, 56, 1989, pp. 17–72

Moore, C., 'Reflections on the new local political economy: resignations, resistance and reform', *Policy and Politics*, 19, 2, 1991, pp. 73–85

Nickson, J. and Foster, J., 'A vision for Scotland', *RSA Journal*, 137, 5400, 1989, pp. 789–809

O'Riordan, T., 'The new environmentalism and sustainable development', *Science of the Total Environment*, 108, 1–2, 1991, pp. 5–15

Pattie, C.J., Russell, A.T. and Johnson, R.J., 'Going green in Britain? Votes for the Green Party and attitudes to green issues in the late 1980s' *Journal of Rural Studies*, 7, 3, 1991, pp. 285–97

Rawcliffe, P., 'Swimming with the tide—environmental groups in the 1990s', *Ecos*, 13, 1, 1992, pp. 2–9

Robinson, G.M., 'Geographical Information Systems (GIS) and planning in Scotland: the RLUIS project and advances in GIS', *Scottish Geographical Magazine*, 1992, 108, 1, pp. 22–8

Royal Town Planning Institute, 'Planning ahead for the next parliament', *The Planner*, 78, 5, 1992, pp. 18–20

Scott, P., 'Rural strategies: a focus for action,' *The Planner*, 78, 18, 1992, pp. 15–16

Selman, P., Davidson, D., Watson, A. and Winterbottom, S., 'GIS in rural environmental planning: visual and land-use analysis of major developmental proposals', *Town Planning Review*, 6, 2, 1992, pp. 215–23

Statham, D., 'New uses for the countryside', *The Planner*, 77, 40, 1991, pp. 83–5

Agriculture

Allanson, P., 'Farm size structure in England and Wales 1939–89', *Journal of Agricultural Economics*, 43, 2, 1992, pp. 137–48

Byrne, P.J. and Ravenscroft, N., 'The role of diversification in restructuring farms and rural estates', *Journal of Royal Agricultural Society of England*, 151, 1990, pp. 51–65

Copus, A. and Leat, P., 'Farm net value added in Scotland and the designation of areas for rural development assistance', *Journal of Agricultural Economics*, 43, 2, 1992, pp. 218–30

Crabtree, J.R. and Appleton, Z., 'Economic evaluation of the Farm Woodland Scheme in Scotland', *Journal of Agricultural Economics*, 43, 3, 1992, pp. 355–67

Dawson, P.J., 'The single analytics of agricultural production quotas', *Oxford Agrarian Studies*, 19, 2, 1991, pp. 127–41

Downs, C.J., 'Milk quotas and the need for a new approach', *Land Use Policy*, 8, 3, 1991, pp. 206–11

Doyle, C.J., Mainland, D.D. and Thomas, C., 'Speculating on long-term changes in UK dairy farming and the implications for research', *Agricultural Systems*, 37, 3, 1991, pp. 243–58

Guy, C.M., 'Urban and rural contrasts in food prices and availability—a case study in Wales', *Journal of Rural Studies*, 7, 3, 1991, pp. 311–25

Hillman, J.S., 'Confessions of a double agent in the EC-US agricultural policy argument', *Journal of Agricultural Economics*, 43, 3, 1992, pp. 327–42

Hope, J. and Lingard, J., 'The influence of risk aversion on the uptake of set-aside: a MOTAD and CPR approach', *Journal of Agricultural Economics*, 43, 3, 1992, pp. 401–11

Ilbery, B.W., 'Farm diversification as an adjustment strategy on the urban fringe of the West Midlands', *Journal of Rural Studies*, 7, 3, 1991, pp. 207–18

Ilbery, B.W. and Stiell, B., 'Uptake of the Farm Diversification Grant Scheme in England', *Geography*, 76, 3, 1991, pp. 259–63

McDonald, J.R.S., Rayner, A.J. and Bates, J.M., 'Productivity growth and the UK food system 1954–84', *Journal of Agricultural Economics*, 43, 2, 1992, pp. 191–204

MacLaren, D., 'The political economy of agricultural policy reform in the European Community and Australia', *Journal of Agricultural Economics*, 43, 3, 1992, pp. 424–39

Marsden, T.K. and Munton, R.J.C., 'The farmed landscape and the occupancy change process', *Environment and Planning A*, 23, 5, 1991, pp. 663–76

Munton, R. and Marsden, T., 'Dualism or diversity in family farming? Patterns of occupancy change in British agriculture', *Geogforum*, 22, 1, 1991, pp. 105–17

Munton, R.J.C. and Marsden, T., 'Occupancy change and the farmed landscape: an analysis of farm level trends 1970–85', *Environment and Planning A*, 23, 4, 1991, pp. 499–510

Oskam, A.J. and Speijers, D.P., 'Quota mobility and quota values: influence on the structural development of dairy farming', *Food Policy*, 17, 1, 1992, pp. 41–52

Pile, S., ' "A load of bloody idiots": Somerset dairy farmers view of their political world', *Political Geography Quarterly*, 10, 4, 1991, pp. 405–21

Robinson, G.M., 'EC agricultural policy and the environment: land-use implications in the UK', *Land Use Policy*, 8, 2, 1991, pp. 95–107

Stott, M., 'CAP reform cuts farm jobs', *Town and Country Planning*, 61, 7–8, 1992, p. 216

Sturgess, I.M., 'Self-sufficiency and food security in the UK and EC', *Journal of Agricultural Economics*, 43, 3, 1992, pp. 311–26

Swinbank, A., 'A surplus of farm land?', *Land Use Policy*, 9, 1, 1992, pp. 3–7

Thirtle, C. and Bottomley, P., 'Total factor productivity in UK agriculture 1967–96', *Journal of Agricultural Economics*, 43, 3, 1992, pp. 381–400

Conservation and protected areas

Adger, N. and Whitby, M., 'Accounting for the impact of agriculture and forestry on environmental quality', *European Economic Review*, 35, 2–3, 1991, pp. 629–41

Barron, S., 'A conservation agency for Scotland', *The Planner*, 78, 7, 1992, pp. 10–11

Bilsborough, S., 'The oven-ready golden eagle: arguments against (economic) valuation (of wildlife)', *Ecos*, 13, 1, 1992, pp. 46–50

Bishop, J. and Rose, J., 'Dependence, independence and interdependence: the resourcing of environmental groups is a poorly explored and often misinterpreted world', *Ecos*, 13, 1, 1992, pp. 14–19

Blankson, E.J. and Green, B.H., 'Use of landscape classification as an essential prerequisite to landscape evaluation', *Landscape and Urban Planning*, 21, 3, 1991, pp. 149–62

Box, J., 'Forty years of Local Nature Reserves', *Ecos*, 12, 3, 1991, pp. 40–3

Brotherton, I., 'The cost of conservation: a comparison of ESA and SSSI payment rates', *Environment and Planning A*, 23, 8, 1991, pp. 1183–95

Brotherton, I., 'Strategies for the conclusion of management agreements in National Parks', *Journal of Environmental Management*, 33, 4, 1991, pp. 395–404

Brotherton, I., 'What limits participation in ESAs?', *Journal of Environmental Management*, 32, 3, 1991, pp. 241–9

Carr, S. and Tait, J., 'Differences in the attitudes of farmers and conservationists and their implications', *Journal of Environmental Management*, 32, 3, 1991, pp. 281–94

Colthurst, D., 'National Parks policy: the failure of success', *Geographical Magazine*, 63, 6, 1991, pp. 10–13

Crabtree, J.R., 'National Park designation in Scotland', *Land Use Policy*, 8, 3, 1991, pp. 241–52

Dwyer, J., 'Structural and evolutionary effects upon conservation policy performance: comparing a UK National and a French Regional Park', *Journal of Rural Studies*, 7, 3, 1991, pp. 265–75

Ebraham, A. and Elliott, G., 'Energy policy and bird species', *Ecos*, 12, 4, 1991, pp. 21–8

Edwards, R., 'Fit for the future: a review of the National Parks', *The Planner*, 77, 40, 1991, pp. 45–50

Evans, P., 'Peat—the flavour of the campaign', *Ecos*, 12, 3, 1991, pp. 32–9

Everett, S., 'The Institute of Ecology and Environmental Management—the first hurdles', *Ecos*, 13, 1, 1992, pp. 43–5

Gaskell, P.T. and Tanner, M., 'Agricultural change and Environmentally Sensitive Areas', *Geoforum*, 22, 1, 1991, pp. 81–90

Gilg, A., 'Planning for agriculture: the growing case for a conservation component', *Geoforum*, 22, 1, 1991, pp. 75–9

Green, C.H. and Tunstall, S.M., 'Is the economic evaluation of environmental resources possible?', *Journal of Environmental Management*, 33, 2, 1991, pp. 123–41

Hodge, I., 'Incentive policies and the rural environment', *Journal of Rural Studies*, 7, 4, 1991, pp. 373–84

Jarman, R., 'The National Trust's environmental audit', *Ecos*, 13, 1, 1992, pp. 37–42

Johnston, B., '(National) Parks in refit for next century', *Planning*, 954, 7/2/92, pp. 14–17

Kayes, R., 'Environmental auditing—the state of play, *Ecos*, 13, 1, 1992, pp. 32–7

Mather, A.S., 'Land use, physical sustainability and conservation in Highland Scotland', *Land Use Policy*, 9, 2, 1992, pp. 99–110

Morphet, J., 'Subsidiarity and EC environmental features', *Town and Country Planning*, 61, 7–8, 1992, pp. 192–4

Penford, N. and Francis, I., 'Common land and nature conservation in England and Wales', *British Wildlife*, 2, 2, 1990, pp. 65–76

Potter, C. and Lobley, M., 'The conservation status and potential of elderly farmers: results from a survey in England and Wales', *Journal of Rural Studies*, 8, 2, 1992, pp. 133–43

Reynolds, F., 'National Parks and the wider countryside—parts of the same whole?' *The Planner*, 77, 40, 1991, pp. 52–4

Rowan-Robinson, J. Livingstone, L., and Cunningham, R., 'SSSIs and Part II of the Wildlife and Countryside Act 1981', *Scottish Planning Law and Practice*, 35, 1992, pp. 10–13

Sheail, J., 'The "amenity" clause: an insight into half a century of environmental protection in the United Kingdom', *Transactions of the Institute of British Geographers: New Series*, 17, 2, 1992, pp. 152–65

Shirley, P. and Knightbridge, R., 'Consultancy and County Trusts—unhappy bedfellows?', *Ecos*, 13, 1, 1992, pp. 27–31

Thorne, J.F. and Huang, Cahng-Shan, 'Toward a landscape ecological aesthetic: methodologies for designers and planners', *Landscape and Urban Planning*, 21 (1–2), 1991, pp. 61–79

Forestry

Adger, W.N., and Whitby, M.C., 'Environmental assessment in forestry: the initial experience', *Journal of Rural Studies*, 7, 4, 1991, pp. 385–95

Edwards, C. and Guyer, C., 'Farm woodland policy: an assessment of the response to the Farm Woodland Scheme in Northern Ireland', *Journal of Environmental Management*, 34, 3, 1992, pp. 197–209

Helliwell, D.R., 'Benefits of multipurpose forestry: who pays and how?', *Arboricultural Journal*, 16, 1, 1992, pp. 5–10

Hummerl, F., 'Comparisons of forestry in Britain and mainland Europe', *Forestry*, 64, 2, 1991, pp. 141–55

McGregor, P.G. and McNicoll, I.H., 'The impact of forestry on output in the UK and its member countries', *Regional Studies*, 26, 1, 1992, pp. 69–79

Mather, A.S., 'The changing role of planning in rural land use: the example of afforestation in Scotland', *Journal of Rural Studies*, 7, 3, 1991, pp. 299–309

Mather, A.S., 'Planning and afforestation in Scotland: the nature and role of afforestation consultations', *Environment and Planning A*, 23, 9, 1991, pp. 1349–59

Stevenson, A.W. and MacKay, A.F., 'Forestry in the Highland Region', *Forestry*, 64, 2, 1991, pp. 103–40

Land-use planning and minerals planning

Adams, D. and Pawson, G., 'Local plan inquiries', *The Planner*, 78, 16, 1992, pp. 12–14

Albrechts, C., 'Changing roles and positions of planners', *Urban Studies*, 28, 1, 1991, pp. 123–37

Allen, T., 'Dormant (mineral) permissions lack appeal for quarry operators, *Planning*, 994, 13/11/92, p. 15

Anon, 'Environmental assessment decisions for period 12 December 1990 to March 31 1991', *Journal of Planning and Environment Law*, August, 1991, pp. 765–71

Breheny, M., 'The renaissance of strategic planning?', *Environment and Planning B*, 18, 2, 1991, pp. 233–49

Campbell, G., 'Telecommunications and the GDO', *Journal of Planning and Environment Law*, March 1992, pp. 222–6

Cherry, G., 'Planning history: recent developments in Britain', *Planning Perspectives*, 6, 1, 1991, pp. 33–45

Curry, N., 'Selling planning permission: a viewpoint', *Town Planning Review,* 62, 3, 1991, pp. v–viii

Denton-Thompson, M., 'Twyford Down—the saga continues', *Ecos*, 12, 4, 1991, pp. 38–41

Elliott, D., 'Yes we have no policy (on wind farms)', *Town and Country Planning*, 61, 7–8, pp. 195–6

Elson, M., 'Green belts for Wales', *The Planner*, 78, 9, 1992, pp. 10–11

Evans, A.W., ' "Rabbit hutches on postage stamps": planning development and political economy', *Urban Studies*, 28, 6, 1991, pp. 853–70

Gatenby, I. and Williams, C., 'Section 54A: the legal and practical implications', *Journal of Planning and Environment Law*, February 1992, pp. 110–20

Harrison, M., 'A presumption in favour of planning permission? (Section 54a)', *Journal of Planning and Environment Law*, February, 1991, pp. 121–9

Home, R.K., 'Deregulating UK planning control in the 1980s', *Cities*, 8, 4, 1991, pp. 292–300

Howe, E., 'Professional roles and the public interest in planning', *Journal of Planning Literature*, 6, 3, 1992, pp. 230–48

Johnston, B., 'Full steam ahead on new plans regime', *Planning*, 954, 7/2/92, pp. 18–19

Jones, A., 'Equal and opposite forces in attitudes to plan' (a discussion on Section 54a of the 1991 Planning and Compensation Act, which makes the provisions of the development plan the first consideration in development control), *Planning*, 940, 18/10/91, pp. 14–15

Larkham, P.J., 'The concept of delay in development control', *Planning Outlook*, 33, 2, 1990, pp. 101–7

Lee, N. and Colley, R., 'Reviewing the quality of environmental statements: review methods and findings', *Town Planning Review*, 62, 2, 1991, pp. 239–48

Manser, M. and Adam, R., 'Putting planning in better shape?', *Planning*, 984, 4/9/92, pp. 24–5

Manser, M. and Adam, R., 'Restoration of democracy mooted as architects remodel (planning) system', *Planning*, 983, 28/8/92, pp. 16–17

Marsden, T. *et al.*, 'Planning for social limits to growth (survey of rural residents in Bucks)', *The Planner*, 78, 4, 1992, pp. 6–7

Marshall, T., 'How green is your region? (progress of Regional Planning Guidance)', *Town and Country Planning*, 61, 1, 1991, pp. 22–5

Nadin, V. and Daniels, R., 'Consultants and Development Plans', *The Planner*, 78, 15, 1992, pp. 10–12

Pacione, M., 'Development pressures and the production of the built environment in the urban fringe', *Scottish Geographical Magazine*, 107, 3, 1991, pp. 162–69

Phillips, M., 'Town and Country Planning Act 1990: new power under Section 187B to apply for injunctions', *Journal of Planning and Environment Law*, May, 1992, pp. 407–13

Phillips, P., 'New strategy needed for tacky (urban) fringe', *Planning*, 993, 6/11/92, pp. 14–15

Poulton, M.C., 'The case for a positive theory of planning. Part I: What is wrong with planning theory?', *Environment and Planning B*, 18/2/1991, pp. 225–32; and 'Part 2: a positive theory of planning', 18/3/1991, pp. 263–75

Salter, J.R., 'Environmental assessment: the challenge from Brussels', *Journal of Planning and Environment Law*, January 1992, pp. 14–20

Salter, J.R., 'Environmental assessment: the need for transparency', *Journal of Planning and Environment Law*, March, 1992, pp. 214–21

Salter, J.R., 'Environmental assessment: the question of implementation', *Journal of Planning and Environment Law*, April, 1992, pp. 313–18

Sheail, J., 'The Opencast Coal Act 1958: the transition from wartime emergency powers to planning for amenity', *Town Planning Review*, 62, 2, 1991, pp. 201–14

Sheail, J., 'Opencast coal mining and the restoration of farmland—the post-war experience', *Journal of Royal Agricultural Society of England*, 152, 1991, pp. 100–11

Sheail, J., 'Opencast coal working and the search for a national land-use strategy in post-war Britain', *Planning perspectives*, 7, 1, 1992, pp. 47–63

Shucksmith, M. and Watkins, L., 'Housebuilding on farmland: the distributional effects in rural areas', *Journal of Rural Studies*, 7, 3, 1991, pp. 153–68

Simmie, J. and Olsberg, C., 'Urban containment and land-use planning', *Land Use Policy*, 9, 1, 1992, pp. 36–46

Smith, H.D., 'The present and future of coastal zone management in the UK', *Land Use Policy*, 8, 2, 1991, pp. 125–32

Stone, C. and Walker, S., 'Environmental assessment in the British planning system', *European Environment*, 2, 1, 1992, pp. 10–13

Wood, C., Lee, N. and Jones, C.E., 'Environmental statements in the UK: the initial experience', *Projects Appraisal*, 6, 4, pp. 187–94

Recreation

Davies, J. and O'Neill, C., 'Discrete-choice valuation of recreational angling in Northern Ireland', *Journal of Agricultural Economics*, 43, 3, 1992, pp. 452–7

Donnelly, W.A., 'A survey in applied environmentrics: the hedonic valuing of environmental amenities', *Environment International*, 17, 6, 1991, pp. 547–58

Evans, N.J. and Ilbery, B.W., 'Farm-based accommodation and the restructuring of agriculture: evidence from three English counties', *Journal of Rural Studies*, 8, 1, 1992, pp. 85–96

Lawson, T., 'Make countryside visitors welcome', *Countryside*, 58, 1992, pp. 4–5

Murdoch, J. and Marsden, T., 'A fair way to plan? Assessing the golf course boom', *The Planner*, 78, 16, 1992, pp. 8–10

Raemaekers, J., 'Piste control: the planning and management of Scottish ski centres, *The Planner*, 77, 37, 1991, pp. 6–8

Wilkinson, D., 'Public access to inland waterways: recreation, conservation and the need for reform, *Journal of Planning and Environment Law*, June, 1992, pp. 525–35

Willis, K. and Garrod, G., 'Valuing open access recreation on inland waterways: on-site recreation surveys and selection effect', *Regional Studies*, 25, 6, 1991, pp. 511–24

Socio-economic

Barlow, J. and Chambers, P., 'Planning agreements and housing quotas', *Town and Country Planning*, 61, 5, 1992, pp. 136–42

Bell, P. and Cloke, P., 'Deregulation and rural bus services: a study in rural Wales', *Environment and Planning A*, 23, 1, 1991, pp. 107–26

Forrest, R. and Murie, A., 'Change on a rural council estate: an analysis of dwelling histories', *Journal of Rural Studies*, 8, 1, 1992, pp. 53–65

Goodchild, B., 'Land allocation for housing: a review of practice and possibility in England', *Housing Studies*, 7, 1, 1992, pp. 45–55

Hill, B. and Young, N., 'Support policy for rural areas in England and Wales: its assessment and qualification, *Journal of Rural Studies*, 7, 3, 1991, pp. 191–206

Lewis, G.J., McDermott, P. and Sherwood, K.B., 'The counter-urbanisation process: demographic restructuring and policy response in rural England', *Sociologia Ruralis*, 31, 4, 1991, pp. 309–20

Lewis, G.J. and Sherwood, K.B., 'Unravelling the counter-urbanisation process in lowland Britain: a case study in east Northamptonshire', *Cambria*, 16, 1–2, 1991, pp. 58–77

Lloyd, G. and Black, S., 'Scottish enterprise—casting a shadow over continuity and accountability', *Town and Country Planning*, 61, 4, 1992, pp. 109–11

Williams, G. and Bell, P., 'The "exceptions" initiative in rural housing—the story so far', *Town and Country Planning*, 61, 5, 1992, pp. 143–4

Wilson, O., 'Landownership and rural development in the North Pennines: a case study, *Journal of Rural Studies*, 8, 2, 1992, pp. 145–58

Wright, S., 'Rural community development: what sort of social change?', *Journal of Rural Studies*, 8, 1, 1992, pp. 15–28

Water

Burgon, J., 'The management of the Coastal Zone', *The Planner*, 77, 40, 1991, pp. 51–2

Downs, P.W., Gregory, K.J. and Brookes, A., 'How integrated is river basin management?', *Environmental Management*, 15, 3, 1991, pp. 299–309

Lloyd, G., 'Planning predicament down on the fish farm', *Town and Country Planning*, 60, 10, 1991, pp. 314–15

Lloyd, M.G. and Livingstone, L.H., 'Marine fish farming in Scotland: proprietorial behaviour and the public interest', *Journal of Rural Studies*, 7, 3, 1991, pp. 253–63

Newson, M., 'Land and water: convergence, divergence and progress in UK policy', *Land Use Policy*, 9, 2, 1992, pp. 111–21

Sheate, W., Buisson, R., Steel, C, Beskine, D., Ormerod, S. and Tyler, S., five articles on water issues, including: 'Water resource management'; 'land drainage'; 'a conservation agenda for the NRA'; 'conservation duties and access rights under the Water Act 1989'; and 'forests and water acidification', *Ecos*, 12, 3, 1991, pp. 3–31

Williams, A.T., 'The quiet conservators: heritage coasts of England and Wales', *Ocean and Coastal Management*, 17, 2, 1992, pp. 151–67

Annual report and accounts

List of annual reports produced by rural planning organisations 1991–2
Published by HMSO

Format: Author, *Title*, HC or Cm. number, Year of Publication, price

Advisory Committee on Pesticides,
   Annual Report 1991, 1992, £7.50
Agriculture, Fisheries and Food, Ministry of
   Agriculture in the UK 1991, 1992, £12.00. 'Total income from farming' fell by 6 per cent, while 'farming income' fell by 14 per cent
Agriculture in Scotland, Department of
   Agriculture in Scotland 1990, Cm. 1648, 1991, £5.50
   ——*Agriculture in Scotland 1991*, Cm. 2020, 1992, £6.55
Ancient Monuments Board for Scotland
   38th Annual Report 1991, HC 7(92–93)
British Tourist Authority
   Accounts 1991–92, HC 168(92–93), £3.50

Chief Planning Inspector's Report
Report for April 1990 to March 1991, 1991, £4.55. Reports a shift towards more local plan inquiry work, and more enforcement appeals as standard appeals fell from 32,281 to 26,692
Countryside Commission
Accounts 1990–91, HC 233(91–92), 1992
—— *Accounts 1991–92*, HC 163(92–93), 1992, £4.70
Crofters Commission
Annual Report 1991, 1992, £5.75
Development Board for Rural Wales
Accounts 1990–91, HC 135 (91–92), 1991, £5.10
—— *DBRW Accounts: Evidence to Committee of Public Accounts*, HC 18–i, 1992, £7.50
—— *Accounts 1991–92*, HC 170(92–93), £5.30
English Tourist Board
Accounts 1991–92, HC 149 (92–93), 1992, £4.10
Forestry Commission
71st Annual Report and Accounts 1990–91, HC 36(91–92), 1991, 12.60. The report noted the increased emphasis placed by the government on achieving multi-purpose forestry, and the fact that the Commission will in future be claiming 25 per cent of the cost of grant schemes aimed at converting farmland to forestry from the EAGGF under EC Regulation 1609/89 which amended the structures Regulation 797/85. During the year the Forestry Enterprise received £34.1 million in grant-in-aid, and grant aided 15,400 ha of private planting and 7.1 million ha of restocking, at a cost of £21.6 million to bring the area under grant-aided forestry to 830,000 ha. The Forestry Authority received £40.3 million, and received 74.1 million from the sales of timber, and produced £12.1 million for the Treasury from sales of land and plantations. It spent £12.0 million on forestry recreation. It planted only 3,500 ha and restocked 7,600 ha to give a total forest area of 903,000 ha. During the year the Commission employed 4,700 staff
—— *Report on Forest Research 1991*, 1991, £15.00
—— *Report on Forest Research 1992*, 1992, £15.00
Highlands and Islands Development Board
Accounts 1990–91, HC 173 (91–92, 1992, £4.10
Highlands and Islands Enterprise
Accounts 1991–92, HC 161(92-93), 1992, £4.70
Historic Buildings Council for Scotland
Report for 1990–91, HC 652 (90–91), 1991, £10.20
Intervention Board Executive Agency
Intervention buying accounts 1989–90, HC 327 (91–92), 1992, £2.95
Land Authority for Wales
Accounts 1991–92, HC 137(92–93), 1992, £3.50
National Heritage Memorial Fund
Accounts 1991–92, HC 139(92–93), 1992, £2.45
Nature Conservancy Council
Accounts 1991, HC 246(92–92), 1992, £3.50
Red Deer Commisssion
Annual Report 1990, 1991, £4.95
Annual Report 1991, 1992, £5.10

Scottish Tourist Board
  Accounts 1991–92, HC 199(92–93), 1992, £3.50
Welsh Tourist Board
  Accounts 1991–92, HC 169(92–93), 1992, £3.50

List of annual reports produced by rural planning organisations 1991–2
Published by the Organisation

Format: Author, *Title*, Year of Publication, price

Agriculture, Fisheries and Food, Ministry of
  Agricultural Marketing Schemes Report for 1989–90, 1991, £3.25
Commission for Local Administration
  Annual Report 1990–91, 1991
  ——*Annual Report 1991–92*, 1992. Reveals that complaints to the 'Ombudsman' about planning fell to 26 per cent of all complaints compared to 32 per
  cent ten years ago
Council for the Protection of Rural England
  1992 Annual Report, 1992. Argues that the CPRE achieved record progress for
  the countryside in 1991. It cites the Planning and Compensation Act 1991 as
  marking a reversal of years of deregulation. Other highlights were progress
  over Environmental Assessment, ESAs, controls over farm buildings and
  roads and a commitment to legislate to protect hedgerows
Countryside Commission
  24th Annual Report 1990–91, CCP 350, 1991, £5.00. Highlights of the year
  included the Countryside Stewardship initiative, choosing the site for the New
  National Forest and transferring staff and assets to the Countryside Council
  for Wales on 1 April 1991. During the year £24,556,791 was spent, of which
  £14,330,669 was spent on grant aid and £6,029, 679 on staff
  ——*25th Annual Report 1991–92*, CCP 385, 1992, £5.00. A year of many
  changes especially in personnel. However in spite of only dealing with England, expenditure rose to £29,249,608, of which £16,574,003 was spent on
  grant aid, and £7,926,330 on running costs. Progress was made across several
  fronts, notably on the development of national policies, and the government's
  acceptance that National Parks should be run by independent authorities. The
  involvement with planning issues had however reached a stage, with 660 issues
  being commented upon, where the work-load was now considerably exceeding
  the Commission's resources. As ever the Commission as it evolves will have
  to asess its priorities and its role
English Nature
  Progress '92, 1992. A 30-page glossy document that records the work of English
  Nature in its first year. It provides a brief review of the issues, and English
  Nature's involvement, and concludes with a diary of achievements, focused on
  designations, agreements and the increase in their grant-in-aid to £36.588
  million for 1992–93. It is a far slimmer and less detailed account than its
  predecessor, see p. 188 and indeed it does not provide any account of how its
  grant is spent

Highlands and Islands Enterprise
  First Report 1991–92, 1992. This is the first report of the body that took over
    from the Highlands and Islands Development Board under the Enterprise and
    New Towns (Scotland) Act 1990 on 1 April 1991. One of the changes this
    brought about was to devolve the work of the organisation into 10 Local
    Enterprise Companies. These are claimed to be a success. During the year
    they collectively approved aid for: 366 industrial developments at a cost of
    £8,126,000; 394 tourism projects at a cost of £5,822,000; 138 Natural
    Resource developments at a cost of £3,259,000; and 190 Land Development
    projects at a cost of £1,456,000
Nature Conservancy Council
  17th Report 1990–1991, 1991. This is the last report of the NCC before it was
    dismembered on 1 April 1991. If the flimsy document produced by its succes-
    sor (see above under 'English Nature') does not improve, it will be a much
    missed publication, because its 126 pages provide a wealth of detail about
    conservation. During the year the NCC spent £38,254,000. Management
    Agreements consumed £7,731,000 of this, and Scientific Support £5,319,000,
    but the lion's share was taken by staff costs at £15,378,000
Priorities Board for Research in Agriculture and Food
  Report for 1992, 1992. Continues to emphasise the need to move research toward
    efficient, profitable and environmentally benign agricultural systems
Rural Development Commission
  Annual Report 1991–92, 1992, £13.50. Reports that although the Commission's
    programme created a total of 3,523 job workplace opportunities, the balance
    shifted away from direct provision towards partnership schemes and incentives
    to encourage private sector workshops. In this regard the report warns that
    planning policies are imposing a constraint on small rural business growth,
    notably in the South-East
Town and Country Planning Association
  Annual Report 1991/92, 1992. A rather bleak year for the Association with falling
    revenues leading to the closure of the Northern Office, and staff reductions
    elsewhere. The Association seems rather to have lost its way in the face of
    competition from more strident environmental groups and single issue groups
Wales Tourist Board
  Annual Report 1991/92, 1992. Although visits and bed nights rose, income fell
    by 4 per cent as a result of a greater use of self-catering

Statistics

*List of periodicals and statistics containing information useful for rural
planning*
Published or sold by HMSO

Format: Author, *Title of Series*, Volume (if relevant), *Year or Period Data
refer to*, Year of Publication, price

Agriculture, Fisheries and Food, Ministry of
Agricultural Statistics UK 1989, 1991, £12.50
——*Farm Incomes in England and Wales*, 1991, *1992 edition*, 1992, £20.00.
Revealed an estimated fall of 6 per cent overall. However cereal farms
increased profits while dairy farms registered a drop for the third year running
Central Statistical Office
Social Trends, 22, *1992*, 1992, £24.75
——*Regional Trends*, 27, *1992*, 1992, £24.75
Environment, Department of
Housing and Construction Statistics 1980–90, 1991, £22.00
——*Housing and Construction Statistics*, 46 Parts 1 and 2, *June 1991*, 1991,
£4.40 and £4.40; 47 Parts 1 and 2, *September 1991*, 1992, £4.40 and £4.40; 48
Parts 1 and 2, *December 1991*, 1992, £4.40 and £4.40; and 49 Part 1, *March
1992*, 1992, £4.95
——*Local Housing Statistics*, 98, *July 1991*, £14.00; 99, *October 1991*, 1992,
£10.50; 100, *January 1992*, 1992, £7.00; 101, *April 1992*, 1992, £10.50
——*Digest of environmental protection and water statistics*, 14, *1991*, 1992,
£13.50
——Office of Population Censuses and Surveys, *Population Trends*, 65,
Autumn 1991, 1991, £7.25; 66, *Winter 1991*, 1991, £7.25; 67, *Spring 1992*, 1992,
£7.75; 68, *Summer 1992*, 1992, £7.75
——*General Household Survey*, 20, *1989*, 1991, £18.50
——*Key Population and Vital Statistics Series. Local and Health Authority
Areas, Series VS 17 and PP1 no. 13 1990*, 1991, £10.30
——*Sub-National Population Projections Series PP3 no. 8 1989 base*, 1991,
£11.10
——*Birth Statistics, Review of the Registrar General on births and patterns of
family building in England and Wales Series FM1*, 1992, £11.80
Office of Population Censuses and Surveys
Leisure day visits in Great Britain 1988/89: a survey for BTA, ETB et al. *by
T.Dodd*, 1991, £4.00
——*1991 Census*: the following *County Monitors* were published during 1992
up till the end of August: Isle of Wight; West Glamorgan; Cambridgeshire;
South Yorkshire; Powys; Tyne and Wear; Oxfordshire; Suffolk; Wiltshire;
Lincolnshire; Gwent; Bucks; Cleveland; Bedfordshire; Cornwall; Cumbria;
Warwickshire; Gwynedd; Derbyshire; Merseyside; North Yorkshire; Clwyd;
Berkshire; Leicestershire; West Sussex; West Yorkshire; Avon; Devon; East
Sussex; Mid Glamorgan; Dorset; Cheshire; Hertfordshire; Humberside; Lan-
cashire; and Surrey; all at £2.00
The following *County Reports* were published during the year: Isle of Wight,
£25.00; Wiltshire, £31.00; and Cambridgeshire, £35.00

Figures 8.1 and 8.2 show and reproduced with thanks, the population changes
between 1981 and 1991; they are derived, from the Office of Population
Census and Surveys Newsletter 17 of 15 October 1991, pp. 4 and 5.

Transport, Department of
Transport Statistics Great Britain 1991, 1991, £24.00

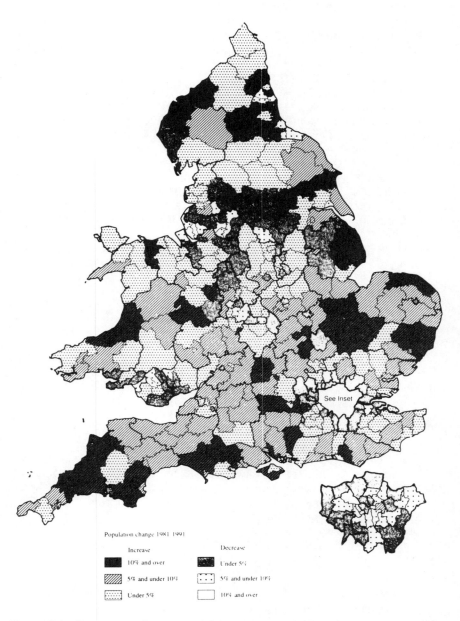

Figure 8.1 *Percentage change in preliminary counts of population present 1981–91: districts of England and Wales*

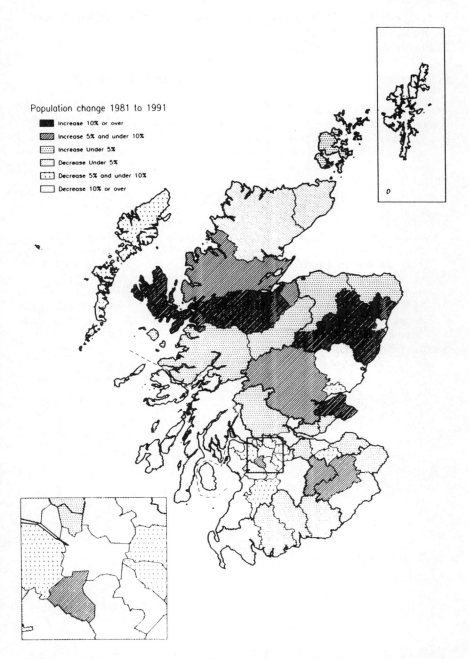

Figure 8.2 *Percentage change in preliminary counts of population present 1981–91:*
Districts and Islands Areas of Scotland

List of periodicals and statistical series containing useful information for rural planners
Published by the Organisations involved

Format: Organisation, *Series or one-off title*, Publisher, Year, price

County Planning Officers Society
  Opencast Coal Mining Statistics 1990–91, County Hall Durham, 1991, £5.00. Opencast coal production remains near the all-time peak of 1989–90 at 18.3 million tonnes. Approval was given for a further 12.7 million tonnes to be extracted in the future
English Tourist Board
  English Heritage Monitor for 1991, the Board, 1992, £15.00. Visitors to historic properties fell by 4 per cent but takings were up by 8 per cent
Environment, Department of
  Land-use change in England, no. 7, DOE, Eastcote, Middlesex, HA4 8SE, 1992, £4.00. Deals with land-use change in 1987, and estimates that about 5,000 ha was transferred from agricultural to urban uses during the year. See Sinclair on p. 173 for an alternative view
  —— *Statistics of Planning Applications Received and decided by County Councils in 1991/92*, 2 Marsham Street, SW1P 3EB, 1992. County Councils made 1,608 decisions, a fall of 8 per cent. The vast majority were for minerals or waste disposal permissions and 81 per cent were granted
Scottish Office
  The Scottish Environment in Statistics, The Office, 1992, £10.00

Section III: Europe

edited by

Mark Blacksell and Andrew Gilg

This year the European section has been edited by Mark Blacksell with the help of Andrew Gilg, the General Editor, who commissioned the articles

Introduction: agriculture and the rural environment in Europe

Mark Blacksell

Agriculture and the rural environment in Europe are in a state of turmoil. In May 1992 the protracted negotiations to reform the EC's Common Agricultural Policy, which had been dragging on for most of the 1980s, were successfully concluded, only for the whole process to be jeopardised a few months later by the discussions on agriculture within the global General Agreement on Tariffs and Trade (GATT) negotiations. The delicate agreements designed to reduce agricultural production within the EC without inflaming the passions of the politically powerful European farmers have been thrown into disarray by the demands of the United States in GATT for further curbs on production. Although the EC Commission has eventually agreed a compromise, this has yet to be ratified by the member states. Farmers across the Community are doing their best to ensure that no such ratification ever occurs, rioting in the streets of several countries, as well as outside the EC headquarters buildings in Brussels and Strasbourg. France has already declared that it will attempt to use its veto in the Council of Ministers to block agreement and a number of other countries, including Belgium, Spain and Ireland, seem to be inclining towards supporting them in the face of intense pressure from their own farmers.

The papers in this European section of *'Progress' in Rural Policy and Planning* expand on a number of different aspects of the pressures now affecting rural areas in Europe. Guy Robinson (University of Edinburgh) and Brian Ilbery (Coventry University) in 'Reforming the CAP: beyond MacSharry' explain the background, meaning and implications of the reforms of the Common-Agricultural Policies (CAP) that were successfully guided through the labyrinth of EC procedures in May by the Irish Commissioner, Ray MacSharry. This introduction is then complemented by a detailed analysis for the financial implications for UK agriculture of the agreement by Andrew Copus (Scottish Agricultural College, Aberdeen) and Ken Thomson (University of Aberdeen) in 'The budgetary effects of the CAP reforms in the UK.' Although their discussion primarily revolves around the impact on UK agriculture, much of their analysis is also highly relevant for the future of the farming industry in other EC countries as well.

It would be a mistake, however, to imply that all the difficulties facing agriculture and the future of rural areas in Europe revolve around the reform of the CAP. As the 25-point declaration by the French Chambers of Agriculture clearly demonstrates, these go far beyond the future of production subsidies and quotas. They want to see a completely new approach to investment in rural infrastructure and a dramatic broadening of the brief for farming, to include meaningful support for new forms of production, for countryside conservation and rural tourism. It is a theme taken up by Nelly Jazra Bandarra, a member of the EC Commission staff in Brussels, writing in her personal capacity on 'The community structural funds and post-Maastricht cohesion'. She explains in considerable detail what the effect of the reform of the structural funds, including the European Agriculture Guidance and Guarantee Fund (EAGGF), in 1989 is having on rural development and how this process is going to be modified, if and when the Treaty on European Union (Maastricht Treaty) is eventually ratified. The cohesion fund, which it is proposed will transfer resources from the richer to the poorer countries in the Community, will have a substantial impact on the whole process of rural development, particularly in the Mediterranean countries.

Lars Olaf Persson (ERU Stockholm) in 'Peripheral labour markets under pressure of change' reports on a piece of research on rural labour markets in Sweden. He reveals that most of the same problems of rural development are also facing Sweden, a country as yet outside the EC, but with an application pending. The CAP cannot be blamed for the decline of rural regions in Sweden, but if it joins the Community it will have to knuckle under its regimes. Persson's report shows that it is only the very heavy public investment in services that has prevented many of the remoter rural areas in Sweden from collapsing. The implication is clear: unless rural development mechanisms are devised to replace the traditional production subsidies of the CAP, the outlook for the majority of rural areas in an EC, enlarged to include first Austria, Finland and Sweden and, later, most of the other countries of the European Economic Area (EEA), is bleak.

Finally, Andrew Gilg (University of Exeter) provides a review of 'Legislative developments in the European Community July 1991—June 1992'. It is an invaluable check-list of the many decisions and regulations emanating from the EC in the past year relating to agriculture and the environment. It is also proof, if proof is needed, that the agreement on the meaning of subsidiarity, concluded in December 1992 at the EC Council of Heads of State in Edinburgh, will have to dismantle a wide range of entrenched interests, if it is to achieve real decentralisation of decision-making in this area of policy.

9 Reforming the CAP: beyond MacSharry

Guy M. Robinson and Brian W. Ilbery

European agriculture is under pressure from a range of economic, social, environmental and political forces to restructure its activities. Recent reforms of the CAP, stemming from proposals by the EC's Agricultural Commissioner, Ray MacSharry, could have important ramifications for the future of agriculture and the countryside.

The MacSharry reforms, and similar proposals agreed by the EC's agriculture ministers in May 1992, represent an attempt to reorientate policy socially and economically so as to maintain a sufficient number of family farms on the land and thereby preserve the natural environment and contribute to rural development. This is to be achieved through substantial cuts in price support (for cereals, beef and milk) and a redistribution of financial support to farmers through income aids; the basis of the reform package is, therefore, the switching of EC support for agriculture from prices to farm incomes. In response to both production and price controls and a continued fall in farm incomes, farmers are having to learn to adjust to a changing policy situation in which they cannot raise incomes by producing more, often unwanted, food.

This paper outlines the background to the CAP reforms, with reference to the chief policy changes effected in the second half of the 1980s. It then considers the MacSharry proposals, arguing that these provided the crucial foundations for the reforms agreed subsequently in May 1992. The latter reforms are outlined and an assessment is made of their likely impact on agriculture. Finally, a statement is made on possible future directions for the CAP.

Establishing co-ordinated agricultural reforms

In 1985 the EC Commission produced a Green Paper, *Perspectives for the CAP*, that initiated a wide-ranging debate on the future of European farming and its role in economic and social development. This debate fostered a sustained questioning of the essential principles of the CAP. For example, in 1986, the European Commission stated, 'European agriculture has to accept economic realities and learn to produce for the market, to adapt to commercial demands and to continue to modernise' (Commission,

1986, p. 8). The situation whereby higher farm incomes could be achieved by increasing output at high guaranteed prices could not be sustained; there were real concerns over the escalating costs of the CAP, especially to store surplus food generated by the system, and the environmental consequences of continued agricultural intensification (Ilbery, 1992a; Robinson, 1991a; 1991b).

The Green Paper suggested guidelines for CAP reform, a basic aim being to reduce surpluses. This was to be achieved through a pricing policy more closely geared to the needs of the market, but with back-up measures to provide protection for the economically weakest holdings and to maintain rural stability. Also suggested as an emergency measure was the use of quotas on production.

Two solutions to the problems of agricultural overproduction presented themselves: first, cuts in price support; and secondly, supply control measures. As the former were politically and socially unacceptable in the mid-1980s, the EC embarked upon a series of policies to control agricultural production. These actually began in 1984, prior to the Green Paper, with guaranteed thresholds for cereals, sunflower seeds, processed fruit and raisins, co-responsibility levies and compulsory production quotas in the milk sector (see Ilbery, 1992b). At the same time, environmental concerns were being expressed and recommendations included Environmentally Sensitive Areas (ESAs) and the withdrawal of land from agriculural production around water bodies and along ecological corridors. ESAs were introduced in 1985 (funding being provided from 1986), together with a farm woodland scheme and an increase in the ceiling for diversification into tourism and crafts in Less Favoured Areas (LFAs). Extensification (Regulation 1760(87)) and set-aside (Regulation 1094(88)) were to follow later in an attempt to cut output and take arable land out of cultivation for five years.

In the late-1980s, building on the Green Paper guidelines, the Commission championed the implementation of three co-ordinated reform measures:

a. A more restrictive pricing policy involving a gradual scaling down of support prices for products in surplus;
b. The application of the principle of producer co-responsibility, in which producers are made to bear a larger share of the costs of disposing of surplus production;
c. Limits on intervention guarantees, coupled with a more stringent policy on quality in order to meet market requirements.

However, slow progress has been made in the application of these reforms. Because of rising agricultural guarantee expenditure, they have tended to be overtaken by other measures, notably the use of budgetary stabilisers (from June 1987), set-aside policies and a pre-pension scheme intended to make it easier for elderly farmers to retire early and so speed up the process of structural change in farming. Nevertheless, in 1988 the EC formally accepted the principles underlying the three measures described above and, subsequently, there have been attempts to establish detailed reforms.

Curbs on spending were seen to be the key to reform, accompanied by financial support for 'weak' regions and a more market-orientated agricultural policy. Reductions in spending were duly implemented in the late-1980s, whilst greater market orientation was encouraged through the use of Maximum Guaranteed Quantities (MGQs) for most crops, sheepmeat and goatmeat. When production exceeds MGQs, then either the price of the particular item or subsidies are automatically reduced. A central aim has been to make producers more subject to market controls by reducing support prices and subsidies, with production above a specified limit resulting in a fall in average returns to the farmer. The reforms proposed by MacSharry and, more recently, by EC farm ministers translated these various ideas into more substantial checks on the price support system.

MacSharry and beyond

The proposals for CAP reform presented by Ray MacSharry in January 1991 included seven main points (Table 9.1). They provided both substantial cuts in support prices for cereals, with smaller cuts for milk, beef and butter, and extensions of the 1980s reforms that had introduced set-aside and championed early retirement for farmers. Furthermore, they proposed curbs on sheep farming. The proposals can be seen as a more concerted attack on the CAP's price guarantee system than the earlier reforms, but with 'safety clauses' for some of the smaller and less efficient producers. Not surprisingly, therefore, they were criticised very strongly by the UK's

Table 9.1   *The MacSharry proposals*

Main Points

1. A 35 per cent cut in the support prices for cereals
2. Ten per cent price cuts for milk producers
3. Fifteen per cent price cuts for beef and butter
4. Individual milk quotas for farmers to be cut by 4 per cent
5. Headage limits of not more than 750 ewes in less favoured areas and 250 ewes in other areas which would be eligible for new subsidies (this would hit UK sheep farmers hardest)
6. Provisions for early retirement of farmers at 55
7. Making the largest and most efficient UK and other European cereal farmers ineligible to full compensation for setting aside at least 15 per cent of their land in order to cut production

Minister of Agriculture, John Gummer, and by several other EC farm ministers who felt their own national interests might be damaged by these proposals. In particular, there was much argument over the suggestion that income aid should be concentrated on smaller and medium-sized farm businesses, leaving the larger businesses to compete in international markets with significantly reduced levels of price support.

Although one of the main intentions of the reforms was to cut the cost of agricultural support, Gummer argued that they would actually add £2.75 million per annum to the cost of running the CAP. Furthermore, he suggested that efficient family farms in the EC would be unfairly penalised to provide extra help to less efficient small producers. This would be brought about by only compensating farmers for up to 50 ha of land set-aside. Yet, this argument overlooks the fact that the larger farms with higher yields would receive the highest amounts of compensation under the reforms, whilst still benefiting from support prices for land remaining under cereals. British objections to the proposals reflected the fact that while an estimated 90.5 per cent of EC holdings with cereals would have no set-aside obligation under these reforms, only 45.4 per cent of UK holdings would escape. Furthermore, only Denmark (72.7 per cent) and France (74.0) per cent) would have figures below the Dutch level of 83.7 per cent. According to the 3rd January edition of *Agra Europe* over 14 per cent of the estimated total UK cereals area would have been subject to set-aside, compared with the EC average (excluding the former East Germany) of 8.9 per cent.

The MacSharry proposals acted as an important catalyst in the continuing discussions over reforms. They filled an important position in the GATT negotiations, showing that the EC not only recognised the need to restrict agricultural support but was willing to put forward concrete proposals for effecting such controls. However, the catalytic effect was most important in encouraging further discussions between EC farm ministers in their ongoing deliberations on what CAP reforms to adopt. On 21 May 1992 agreement was reached by these ministers after eighteen months of negotiation on restructuring the CAP. They claimed that the agreement would bring lower farm-gate prices and, therefore, perhaps cheaper food prices which would more closely reflect world market prices. It was also argued that from 1993 agricultural spending would be less than 50 per cent of the EC budget for the first time in the CAP's history.

The agreement was generally agreed to be a move away from supporting farmers through high produce prices towards giving them direct income supports. However according to reports in the media reactions to the agreement varied widely. For example, John Gummer stated, that it was a great change that enabled the CAP to deal with times of surplus when it had been designed to deal with times of shortage. In contrast, David Clark, Labour's agricultural spokesman, pronounced that the deal would increase the cost of agricultural support to the taxpayer, perhaps by as much as an extra £3 billion over five years. There was some agreement, though, that consumers would pay less for certain types of produce and that the burden of CAP support would shift towards taxpayers as opposed to consumers. For example, MacSharry claimed that, as a result of the agreement, food prices would come down speedily within one year. It was also suggested that the reforms could mean the equivalent of 3p off the basic rate of income tax per European consumer, through cheaper food prices. The Ministry of Agriculture Fisheries and Food (MAFF) however estimated that savings to consumers would be in the order of 2 per cent when compared with current prices for food.

These proposals were not the full package proposed by MacSharry (see Table 9.2). The main point was a 29 per cent cut over three years in the price paid to farmers for cereal production, but with compensation to be paid irrespective of farm size. In contrast, the original MacSharry proposals would have linked compensation to farm size, in favour of smaller farmers and thereby disadvantaging many UK cereal producers. To qualify for income aid, all but the smallest producers must take 15 per cent of their arable land out of production. In addition, there will be grants to encourage more farm forestry, early retirement schemes and diversification programmes. The proposals link farmers' compensation payments to acreage and average yields, so that prices will be allowed to balance demand and supply, with compensation to farmers through tax-funded subsidies. Other proposals include cuts of 15 per cent in support to beef

Table 9.2   *Reforms proposed by EC farm ministers, May 1992*

Main points

1. 29% cut in cereal support over the next three years
2. £80/t feed wheat intervention price in 1995
3. Compensatory aid payment of £209/ha for cereals harvested in 1995
4. Compensatory aid payment of £300/ha for protein peas and beans harvested in 1995
5. Payment of compensatory aid:
   a) conditional upon rotational set-aside of 15%
   b) restricted to the remaining 85%
6. Base area is calculated from average area of cereals, peas, beans, rape and permanent set-aside in 1989, 1990 and 1991. This will be based on current exchange rates and estimated average regional yields
7. Compensation for rotational set-aside of £209/ha in 1995
8. Oilseeds support regime to be incorporated within package
9. Crops not eligible for inclusion in the base area are potatoes, sugar beet, linseed, permanent pasture, fruit and vegetables
10. Co-responsibility levy abolished
11. Additional environmental aid
12. New non-rotational set-aside to be introduced

Source: Crops, 6.6.92

and poultry producers so that there will be reductions in the size of herds and flocks. Cuts of 5 per cent for dairy products are also proposed.

The suggested level of payments for cereals is 110 ECUs per tonne (£77 per tonne), which could put the market price on a par with the current world price. Consequently, grain prices could fall from double the world price to about 15 per cent above it. The cost of subsidising exports down to the world price will, therefore, fall and so will the disruptive effects on unsubsidised food exporters. There is certainly the potential for agricultural imports from Developing Countries to become more competitive in the EC and produce an overall diminution of trade distortion. As the stated intention is gradually to phase out export refunds, this is a goal that could influence the current round of GATT negotiations in which the United States has been highly critical of such practices adopted by the EC.

The proposals could also translate into a 15 per cent decrease in meat prices because of grain's role as an animal feed, and a 5 per cent decrease in the prices of dairy produce. It remains to be seen, though, whether these measures will be sufficient to reduce surplus production. Grain farmers will still have, in effect, a quota of 85 per cent of their current arable area. This will affect both efficient, low-cost producers and inefficient producers and so the costs of production might not be greatly reduced.

Despite the extravagant claims of some of the agricultural ministers, the reforms do not represent the removal of the basic support system of the CAP. The 'driving engine' of price guarantees to farmers will only have lost a little of its force. The cost to the EC budget will still be high, and may even be higher in the short term. The burden for payment will simply have been moved more from consumers to taxpayers. Furthermore, the reforms may not seriously reduce production. Although 15 per cent of arable land per holding may be removed from production, the drop in production overall will certainly be less than 15 per cent. It seems probable that many farmers will set aside marginal land in order to obtain income aid whilst intensifying production on their remaining land in order to compensate for lower prices (a problem known as slippage). Moreover, there is likely to be little effect on livestock production because the potential cut in livestock prices will reflect the lower cost of feedstuffs, so that the profitability of the livestock sector should remain about the same. Consequently, livestock production may also be little changed. So if the overall quantity of production of cereals and livestock is not greatly affected, then prices might not fall. The continuing imbalance between these EC prices and the world market price may, therefore, continue to foster conflicts with both the Americans and Developing Countries over their lack of access to the European market.

John Gummer has suggested that the reforms will bring about a 2p drop in bread prices over a three-year period. Similarly, the Consumers in the EC Group have predicted cuts of 3p for a loaf of bread, 18p per lb for beef, 3p for a 250g packet of butter, some reductions in the prices of poultrymeat and pork, but with little effect on milk and sugar prices. However, bakers have already discounted the idea of the cut in cereal prices being passed on to consumers in the form of lower bread prices. At present, for a loaf of bread retailing at 65p only 8.5p goes to the farmer. The remaining costs are incurred in baking, milling, marketing, packaging and delivering to retailers. There are many other instances where farm prices negotiated in Brussels play only a small role in determining the price of food in the shops. It seems more likely that price rises in the mid-1990s will occur at a slower rate rather than there being outright price reductions.

In fact, farm-gate prices are actually lower than they were ten years ago: in real terms by 50 per cent or more. Retailers have widened their margins by cartel-like control on supply side prices and by raising retail prices. This has been especially effective in the fresh food sector because of the perishability of this food and the need for farmers and wholesalers to sell this produce quickly. A good example is the collapse of farm-gate lamb prices in 1992, which retailers did not pass on to consumers in lower retail prices in the supermarkets.

The proposed reforms have received a very mixed reception from farmers' organisations. The main focus of attention initially was upon the response of French farmers, who protested through direct action, blocking roads in conjunction with truck drivers who were demonstrating about new motoring penalties. The main farm protests in France came from Rural Co-ordination which rejects the reforms outright. This organisation's support base is concentrated in south-west France where the road blocks were first started in June 1992. Their protest highlights the fear of many farmers in the EC that, in the face of a continued cost-price squeeze, farmers' incomes will continue to fall sharply if price guarantees are reduced (Gasson and Potter, 1988; Koester, 1989). Compensatory payments for set-aside land or planting trees are not seen as adequate recompense for these reductions. In both France and the UK, fears have been expressed that only the largest producers in the best endowed areas for cereal growing will be able to take full advantage of the reforms. Meanwhile, elsewhere there will be a continuing exodus of other farmers from the land, leading to increased rural poverty and depressed rural economies. The gap between rich and poor regions may also be accentuated.

Conclusions: towards European agriculture 2000 and beyond

In the mid-1980s, reforms to the CAP, in the form of milk quotas and budgetary stabilisers, were achieved through a widespread agreement that the CAP's budget had to be contained (Moyer and Josling, 1990, p. 100). The details of these reforms involved protracted negotiations and with some recognition that the measures adopted had certain deficiencies. These have now become most evident in the operation of milk quotas

(Downs, 1991). Subsequently, although the issue of controlling the budget has remained highly significant, some additional considerations have motivated fresh proposals for CAP reform. These have included the need to reduce farm subsidies to help facilitate agreement in the current GATT negotiations, the need to reduce surplus production and the need to tackle environmental 'disbenefits' consequent upon the CAP's promotion of increased output.

Growing pressures for CAP reform have spawned a number of policy measures aimed at achieving different targets, resulting in a rather confused picture of new objectives for agricultural policy. A number of measures have encouraged less intensive farming and the adoption of 'environmentally friendly' farming. Others have promoted reduced cereal production, diversification of the farm enterprise and an increase in farm forestry. However, until the MacSharry proposals of 1991, none of the measures made a sustained attack on the levels of price support available to farmers. The adoption of budgetary stabilisers and MGQs introduced some controls on spending, but only to a marginal extent and without fundamental alteration of the support mechanism.

The MacSharry proposals and the subsequent reforms agreed by the EC farm ministers have now carried agricultural policy reform a stage further, representing a fundamental change in the CAP and thus in the future of European agriculture. There should be a significant shift in the basis of EC farm support to arable producers: from crop prices to acreage payments. It shifts the burden of support and lends encouragement to the idea that European agriculture is moving away from a 'productionist era', maintained by substantial price guarantees, and towards a 'post-productionist era' in which farmers are paid 'to produce countryside'. Under these reforms the intention is to cut cereal prices to move into line with world prices whilst more extensive farming practices are advocated. Greater response to market demands is intended, but with less exchequer commitment.

Earlier attempts to curb surplus production, through different supply control measures, had limited short-term effects and in 1991 the EC had 25 million tonnes of cereals in store, 800,000 tonnes of beef, 700,000 tonnes of dairy produce and 2,200 million litres of wine. The measures did little either to improve the social and economic efficiency of the CAP or to solve the increasing divergence of incomes within the agricultural community. For example, neither set-aside nor the promotion of farm diversification had real impacts on agricultural production or farm incomes. Their uptake has been low and geographically varied, reflecting the distribution of marginal cereal areas and real differences in the market opportunities for the various types of farm diversification (Ilbery, 1990; Ilbery and Stiell, 1991).

For most farmers, the concept of obtaining income from setting aside land and diversifying into alternative, non-agricultural enterprises on the farm is still novel. In relation to farm diversification specifically, its adoption should increase, but there are certain limiting factors. Farm diversification represents only one in a set of development options on farm income available to farmers; at present significant numbers of farmers are selecting alternatives connected directly with agricultural production as their preferred business change, rather than diversification. Many farmers are also electing to develop their incomes through economic activity off the farm (other gainful activities) (Gasson, 1988; Shucksmith *et al.*, 1989). Yet others are doing nothing. These tend to be farmers nearing retirement who have no children interested in continuing the farm business and low levels of indebtedness; they are becoming increasingly marginalised.

The current reforms to the CAP have not really gone far enough in either reducing agricultural income differences between the regions or integrating environmental objectives into policy measures. In this context, three requirements are necessary for the future of agriculture in rural areas:

a. Special help needs to be directed towards the poorer farmers and marginal areas in the EC. In association with price cuts, this could be done by making income aids degressive, whereby the rate of compensation decreases with increasing farm size. This was part of the original MacSharry proposals, but was dropped in the final reform package.
b. The CAP needs to be part of a much wider rural development strategy, where agriculture is just one element alongside tourism, forestry, industry and services. Agriculture should be integrated into a coherent rural development programme which is based on social and environmental, as well as economic, criteria. More specifically, rural policies need to be regionally-based, to take account of the great diversity and range of socio-economic conditions which exist in the EC and the real problems facing farming in the lagging regions of the Community.
c. Sustainable and environmentally-friendly agriculture should be encouraged. This would necessitate an integration of environmental objectives into agricultural and rural development policy; unfortunately, no framework currently exists in the EC for reconciling agricultural and environmental objectives.

A start has been made in reforming the CAP, but policy-makers have not really moved very far away from the idea of supporting farmers in one way or another. Yet much of this support has been misdirected and has not benefited those farmers most in need of assistance. The strong reactions to the MacSharry proposals and to those of the EC farm ministers indicate profound concern throughout the Community as to their detailed repercussions. The prospect of differential regional and sectoral responses to the reforms is producing renewed debate as to the likely character of European agriculture by the end of the century. The uncertainty about this future comes at a time when many farm incomes are greatly reduced from their level of ten years ago and when continued loss of full-time farm labour is occurring (Britton, 1990; Hill, 1990). So the turmoil of unfolding events offers the prospect of sustained opposition from many farmers and further political bargaining as member countries seek to maximise their own interests.

There are still numerous stumbling—blocks on the way to implementing the farm ministers' reforms. For example, in the UK farmers have complained that the government is already undermining the reforms by failing to say whether or not it would match money released by Brussels to pay farmers to set aside land. The grants offered to farmers throughout the EC amount to £400 million, but individual Treasuries have to match the money offered by the CAP. Furthermore, as yet the Commission has not set the terms of the schemes to be implemented. As with the establishment of the CAP itself, the birth of a reformed CAP seems likely to be a protracted and difficult process.

References

Britton, D. 1990, 'Recent changes and current trends' in D. Britton (ed.), *Agriculture in Britain: changing pressures and policies*, CAB International, Wallingford, pp. 1–33

Commission of the European Communities (CEC), 1986, *Europe's Common Agricultural Policy*, CEC, Brussels

Downs, C.J., 1991, 'EC agricultural policy and land use: milk quotas and the need for a new approach', *Land Use Policy*, **8**: 206–10

Gasson, R.M., 1988, 'Farm diversification and rural development', *Journal of Agricultural Economics*, **39**: 175–81

Gasson, R.M. and Potter, C., 1988, 'Conservation through land diversion: a survey of farmers' attitudes', *Journal of Agricultural Economics*, **39**: 340–51

Hill, B., 1990, 'Incomes and wealth' in D. Britton (ed.), *Agriculture in Britain: changing pressures and policies*, CAB International, Wallingford, pp. 135–60

Ilbery, B.W., 1990, 'Adoption of the arable set-aside scheme in England', *Geography*, **75**: 69–73

Ilbery, B.W., 1992a, 'From Scott to ALURE—and back again?', *Land Use Policy*, **9**: 131–42

Ilbery, B.W., 1992b, 'Agricultural policy and land diversion in the European Community' in A. Gilg (ed.), *Progress in Rural Policy and Planning*, Volume 2 Belhaven Press, London and New York, pp. 153–66

Ilbery, B.W. and Stiell, B., 1991, 'Uptake of the Farm Diversification Grant Scheme in England', *Geography*, **76**: 259–63

Koester, U., 1989, 'Financial implications of the EC set-aside programme', *Journal of Agricultural Economics*, **40**: 240–8

Moyer, H.W. and Josling, T.E., 1990, *Agricultural policy reform: politics and process in the EC and USA*, Iowa State University Press, Ames

Robinson, G.M., 1991a, 'The environmental dimensions of recent agricultural policy in the United Kingdom' in G.E. Jones and G.M. Robinson (eds), *Land-use change and the environment in the European Community*, Biogeography Monographs, No. 4, Institute of British Geographers, pp 63–76

Robinson, G.M., 1991b, 'The environment and agricultural policy in the European Community: land-use implications in the United Kingdom', *Land Use Policy*, **8**: 95–107

Shucksmith, D., Bryden, J., Rosenthall, P., Short, C. and Winter, D., 1989, 'Pluriactivity, farm structures and rural change', *Journal of Agricultural Economics*, **40**: 345–60

10 The budgetary effects of the CAP reforms in the UK

A.K. Copus and K.J. Thomson

Introduction

The financial cost of the EC's Common Agricultural Policy has been of concern since the early days of the CAP in the 1960s. Successive budgetary crises in both national contributions and overall expenditure have given rise to various attempts at adjustment and control, including co-responsibility levies (producer taxes), the UK budget rebate, milk quotas and the 'stabiliser' mechanism for reducing market support prices as EC production exceeds a 'guarantee threshold'. However, none of these attempts has prevented the CAP budget (which is spent mainly on market intervention by export subsidies and public purchase and storage, with smaller amounts on a variety of price subsidies and on structural assistance) reaching 30 billion ECU (about £25 billion) in 1991.

Furthermore, CAP spending has failed to prevent a continuing exodus from European farms, with per capita agricultural incomes being more or less maintained in real terms while incomes elsewhere have risen. The distribution of support, linked as it has mainly been to quantities of production rather than to regional, social or environmental criteria, has been far from satisfactory. Finally, the *economic* (as opposed to financial) consequences of CAP market support, in terms of distorted resource use and consumer choice, have been calculated as one to two times the budgetary cost, giving a total annual transfer associated with EC agricultural policies of over 100 billion ECU (about £80 billion), or some 331 ECU (£265) per head of population (OECD, 1992).

The reforms agreed in May 1992 represent a significant change in a number of CAP commodity regimes, although only some 50 per cent of total EC final agricultural production is directly affected. The main element is a substantial reduction in cereal intervention (market support) prices, which in turn will allow falls in most meat products, in the case of beef via a parallel cut in beef support prices. These price measures will reduce the market support cost of the CAP regimes affected, in three possible ways: increased consumption, reduced production (both reducing EC surpluses) and diminished export subsidy rates, possibly assisted by rises in world market prices in response to lower Community exports. However, these effects may be less than anticipated, due to slow and limited reactions on the part of consumers and producers to the changed price incentives. EC-world price ratios may also not diminish as much as expected, due to dollar-ECU exchange-rate movements and to competitive price reductions on the part of extra-EC suppliers.

The other main component of the May 1992 reforms, the compensation to be paid to producers, will give rise to a major switch from indirect (market) support to direct (producer) support. Other things being equal, the very substantial amounts to be paid out in this way (see below) would be expected to increase the efficiency (and thus might reduce the budgetary cost in level and rate over time) of the policy as a whole. However, much depends on the administration of the compensation measures. Determination of eligibility for total and set-aside arable areas and for livestock headage numbers will be complex, and the rates of compensation payments will be subject to Council and Commission determination. As conditions change over the years, these bodies will need to balance the competing demands of budgetary control, farm-income maintenance and supply limitation.

The expenditure estimates below have been calculated under a number of necessary assumptions, the most important of which relates to the level of CAP market support still considered necessary after EC support prices have been reduced, and the level of the 'green' pound which converts the pre-announced ECU levels to national sterling prices. The extent of market support reduction is described for the cereal and beef sectors below, while a sterling-ECU exchange rate of 1 ECU = £0.795 has been taken.

The arable sector

The reform of the arable regime of the CAP involves a 29 per cent reduction in cereals support prices for cereals over three years, for which farmers will be compensated by area payments.[1] In order to qualify for this aid 'professional growers'[2] will be required to set-aside 15 per cent of their cereals, oilseeds and protein crops (COPs) area. Set-aside land will also attract area payments. Smaller producers will have no set-aside requirement. Co-responsibility levy will be abolished, effectively raising the market price of cereals by approximately 5 per cent.

Table 10.1 shows the costs of market support and direct subsidies under the CAP arable regimes for the UK in 1991, and estimates of cost under the reformed arrangements. In 1991, the largest share of the £521m cost of supporting the UK arable sector, was accounted for by oilseeds (£252m). Cereals accounted for a net £184m, comprising payments of £241m on export refunds and £43m on intervention, against which was offset £101m generated by co-responsibility levy. Market support for protein crops totalled £43m, whilst set-aside (the only support paid directly to farmers) accounted for £25m.

Table 10.1   *Market support and direct subsidies to the UK arable sector in 1991 and after CAP reform*

	1991 (£m)	Post-reform (£m)	Change (£m)
Market support	476.0	120.4	−355.6
Direct subsidies	25.3	951.0	+925.6
Total	501.3	1,071.3	+570.0

Note: 1991 data were calculated as a weighed average of data for 1990/91 and 1991/92 financial years.

Source: MAFF, 1992; IBAP, 1992; and estimates

Table 10.2   *UK COPs and set-aside area, and compensation expenditure, after CAP reform*

	COPs area (ha)	Set-aside area (ha)	Price compensation (£m)	Compensation set-aside (£m)	Total (£m)
England	3,557,201	515,867	715.2	109.5	824.7
Wales	55,133	4,887	8.5	0.8	9.3
Scotland	520,768	71,123	95.1	13.7	108.8
N. Ireland	47,211	3,082	7.7	0.5	8.2
UK	4,180,313	594,959	826.4	124.5	951.0

Source: Agricultural Census and estimates

In Table 10.1 it is assumed that, following CAP reform, the improved market situation will mean that intervention costs in the arable sector will be minimal, whilst export refunds for cereals will be halved. The bulk of post-reform arable sector support (roughly £1 billion) will be paid direct to farmers, representing a total increase on the 1991 payment of more than 100 per cent. By far the largest share of this (£587m, 54 per cent) will be accounted for by price compensation paid to professional cereal growers. A further £41m (4 per cent) will be spent on small producer price compensation, £125m (12 per cent) on set-aside, and a little over £200m (19 per cent) on oilseeds and protein crops compensation.[3] Table 10.2 shows the estimated direct subsidy expenditure by constituent country in the UK.

The livestock sector

Very modest changes were agreed for the sheep and milk sectors in 1992, and these are unlikely to result in significant changes in CAP expenditure.

The original reform proposal for the ewe premium, which would have deprived larger and more intensive producers of a significant proportion of the subsidy they currently receive, was very much watered down. Individual quotas based on premia claims in 1991 will be introduced, together with arrangements for the trading of premia rights and a national reserve to cater for new entrants, and to prevent the loss of premia rights from 'sensitive areas'. Current headage limits (1,000 ewes in the Less Favoured Areas and 500 in lowground areas) will remain, with 50 per cent premium to be paid on sheep in excess of these limits. These arrangements will act as a brake to structural changes within the industry, and give sheep farmers a new capital asset, their quota entitlement. Milk quotas are to remain, with no reduction in 1992–3, although the Commission is to review the situation for the following two years. There will be a small (2.5 per cent) reduction in butter support prices in 1993–4 and 1994–5, but skim milk prices will remain unchanged.

For the beef sector, the policy changes and expenditure calculations are quite complex. In 1991, expenditure on market support for beef within the UK (Table 10.3) totalled £295m. Over 90 per cent (£273m) of this expenditure related to intervention, with export refunds and food aid accounting for a mere £22m. CAP reform will result in a 15 per cent reduction in support prices.[4] In addition, a progressively lower limit will be placed upon the tonnage which will be accepted for intervention each year, effectively halving intervention purchases by 1997.

In Table 10.3 it was assumed that the reforms will have intervention costs, to £136m, and reduce export refunds by 15 per cent to £18.5m. Thus total market support for beef after the reforms is estimated at £155m, a reduction of almost 50 per cent compared to 1991.

The Beef Special Premium (BSP) is currently paid at slaughter on up to 90 head of male beef cattle per producer. Under the reformed regime, two rather larger[5] 'on-farm' payments will be made at 10 and 22 months. These will be subject to stocking density limits, individual headage limits, and regional quotas.[6] Producers with extensive systems will be eligible for an additional 'extensification premium', and producers in Northern Ireland

Table 10.3 *Market support for beef, 1991, and post-reform*

	1991 (£m)	Post-reform (£m)
Intervention	273	136
Export Refunds	22	19
Total	295	155

Source: IBAP, 1992; and estimates

Table 10.4 *Beef Special Premium payments in the UK, 1991, and post-reform*

| | No. of premia ('000 hd) | | 1991 | Post-reform BSP | Value of payments | | Total post-reform payment |
	1991	Post-reform	(£m)	(£m)	Extensification premia (£m)	DSP (£m)	(£m)
England and Wales	940	1,212–1,671	30	87–120	7.2	n.a.	94–128
Scotland	245	354–486	8	25–35	2.1	n.a.	27–37
N.I.	235	315–354	7	23–25	1.9	5[1]	30–32
U.K.	1,419	1,881–2,511	45	135–180	11.2	5	151–197

Note: Estimate supplied by the Department of Agriculture Northern Ireland; adjustments in the seasonal pattern of cattle marketing would probably disqualify Northern Ireland from this premium within less than five years

Source: Agricultural Departments and estimates based upon Agricultural Census

will be encouraged to avoid marketing their cattle during the autumn peak period through the payment of a 'De-seasonalisation Premium' (DSP).

In 1991, BSP totalling £45m was paid on 1.4 million cattle in the UK. The impact of the reforms is not easy to predict with any degree of accuracy, although it has proved possible to estimate minimum and maximum possible outcomes (see Table 10.4). The minimum estimate (£146m) is based upon the assumption that beef producers continue with their current production systems, and that the reforms would not prompt any changes in the age structure of male beef cattle within the UK. Under this scenario the number of second (22 months) BSP payments would be only 45–50 per cent of the number of first (11 months) payments, since a large proportion of male beef cattle are finished at 15–18 months. The maximum estimate (£195m) assumes that all beef finishers are able to adapt their systems in order to maximise their claims of the second BSP payment.[7] Both estimates assume that 5 per cent of 10-month-old cattle and 20 per cent of 22-month-old cattle would be excluded by stocking density limit, that 25 per cent would be eligible for extensification premium,[8] and that the 90 head limit would effectively be circumvented by careful marketing.[9] Clearly, even the minimum estimate represents a very substantial increase in expenditure (224 per cent on 1991 levels).

The EC contribution towards Suckler Cow Premium (SCP)—payable on cows used for breeding beef calves of farms without a commercial dairy herd—is to be substantially increased, and supplemented by an extensification premium.[10] Individual quotas and stocking rate premium eligibility limits will be introduced.[11]

In 1991, roughly 1.4 million Suckler Cow Premia were paid in the UK, totalling £70.4m (Table 10.5). On the basis of average stocking rates for suckler cow enterprises produced by the Meat and Livestock Commission (MLC) (1992), we may assume that very few suckler cows, say 5 per cent, will be excluded from premium by the stocking density limits. This means

Table 10.5 *Suckler Cow Premium payments in the UK, 1991, and post-reform*

| | No. of payments | | Value of payments | | | |
	1991 ('000)	Post-reform ('000)	1991[1] (£m)	Post-reform[1] (£m)	Extensification (£m)	Total[1] (£m)
England	574	588	28(23)	58(53)	1.4	59(54)
Wales	182	186	9(7)	19(17)	0.4	19(17)
Scotland	447	456	22(18)	45(41)	1.9	47(43)
N.I.	264	280	11(11)	26(25)	0.7	27(26)
U.K.	1,466	1,510	70(58)	148(136)	3.6	152(140)

Note: 1. EC contributions shown in brackets

Source: Agricultural Departments and estimates based on the Agricultural Census

Table 10.6   *Net change in expenditure on the UK beef sector*

	1991 (£m)	Post-reform (£m)	Change (£m)
Market support	295	155	−140
Direct subsidies[1]	120	331[2]	+211
Total expenditure	415	486	+71

Notes: 1. Includes EC contributions to BSP, SCP and to cattle HLCA payments
2. Assumes that post-reform BSP expenditure will be midway between the minimum and maximum estimates given in Table 10.4

Source: Tables 10.3–5

that the total payment implied by the new rates would rise to £148m. Farm Accounts Scheme[12] data indicates that approximately 10 per cent of Scottish suckler cows were in herds with stocking densities of less than 1.4 livestock units per forage hectare. Extensification premia on suckler cows are likely to generate in the region of £2.6m.

Table 10.6 summarises the impact of CAP reform on expenditure on the beef sector in the UK. Clearly, the increase in direct subsidies (£211m, 180 per cent of the 1991 expenditure is only partially offset by the reduction in market support (£140m, 47 per cent of 1991 expenditure). The net effect upon total expenditure is an increase of £71m (17 per cent).

Summary, discussion and conclusions

Table 10.7 shows that the reforms are likely to increase EC agricultural expenditure (excluding capital grants) in the UK by approximately 30 per cent, from £1.4 billion to £1.9 billion. This suggests that unless there are substantial savings elsewhere within the Community, they will have limited success in controlling or curtailing the agricultural budget.

Table 10.7 also indicates that the proportion of EC expenditure spent on direct subsidies is likely to increase from 45 per cent to more than 80 per cent. This clearly has implications in terms of transparency, and of public perception of agricultural support. It may well prove more difficult to defend direct income aids than it has been to defend the more remote and anonymous market support.

If the CAP reforms are to be implemented, effective monitoring and control will be necessary to prevent widespread misuse of the system. The level of monitoring required to ensure that set-aside commitments are adhered to, and that reference flock numbers and stocking rates are not

Table 10.7   *Overall EC budgetary impact of CAP reform in the UK*

	1991 (£m)	Post-reform (£m)	Change (£m)
Market support	786	292	−494
Direct subsidies	656[1]	1,569[2]	+913
Total expenditure[3]	1,442	1,861	+419

Notes: 1. Includes EC contributions to Set-Aside, SAP, SVP, HLCAs, BSP, SCP and Milk Outgoers Scheme/Quota Compensation
2. Includes EC contributions to Set-Aside and arable area payments, SAP, HLCAs, BSP, SCP and Extensification Premia
3. Excludes EC expenditure on capital grants and environmental schemes

Source: MAFF, 1992; IBAP, 1992; and estimates

exceeded, will be far greater and more costly than for existing schemes. It is possible that the introduction of the reforms could provide an opportunity for the rationalisation, harmonisation and simplification of complicated and sometimes unrelated administrative mechanisms which have been created piecemeal as new policies have been introduced. However, this would require a radical rethink of current procedures, which the regulatory authorities (principally MAFF for the UK) may not be prepared to contemplate. The European Commission is likely to allocate some funds to help member states set up an Integrated Administration and Control System, but the major proportion of the public-sector costs involved is likely to fall on national exchequers, while farmers themselves will have substantial costs in providing and checking eligibility data and possibly in pursuing grievances through political and legal channels.

The above estimates have been made using green exchange rates current before the pound was taken out of the Exchange Rate Mechanism (ERM) in September (1 ECU = £0.795423). Since 'Black Wednesday', the green pound has already been devalued once, and given the continued slide of sterling further changes appear inevitable. Furthermore, the green money system is due to be dismantled from 1 January 1993, as part of the arrangements for the creation of the Single European Market. Whatever the details of the transitional arrangements, it is clear that by the time the CAP reform is complete in 1996/7 agricultural subsidy rates are likely to be converted into pounds at exchange rates close to those of the currency markets. It would of course be foolish to attempt to predict the precise impact of such a change, although it seems highly likely that farmers in the UK will receive a 'windfall gain' not available to those in countries remaining within the narrow band of the ERM. It has recently been suggested that by early 1993 the green rate will approximate 1ECU = £0.95.[13] Such a green rate would result in a substantial rise in the value of EC-funded direct subsidies within the UK, to over £2.2 billion, an increase of over £781m compared to 1991. It would also go a long way towards offsetting the reduction in intervention (and hence farm-gate) prices, although the precise impact here would depend upon a number of trade considerations which are very difficult to predict.

This chapter has discussed the nature of the change in the budgetary aspect of the CAP after reform, and presented some estimates of CAP expenditures in the UK beforehand and afterwards. The overall financial impact of the reforms is seen to be highly dependent on the continued need for EC market support expenditure despite the reduction in cereal and beef support prices, but can be expected to increase public expenditure on UK agriculture by around 30 per cent (see also the Chancellor's public expenditure estimates, 11 November 1992 H.C. 231 and 232 (92–93). At Community level, the budgetary effects may be somewhat less, since the agricultural structure is more fragmented, and market support is concentrated in certain countries. However, most authorities (including the Commission itself) are assuming a substantial rise in total CAP spending, as well as in administrative complexity, and this rise in cost must be set against the reduction in consumer burden and the improvement in distribution of policy benefits amongst producers.

Notes

1. This compensation will be paid according to the area sown with cereals, oilseeds and protein crops (peas, beans and lupins), at rates which will vary from region to region, higher in high-yielding areas, and vice versa. For cereals an ECU 45 (£36) per tonne standard rate will be translated into per hectare payments using average regional yields. Oilseeds will receive ECU 152 (£121) per tonne multiplied by the regional oilseeds yield, whilst protein crops will receive ECU 65 (£52), multiplied by the regional cereals yield.

2. Defined as those with an area of COPs capable of producing more than 92 tonnes of cereals per annum at the average regional yield.

3. A number of assumptions underlie these estimates of post-reform expenditure. All set-aside is assumed to be rotational. The addition of a non-rotational scheme will have an at present unknown impact upon both the price compensation and the set-aside compensation payments. It is also impossible to predict how long the compensation rates stated in the reform agreement may remain in force. It is widely feared in the industry that their real value will be rapidly eroded after the completion of the transitional period.

4. The 15 per cent reduction in support prices does not necessarily imply an equivalent fall in farm-gate cattle prices. However, the strict limits to be imposed on intervention may well result in large volumes of Irish beef,

currently sold into intervention, appearing on the UK market and adding to the downward pressure on prices.

5. Each payment will be of ECU 90 (£72), compared with the current single payment of £32.

6. Premium eligibility on all but the smallest farms (under 15 livestock units) will be subject to a stocking density limit of 2 livestock units per forage hectare. Individual producers may claim special premium on up to 90 head of male beef cattle in each age group. However, within each region (constituent countries in the UK) the total number of payments in the 10-month age group is to be limited to the number paid in the reference year (1991 in the UK). If the number of requests for (10-month) premium exceeds the reference herd, individual claims for both first and second payments will be proportionately reduced. Producers with stocking rates less than 1.4 livestock units per hectare will be eligible for an additional ECU 30 (£24) 'extensification premium'.

7. The proportion of farmers currently finishing cattle 15–18 months who will change their system in order to collect the second Special Premium payment is uncertain. The Meat and Livestock Commission have estimated that keeping the cattle on would result in a 10 per cent increase in gross margin per hectare, and a 40 per cent increase per calf. However most beef specialists agree that there would be considerable non-economic barriers to such a change, including the need for additional winter accommodation, and more difficult worm control. There may well be pronounced regional variations in response. In Northern Ireland, where the milder climate allows fat cattle to remain outside in winter with little loss of condition, a large proportion of cattle already reach 22 months before slaughter, 90 per cent of cattle are anticipated to receive the second premium payment. Elsewhere the take-up rate may be nearer 40–50 per cent.

8. Meat and Livestock Commission estimates (MLC, 1992) suggest that the majority of intensive, cereal-based, producers would forfeit all premium entitlement since their forage area is minimal. Systems heavily dependent upon grass silage generally have stocking rates averaging over 5 livestock units per hectare, and would also lose a large proportion of their entitlement. More extensive, grass-based systems, by far the most common in the UK, had average stocking rates of slightly over 2 units per hectare, and would therefore retain the majority of their entitlement. An analysis of data from the Scottish Farm Accounts Survey suggests that approximately 90 per cent of cattle would retain Special Premium eligibility on grounds of stocking density. Furthermore, over 50 per cent would be eligible for the Extensification Premium. Both these figures may be somewhat lower across the UK as a whole since Scottish systems tend to be more extensive than those in England and Wales.

9. It is assumed that any producer who has reached the annual limit of 90 premia in either age-group will be able to sell remaining cattle to smaller producers (who will be able to claim the premia) at a higher price than those upon which the premium has already been paid. There will thus be a dual market in male beef cattle, distinguished by a roughly £90 price margin.

10. The current rate is ECU 50 (£40); the new payment will be ECU 120 (£95). In addition, national governments may elect to pay a supplement of up to ECU 20 (£35). Current rates (including national supplements) are £60 in the LFA and £55 in lowground areas. If the national supplements are maintained the

post-reform rates would be £115 and £110 respectively. However, it is possible that the UK government may take the opportunity to remove the supplements, giving a single rate of £95. Producers with stocking rates under 1.4 livestock units will be able to claim the ECU 30 (£24) extensification premium.

11. Individual producers will not be able to claim more than 99 per cent of the number of premia that they received in the reference year (1992 in the UK), or to exceed the density limit of 2 livestock unit per forage hectare. However, as with the ewe premium, premium rights will be tradable, and will therefore acquire a capital value, and there will be similar arrangements for a national reserve.

12. The Farm Accounts Scheme is the Scottish component of the EC Farm Accountancy Data Network.

13. *Agra Europe*, 30 10 93.

References

Intervention Board for Agricultural Produce (IBAP), 1992, *1991–92 Annual Report*, IBAP, Reading

MAFF 1992, *Agriculture in the United Kingdom 1991*, HMSO, London

Meat and Livestock Commission, (MLC) 1992, *Cattle market outlook* (MLC), July 1992

OECD, 1992, *Agricultural policies, markets and trade: monitoring and outlook 1992*, Paris

11 Agriculture and rural areas: a 25-point declaration by the Permanent Assembly of the French Chambers of Agriculture (APCA), June 1992

Assemblée Permanente Chambres d'Agriculture, translated by Mark Blacksell

The 25-point declaration set out below has been drawn up in the belief that the balanced development of rural areas is one of the key challenges facing the French government at the turn of the twentieth century. Positive action is required if the countryside is not to slip into irrevocable decline. The declaration is reprinted here, because it may well be that other European countries would benefit from working to such a clear and uncompromising agenda.

1. The drawing up of a national framework planning law
2. Agreement of regional master plans
3. Stronger protection for farmland, forests and sites of ecological importance so as to ensure greater clarity in the way they are defined; enhanced protection and more legal safeguards over land ownership
4. The encouragement of a spirit of inter-communal co-operation
5. The establishment of truly uninhabited zones in particularly difficult rural areas
6. Improvement in the quality of services in the 'rural desert' by installing water supplies, mains drainage and electricity
7. Change education policy so that the flawed logic of closing rural schools is abandoned
8. Make up for lost time in building rural housing
9. Link rural areas into the wider infrastructure of communications and telecommunications
10. Modify the tariff structure for long-distance and local telephone calls so that the time allocated is not solely determined by distance

11. Improve public services in rural areas
12. Strengthen the role of the Chambers of Agriculture in developing planning policies for rural areas
13. Devise policies at the Community, national and regional levels
14. Promote the investment of financial and human capital in rural areas
15. Correct the spatial disequilibria caused by the reform of the CAP
16. Increase the outlets for agricultural products
17. Make the sale and transfer of farms easier
18. Reduce the taxes on farmers
19. Support the setting up of an Association of Agricultural Landowners
20. Remove the obstacles to pluriactivity
21. Remove the fiscal and social obstacles to developing farm tourism
22. Draw up a scale of payments to remunerate those farmers who conserve nationally recognised 'natural' landscapes of ecological or historic interest
23. Adapt the tools available to landowners (the statute on tenant farming, and the multi-annual convention on agriculture) to enable the funds borrowed to be used in ways that are more environmentally friendly
24. Adapt the funding policies for agriculture so that they are better fitted to the ways in which farmers actually need to manage the land
25. Integrate the principles of land management into the relevant legislation on farm structures.

12 The Community Structural Funds and post-Maastricht cohesion

Nelly Jazra Bandarra*

The Community's structural policy is at a turning-point, facing a further challenge after the reform begun in 1989. This chapter reviews the impact of this reform on the rural areas of the EC and then goes on to consider the further changes that will be necessary when the Treaty on European Union (Maastricht Treaty) is finally ratified, probably in the latter half of 1993.

Assistance is provided by the three Community structural Funds: the Guidance Section of the European Agricultural Guidance and Guarantee Fund (EAGGF), the European Regional Development Fund (ERDF) and the European Social Fund (ESF). For various reasons, the Commission and the member states have been obliged to reflect on the guidelines for the activities of the Funds, to integrate them into the framework created by the Maastricht Treaty on European Union and to decide on new budget appropriations for the 1993–97 period (Table 12.1).

The reform of the structural Funds only came into force for regions under Objective 1 (regions lagging behind in their development) more than a year after formal approval in 1989 and approximately two years after for regions under Objective 5b (rural areas). The first stage of the reform ends in 1993, as does the deadline for implementing almost all programmes.

For several months, therefore, the Commission has been preparing new proposals for inclusion in the so-called 'Delors II' package (to distinguish it from 'Delors I' which covered the 1989–93 period and involved doubling the money available under the structural Funds at 1989 prices). Delors II provides for an appreciable increase in all the Funds, with the amount available for Objective 1 once again doubling. The resources of the structural Funds rose from 9.1 B. ECU of the total Community budget in 1987 to 18.6 B. ECU in 1992, and is planned to reach 29.3 B. ECU in 1997. It must be stressed, however, that this is not going to be achieved by a reduction in expenditure on the CAP, which rose from 32.7 B. ECU of the Community budget in 1987 to 35.3 B. ECU in 1992 and is set to reach 39.6 B. ECU in 1997 if the Commission proposals on the reform of the CAP are adopted (see Table 12.2).

*This chapter represents only the personal views of its author.

Table 12.1   *Structural Funds, breakdown by objective*

	Billion ECU 1989 prices	%	% of Community population covered
Objective 1 (lagging regions)	38.3	63.4	21.5
Objective 2 (industrial decline)	7.2	11.9	16.0
Objectives 3 + 4 (labour market)	7.5	12.4	(a)
Objective 5a (agricultural structures) (b)	3.4	5.6	(a)
Objective 5b (rural areas)	2.8	4.6	5.0
Transitional measures and Community initatives	1.1	2.0	(a)
TOTAL	60.4	100.0	42.5

Notes: a. Objectives 3 and 4 and 5a and transitional measures being 'horizontal' do not relate to specific sections of the population
b. Data on Objective 5a do not include Objective 1 regions

Source: Commission services

Table 12.2   *Financial outlook, 1987–97*

	1987	1992	1997
Commitment Appropriations (billion ECUS 1992)			
I. Common agricultural policy	32.7	35.3	39.6
II. Structural operations (including the Cohesion Fund)	9.1	18.6	29.3
III. Internal policies (other than structural operations)	1.9	4	6.9
IV. External action	1.4	3.6	6.3
V. Administrative expenditure (and repayments)	5.9	4	4
VI. Reserves	0	1	1.4
TOTAL	51	66.6	87.5
PAYMENT APPROPRIATIONS REQUIRED	49.4	63.2	83.2
as % of GNP	1.05	1.15	1.34
Own resources ceiling as % of GNP	(none) (except VAT = 1.40)	1.20	1.37

Note: Average annual GNP growth
— 87–92 (actual)   3.1%
— 92–97 (projected)   2.5%

The assistance provided by the Funds during the 1989–93 period raises a wide range of issues, as do the proposals for the period up to 1997. For the most part, they are beyond the scope of this chapter; the analysis here concentrates on rural development and the call it will have on Community aid in the future, as well as its likely contribution to economic and social cohesion in the EC.

The Delors II package is related to the Maastricht accords on political and monetary union, which reaffirm the principle of economic and social cohesion (Article 130b of the Treaty of Rome). The implementation of this principle, the purpose of which is to reduce the disparities in levels of development and living standards, will make it possible to spread the advantages of the Single Market more widely, and to apply competition policy more rigorously. The reform of the CAP and a policy more focused on rural development policy are essential for rural areas but neither will have any effect on the financing of major investment and infrastructural projects, which absorb the bulk of Community aid.

Extensive discussions are taking place on all these topics, but very little information is filtering out to the public domain. The issues are not always very clear-cut, even to those concerned with the actual implementation of structural Fund policies. The wider issues will, of course, depend on the Maastricht Treaty being ratified by the member states.

Impact of structural Fund aid on rural areas

Can the impact be measured?

The whole history of the structural Funds is dealt with elsewhere,[1] but there are some questions of a general nature which need to be examined here, as well as other issues associated directly with the impact of aid schemes. One fundamental question is whether Community projects have brought about any reduction in the disparities between the regions in the Community and therefore have led to an improvement in the living standards. If one takes an overall indicator such as per capita GDP, it is quite clear that the countries with the lowest figures have actually moved closer to the Community average in recent years but it will still be a long time before they catch up completely. Portugal has made appreciable progress, from 48.9 per cent of average Community GDP in 1970 to 56.3 per cent in 1992. It is much the same for Ireland, which has improved from 59.5 per cent in 1970 to 68.9 per cent in 1992. On the other hand, Greece has not seen much change: 51.6 per cent in 1970 and 52.1 per cent in 1992 (see Table 12.3). By contrast, more developed countries such as Denmark, the United Kingdom, the Netherlands and Luxembourg have seen a decline in per capita Gross Domestic Product (GDP) in relation to the Community average.

Table 12.3 *Gross Domestic Product at current market prices per head of population*

	B	DK	HD	GR	E	F	IRL	I	L	NL	P	UK	EUR12
1960	95.4	118.3	117.9	38.6	60.3	105.8	60.8	86.5	158.5	118.6	38.7	128.6	100.0
1980	104.1	107.8	113.6	58.1	74.2	111.6	64.0	102.5	118.5	110.9	55.0	101.1	100.0
1981	103.2	107.2	113.8	57.8	73.4	112.6	65.4	103.5	117.1	109.7	55.6	100.0	100.0
1982	104.1	109.8	112.5	57.3	73.5	113.9	65.8	103.0	118.7	106.9	56.0	101.2	100.0
1983	103.0	111.1	113.0	56.4	73.4	112.6	64.3	102.3	118.3	106.5	54.7	103.4	100.0
1984	103.0	113.6	114.2	56.4	72.8	111.5	65.2	102.9	120.7	107.1	52.1	103.2	100.0
1985	101.6	115.8	114.2	56.7	72.5	110.6	65.2	103.1	122.4	107.0	52.0	104.2	100.0
1986	100.6	117.0	114.0	55.9	72.8	110.1	63.4	103.0	126.2	106.0	52.5	105.4	100.0
1987	100.1	114.2	112.9	54.2	74.7	108.9	64.5	103.2	123.1	103.4	53.6	107.2	100.0
1988	100.9	110.7	112.3	54.3	75.7	108.4	64.7	103.5	124.4	101.7	53.7	108.0	100.0
1989	101.3	108.8	111.7	54.1	76.9	108.6	67.0	103.6	129.7	102.2	54.9	106.9	100.0
1990	102.6	108.2	112.8	52.6	77.8	108.6	69.0	103.1	125.6	103.1	55.7	105.1	100.0
1991	103.0	109.0	114.2	52.5	79.0	108.7	68.9	103.1	127.8	103.9	56.3	102.1	100.0
1992	103.4	110.2	113.6	52.1	79.9	108.8	68.9	103.2	130.0	102.7	56.3	102.1	100.0

Note: Reference to GDP may overstate progress to the extent that income transfers to abroad may have outpaced nominal GDP growth

Source: Statistical Annex of European Economy, November 1991, Commission Services

These figures are essential for understanding the way in which regions are classified. The gap between the richest regions and the poorest regions decreased slightly in the 1980s, in part due to the fact that some regions improved their positions but in part also because many of the richer regions, have suffered seriously from the effects of recession and industrial decline (see Table 12.4). Community structural assistance has helped reduce divergences between regions, but it is difficult to quantify the effects and they were not fundamental, unlike the situation after 1989, since when there have been clearer guidelines.

There are no appropriate data for measuring specifically the situation of rural areas but one can assume that the trends there have been much the same, though there are some indications that they are less influenced by short-term fluctuations. However, taking into account the decline in farm prices and the concomitant fall in farm incomes over recent years, the majority of these regions are now facing a more difficult situation than during the previous decade. This must be set in the context of the long-term decline of rural areas which are increasingly isolated and have growing problems caused by depopulation.

The most useful indicator is that showing the changes in income levels, especially if total income is taken into account, i.e. both agricultural and non-agricultural earnings, although there are few data on the latter available. The indicators showing the contribution of agriculture to GDP or the decline in the number of people working in the agricultural sector, both of which are strictly agricultural criteria, should not necessarily be viewed negatively. On the contrary, they can be seen as showing that rural development is no longer based on agriculture alone, but is seeking to diversify into new areas, such as tourism, the new technologies and services.

Community support framework programmes are documents summarizing the priorities of the approved schemes, the amount of finance to be made available, the effects on macroeconomic variables, in particular the growth in GNP (gross national product) and investment. However, only in the Objective 1 regions is the volume of aid sufficiently large to enable any meaningful assessment to be made. The results of the Commission's own forecasts show that the effects are expected to be most significant in Portugal, where growth should increase by 0.7 per cent, and in Greece, where the figure should be 0.5 per cent. For the Objective 1 regions as a whole the figure should be approximately 0.3 per cent. The growth expected in the rate of investment is appreciably higher, of the order of 2–3 per cent. The real effects, however, will only become clear as the schemes are implemented, and the full picture will probably not emerge until the programmes are completed (between 1993 and 1995).

Until the regional development programmes were launched and before the reform of the structural Funds became operational, the richest regions of the Community were awarded most of the unrestricted socio-structural

Table 12.4 *Disparities in GDP per inhabitant between the regions[1] of the Community 1980–89 (in PPS, EUR 12 = 100)*

	1980	1981	1982	1983	1984	1985	1986	1987	1988	1989
Average 10 weakest regions	47	46	46	45	45	45	45	45	45	47
Average 10 strongest regions	145	146	147	149	149	150	151	151	151	151
Average 25 weakest regions	57	57	58	56	55	56	55	56	56	57
Average 25 strongest regions	135	136	136	136	137	138	138	137	137	138
Disparity[2]	26.1	26.5	26.8	27	27.2	27.5	27.9	27.5	27.5	26.9

Note: 1. Includes French overseas Territories. Azores and Madeira not included
2. Weighted standard deviation

Source: Fourth Periodic Report, 1991, Statistical annexes, p. 87; Commission services

schemes, applicable in all the member states. The explanation is that, first of all, they were better informed, and secondly, they had a greater capacity for initiating and implementing projects. Since 1989, the situation with regard to the distribution of the structural Funds has changed; priority is now given to regions with less than 75 per cent of the average per capita GDP in the Community, even though there may be great differences *within* a single Objective 1 country or region.

To measure the impact of Community assistance, one must first establish the kind of aid involved, starting with the assumption that investment in the manufacturing and service sectors will have a greater immediate effect than investment in infrastructure (see Table 12.5). This explains why the European Regional Development Fund wants member states to submit more proposals for the manufacturing and service sectors than for infrastructure. It will be a major shift, because, except for Italy with 29 per cent of investment in the manufacturing and service sectors, the Objective 1 countries have not got above 17 per cent. On the other hand, the proposed expenditure on infrastructure has reached 53 per cent in Spain—1,600 km of motorway receiving Community aid—47 per cent in Italy and 31 per cent in Greece. Irrigation and drainage schemes also absorb a large part of the investment in the regions in the South.

Infrastructural investment may not have an immediate effect, but it is none the less fundamental, because it is generally a prerequisite for the establishment of manufacturing and service activities in a region. Often, new communications links are the only way to open up the access to remote rural areas and the same applies to programmes for the various islands in the EC.

Table 12.5 *Community Structural Funds: expenditure by category* (in percentage)

Category	Greece	Ireland	Portugal (%)	Spain*	Italy*
Infrastructure	31.3	25.4	27.3	53.1	47.3
Aids to productive investment	7.0	16.2	17.0	9.9	29.0
of which industry	5.9	8.4	13.5	7.9	17.9
Agriculture	13.3	18.0	11.9	14.0	8.3
Manpower	13.7	39.6	28.0	22.7	14.8
Regional programmes	34.5	**	15.6	**	**
Others	0.4	0.6	0.2	0.3	0.6
Total public expenditure	100.0	100.0	100.0	100.0	100.0

Note: *Objective 1 regions
      **Included in other categories

Source: CSF, Commission services

The situation is different in the rural areas classified under Objective 5b. Aid there has been provided primarily for diversification schemes, and not only within the agricultural sector. Approximately one-third of the total is for non-agricultural schemes in areas such as the environment (12 per cent) and tourism (approximately 10 per cent). Projects in the service sector are still few and far between, even though these are essential for maintaining population levels in rural areas. The concentration of measures in these categories of investment is a direct result of the guidelines emanating from the various departments in the Commission. There is moreover no question of financing major infrastructure projects, because of the small amount of money allocated to each programme.

The difficulties to be overcome in assessing the efficacy of EC development schemes

Before the share of the budget for the structural Funds can be increased, progress to date needs to be assessed, something that is rather difficult, given that the present arrangements only apply to the period of 1989 to 1993, or rather 1989 to 1992. Indeed, most programmes were not approved until 1990 or even 1991, so that it is only possible to evaluate properly their initial stages and any forecasts must be based on the results of other, similar, projects. Any conclusions about the effects of the structural measures on cohesion in the EC can only be drawn when long-term data are available, covering at least a ten-year period. The analyses referred to above were for the periods 1980 to 1990 and 1960 to 1990 respectively. The Commissions's own studies of Community support suggest that fifty years or more will be required before the requisite catching up process is complete.

The programmes currently under way are already showing significant results, but it is too early yet to evaluate them. Those that began before the reform of the Funds should yield more results. They are numerous and absorbed the bulk of the available finance in 1990 and 1991. They account for more than 50 per cent of the Objective 1 programmes and approximately 60 per cent of the Objective 5(b) ones. Few have yet been evaluated, but results are starting to emerge from some of them (West of Ireland, the Highlands and Islands, the regions covered by the Integrated Mediterranean Programmes, etc.).

The difficulty of gauging the impact of the Community measures remains a major obstacle to formulating a progress report. In most member states Community measures are linked to national programmes and it is difficult to disentangle their respective impacts. Then there are the problems of making an 'objective' evaluation and the fact that this cannot be done in isolation. A region's state of development is primarily determined by more general factors, such as the socio-economic situation of the country and the state of the world market. In addition, the results of most (though admittedly not all) the evaluation studies carried out so far are rather disappointing. They tend to overlook the concrete results and too often only comment on physical indicators, or the impact of new infrastructural investment, in particular communications. There is a great need for more emphasis on evaluation with more precise guidance given by the Commission to evaluators.

Some impact assessment studies of current structural and rural development measures[2] cite the trends in agricultural prices and in EAGGF subsidies for agricultural products as the crucial engines of change, even though agriculture remains predominant. It is difficult to judge the true impact of non-agricultural activities, either on individual households or on the rural economy as a whole, but their importance is increasing. Not only is a growing number of farms diversifying, but farms of all sizes and income level are involved. The new activities are now vital for sustaining farms in business; many would have disappeared without an additional external income.

There are data from which the number of beneficiaries of horizontal measures (Community regulations classified under Objective 5a) can be calculated. It is clear that some of these measures have a significant impact: for instance, the compensatory allowance for which 1,200,000 farmers qualify. Approximately 60,000 farmers receive farm investment aid annually and 20,000 young farmers receive start-up assistance. However, it is difficult to know if these measures, which are spread thinly across the Community, do in fact boost agriculture as a whole in a given region. The same applies to the afforestation measures outside the formal forestry programmes.

Moreover, the number of jobs actually created by the structural Funds' investment remains an open question. We need to know whether the target of 500,000 jobs for the period 1989 to 1993 has been reached, whether the acceleration of growth has had the positive effects envisaged, and what the effects have been on the member states providing the capital for the Funds. On the latter point, according to a Commission report,[3] for every ECU 1 invested in work in Portugal, ECU 0.45 returns to the investors in the form of orders. Even if this is something of an over-exaggeration, it is still the case that numerous capital goods are imported from the more developed member states and that their firms often win contracts for work, especially for infrastructural development.

A preliminary appraisal

A preliminary appraisal of specific aspects of the structural Funds has already been made, including issues like the types of assistance available from the structural Funds and the way in which the principles underlying the reforms have been applied.

The types of assistance available   The overall assessment has perhaps concentrated too much on this point so far. In April 1991, a Commission document on ways of improving on the types of assistance available through the structural Funds and the whole question of access to aid mentioned specifically the difficulties in operating extremely complex procedures, which in some cases actually obstruct aid measures. It recommended that programme procedures be simplified, that co-ordination between the Commission departments be improved, and that there be a clearer definition of the financial rules and the conditions under which the principle of additionality applied. A number of improvements in implementation procedures have now been approved by the Commission, but they remain extremely complex.

The principles underlying the reforms   The most recent reforms of the structural Funds were not a thoroughgoing review, but they did clarify and integrate the underlying principles into a more general approach. The most important of these principles were those relating to the concentration of aid in the least developed regions; programming; partnership, and additionality.

The principle of concentration resulted first in the identification of geographical areas, based on Community criteria, which form the basis of the current pattern of Objective 1, 2 and 5b regions. Experience so far has shown that administrative boundaries must be made to correspond to regions that are geographically and economically significant. Decisions about concentration were also based on a range of other criteria, not all of which were taken into account in each case, given that those espoused by the Commission must also fit with other aspects EC policy. It means that in some cases the best options are not always very clear.

It soon became apparent that schemes submitted by the regions and by the member states needed to be accompanied by others, which took in to account such things as the environment or vocational training. At the same time, compatibility with other Community policies, such as the CAP and competition policy, had to be assured. The Commission has been able to intervene actively in some fields, but in others, in particular those involving major infrastructural developments (motorways, bridges, power stations, etc.), the criteria enabling it to do so are not formulated sufficiently clearly, or are non-existent. In some instances, the Commission also advised the member states to seek loans from the EIB (European Investment Bank). Schemes may also conflict with national plans or with public investment that has already been sanctioned. Co-ordination between different bodies in charge of schemes at EC level and at national level is not always easy, nor is it always possible to reconcile all the various options available for developing regarding European transport or telecommunications networks and the like. The Europe 2000 studies[4] undertaken by the Commission are designed to contribute to a better specification of Community projects in these priority fields and to the design of common guidelines for the future.

Most Community assistance is now directly related to general development programmes, which is a considerable advance. However, it requires additional effort on the part of the regions to present all the various schemes for a given region in a coherent and supposedly integrated form and, in practice, this is often difficult to achieve.

The five-year duration of the new programme is considered reasonable, as long as the period is counted from the date of approval and not the date when the reforms came into force. The most recent schemes, including some Community initiatives, will only have been in operation for less than two years in 1993.

One question that keeps cropping up is how precisely to define the measures provided for in the individual programmes. If the specifications are too detailed, they will have to be constantly adjusted to take account of new factors. On the other hand, if they are too generalised it will be difficult to say exactly what they mean. In fact, the situation differs greatly from one programme to another, even in rural areas (Objective 5b), where the member states have had to follow a precise guidelines worked out by the Commission.

The emphasis on programming explains the low uptake of other forms of assistance, such as the global grants which enables a scheme to be presented and managed by a non-governmental organisation. The global grant is only available for a few Community initiatives (schemes proposed by the Commission independently of the proposals put forward by the member states; they account for 15 per cent of the total finance available to the structural Funds), e.g. the Community rural development initiative (LEADER).

The partnership approach is regarded as a success by the Commission,[5] especially as regards relations with the member states and the regions. It is overseen by a monitoring committee representing the various parties involved in the implementation of the programmes (the responsible national administrative agencies, EC agencies and, in some instances, social scientists and other professionals). The structure appears generally to have worked well, but in some regions there have been operational problems that have limited its effectiveness. Partnerships with the member states have been in existence for some time, but the systematic and active participation of the regions represents an important innovation. It has been particularly significant in those countries with centralised administrative structures, although there have also been some problems, not least of which is the reluctance of central governments to share some of its prerogatives with the regions.

Partnership has not affected programmes at local level, except for those Community initiatives specifically intended to address local needs. Nor has it had much effect on the relationship with bodies like trade organisations and trade unions, consultation with whom varies widely from region to region. At Community level, an advisory committee including such bodies has met regularly.

Checking for additionality is more difficult. The principle requires member states to increase their own financial input into schemes covered by the new EC programme, so that the level of national aid is higher than when public funds were only available from national sources. The information necessary to check that this principle is being applied has so far been inadequate and difficult to obtain. At the very least, member states must have a budget covering the same period as the Community support frameworks, otherwise the additionality principle can be applied only *a posteriori*, which is likely to be too late.

The new aid measures and the underlying structural Funds reforms have made necessary better co-ordination and clearer goals for both the Commission and national and regional governments. This has led to major difficulties and constitutes a serious obstacle to implementing new schemes, with major bureaucratic complications and serious delays.

There are a number of innovations in the reforms which need to be stressed. The first is approval for specific integrated rural development programmes (including, for the first time, agricultural schemes where agriculture itself is not the main focus) in about fifty regions, as well as over 200 local initiative projects (under Objective 5b and LEADER). Even if the results are not yet apparent, the interest they have aroused points to them ultimately producing positive results. The diversification which is at the core of such aid is essential for progress and the survival of numerous rural areas, directly benefiting the populations concerned.

It is still too early to judge the impact of the new rural development programmes and projects, but it is possible to make a financial and structural assessment of the programmes funded under Objective 1 and of the other schemes already in operation.

Allocation of resources to rural development

The progress on the new programmes so far means that the overall achievements of the structural Funds can already be assessed from both the financial and the physical (i.e. based on some important physical indicators) points of view. The socio-economic assessment will have to come later, for the reasons already mentioned.

In this analysis, the assessment will be limited to rural development schemes, which are financed in part by the EAGGF Guidance Section, but mainly by the ERDF (small and medium-sized enterprises, rural tourism, rural infrastructure, services in rural areas, etc.) and the ESF (vocational training). The EAGGF Guidance Section has accounted for approximately 16.7 per cent of the total of Community aid, the total value of which has risen from ECU 938 million in 1987 and ECU 2,488 million in 1991 (Figure 12.1). An assessment undertaken by the Commission in 1992, gives an estimate of the importance of EC aid in financial terms (payments/commitments):

—70 per cent for Objective 1; except for Italy, where the rate is 46 per cent, the rates for member states range from 68 per cent to 88 per cent. The EAGGF Guidance Section is the most important of the Funds, contributing 78 per cent of the total;
—86 per cent for Objective 5a; the rate is the usual 'horizontal' one for structural measures applied in each member states and is highest in Germany where the rate is 93 per cent;
−62 per cent for Objective 5b; rates vary greatly from one member state to another and from one Fund to another. The rates tend to increase progressively and rapidly as programmes get under way.

These figures are merely an indication of the progress in the implementing Community aid, not of the actual work done. The fact that payments have been made by the Commission does not necessarily mean that the money has actually reached the beneficiaries. In most countries the process takes more than six months. Other factors also pay a part: the number of projects submitted; the effectiveness of the government administration; the priority given to a programme; and the effort put into making it a success.

The member states which benefited most from funding by the EAGGF Guidance Section between 1987 and 1991 are:

France   : 19.0 per cent
Spain   : 15.5 per cent
Italy   : 14.3 per cent
Greece   : 13.0 per cent
Portugal : 11.6 per cent

As the importance of regional programmes grows relative to horizontal measures, the countries covered by Objective 1 will receive the largest amounts of money.

A more detailed breakdown of expenditure is provided by Tables 12.6, 12.7 and 12.8 which show expenditure by the type of programme, expenditure by country and the impact of these and previous programmes as measured by the value added per Agricultural Work Unit (AWU).

It would take too long to review all the physical indicators associated with each programme. Moreover, this could be done only for certain

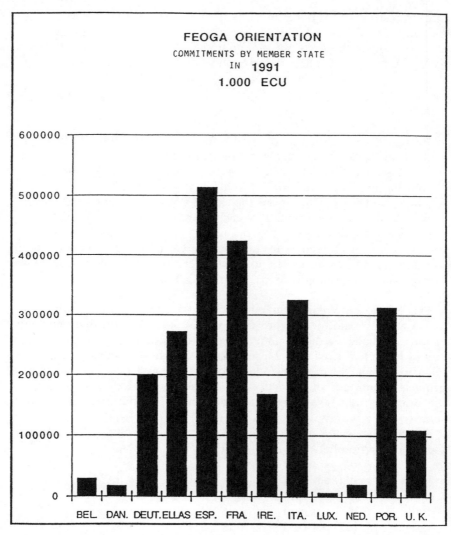

Figure 12.1   *EAGGF Guidance Section: commitments by member state in 1991*

programmes in Objective 1 regions and for the horizontal measures for rural development. It is too early to do so for Objective 5b or for the LEADER projects which have only recently become operational. These schemes have been well received by the member states and rural development associations, but the amounts allocated to them remain small (for the three Funds, ECU 2,607 million for Objective 5b from 1989 to 1993, of which ECU 400 million is earmarked for the EC's LEADER initiative).

The overall monitoring indicates that most programmes have been well managed and that they have benefited a wide range of different activities:

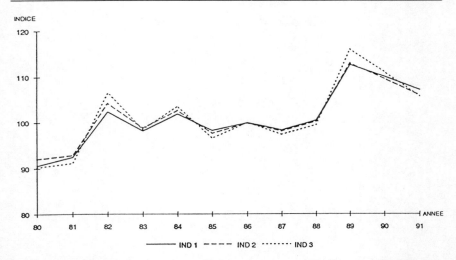

Figure 12.2 *Agricultural income indicators 1, 2 and 3 for the Community from 1980 to 1991 (1984–6 = 100)*

conversion of crops, restructuring of plantations, diversification, producer groups, rural infrastructure, etc. Agricultural investment presents more of a problem on account of the recent proposals for reforming the CAP. These have engendered uncertainty about the future of certain types of agricultural production and about the guidelines that should be given to farmers, but as Figure 12.2 shows income has risen.

The forestry measures would seem to have been a definite success (with Greece benefiting from a whole range of new proposals). The measures relating to the environment will take longer to implement and require time to gain public acceptance, although there has already been an increased uptake. The early retirement will also take some time to take effect.

The range of horizontal measures is also expanding, especially compensatory allowances for the newly redefined Less Favoured Areas. The same is true of the marketing and processing of agricultural and forestry products; programmes for both of these have been approved recently.

It emerged from the most recent discussions with the various member states that demand for financial aid for these measures is increasing, but there are still a number of problems to be overcome.

—There needs to be better co-ordination between the horizontal and the regional measures and between these and the general EC initiatives— an issue which has cropped up before and one on which efforts have been made to effect improvements.
—The questions of control and of management, both of which become very important when there are a large number of programmes (545 cases of assistance between all the Funds, 72 of which are for Objective 1 with

Table 12.6 *EAGGF Guidance Section: breakdown of commitments by scheme, 1987–91*

1	1987		1988		1989		1990		1991	
	1.000 ECU	%	1.000 ECU	%	1.000 ECU	%	1.000 ECU	%	1.000 ECU	%
	2	3	4	5	6	7	8	9	10	11
Total	938.938	100.00	1.180.000	100.00	1.461.991	100.00	1.925.676	100.00	2.408.159	100.00
797/85[1]	275.546	29.35	452.631	38.36	451.152	30.86	813.202	42.23	859.229	35.68
Regionalise[1] & PIM[2]	103.442	11.02	216.187	18.32	379.675	25.97	513.969	26.69	1,198.841	49.78
Processing and Marketing[3]	307.359	32.73	280.903	23.81	367.615	25.14	365.948	19.00	203.385	8.45
Socio-structur.[4]	122.397	13.04	119.864	10.16	221.662	15.16	103.919	5.40	55.773	2.32
R. 1096/88–	128.014	13.63	107.336	9.10	39.474	2.70	103.684	5.38	65.171	2.71
PRER.[5] ART. 8	0	0.00	0	0.00	0	0.00	23.468	1.22	15.060	0.63
R. 4256/88[6]	2.180	0.23	3.073	0.26	2.413	0.17	1.486	0.08	10.700	0.44

Notes: 1. Improvement of agricultural structures
2. Regionalised programmes and Mediterranean Integrated Programmes
3. Processing and marketing of agricultural products
4. Other structural actions
5. Early retirement for farmers
6. Pilot projects and technical assistance

Table 12.7 *EAGGF Guidance Section: breakdown of commitments by member state, 1987–91*

Member States	1987		1988		1989		1990		1991		1987–1991	
	1.000 ECU	%	1.000 ECU	%	1.000 ECU	%	1.000 ECU	%	1.000 ECU	%	1.000 ECU	%
1	2	3	4	5	6	7	8	9	10	11	8	9
Luxemburg	3.889	0.41	2.140	0.18	3.577	0.24	4.603	0.24	6.666	0.28	20.875	0.26
Netherlands	13.796	1.47	5.260	0.45	20.663	1.41	10.708	0.56	20.496	0.85	70.923	0.90
Denmark	11.602	1.24	12.752	1.08	17.294	1.18	16.920	0.88	18.038	0.75	76.606	0.97
Belgium	21.131	2.25	18.340	1.55	31.579	2.16	23.055	1.20	30.488	1.27	124.593	1.57
U.K.	83.741	8.92	82.209	6.97	78.028	5.34	96.548	5.01	110.243	4.58	450.769	5.70
Ireland	96.556	10.28	81.199	6.88	121.737	8.33	124.768	6.48	168.501	7.00	592.761	7.49
Germany	121.924	12.99	124.607	10.56	127.155	8.70	183.285	9.52	200.192	8.31	757.163	9.57
Portugal	62.165	6.62	121.945	10.33	179.395	12.27	241.612	12.55	313.402	13.01	918.519	11.61
Greece	105.141	11.20	148.609	12.59	235.297	16.09	270.165	14.03	274.205	11.39	1.033.417	13.06
Italy	95.878	10.21	178.381	15.12	263.610	18.03	269.259	13.98	326.511	13.56	1.133.639	14.32
Spain	79.359	8.45	133.603	11.32	203.890	13.95	301.827	15.67	514.155	21.35	1.232.834	15.58
France	243.756	25.96	270.955	22.96	179.766	12.30	382.926	19.89	425.262	17.66	1.502.665	18.99
Total	938.938	100.00	1.180.00	100.00	1.461.991	100.00	1.925.676	100.00	2.408.159	100.00	7.914.764	100.00

Table 12.8 Indices of real net value added at factor cost, per AWU, from 1973 to 1991, with 1984–86 = 100

	B	DK	D	GR	E	F	IRL	I	L	NL	P	UK	EUR12
1973	102.4	65.4	122.5	73.1	74.1	110.6	95.4	94.3	71.3	91.1	—	119.1	—
1974	81.9	63.7	104.6	71.0	63.4	102.0	87.4	87.8	59.4	77.0	—	108.5	—
1975	85.7	53.3	118.8	72.4	71.3	94.8	107.2	90.1	65.3	82.9	—	105.2	—
1976	101.1	55.1	123.4	78.5	76.3	93.8	101.8	84.3	57.8	90.3	—	112.9	—
1977	84.1	64.4	118.2	75.4	86.8	91.6	125.3	88.9	72.0	86.0	—	105.4	—
1978	90.7	70.0	113.3	85.3	87.9	95.0	129.8	89.9	71.7	84.7	—	100.2	—
1979	82.1	60.8	101.3	80.8	80.0	97.2	108.2	96.0	74.5	78.1	—	96.9	—
1980	86.8	65.8	90.3	92.0	85.9	88.0	88.3	109.3	68.8	75.2	95.7	90.7	90.6
1981	95.3	75.4	91.1	97.4	76.5	91.2	88.6	106.7	77.4	92.3	90.0	96.1	92.5
1982	100.4	91.2	111.0	100.1	88.6	107.6	96.7	106.9	106.6	96.9	100.5	104.6	102.3
1983	108.3	78.1	89.4	90.9	89.0	100.3	101.1	112.0	94.3	93.4	97.3	93.3	98.2
1984	104.3	104.0	102.4	98.8	100.0	99.4	112.3	101.0	97.7	100.9	99.6	112.7	101.8
1985	99.4	95.7	92.6	101.3	102.1	100.0	97.7	101.4	99.9	95.6	98.4	90.0	98.3
1986	96.2	100.3	105.0	99.9	97.9	100.5	89.9	97.5	103.3	103.5	102.1	97.3	99.9
1987	90.8	80.3	87.8	102.2	104.3	101.5	109.9	98.8	104.2	99.6	99.8	95.4	98.3
1988	98.6	81.0	109.1	112.4	118.8	97.7	128.6	93.3	106.2	101.2	84.0	85.3	100.4
1989	122.5	97.1	129.7	124.4	120.9	112.3	131.5	99.2	123.2	119.8	98.2	97.3	112.6
1990	111.0	95.3	113.8	113.8	126.8	117.2	133.7	90.6	117.2	119.0	104.7	96.0	110.0
1991	108.7	85.4	99.3	122.4	127.6	104.2	122.9	98.7	95.3	122.5	89.6	88.5	107.1
91/90 (%)	−2.1	−10.4	−12.8	8.2	0.6	−11.0	−8.1	8.9	−18.7	2.9	−14.5	−7.9	−2.6

the participation of the EAGGF Guidance Section and 74 for Objective 5b), should be discussed at the regular meetings of the monitoring committees. Further improvements are needed if delays in implementation are to be avoided.

—There is the fundamental problem of the compatibility of structural measures with other Community policies, especially competition policy. The advent of the Single Market will make this an even more important issue.

The link between the CAP and the environment has also raised questions about both policies, causing them to be reviewed and, where appropriate, revised.

Cohesion after Maastricht

One of the principal issues in the Maastricht document and the budgetary proposals now under discussion, to give concrete expression to the Treaty on European Union, is economic and social cohesion. To translate the Commission's objectives into reality, the guidelines laid down at the time of the reform of the Funds are, for the most part, retained in the new treaty. The resources allocated to the structural Funds are actually going to be increased and further new funds are planned (Cohesion Fund, appropriations to compensate for restructuring in the fisheries sector, Community initiative programmes for industrial change).

Preserving the present guidelines but increasing the available resources

The importance of Objective 1 has been reaffirmed and resources will continue to be allocated as a matter of priority, since there is still so much to be done. A doubling of funds is planned so that similar schemes can be implemented in Greece, Portugal, Ireland and Spain (Table 12.9). An increase of two-thirds is planned for the other Objective 1 regions. Special attention is to be paid to the remotest regions, particularly the islands. The provision of such large amounts of money will enable extensive investment to be made in infrastructure, as well as improvements in production facilities in rural and other areas.

Even greater changes are planned for the horizontal structural measures, not least because of:

—proposals included in the review of the CAP, in particular the associated measures. Environmental measures, early retirement and forestry schemes are all enhanced. They are currently covered by Community

Table 12.9 *Relative macroeconomic importance of the CSFs and Community Structural Funds (1989–93)*

	CSF public expenditure (structural funds and national finance requirement)		Structural Funds	
	MECU 1989 prices	% of region GDP	MECU 1989 prices	% of region GDP
Italy (Mezzogiorno)	14,062	1.5	7,583	0.8
Ireland (entire country)	6,126	3.8	3,672	2.3
Greece (entire country)	12,995	5.2	7,193	2.9
Spain (70% of the country	16,507	2.0	9,779	1.2
Portugal (entire country)	14,026	6.6	7,368	3.5

Source: CSFs, Commission services

regulations, but in the future they will have to be incorporated into regional programmes;

— the need for all aspects of EC aid to be integrated into regional programmes; the incorporation of horizontal measures into programmes, thus enabling all aspects of rural development relating to a region to be better integrated and adapted to specific conditions in individual regions;

— the request by member states for increased expenditure on improving agricultural structures.

The rural development programmes for Objective 5b regions and Community initiatives are to be expanded. It is proposed that the budget for the programmes be increased by 50 per cent of the amounts currently allocated to these regions; the funds for the EC LEADER initiative would be doubled. The definition of 5b regions would remain unchanged, but there could be some adjustments to boundaries, though the existing criteria would still apply.

Creation of the Cohesion Fund

New resources are envisaged in two fields where investment is expensive and affects more than one Community country:

— trans-European communications networks, in particular investment in

 transportation infrastructure;
—the environment.

This Fund will be targeted towards Greece, Ireland, Portugal and Spain; the rates of Community finance available may be as much as 90 per cent (compared with a maximum rate for other measures of 75 per cent). The programme of the Cohesion Fund, to which ECU 1.5 billion will be allocated, rising to ECU 2.5 billion in 1997, will have to comply with the convergence conditions agreed by the Community, in particular as regards public sector debt.[6]

The detailed rules on eligibility

The review of the management of the structural Funds has introduced further changes which seem likely to complicate further their procedures. The new rules will affect all the activities supported by the structural Funds—operational programmes, horizontal measures, associated measures and local initiatives. The rules must not diverge too much from each other and all must be subject to the same processes of presentation, discussion, approval and control.

The richer member states which effectively fund the EC's budget regard the new proposals for the structural Funds as too ambitious and would like to see only modest increases in the funds allocated to them. They are calling on the Commission to put forward a more convincing case for new appropriations and to check that commitments already made are being properly implemented.

Some countries are expecting to lose out as a result of the CAP reform and want to see their farmers fairly compensated for any losses resulting from lower prices. It was probably the most difficult issue to be resolved at the Council of Heads of States held at Edinburgh in December 1992, agreement being reached on a larger cohesion fund to benefit Spain, Portugal, Greece and Ireland. It should endow the structural Funds with sufficient resources to enable them to have a real impact on the Community's least developed regions, enabling them to benefit more from the Single Market. There needs to be a balance within the Community, allowing common rules on convergence leading towards monetary union to be adopted and the rapid development of the peripheral regions, even though an increase in expenditure on the structural Funds might seem to be in conflict with the aims of the Single Market.

The Community has also taken important new decisions on enlargement at the Edinburgh Council meeting, agreeing to open negotiations with Austria, Finland and Sweden immediately and then to consider an application from Norway later in 1993. In due course there will also be requests for membership from central Europe, prompted by the integration of the new German Länder in what was the DDR. The agenda is massive and it would be unrealistic to expect these developments to proceed without giving rise to contradictions, conflicts of interests and many other difficulties.

Notes

1. Jazra Bandarra, N., 'Reform of policy on the EEC structural Funds: institutional or structural change?', presented to an INA seminar in Portugal, 15 November 1989, Lisbon.
   Jazra Bandarra 'Los "elegidos" de la reforma de los fondos structurales', *Agricultura y Sociedad*, October 1991, Madrid.
2. Arkleton Research, 'Rural change in Europe', summary reports to the Community in 1989 and 1990, CEE.
   INRA, Dijon, 'Report on the evaluation of horizontal structural measures: the installation of young farmers in the Community countries'.
   CEAS, CEP AND FAL, 'Monitoring and evaluation of Objective 5b regions, final report', April 1991, Report to the Commissions Services.
   Various evaluation reports to the Commission on the CSFs for Objective 1 regions (not published)
3. EEC 1992, 'Community structural policies—assessment and outlook', (Commission document) COM(92) 84/2 of 13 March 1992
   Improvement of the mechanisms and of the procedures of implementation of the structural assistance, COM (Commission document), 20 September 1991.
4. EEC, 1991, Europe 2000—Outlook for the development of the Community's territory, 1991.
5. EEC, 1992, *Second annual report on the implementation of the reform of the structural Funds, 1990*, Brussels.
6. EEC: From the Single Act to Maastricht and beyond, COM (92) final, 11 February 1992.
   Implementation of the Inter-institutional Agreement of 29 June 1988 on budgetary discipline and improvement of the budgetary procedure, COM(92) final, 10 March 1992.
   EAGGF-Guidance Section: Annual financial reports.

13 Peripheral labour markets under pressure of change

Lars Olaf Persson

The general economic scene

General economic conditions in Sweden have changed rapidly during the last few years. A period of unbroken expansion, which started in the early 1980s has come to an end. The growth in domestic demand which supported the upswing has declined. At the same time, Swedish producers' market share is being lost due to a lack of competitiveness, which in turn means that little support for growth can be expected from abroad. As a result, the current Swedish economy is considered by both external and internal observers to have severe problems (OECD, 1991; SOU, 1992, p. 19). The general growth rate is lower than in most other European countries. For several years the balance of foreign trade has been negative and, until recently, the rate of inflation was running at a high level. The level of investments both in industry and in infrastructure has been lower than that in many other European countries. In only the last two years unemployment has increased from less than 3 per cent to 7 per cent, the highest rate being reported from the northernmost county of Norrbotten.

Many of these distortions are considered to have been caused by the Swedish public sector and the way it is financed—by taxes on consumption, incomes and labour. The latter in particular is considered to be the major reason for the high production costs of Swedish firms. The public sector is the largest in Europe in relative terms and its influence on the private sector is profound. In the late 1980s, the Social Democratic government started implementing measures to improve efficiency in general and particularly in the public sector. The present Conservative-Centre-Liberal-Christian Democratic government has proposed a sharp reduction of public expenditures and has begun to privatize some sectors. According to one recent estimate, the budget deficit in 1992 will correspond to as much as 12 per cent of GNP. The economic problems are expected to continue for several years, with a slow rate of growth, reductions in the state budget and static, or even increasing, levels of unemployment.

At the same time, there are some facets of the Swedish economy that are generally considered to be strong. The industrial sector is highly developed and relatively R&D intensive. Foreign investment in Sweden has increased during the last few years while investment abroad by Swedish firms has decreased. Extensive intervention in the labour market—

following the principles of the so-called 'labour line' and including education programmes—mean that unemployment is still lower than in many other European countries. The labour market is considered to be quite efficient and the welfare system remains comprehensive and accessible to all the different social groups and regions. Tax reforms have reduced some of the distorting effects of high levels of taxation.

During the first four decades following the end of World War II, Sweden systematically promoted what was then a unique welfare model. 'The People's Home' and 'the Strong Society' were the key concepts which received broad approval from voters from the generations born up to the end of World War II (Johansson and Persson, 1991). The Social Democrats were largely secure in government for an unbroken period of 44 years (though sometimes depending on support in Parliament from the Communists), a dominance that only came to an end with the formation of Liberal-Centre-Conservative governments in the late-1970s, but even this change did not seriously bring into question the legitimacy of the welfare model. Not until around 1985, when growth in productivity began to decline and the state budget deficit began to increase during the present deep recession, did the Liberal-Centre-Conservative-Christian Democratic government show any inclination to question the 'ideological basis' of the welfare model.

The regional picture

Even as recently as the late 1940s, most regions in Sweden retained much of their traditonal rural character, but since then industrialization, urbanization and structural transformation have become the dominant features. In a country with a vast land area and a small population, this also put intense pressure on the regional equilibrium; on one hand, between the forest-dominated counties in the north and the urban centres in the south and, on the other, between rural areas and urban centres all over the country. The present active regional policy was introduced in the 1960s, based mainly on investment support for manufacturing firms in the north-western periphery, aiming to compensate them for the problems they faced associated with remoteness and sparse populations. An agricultural policy largely based on income support, but which includes some regional elements, i.e. price support for dairy farms in northern Sweden to compensate them for difficult natural conditions, has been in effect during the whole of the post-war period (OECD Observer, 1991). However, it is probably fair to say that the effectiveness of regional and agricultural policies in maintaining or creating new jobs in the regions attracting support has probably been limited.

Fortunately, the regional imbalances in service supply and employment were largely counteracted by the continuous growth of the public service sector, providing jobs and services equally to individuals and households in all regions. In most cases, the local labour markets even in the peripheral regions seemed to function quite well until the end of the 1980s. Certainly, the level of the available jobs was generally inferior in these regions, but this was to a large extent compensated for by the flat rate wage structure operating across the different sectors and professions and by the progressive income tax system. International comparisons show the gap between Swedish regions—measured in terms of buying power per capita—was and is still smaller than in almost all other European countries. Only recently has it become evident that the increasing dependency on state transfers to individuals, municipalities and enterprises, as well as the subsidies available for communications, has actually made the peripheral regions more rather than less stable (Persson, 1990). The Swedish concept of 'security', which has a specific connotation of safety, patronage and cosiness, is supposed to be almost a basic human right for all Swedish households. It is considered a key responsibility of both central and local government to see that it is actually realized, but quite obviously success at all levels has fallen short of the ideal, something that is becoming increasingly obvious as Sweden approaches full membership of the EC and the liberal trade principles of the Single Market.

The Swedish economy became increasingly international in the 1980s, with a substantial proportion—approximately 30 per cent—of the investment by Swedish firms going abroad, mainly to the EC. For at least the last 30 years, more than 50 per cent of both Swedish exports and imports have been to and from the present EC-countries (SOU, 1992, p. 19). The traditional Swedish reservations to European integration largely, but not totally, disappeared when Sweden applied for full membership of the EC in 1991.

Peripheral and/or rural areas

The decreasing market share of resource-based industries, rising levels of unemployment, cut-backs in public services and diminishing returns from a deregulated agricultural industry, mean that many households and labour markets in the northern peripheral regions are facing a difficult time. Local jobs in the service sector are getting scarce as municipalities reorganize and centralize their public services, though as much as 40 per cent of the jobs available are still in public services in many of these labour markets.

At the same time, individual values are beginning to take precedence over collectivist values; there is more emphasis on private rather than public activities; and an overall increase in mobility. Many families—often professionals with small children—are leaving the urban areas, mainly to find attractive places to live in rather than new sources of local income. To this extent, small towns and those rural areas that are not too remote locations are enjoying a new climate of comparative advantage. As a result, rural areas are becoming more divergent and the justification for protecting and compensating them financially by means of state transfers has to be scrutinized, not least in terms of spatial extent, in each case (Newby, 1987; *Future of Rural Society*, 1988).

As a response to the changing macroeconomic conditions and the way different households have reacted to these changes, four types of rural labour market areas seem to have emerged in Sweden in the course of the 1990s (Persson and Westholm, 1992). In the urban fringe there are areas of spontaneous growth; there are intermediate zones with both urban and rural characteristics and with adequate infrastructures; peripheral regions with unique natural and cultural assets, which have attracted permanent and/or temporary new residents; and areas with declining populations, i.e. marginal or peripheral areas with few of the attractions and competitive potential of the other regions mentioned.

In this chapter, we concentrate on the last category of region, though the whole concept of rurality must be used with caution, as it can falsely imply that the rural sector is somehow separated from the general economic and social processes at work in the country (Persson and Wiberg, 1988). A closer examination of the prospects for rural areas in Sweden makes it obvious that changing micro-economic conditions and the present political shift, from policies based on the dominance of welfare programmes within the Swedish model, towards increasing market orientation, may well have profound effects in these areas. We shall argue that it is the unintended spatial effects of changing state expenditure that is likely to determine the future of rural areas more than any agricultural or regional policy. We shall also argue that any political strategy for rural areas must consider the impact of these changing conditions and forecast the prospects of different types of peripheral and/or rural area.

Dynamics of declining labour markets

In general policy debate in Sweden, negative population development is considered to be the main symptom of regional dysfunction. In spite of the overall economic growth during the second half of the 1980s and the general regional equilibrium, more than 50 per cent of all labour market areas (LMA) in Sweden (60 out of 111) underwent a decrease in population during the period 1985–90. Many of these LMAs are located in the northern part of the country, but by no means all. These declining regions have been studied and classified by means of a cluster analysis, the clusters of variables describing four characteristic problems:

Demography   (variables: percent age of whole population in the
                      age group 25–44 years; percentage of females in the
                      whole age group 25–44 years).

Population dynamics	(variables: net migration 1985–90 as a proportion of total population; net birth minus death ratio).
Spatial structure	(variables: proportion of population living in urban areas, i.e. in localities with more than 200 inhabitants; population density, inhabitants/sq.km).
Dependency on public resource transfers	(variables: state transfers to individuals within social and welfare programs (SEK/capita); resources to compensate for regional labour market problems (SEK/capita).

These variables have been chosen to describe four aspects of the problems occurring in declining or disadvantaged regions;

—the deformation of the age structure in terms of deficits of labour in 'productive' age groups
—the components of population change in terms of the balance between migration and 'natural' change
—the physical preconditions for service and infrastructure provision
—the demand for compensatory provisions within the social welfare, labour market and regional policies

After 25 iterations of the cluster analysis we arrived at seven clusters describing declining LMAs. No weights were assigned to the variables, but as two of the variable groups related to population (Demography; Populations Dynamics) there is an implicit weighting. The variables are not all scaled in the same way—e.g. percentage of females in the age group 25–44 years, and transfers SEK/capita—and to overcome this problem the variables were standardized (Z_{ij}). This means that they are transformed so that they all have a zero mean and a standard deviation of 1 (see formulas below):

$$Z_{ij} = \frac{(x_{ij} - \bar{x}_j)}{s_j}$$

Where

$$\bar{x}_j = \frac{\sum\limits_{i=1}^{n} x_{ij}}{n}$$

and

$$s_j = \frac{\sum\limits_{i=1}^{n} (x_{ij} - \bar{x}_j)^2}{n-1}$$

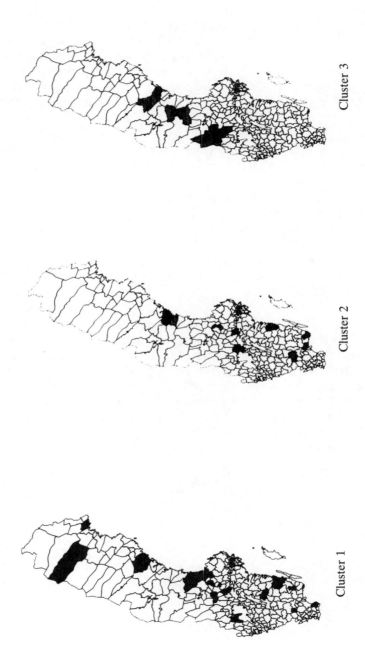

Cluster 3

Cluster 2

Cluster 1

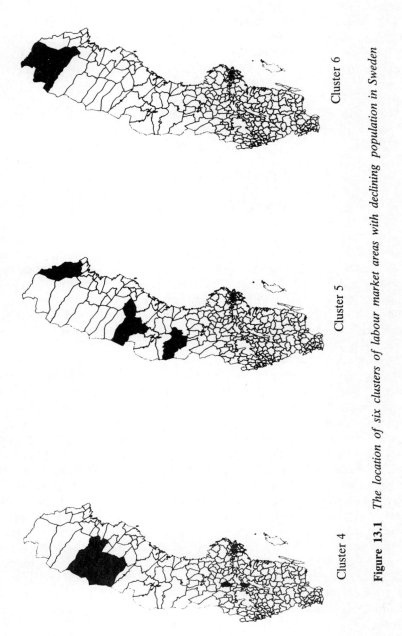

Cluster 4   Cluster 5   Cluster 6

Figure 13.1   *The location of six clusters of labour market areas with declining population in Sweden*

The clustering alogrithm we found most useful for our purposes was Ward's method, which aggregates those cases which produce the smallest increase in the within-group sum of squares.

The clusters have been labelled based on a few distinguishing characteristics. However, it should be remembered that the clustering procedure in itself means that the components of each cluster are more similar to each other in 'all' respects than to the components of any other cluster.

0 Small Towns (ST): 4 LMAs, all in southern Sweden
1 Medium Size Decentralized (MSD): 17 LMAs, six of them in Norr-land (the five northernmost counties)
2 Medium Size Urban (MSU): 12 LMAs, two in Norrland
3 Small Decentralized (SD): 9 LMAs, four in Norrland
4 Small Dependent Towns (SDT): 7 LMAs, five in Norrland
5 Small Dependent Peripheries (SDP): 7 LMAs, all in Norrland
6 Mining Areas (MA): 2 LMAs, both in Norrland.

Figure 13.1 shows the location of the LMAs in each cluster 1–6. The Small Towns are excluded from the subsequent analysis since they represent LMAs exhibiting little population decline and few rural characteristics. Figures 13.2–5 show the basic profiles of each cluster. The age group 25–44 is over-represented in the Mining Areas, but the other five clusters show little variation, all lying some 5 per cent below the national average (28.5 per cent), indicating that demographic distortion is strongly correlated with population decline.

Figures 13.2–5 show the basic profile of each cluster. The age group 25–44 years is most under-represented in the Small Towns in the south and most over-represented in the Mining Fields, while the other five clusters show a similar structure (Figure 13.2). All these have some 5 per cent of units below the national average (28.5 per cent) which means that demographic distortion is strongly correlated to population decline. Furthermore, the proportion of females in this age-group is under-represented in all the clusters representing decline, especially in those clusters containing LMAs in Norrland. In LMAs with increasing or stable populations, females usually outnumber males in this particular age-group. The female labour force is generally associated with service jobs in Sweden and this regional pattern tells us something about the relatively short supply of attractive service jobs in these peripheral labour markets. Within the framework of growth in the service sector during this period in all regions, it is probably true that the more attractive jobs were created in urban regions, influencing young women from the peripheries to migrate to these regions. The location of educational facilities in these central regions has further favoured this process.

The high level of dependency on transfers of state aid is strongly apparent in clusters 3, 4 and 5, the Norrland-dominated clusters except for

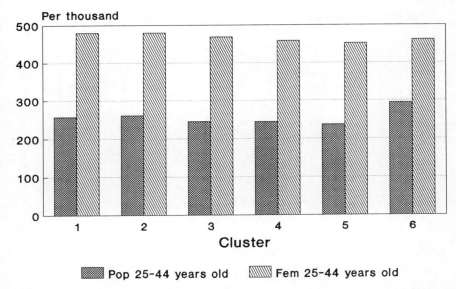

Figure 13.2 *Age-group 25–44 per thousands of total population (A) and* pro mille *females in the same age-group (B) 1990.* Six clusters of labour market areas (LMAs) with declining population in Sweden
Source: FORA, 1992

the Mining Areas (Figure 13.3). The compensation programmes are primarily oriented towards the three Norrland clusters, in increasing order of importance: the Small Dependent Towns, the Small Dependent Peripheries and the Mining Areas. This reflects the prevailing spatial structure of the regional economic problem.

The density variable separates out two sets of clusters with entirely different characteristics; the densely populated clusters 1, 2 and 3 in southern and central Sweden, and the remaining sparsely populated Norrland clusters (Figure 13.4). It should be remembered that in Scandanavia as a whole, low population density is effectively synonymous with peripherality.

The settlement structure has a less differentiated pattern: clusters 2, Medium Size Urban, 4 Small Dependent Towns and 6 Mining Areas, are all equally urbanized, while clusters 3, Small Decentralized and 5 Small Dependent Peripheries, in particular have rural characteristics (Figure 13.4).

Finally, the Norrland clusters come out as the most subject to decline in terms of total population (Figure 13.5). These clusters all show an annual population loss of more than 0.5 per cent during the second half of the 1980s, while the other three clusters show an average annual loss of 0.15–0.35. The latter three clusters also show an across-the-board decrease

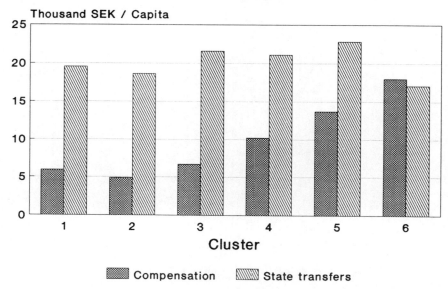

Figure 13.3   *Governmental transfers and resources for compensating regional problems,* SEK/capita. Six clusters of labour market areas (LMAs) with declining population in Sweden
Source: FORA, 1992

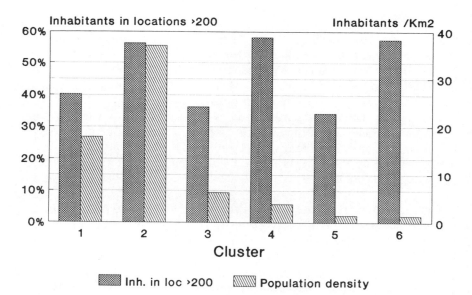

Figure 13.4   *Population density inhabitants per square kilometer and percentage of all inhabitants in localities with more than 200 inhabitants, 1990.* Six clusters of labour market areas (LMAs) with declining population in Sweden
Source: FORA, 1992

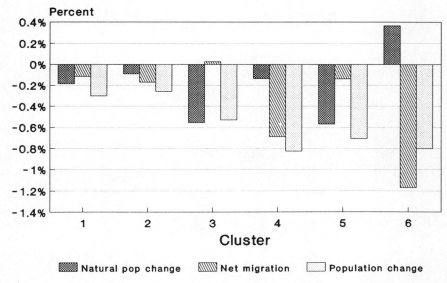

Figure 13.5   *Annual population changes, 1985–90, net migration and birth–death ratio, relative to total population.* Six clusters of LMAs with declining population in Sweden
Source: FORA, 1992

in both birth-death rate and net migration, while depopulation is mainly explained by negative net migration in clusters 4 (SDT) and 6 (MA) and by a negative birth-death ratio in clusters 3 (SD) and 5 (SDP).

Figures 13.6 to 8 show some of the dynamics of the six clusters of LMAs during the second half of the 1980s. The relative decline in the proportion of the population economically active in agriculture and forestry is more rapid in most of these clusters than in the country as a whole. It indicates that in these areas structural transformation in this sector is still a reality, and that the same is true even more so in clusters 4 (SDT) and 5 (SDP), i.e. clusters with rapid decline in population over the same period. This illustrates the continuing importance of agriculture in general, and forestry in particular, on the dynamics of peripheral LMAs, reflecting the fact that this sector is over-represented in most of these labour markets (except clusters 2 and 6) compared to Sweden as a whole. With close to 10 per cent of employment in this sector in clusters 3, 4 and 5 we anticipate that the restructuring in this sector due to recession and reduced subsidies will continue to underline its importance for the dynamics of the labour market.

The process of industrialization still seems to continue in the latter clusters, while the more urban and southern clusters are closer to the national picture of 'deindustrialization' in terms of employment (Figure 13.7). It is evident from these findings that industrialization is fully compatible with population decline.

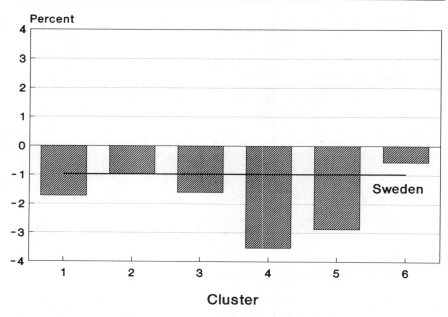

Figure 13.6   *Change of employment in agriculture and forestry as a proportion of total employment, 1986–90.* Six clusters of LMAs with declining population in Sweden
Source: FORA, 1992

In the second half of the 1980s, all these clusters (except the Mining Areas which went through a dramatic restructuring of the mining industry in the early 1980s) experienced relative gains, above the national average of employment in public services such as health care and social services (Figure 13.8). In these services, the process of growth and decentralization continued to be active even during this most recent period.

The last sequence of Figures (13.9–11) illustrates the turnover of three specific categories of labour in these clusters, plus—as a point of reference—a large, differentiated and 'normal' LMA (Skellefteå, an urban centre in the north-east on the Baltic coast). In each graph the *net migration* variable is the number of employed in each category moving from other LMAs to work in this LMA during the period 1986–89, *minus* the number of employed moving in the other direction. The *local net* flow consists of all those who enter the local labour market—from school or unemployment—during this period *minus* those who leave the labour market entirely, whether for retirement or for any other reason. *Total* is the change in the numbers employed in each respective category from 1986 to 1989. The booming demand for labour in Sweden as a whole and in these clusters of LMAs is evident from the Figures. In practically all

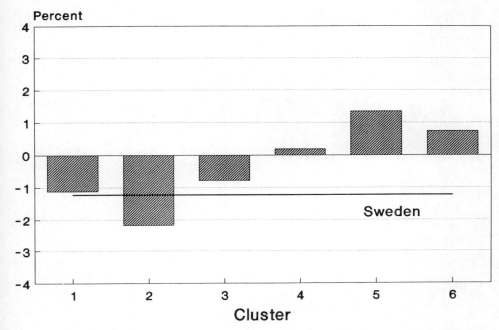

Figure   13.7 *Change   of   employment   in   manufacturing   industry   as   a proportion   of   total   employment,   1986–90.   Six   clusters of   labour   market   areas   (LMAs)   with   declining   popula-tion in Sweden*
Source: FORA, 1992

clusters and all categories of labour an increase in the number of employed is recorded, surely making this period a unique one.

Figure 13.9 shows the dynamics of the category of married females with children 2–15 years, i.e. a low mobility group. The flows of labour from this category to and from the LMAs are in balance in most clusters. Cluster 5 (Small Dependent Peripheries) has benefited from the overall growth in the number of employed in this group of almost 10 per cent during the five-year period. It is a development that is to some extent explained by net in-migration, but more by a net expansion of local recruitment. In this period with substantial growth in the service sector in all these clusters, it is clear that the available local reserves of labour were mobilized. Figure 13.10 shows the group of married females 25–50 years without post-secondary education working in public services, i.e. a low-skill group but one which would be expected to be attracted to LMAs showing expansion in public services. None of these clusters shows any increase in the numbers of women from this group migrating and some of the clusters reveal substantial losses (4 and 6). Local recruitment is very similar in all these clusters and also in the reference LMA of Skellefteå.

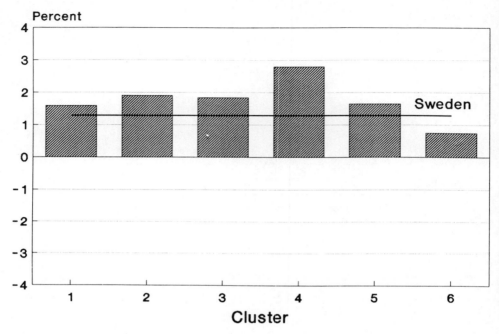

Figure 13.8   *Change of employment in health care and social services as a propor-*
tion of total employment, 1986–90. Six clusters of labour market areas
(LMAs) with declining population in Sweden
Source: FORA, 1992

An example of a high mobility group, technicians 25–34 years old with
a university degree (Figure 13.11), shows a negative net migration pattern
in clusters 1, 2 and especially 4 (SDT) and 6 (MA), as well as in the
reference LMA. In a period of overall growth in this type of employment
in most clusters, it is mostly local labour that is being recruited. Only in
clusters 3 (SD) and, in particular, 5 (SDP) have the new jobs also been
filled by in-migrating labour.

There are a few remarks to be made about the results of this analysis
of clusters of declining LMAs. Firstly, in spite of a total growth in the
number of jobs in these labour markets, they have continued losing
population. This indicates that to reverse the depopulation trend, especially in a period of recession, it is not enough just to try to attract new
employment opportunities. The data show that neither increases in
employment in manufacturing nor in services have altered the depopulation trend during the period under review. It is also evident that low-skilled
jobs in the local service sector have attracted local female labour and it is
probably true that the greater availability of service jobs for more highly
qualified personnel in central and urban labour markets has caused out-

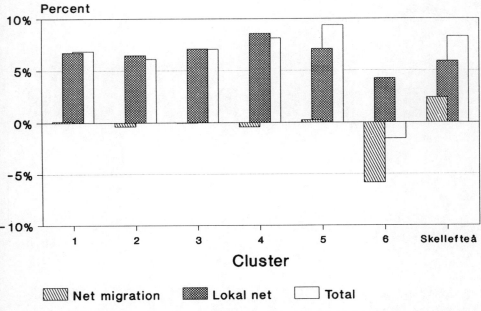

Figure 13.9   *Married women with children 2–15 years.* Labour flows in six clusters of labour market areas (LMAs) with declining population in Sweden plus reference LMA of Skellefteå.
Source: FORA, 1992

migration of young women. There are indications that small and peripheral labour markets usually show a larger turnover of labour, which means that even when population is declining, the labour market is very fluid, a feature that is expressed in flows of labour both to and from the LMA in question.

Regional policy—a minor item in the national budget

One problem which makes it difficult to evaluate the present regional policy is its limited influence on the development process. It seems that geographically the redistribution of the state budget is more powerfully affected by decisions within other sectors than by 'international' regional policy. It is calculated that resources for regional policy in Sweden correspond to less than 0.7 per cent of the total government resources to the average region (SOU, 1989, p. 65). Furthermore, rural policy represents—in resource terms—only a fraction of overall regional policy. Direct welfare transfers account for almost 50 per cent of total transfers and another 11 per cent is made up of compensation payments for the generally

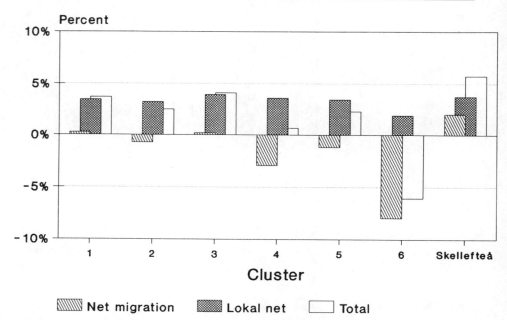

Figure 13.10   *Females 25–50 years without post-secondary education working –*
public services. Labour flows in six clusters of LMAs with declining
population in Sweden plus reference LMA of Skellefteå.
Source: FORA, 1992

weak conditions in the regions, e.g. as expressed by high levels of unemployment.

Regional policy in Sweden was largely implemented on the assumption of permanent growth. Today the recession and budget problems, together with the prospect of European integration, mean that the existing regional priorities are, and will continue to be, questioned. The ambitious objectives of a regional equilibrium and equal conditions for all households throughout Sweden have already been severely compromised.

To conclude, any examination of the future of peripheral and/or rural areas must not be limited only to existing regional policy. The latter is founded on ideas and a perception of reality that seems to be largely out of date. The influence of regional policy on the spatial distribution of people and economic activities is limited, compared to the influence exerted by other areas of the public expenditure. Furthermore, regional policy is built around economic and social structures from the past and has not been adapted to important recent changes.

A successful regional policy will have to take into account, and make use of, these changes both on a national level and in the different individual localities. It will also be necessary for those designing the policy to consider the impact of general changes in society, such as the interna-

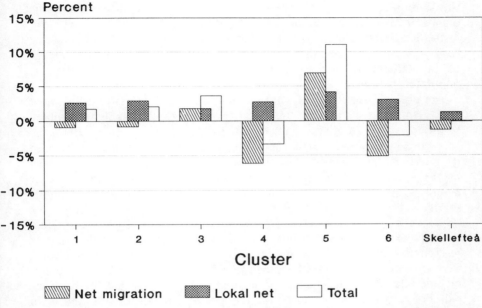

Figure 13.11   *Technicians 25–34 years with university degree.* Labour flows in six clusters of LMAs with declining population in Sweden plus reference LMA of Skellefteå.
Source: FORA, 1992

tionalization of the economy, European political integration and political changes at a national level. In the next section we shall highlight some general economic and political changes which will affect the options for peripheral and/or rural areas. Finally some of the implications for regional policy will be highlighted.

A governmental strategy with regional implications

All the main political parties agree on three fundamental elements in the current strategy for Swedish economic policy. They can be summed up as follows: first, to take a more active part in the European integration process (Prime Minister's Declaration, 1991); second, to reduce production costs, mainly by limiting wage increases, and improve competitiveness in order to avoid unemployment and safeguard the basic elements of the welfare system; and third, to revive growth by government and private investment in infrastructure, job training and improving the skill levels of the labour force.

The increasing pressure to achieve international competitiveness, the challenges introduced by the EEA agreement (and possible EC membership), and the technological revolution in industry have all intensified the debate in Sweden on regional development. The specific geographical, institutional and economic conditions are at the heart of the discussions: with 21 inhabitants per sq. km, as compared with the European average of 147 inhabitants per sq. km, Sweden is one of the most sparsely populated nations in Europe.

The political shift towards market solutions, the process of adjustment to EC rules and the national budgetary problems are all likely to combine to produce a substantial reduction in the state budget (Tapper, 1992).

According to one estimate (assuming a SEK 80,000 million cut-back of the present SEK 500,000 million state budget), the per capita net effect means that the central regions, especially the big cities, will actually benefit, with tax reductions and only a limited contraction in public services. The main reason for the negative effect on the periphery is its high level of dependency on public services and transfers from the national exchequer, plus the relative low level of incomes, which mean that any tax reductions have a relatively small positive impact on overall buying power. The expected cut-backs (the positive effects of tax reductions are not included here) for our clusters of declining LMAs show that the pressure will be very great, especially on the peripheral clusters of LMAs in Norrland:

1 Small Towns (−1,640 SEK/capita)
2 Medium Size Decentralized (−1,946)
3 Medium Size Urban (−3,847)
4 Small Decentralized (−4,039)
5 Small Dependent Towns (−7,257)
6 Small Dependent Peripheries (−8,727)
7 Mining Areas (−9,157)

The figures are hypothetical and can only be looked at as examples of what would happen if proposed budget reductions were carried through. Nevertheless, the example above indicates that a spatial perspective on the present changing macroeconomic conditions is needed. The redistributional effects of policy changes will have to be taken into consideration, as well as the varying needs and possibilities of the different kinds of peripheral and rural area. Such a policy cannot be restricted to traditional regional policy; it must embrace all sectors and be strategic and progressive. From one perspective, the major challenge is to create the conditions that will enable peripheral areas to participate in the growth sectors of the economy. From another especially in terms of the long-term demographic processes operating in these regions, the major task is to develop ways and means to facilitate economic and social adjustment to these processes.

Conclusions—emerging types of peripheral and/or rural labour markets

The development of a 'Swedish welfare model', directed towards individuals, rather than regions, has meant that jobs and services have been provided on an equal basis in all regions. A system which provided for education, health care, social welfare etc. equally across the country generated jobs and services in regions which would otherwise have lagged behind. These spatial effects of the welfare system have never been studied in detail and, when the welfare model comes under scrutiny and state transfers to individuals and municipalities are to be cut back, the negative effects in many peripheral and rural areas come as something of a shock. Structural changes determining the future of these areas will also occur in other parts of the system—in the economy and in other areas of politics.

In order to understand the processes at work, we have to focus on the different problems and prospects for different localities. Tentatively we may recognize three types of peripheral and/or rural regions emerging in Sweden.

Intermediate zones with both rural and urban characteristics and adequate infrastructure

These zones are normally characterized by net out-migration and by an internal migration to towns and municipalities within the region (Wiberg, 1990). Population decline, service problems and a predominance of declining sectors are some of the standard features, expressed largely in our clusters 1–4, i.e. ST, MSD, MSU and SD. Some of these regions, however, are taking advantage of a perceived new attractiveness, as places to live, to invest in and to spend holidays in, etc. A social, as well as an economic, change is taking place with traditional farming in decline.

The labour markets in intermediate zones in Sweden are generally small, but are able to offer almost as much employment as the larger regions. Average employment and unemployment levels are a few percentage units lower than in other regions in the country.

Peripheries with unique natural and cultural assets, attracting permanent or/and temporary residents

Dispersed amongst the intermediate and marginal zones there is an archipelago of rural localities and small towns which have specific scenic, sporting and/or wilderness characteristics. In spite of a slow-down during the present recession, there has been a long-term trend towards population growth in these localities, in some cases based on permanent residents, in others more on second homes. The increasing numbers of relatively well-off retired people will boost the demand for attractive sites with good infrastructure and service facilities. It is likely that the marketing in central Europe of specific Nordic sites with unique environmental assets will result in a growing tourist business. The long-term increase in individual mobility amongst major sections of the population in the advanced economies of Europe will add to the dynamism of these rural localities. Our method of clustering LMAs do not allow these LMAs to be distinguished and identified.

Marginal areas lacking much of the attractiveness and potential of zones a and b

Marginal areas with sparse and often ageing and declining populations, with small or no attraction for private investment, as well as limited potential for infrastructure investment face severe structural problems, because of the large share of their employment that is in declining sectors. Rising costs for maintenance of public service such as schools, health care, post delivery, etc. add to the insecurity of their future. Traditionally they are subsidized by other regions, but with a political shift towards market solutions they may in the future face new difficulties, accelerated by increased competition as a result of Sweden's integration into the EC. Most of the interior of Norrland and also some other regions are dominated by these kinds of problem.

On the whole, marginal areas are vulnerable because of their dependence on subsidies and/or a strong public sector. Traditionally they have gained all round from the welfare model, but there is now a diminishing political interest for subsidizing marginal areas, a trend fuelled by the moves towards European integration. We believe that many LMAs in our clusters 4–6 (SDT, SDP and MF) are regions of this type.

References

Chang, J., Gade, O. and Jones, J., 1991, 'The intermediate socioeconomic zone: a North Carolina case study' in O. Gade, V.P. Miller and L. Sommers (eds), *Planning in marginal areas*, Occasional Papers, Vol. 3 (Spring, 1991), Department of Geography, Appalachian State University, Boone NC, pp 149–68

FORA (Forskningsgruppen för regionl analys Research Group on Regional Analysis), Royal Institute of Technology, Stockholm

Johansson, M. and Persson, L.O., 1991, *Regioner för generationer*, Allmänna Förlaget Publica, Stockholm

Newby, H., 1987, *Country life. A social history of rural England*

OECD, 1991, *OECD Economic Surveys: Sweden*, Paris

Persson, L.O. 1990, 'Urbanization processes in peripheral areas in a welfare state', *Journal of Rural Studies*, Vol 6, No 4, pp 437–42

Persson, L.O. 1992, 'Rural labour markets meeting urbanization and the arena society' in T. Marsden *et al.* (eds), *Critical perspectives in rural change labour and locality*, Fulton, London

Persson, L.O. and Westholm, E, 1992, *Turmoil in the welfare state reshapes rural Sweden*, not yet published

Persson, L.O. and Wiberg, U., 1988, 'Policy and planning for the urbanized rural areas', *Scandinavian Housing and Planning Research*, Vol 5, No 4, November 1988

Statens Offentliga Statistik (SOS), Statistiska Centralbyrån (SCB)

Statens Offentliga Utredningar (SOU), 1989;65 *Statenigeografin* (The state in geography), Stockholm, p. 65 (Vol 65)

Statens Offentliga Utredningar (SOU), 1992:19 *Långtidsutredningen 1992*

Statens Offentliga Utredningar (SOU) 1992:19 Bilaga 5 till Långtidsutredningen 1992 *EG och den regionala utvecklingen i Sverige.*

Swedish Governments, *Financial Plan 1991/92*, Stockholm

Tapper, H., 1992, *EG, statsbudgeten och den regionala balansen*, Departement-sskrift (Ds) 1992:80

The Prime Minister's 1991, Declaration to Parliament', Prime Minister's Office, 6 June 1991

The Future of Rural Society, 1988 Bulletin of the European Community, Supplement 4/88

The OECD Observer, Aug/Sept 1991, *The resistance to agricultural reform*, Viatte, G. and Cahill

Wiberg, U., (ed.), 1990, *Characteristics of the intermediate socio-economic zones in Sweden and USA*, Umeå, University of Umeå, CERUM Working Paper, CWP-1990 no. 8

14 Legislative developments in the European Community, July 1991- June 1992

Andrew W. Gilg

This review is based on two main sources: first, the biannual publication *Developments in the European Community* published by HMSO (Cm. 1857 and 2065) and second, the weekly bulletin of the Commission of the European Communities. It is divided into four areas: Finance; Agriculture; the Environment; and Wildlife Conservation.

Outline of developments in finance and agriculture

In February 1992 the Commission published its proposals for the future financing of the Community. These included an increase in the own resources ceiling from 1.2 per cent of Community GNP to 1.37 per cent, permitting a real-terms increase in expenditure of more than 30 per cent, from 63.2 billion ECU (£44 billion) in 1992 to 83.2 billion ECU (£58 billion) in 1997 (all at 1992 prices). It also proposed some reforms to the system of Own Resources, and renewal of the Inter-Institutional Agreement on Budgetary Discipline. The June 1992 Lisbon European Council did not reach agreement on any specific figures for spending, either on individual policies or in total, but concluded that it would reach decisions at its meeting in Edinburgh in December 1992.

Between July and December 1991 the Agriculture Council discussed GATT and the Commission's proposals for reform of the CAP. Council reached agreement on the principles of a transitional oilseeds regime to meet the criticisms of the GATT soya panel, pending agreement on CAP reform. Agreement was also reached on the welfare of animals in transit, welfare standards for calves and pigs, on two plant health Directives representing significant progress towards the Single Market, on a further moratorium on the use of bovine somatotrophin and also on an increase in the maximum level for 1991 suckler cow premium.

Between December and July 1992, the Agriculture Council reached agreement on reforming the CAP. The reform package involved a fundamental change to support arrangements, a commitment to pursue environmental protection as an integrated part of the CAP and measures on forestry and support prices for the 1992/93 marketing year. Strict anti-rabies measures were agreed for commercial imports of cats and dogs as were important measures on the marketing of meat products and on milk hygiene.

Developments in agriculture in detail, July-December 1991

Reform of the CAP

In July 1991, the Commission published a paper outlining its ideas for reform of the CAP. This was discussed by the Agriculture Council in September. Formal proposals followed for major changes to the regimes for arable crops (cereals, oilseeds, protein crops), tobacco, beef, sheep-meat and milk, together with accompanying proposals for an agri-environmental scheme and for measures on forestry and to encourage early retirement. These were considered by the Agriculture Council in November and December.

Plant Health

On 19 December 1991, the Council adopted a Directive laying down the principles governing the organisation of plant health controls following the establishment of the Single Market. Once implemented, the Directive will require certain plants, plant products and other objects to be identified as meeting the plant health standards of the European Community by way of a plant passport, usually in the form of a label. Producers, wholesalers and importers dealing with such material will be registered and inspected to ensure compliance. (There is scope to exempt small exclusively localised operations.) Material entering the Community from third countries which currently requires a phytosanitary certificate will continue to do so. After inspection the phytosanitary certificate will be replaced by a plant passport and the material will be able to circulate within the Community on the same basis as passported material originating within it. Where a higher plant health status can be shown to exist within discrete parts of the Community, protected zones may be established in order to maintain these. Passported material entering such zones will need to meet their stricter plant health standards and be identified accordingly. The Directive to be implemented by 1 January 1993.

Animal Welfare

In the autumn of 1991 the Agriculture Council adopted a Directive for the protection of all animals in transit. It provides a framework of safeguards to fulfil the needs of the Single Market whilst setting specific conditions for individual species. Some of the detailed implementing rules had to be decided by the Council by the end of 1992, taking account of a report in preparation by scientific advisors covering points such as feeding, watering and resting intervals for farmed species.

The Directive provides for additional requirements to be drawn up to protect certain vulnerable species in trade, such as wild birds and horses. Meanwhile national provisions may apply.

The Maastricht summit in December 1991 agreed a declaration on the protection of animals. As a result, in future all Community legislation on agriculture, the internal market, transport and research will need to take account of animal welfare concerns.

Animal Health

On 11–12 December 1991 the Agriculture Council adopted a package of measures amending existing legislation, consisting of 3 Directives and a Council Decision, on Classical Swine Fever. They include the introduction of community-wide measures for dealing with outbreaks of the disease by the adoption of a slaughter and compensation policy, in a similar way to that recently established for Foot and Mouth Disease. Member states have to submit to the Commission contingency plans for dealing with the disease, again in a similar way to that recently done for Foot and Mouth Disease.

Amendments to intra-Community trade rules discontinue the concept of 'Officially Swine Fever free' and 'Swine Fever free' member states, regions and holdings. Member states will in future be responsible for controlling movements of pigs, pigmeat and pigmeat products out of a zone where Classical Swine Fever exists or is suspected. In line with the reduced incidence of Classical Swine Fever in the Community, amendments to the third-country import rules for pigs, pigmeat and pigmeat products prohibits imports from those countries which have not been free of the disease and/or which have permitted vaccination during the previous 12 months.

Oilseeds

On 11 December 1991 the Agriculture Council adopted a regulation establishing a new oilseeds scheme, to run from the 1992/93 marketing year. Under the new scheme, producers receive per hectare payments. The scheme replaces the present one, under which aid is paid to oilseed processors.

Beef

On 11 December 1991 the Agriculture Council adopted a regulation increasing for the 1991 scheme year only, both the EAGGF and the permitted national contributions to the suckler cow premium and increasing EAGGF funding of this premium in Northern Ireland, Ireland and Greece.

On 25 July 1991 the Council adopted a regulation opening for 1991 an autonomous high quality beef quota for 11,430 tonnes as compensation for countries that would normally export to the Community under the manufacturing balance sheet, which was set at zero for 1991. On 11 December the Agriculture Council adopted regulations opening import quotas for 1992 covering 53,000 tonnes of frozen beef and veal, 34,300 tonnes of high quality beef, 2,250 tonnes of buffalo meat and 1,500 tonnes of thin skirt (diaphragm muscle).

Sheepmeat

On 19 December the Council adopted a regulation applying for the 1992 marketing year the existing definitions of 'eligible ewe', 'eligible she-goat' and 'eligible female other than eligible ewe' for the purpose of sheep annual premium payments. The regulation ensured that an essential element of the sheepmeat support arrangements remained in place pending agreement on the new definitions proposed in the context of CAP reform.

Developments in agriculture in detail, January–June 1992

Reform of the Common Agricultural Policy

On 21 May 1992, the Agriculture Council reached agreement in principle on reform in the CAP. This agreement shifted the emphasis on support from the product to the producer and represented the most fundamental reform of the CAP yet achieved. The agreement also trod new ground in bringing environmental issues into the heart of the CAP.

The agreement significantly cut support prices and reduced the role of intervention. A central element was the reduction in cereal prices of up to 35 per cent over three years from 1993. To compensate, arable producers receive direct aid paid on an area basis, providing they set aside 15 per cent of their arable land. Smaller producers will not have to set land aside in order to claim aid. This combination of price cut and set-aside is designed to reduce over production and to curb Community expenditure on surpluses.

Beef support prices will be cut by 15 per cent over three years from 1993. Those rearing livestock intensively will benefit from the reduced cereal prices; extensive rearers will—subject to stocking limits—receive an increase in premium payments. Additional restrictions will reduce the attractiveness of intervention. A quota system for entitlement to ewe premium will be introduced to curb expenditure in the sheep sector, with special measures to protect sensitive areas dependent on sheep production. For milk, the intervention price for butter will be reduced by 5 per cent over two years, while quotas will be cut by 1 per cent in 1993 and 1994, although this decision will be reviewed in the light of the market situation at the time. To reduce the very high cost of supporting the tobacco sector, quotas will be introduced on premium payments at levels considerably below current production. Steps are also being taken to discourage the production of less marketable varieties.

An important part of the settlement was the agreement of an agri-environment regulation. All member states will now operate schemes to encourage environmentally sensitive farming. This builds on the success of the United Kingdom's Environmentally Sensitive Areas scheme. Member states have a year in which to draw up their programmes. At the United Kingdom's insistence, the settlement also included a commitment by the Agriculture Council to pursue environmental proctection requirements as an integral part of the CAP.

The Commission confirmed that the costs to reform including the accompanying measures could be met from within the existing guideline.

The agreement also included support prices for agricultural products for the marketing year 1992/93. Prices were frozen for most commodities.

Arable crops Support prices for cereals were cut by 3 per cent by application of the stabiliser mechanism. The co-responsibility levy was abolished from the start of the 1992/93 marketing year. A new price structure for cereals will come into effect from the start of the 1993/94 marketing year, with a target price reducing over three years to 110 ECU/tonne (£87/tonne) and, as now, an intervention price setting the minium support levels for cereals; there will be no support prices for oilseeds and proteins under the reformed regimes. Direct aids will be payable to arable producers on an area basis, subject to a 15 per cent set-aside requirement.

Dairy products Support prices were frozen for 1992/93, but cuts agreed in the butter support price of 2.5 per cent per year in 1993/94 and 1994/95, subject to the market situation at the time. The existing milk quota system is extended to the year 2000. There was no quota cut for 1992/93 but cuts of 1 per cent were agreed in principle for the following two market years, again subject to review. An additional quota was granted to Spain and Greece on condition that the quota system is fully implemented. The dairy co-responsibility levy is to be abolished in 1993.

Beef The intervention price for 1992/93 was frozen, but from 1 July 1993 will be reduced by 15 per cent over 3 years. Ceilings are to be introduced on the amounts—to be reduced progressively to 350,000 tonnes—which may be purchased into intervention. The suckler cow premium is to be increased progressively to £95.45 per head by 1995 and made subject to individual producer quotas. From 1993, it will cease to apply to cows of dairy breed. There is also an increase to the beef special premium (to £71.58 per head by 1995), which will become payable up to twice per head in the life of the animal and which will be subject to regional ceilings on the number of claims. For regions where pronounced seasonality of slaughtering occurs, including Northern Ireland, there is also an additional premium available to producers to encourage slaughtering outside the peak period. Both the suckler cow premium and the beef special premium are made subject to stocking limits and, to encourage extensification, producers with stocking rates of less than 1.4 livestock units per hectare will be able to claim an additional premium. As a step towards reducing quantities bought into intervention, member states must introduce either an early disposal scheme for male dairy calves or intervention for light-weight carcasses.

Sheep Basic support prices remain unchanged. A new definition of the eligible ewe premium will be introduced from the 1993 marketing year. Individual producer quotas for ewe premium are to be introduced from the start of the 1993 marketing year, with provision for new entrants and special cases. Quotas are to be transferable, subject to provisions to ensure that quotas are not transferred out of areas dependent on sheep production.

Tobacco Support prices remain unchanged. Quotas are to be introduced on tobacco premia and will be progressively reduced to 350,000 tonnes, well below current production. Measures are also being taken to encourage the production of more marketable varieties.

Cotton A 7 per cent rise in the guide price and an increase in the standard quality are offset by a reduction in the maximum guaranteed quantity to give a budgetarily neutral effect. The reduction in aid in any year is limited to 15 per cent; however, any excess up to 5 per cent may be carried forward to the next marketing year. The small producer scheme is extended to 1995/6.

Olive Oil An increase in production aid of 19 per cent is partly offset by a decrease of 15 per cent in consumption aid.

Fruit and vegetables The Council agreed to measures to improve the structure and competitiveness of the raspberry processing sector, from which Scottish producers in particular should benefit. Market stability for processed tomatoes will be ensured by means of a guarantee threshold coupled with in-year reductions in production aid; market management by means of a quota system will, however, be reintroduced for 1993/94.

Wine The Commission made a commitment to consider, in the context of reform of the wine regime, the possibility of allowing quality wine to be made from hybrid wine varieties.

Stop-press

On 4 December 1992 *Farmers Weekly* reported that as a result of the draft GATT deal (see UK section p. 146) that the CAP reforms would be modified as follows:

a. For beef, a reduction in EC exports from 1,034 million tonnes to 817,000 by 1999. Export subsidies and import tariffs to be cut by 36 per cent;
b. For dairy, a cut in export of milk products from 2.35 million tonnes to 1.85 million tonnes by 1999. An increase in imports of 193,000 million tonnes. Export subsidies and import tariffs to be cut by 36 per cent;
c. For pig and poultrymeat, a cut of 21 per cent in subsidised exports. But it is expected that most exports will be able to take place without subsidy;
d. For cereals a reduction in exports from 29.6 million tonnes to 23.4 million tonnes. Export subsidies and import tariffs to drop by 36 per cent;
e. For oilseeds, the main change, a limit of 5.128 million hectares, extra for industrial use.

It was forecast that this would increase the set-aside area for each country as follows, with the new forecast second: Germany 8 to 15; France 12 to 23; Italy 4 to 7; Belgium 8 to 15; Denmark 13 to 25; UK 16 to 29; and Spain 7 to 13.

Other measures

Beef On 27 January 1992, the Council adopted a regulation opening a quota of 198,000 head of young male bovine animals for fattening for 1992 and agreed a nil Manufacturing Balance Sheet quota for 1992 (the same as 1991). On 27 May, the Council adopted a regulation opening an autonomous quota of 11,430 tonnes of high quality (Hilton) beef as compensation to supplying countries for the loss of Manufacturing Balance

Sheet imports. An import quota for 1992 covering 47,600 head of certain breeds of Alpine and Mountain cattle was proposed.

Sheepmeat On 3 March 1992, the Council adopted a Decision extending until 31 December 1995 the period of application of Decision 82/530/EEC authorising the United Kingdom to permit the Isle of Man authorities to apply a special import licensing system for sheepmeat, beef and veal.

Fruit plants marketing scheme On 28 April 1992, the Internal Market Council agreed a Directive establishing the framework for the harmonisation of Community rules on the certification of fruit plants and planting material intended for fruit production. In addition to a minimum grade, there will be three optional higher grades and labelling requirements. Material marketed at one of the higher grades must belong to a registered variety. Material may be registered provided it satisfies certain conditions. Specifications for the main commercial groups of varieties will be prescribed in schedules. Suppliers of varieties covered by a schedule must comply with its specifications. Suppliers of such varieties, including retailers, will be inspected and accredited by the appropriate national authority. (There is scope to exempt small, exclusively localised operations.) Imports from third countries must meet the same requirements.

Health rules for milk and milk products On 15 June 1992, the Agriculture Council adopted a Directive on the production and placing on the market of raw milk, heat-treated milk and milk-based products. It sets out microbiological standards and hygiene rules for production holdings, processing and manufacturing establishments and also includes provisions on packaging, labelling, transport and storage of milk and milk products.

Health rules on the marketing of meat products On 10 February 1992, the Agriculture Council adopted a Directive laying down common public health rules for the marketing of meat products and certain other products of animal origin intended for human consumption. This Directive will include hygiene rules, structural requirements and supervision arrangements in premises.

Public and animal health rules for wild game meat On 15 June 1992, the Agriculture Council adopted a Directive which harmonises the public and animal health rules for the killing, preparation and marketing of wild game. It includes rules on the provenance, post-mortem inspection, certification, transport, storage and hygiene handling of wild game meat; approval and inspection of processing establishments; and arrangements for third-country imports.

Annotated list of Major Commission documents issued between July 1991–June 1992

Council Regulation 2329/91—opening and providing for the administration of a special autonomous quota for high quality fresh chilled or frozen meat from certain countries.

Council Regulation 3605/91—derogates from Article 3 or Regulation 1357/80, for applications for the suckler cow premium scheme, and provides for an increase in the maximum rate of premium payable by member states for applications lodged in respect of the 1991 scheme.

Council Regulation 3667/91—opening and providing for the administration of an import quota for frozen beef and veal.

Council Regulation 3668/91—opening and providing for the administration of an import quota of high quality fresh, chilled or frozen meat of bovine animals from certain countries.

Council Regulation 3669/91—opening and providing for the administration of an import quota for frozen buffalo meat.

Council Regulation 3670/91—opening and providing for the administration of an import quota for frozen thin skirt meat.

Council Regulations following Commission Document COM(92)94 on support prices for the 1992/93 marketing year.

Council Regulations following Commission Document COM(91)258 on the Reform of the Common Agricultural Policy.

Council Regulation 916/92—on the transfer to Portugal of 382,000 tonnes of cereals held by various intervention agencies.

Council Regulation 1333/92—on the system of minimum import prices for certain soft fruits originating in Hungary, Poland and the Czech and Slovak Federal Republic.

Council Regulation 1404/92—opening and providing for an autonomous high quality (Hilton) beef import quota for 11,430 tonnes as compensation to third countries who normally export beef under the Manufacturing Balance Sheet, which has been set at nil for 1992.

Council Regulation 1568/92—concerning the import arrangements applicable to certain third countries in the sheepmeat and goatmeat sector.

Council Regulation 1600/92, 1601/92 and 1603/92—introducing specific measures for the agriculture sectors in the Canary Islands and in Madeira and the Azores.

Council Regulation 1756/92—on the support system for producers of certain arable crops.

Council Regulation 1766/92—on the common organisation of the market in cereals.

Council Estimate 92/60—concerning beef and veal intended for the processing industry for the period 1 January to 31 December 1992.

Annotated list of other Commission documents issued between July 1991–June 1992

COM(91)415—On 8 November the Commission submitted a proposal for Council regulations on agricultural production methods compatible with protection of the environment and the maintenance of the countryside and to institute Community aid schemes for forestry measures in agriculture and for early retirement from farming.

COM(91)454—On 20 November the Commission submitted a proposal for a regulation amending Regulation 1411/71 laying down additional rules on the common market organisation in milk and milk products for drinking milk.

COM(91)467—On 21 November 1991, the Commission submitted a proposal for a Council regulation estimating the number of young male bovine animals weighing 300kg or less intended for fattening for 1992 and the amount of beef and veal intended for processing in 1992. The Commission also submitted a proposal for a Council regulation to open an autonomous high quality (Hilton) beef import quota for 11,430 tonnes as compensation to third countries who normally export beef under the Manufacturing Balance Sheet, which has been proposed at zero for 1992.

Developments in the field of environmental legislation

Vehicle emissions

On 1 October 1991 the Environment Council formally adopted a Directive tightening emission standards from large diesel-engined vehicles, which was agreed in principle earlier in the year. The new controls will come into effect in 1995 and 1996.

Standardised reporting

On 1 October 1991 the Environment Council agreed a directive to introduce new standardised reporting arrangements into a large number of existing environmental Directives. Member states will be required to submit information to the European Commission in a prescribed format every three years on the implementation of the Directive concerned, with one exception. In the case of the Bathing Water Directive, reports will be produced annually. Commission reports will be based on this information.

Eco-labelling

Agreement was reached at the 12–13 December 1991 Environment Council on a regulation which will introduce a Community-wide eco-labelling scheme. This scheme will inform consumers, encourage the development of less environmentally damaging products and facilitate trade. It will be voluntary; assess products over the whole of their life-cycle; demand a high level of environmental protection; work on a pass/fail basis; and exclude food and drink. Criteria for the award of the label will be valid throughout the Community. Primary responsibility for awarding labels will rest with individual member states, although there will be safeguards to ensure criteria are uniformly applied across the Community.

Carbon energy tax

On 13 December 1991, a joint session of the Environment and Energy Councils met to discuss the Commission's recent communication on a Community strategy to limit carbon dioxide (CO_2) emissions and to improve energy efficiency. Conclusions were agreed which recognised the need for a strategy at Community level based on a wide-ranging package of Community and national measures. It was agreed that national programmes should be formulated for limiting CO_2 emissions and that specific measures at Community level and a move to higher energy pricing through the use of fiscal instruments might form useful parts of a global policy. The Council invited the Commission to put forward formal proposals for measures arising from the Community strategy, taking into account the further studies needed and the conclusions of separate discussions by Finance Ministers. The Council recognised that the introduction of Community-wide taxation would pose a wide range of complex issues requiring further studies.

Life

The Environment Council on 12–13 December agreed a regulation to establish a new Community fund for the Environment (LIFE). This brings together several existing funds and also incorporates a number of new areas for Community support.

United Nations Conference on Environment and Development (UNCED)

The Joint Environment/Development Council on 5 May 1992 discussed Community preparations for the UNCED summit in June and agreed

Conclusions on most of the aspects under debate. The Council adopted Conclusions on 26 May on the Framework Convention on Climate Change and the Community signed the Convention during the UNCED summit. The Convention commits developed countries to take measures aimed at returning carbon dioxide and other greenhouse gas emissions to their 1990 levels by 2000 and represents a significant first step in a global response to the threat of climate change. The Community also signed the Convention on Biological Diversity and agreed to provide financial assistance under the Agenda 21 programme (an action plan for future work on the environment and development). The Biological Diversity Convention aims to safeguard eco-systems and will provide a package of measures for the conservation and sustainable use of the global variety of plant and animal species. The Agenda 21 programme will encourage sustainable development in developing countries.

At the Lisbon European Council on 26–27 June 1992, the Council invited all states participating in UNCED to proceed rapidly to the implementation of measures agreed. The Community and its member states agreed to a plan for follow-up action involving the following commitments:

— to ratify the Climate Change Convention and to establish the basis of ratification of the Biological Diversity Convention;
— to publish national plans to implement UNCED agreements;
— to give financial support to developing countries for the implementation of Agenda 21 through ODA and for the replenishment of the Global Environment Fund (GEF);
— to take the lead at the 1992 UN General Assembly in the establishment of the Sustainable Development Commission;
— to put weight behind establishing an international review process for forestry principles; and
— to take the lead in the restructuring of the GEF.

Ozone depletion

On 23 March 1992, the Environment Council reached agreement on a Community negotiating position for the forthcoming revision of the Montreal Protocol on ozone depletion. The Community will work towards the phasing out of chlorofluorocarbons (CFCs) and other ozone depleting substances by the end of 1995 with intermediate cuts by the end of 1993. The Council also agreed proposals for control of halogenated chlorofluorocarbons (HCFCs).

Air pollution by ozone

On 26 May 1992, the Environment Council adopted a common position on a Directive on air pollution by ozone. This requires monitoring to be carried out throughout the EC on a consistent basis, sharing of information and the issuing of health warnings to the public if specified ozone levels are exceeded. Within four years of the Directive coming into force, the Commission must report to the Council on data collected and put forward proposals for control of ozone pollution.

Annotated list of Commission documents, July 1991–June 1992

COM(91)220—On 2 July 1991, the Commission submitted a proposal for a Council directive on air pollution by ozone. This would implement Community-wide standards for the monitoring of ground-level atmospheric concentrations of ozone.

COM(91)268—On 23 July 1991, the Commission submitted a proposal for a Council decision on accession to the NO_x Protocol to the Geneva Convention. This is concerned with the reduction of emissions of nitrogen oxides or their transboundary fluxes.

COM(91)177—On 31 July 1991, the Commission submitted a proposal for a Council Directive laying down minimum standards for the keeping of animals in zoos.

COM(91)448—On 6 December 1991, the Commission submitted to the Council a proposal for a regulation laying down provisions with regard to possession of and trade in specimens of wild fauna and flora. This would replace Regulations 3626/82 and 3418/83 which currently implement the Convention on the International Trade in Endangered Species of Wild Fauna and Flora (CITES) within the Community.

COM(91)459—On 6 March 1992, the Commission submitted a proposal for a Council regulation allowing voluntary participation by companies in the industrial sector in a Community eco-audit scheme. This would establish a Community-wide scheme to encourage positive and effective environment management of industrial operations.

COM(92)106—On 20 March 1992, the Commission submitted a proposal for a Council Regulation amending Regulation 594/91 in order to speed up the phasing-out dates of ozone depleting substances amending dates set in Regulation 594/91.

COM(92)181—On 27 May 1992, the Commission submitted a proposal for a Council decision for a monitoring mechanism of Community carbon dioxide and other greenhouse gas emissions. This proposal would require member states to draw up and send to the Commission national programmes for limiting their carbon dioxide emissions.

COM(92)23—On 27 March 1992, the Commission submitted a proposal for a council resolution on a Community programme of policy and action in relation to the environment and sustainable development ('The Fifth Action Programme'). This will set the strategic framework for the Community's environmental policy until the year 2000.

A commentary on this proposal was provided by the weekly Bulletin of the Commission on the 21 July 1992, parts of which are reproduced below:

Fifth Environmental Action Programme

At the end of March 1992, the European Commission adopted the fifth of its environmental action programmes designed to protect and enhance the quality of the environment in the European Community. Due to run from 1993 to 2000 the fifth programme, entitled 'Towards Sustainability' is a departure from the four previous programmes: the adoption of the Single European Act has for the first time given the Community a constitutional mandate to take environmental protection measures. The previous programmes were very reactive, 'end of the pipe' strategies which responded to environmental problems after they had occured. But the fifth action programme is much more proactive, based on the thesis of 'sustainable development' as put forward by the 1987 Brundtland Report, whereby the root causes of environmental degradation are addressed before the problems become so pressing that they can no longer be ignored. Furthermore, the programme recognises that the full economic benefits of the single European market, in terms of continued growth and efficiency, are limited by environmental constraints, and that the whole internal market programme could be jeopardised if the tolerance levels of the natural environment are breached.

The main strategy behind the action programme is based on the realisation that environmental damage will never be halted, let alone prevented if behavioural patterns of producers and consumers, governments and citizens are not altered to take the environment more into account.

The Fifth Environmental Action Programme itself is in three volumes: COM(92)23 Final. Volume I is a Proposal for a Resolution of the Council of the European Communities on a Community programme of policy and action in relation to the environment and sustainable development.

This proposal for a Resolution would, if adopted, basically mean that the Council of Ministers approves and supports the Commission's strategy outlined in 'Towards Sustainability' and would give the Commission the go-ahead to come forward with futher proposals to put the programme into effect.

Volume II entitled 'Towards Sustainability', A European Community Programme of Policy and Action on Relation to the Environment and

Sustainable Development, contains the Commission's suggestions for action. Greater detail is given below.

Volume III—The State of the Environment in the European Community, Overview is in three parts. Part One looks at the state of air; water; soil; waste; quality of life in Europe; high-risk activities for the environmental, and biological diversity. Part Two looks at the causes of environmental degradation in the five key areas targeted for action in the programme, namely agriculture: forestry and fisheries: energy; industrial activity; transport; and tourism. The final part looks at the economic aspects of environmental damage—the costs incurred by not protecting the environment and benefits of protection, such as avoidance of damage and resulting cost; an improvement in the competitiveness of industry and a reduction in unemployment (eg. through a boom in the clean technologies and environment-related industries). Also included in the document are environmental statistics for 1991 as compiled by Euro-stat.

Having outlined the contents of the three main volumes, attention is now turned to Volume II, 'Towards Sustainability'. This is divided into three parts. Part One forms the bulk of the document and is entitled 'A Policy and Strategy for the Environment and Sustainable Development within the European Community'. It looks at the need for change and the strategy to achieve this. Part Two looks at the Community's role in the wider international arena; and Part Three briefly assesses priorities, costs and the review process. In essence, the main goal of the Fifth Action programme as set out in these three parts is to raise public awareness of the problems facing the environment and to change people's attitudes and behaviour to become more environmentally friendly. Three main groups of actors are identified:

—Public Authorities (central and local government) who have a crucial role to play not only in enforcing legislation, but also in making planning decisions, and informing and educating the public;
—Public and Private Enterprise as huge consumers of materials and producers of waste who must be both encouraged and obliged to take their responsibilities towards the environment seriously;
—The General Public, who as voter, producer of pollution and consumer of goods and services can also exert a great influence on the future quality of the environment.

In addition to the three groups of actors, selected target sectors include: Industry; Energy; Transport; Agriculture; and Tourism; but space precludes all but a brief presentation of the agricultural sector here.

The agricultural sector has undergone drastic changes in the last few decades, many of which have been as a direct result of the Common Agricultural Policy, and many of which have had a negative impact on the environment, for example the demands for ever higher yields. This has led to soil and water pollution problems; loss of top soil; an increase in plant and animal diseases; drainage of wetlands; and clearance of forests, to name but a few of the problems. The strategy now put forward aims to minimise the impact of agriculture on the environment by encouraging farmers to see themselves as guardians of the countryside. Objectives include:

—reducing pollution from nitrates, phosphates, pesticides and livestock units by strict controls;
—financial incentives to encourage farmers to farm in an 'environmentally friendly' way, complemented by training measures; and
—new afforestation projects (mixed forests) and action to prevent forest fires.

In the wider international arena 'Towards Sustainability' looks at the European Community's role in the wider international arena and points out that:

—it is a major contributor to global issues such as climate change and deforestation and must therefore be instrumental in addressing these issues;
—it has responsibilities towards the developing countries and must show that it is not just preaching at those countries but willing to change life-styles and cut consumption levels. Partnership with the developing countries to achieve sustainable development at a global level is essential;
—the newly democratised countries of Central and Eastern Europe are understandably looking to the Community for assistance in clearing up their many environmental disasters;
—the 1992 United Nations Conference on Environment and Development in Rio de Janeiro and the preparatory and follow-up work are providing the Community with the opportunity of showing the rest of the world just how committed Europe is to achieving sustainable development.

Part Three of the document acts as a summing up of the whole strategy, reiterating the selection of priority fields of action, and comparing the economic costs of environmental protection with the global environment costs of maintaining the *status quo*. It finishes by saying that the road to sustainable development will be long and that a review of the strategy will be necessary during the programme, by the end of 1995. The final message is that 'the environment is dependent on our collective actions; tomorrow's environment depends on how we act today'.

Developments in the conservation field, July 1991–December 1992

Habitats

On 12–13 December 1991, the Council reached agreement on a Directive to protect natural and semi-natural habitats and wild flora and fauna. The principal aim of the Directive is to contribute towards ensuring bio-diversity by safeguarding Europe's natural heritage through the establishment of a network to be known as 'Natura 2000' of protected sites or Special Areas of Conservation (SAC). It will be the responsibility of each member state to implement the Directive on its own territory but the Directive recognises the disproportionate burden which may be faced by some member states by setting up a limited co-financing mechanism for the protection of habitats and species in danger of extinction.

Member states have two years to bring forward the laws, regulations and administrative provisions necessary to implement the Directive. They have three years in which to submit to the Commission a proposed national list of sites, from which the sites to be designated as SACs will be selected. Member states have the discretion to select sites to maintain certain habitats and species at a favourable conservation status. The Directive imposes a responsibility to afford SACs a high level of protection and to maintain the coherence of the 'Natura 2000' network but member states may also weigh in the balance the potentially conflicting demands of nature conservation and other overriding public interests on individual sites.

The Annexes to the Directive identify the habitat types and animal and plant species which by virtue of their rarity and vulnerability merit protection. In the case of animals and plants, this can include strict species protection, habitat designation and management measures.

The following review of the Directive was provided by David Baldock writing in *Ecos*, **13** (1), 1992, on page 57.

High political drama preceded the final act of many years of negotiations over the EC's Habitats Directive. The Directive was agreed on 12 December at the last Environment Council meeting under the Dutch Presidency.

As predicted in *Ecos*, **12** (3), disagreement over the need for contributions from the EC budget nearly capsized progress made under the Luxembourg Presidency in negotiating a compromise text. The Spanish government led arguments for a substantial contribution from EC funds to offset the costs of complying with the Directive, which could require protection of a significant proportion of the land area in Spain and some other member states. At the same time, the Spanish government was threatening to block agreement at Maastricht on political union unless substantial new funds were made available for the poorer member states. From their perspective, the Habitats Directive was not an isolated example; EC funds should be made available to support implementation of other environmental Directives as well. However, several Northern member states remained opposed to conceding the general principle that Community funding should be provided when new environmental legislation is agreed.

Following Ministerial meetings in the run-up to Maastricht, the Spanish won the argument over EC funds for the Directive, which was duly agreed. In the same week, two significant new EC funds were agreed. One for the environment (known as LIFE), and another specially for infrastructure works and environmental projects in the four poorest member states. However, there remain tensions over which of these will be used for the Habitats Directive and many governments will be loath to attach special funding to future environmental Directives.

The aim of the Directive remains the establishment of a European network of 'special areas for conservation' (SACs) which are broadly equivalent to Special Protection Areas (SPAs) under the Birds Directive. The sites will consist of both habitats of Community importance and the habitats of species of Community importance, as listed in Annexes. In due course, a pan-European network of such sites will be established under the title Natura 2000. This process will be protracted and may not be completed until 2004.

Although less ambitious than earlier drafts, the Directive is a notable step forward in EC legislation. One Article that has received little attention but will come into effect in 1994 is an amendment to the Birds Directive, which deals with the protection of SPAs. This stems from concern by the UK and other governments about a European Court of Justice ruling which greatly restricted the kind of projects which could be permitted to damage SPAs, effectively requiring more protection for these sites than that given in most member states. The new Article opens the door a little wider, but only allows projects required for reasons of overriding public interest where there is no alternative available. This will be the rule for the new SACs as well as SPAs.

Section IV:
Canada

edited by
Robert S. Dilley

Introduction
Robert S Dilley

Rural Canada has not made quite the same impact on the media as it had at this time last year; not least because the national constitutional debate superseded every other news item. However, problems remain and developments are still occurring. In this issue one of the recurrent problems is addressed: that of preserving agricultural land. As I reported last year, there is a growing realisation in the world's second largest country (there was disappointment in some quarters that the breakup of the Soviet Union did not lead to Canada becoming the *largest* country) that resources are not infinite. Among other things, this has led to a realisation that prime agricultural land is being lost at an alarming rate. The chapter by Pierce and Séguin examines the efforts of two major agricultural provinces to slow this loss.

Volumes I and II each contained pieces on organisations involved in rural research and education. This volume should have included a chapter on the operations of the Quebec-Labrador Foundation. Unfortunately, the manuscript never arrived. However, I remembered that some time earlier a colleague from the Department of History had asked permission to have the cartographer in the Geography Department at Lakehead draw a map for a conference paper he was giving on continuing education. At the eleventh hour (or, as the General Editor would doubtless concur, somewhat after) I got hold of this paper, pleaded successfully for information on distance education (not in the original) and did some heavy editing. The result is, I hope, an enlightening picture of a small university striving to bring post-secondary education to an area more than twice that of the United Kingdom.

One of the major problems currently facing rural Canada is the decline of the Atlantic fishing industry. I was unable to persuade Newfoundland Premier Clyde Wells to write a piece on the effects this decline was having on the rural communities of his province, but I am hopeful of obtaining something along those lines for Volume IV. This perhaps is a good point to explain the policy I am applying to papers submitted for the Canadian section of PIRPAP. Major papers (such as that by Pierce and Séguin in this issue) are subjected to double-blind refereeing by at least two external referees. Shorter informational and discussion papers, such as that by Zimmermann and Pakulak, are edited, but not refereed unless the author(s) specifically so request. Potential authors are encouraged to contact me to discuss possible contributions to either category of paper.

Once again the review of Canada's rural scene has depended heavily on contributions from a national network of correspondents. Coverage is extensive, and presented by thematic topics, but still not complete. Requests for information from Prince Edward Island and (once again) Quebec went unanswered. I received a very courteous reply from Newfoundland, but did not discover until too late that the material which was supposed to have accompanied the letter was not there. Next time, I hope, every province will be represented: though I am not very optimistic about obtaining a response from Quebec.

15 Exclusive agricultural zoning in British Columbia and Quebec: problems and prospects

John T. Pierce and Jacinthe Séguin

Introduction

British Columbia (BC) and Quebec are currently managing their agricultural land bases with the most protective and exclusionary approaches in Canada. In both cases agriculture is given priority rights to the use of land, within specially designated reserves. However, pressures for land-use change within and adjacent to these reserves, along with a changing economic environment for agriculture, suggest a need for a re-examination of the function and operation of these programs as they are presently constituted.

In this chapter, the agricultural land preservation programs in both jurisdictions are analysed and compared with respect to their record of protecting the land base and the factors which directly and indirectly shape that record. The factors are divided into two general categories: internal, representing the conditions set out in the acts along with complementary legislation; and external, representing the demographic, economic, social and political forces which affect the viability of farming and influence the demand for rural lands. The conclusion builds upon these findings to construct recommendations for improving and redesigning agricultural land preservation programs, so as to take account of the changing economic environment for agriculture, and the need to balance a larger body of interests and constituents in the rural land-use scene.

The changing context of agricultural land preservation

The pressure to preserve agricultural land in Canada and the responses thereto have varied significantly over space and time. This is due to at least three factors. First, the management of land resources is a provincial responsibility and therefore subject to different political agendas. Particularly important is the variation in the dominant values and assumptions of decision-makers regarding individual versus collective property rights; the efficiency and equity of the market; and relative merits of 'top-down' versus 'bottom-up' strategies for protecting land (Bryant and Russwurm, 1982). Second, there is variation in the regional adequacy of prime agricultural land, the rate of loss of that land and perceptions of its continued importance to food security. In Canada, for example, of the 250 million hectares (ha) of land with the potential for agriculture, only 18 per cent or 46 million ha have prime capability to produce crops. However, this prime agricultural land accounted for more than 60 per cent of all rural land converted during the last two decades (Environment Canada, 1989). To replace the productive potential of these lands would require more than double the area of secondary capability lands. The situation was particularly alarming in BC and Quebec because their major urban growth centres were located on prime agricultural land. Third, irrespective of these regional variations, there has been a change in the context within which society demands, values and uses resources. In the case of the arable land resource, and the goods and services society derives from the use of that resource both for agriculture and other activities, the context is framed by such things as technology, production costs, population and income growth, international competition, agricultural/macroeconomic policy and how society values non-monetary aspects of the environment.

During the 1960s, beginning with the Resources for Tomorrow Conference and later through the creation of the Canada Land Inventory (which documented the quantity and quality of the nation's agricultural land) attention was increasingly being focused on the excessive loss of prime agricultural land, its implications for food production potential and the negative externalities associated with non-farm development of agricultural lands. Arguably, society's concern over the conservation of resources reached its apogee in the early 1970s. A combination of macro and meso-scale forces including the energy crisis, rising crop prices and rapid regional consumption of prime agricultural land, signalled the need for increased protection of the arable land base (Furuseth and Pierce, 1982; Lockeretz, 1987; Troughton, 1981). The differential response to this need generally reflected different government priorities. For example, farmland preservation was an important part of the BC New Democratic Party's (NDP) provincial election platform in 1972. Soon after being elected the NDP implemented exclusive agriculture zoning. Similarly the Parti Québecois promised to protect farmland in the 1976 provincial election. After defeating the Liberals they instituted comparable farmland protection legislation. Ontario, on the other hand, retained a Conservative government throughout the 1970s. Despite large-scale losses of prime agricultural land there was no attempt to use clear boundaries demarcating urban and agricultural uses of the land (Bryant and Russwurm, 1982). It was only with election of the NDP (which had promised to preserve agricultural land) as the official opposition in 1975, and the creation of a minority government, that guidelines for the protection of agricultural land were released. These became official Ontario policy in 1978. Other NDP governments were elected in Saskatchewan and Manitoba, but the loss of agricultural lands in these provinces was not severe and the respective governments reacted with very 'soft' measures.

The 1980s presented a very different set of challenges for the agricultural sector. With an energy glut, increased international competition for markets, declining crop prices, a record level of farm debt and bankruptcies and a slow-down in rates of urbanisation of agricultural land (the first half of the 1980s had the lowest conversion of agricultural land compared to the two preceding quinquennial periods in Canada) issues related to resource adequacy lost much of their popular appeal. Consequently there have been no new farmland preservation initiatives in Canada since the 1970s. This situation is somewhat ironic given the growth in public concern over and government acknowledgment of the importance of conservation issues, and the need to protect the environment. For example, during the 1980s sustainability became the new criterion for judging growth options within society. It has been contended that public policy in agriculture should aim at balancing the triple concerns of stewardship of the land, food sufficiency and social and economic viability of the farm unit (Brklacich et al., 1991). It was also argued that land should be valued for many of the diverse functions it provides society above and beyond its purely commodity function for agricultural production (Manning, 1986; Crosson, 1990; OECD, 1989a). In other words, the consumption or amenity values of the countryside were gaining increased importance.

Despite the attractiveness of these concepts, particularly among academics, the short-term economic survival of family farms is currently uppermost in the minds of policy-makers and the public alike. The most pressing issue confronting the industry is the shift towards increased levels of international competition as a result of the technology and trade-driven oversupply of food. On the horizon are more long-term threats to market shares through the North American Free Trade Agreement (NAFTA) incorporating Canada, the United States and Mexico, and proposed changes to agricultural policy under the Uruguay Round negotiations of the General Agreement on Tariffs and Trade (GATT). While NAFTA did not directly threaten supply management programs in Canada, the proposed changes to GATT (through the substitution of tariffs for quotas) would certainly make them redundant.

The clear focus of attention therefore is now on the large-scale restructuring of the agri-food industry and the national and regional implications of a more liberal trade in agricultural commodities rather than the adequacy of the resource base to sustain agricultural production. Land represents but one of a number of important dimensions affecting the viability of agriculture. In this regard Bryant (1986) has argued that change to and loss of agricultural landscapes can only be understood from a wider perspective in which consideration is given to non-urban based forces for change as well as the distinct mosaic of modes of production and systems of exchange which exist in peri-urban regions. All these parameters will have an important effect upon the future support for and success of farmland preservation programs such as the ones in BC and Quebec. These programs have to contend with one of their universal weaknesses, which is that farmland preservation is a necessary but not a sufficient condition for promoting the continuation of a healthy agricultural sector.

Exclusive agricultural zones in British Columbia and Quebec

How do the two provinces compare with respect to the quality of their agricultural land, population size and distribution, and structure of agriculture? Quebec has approximately twice the population of BC. Their respective arable land bases are similar–3.7 million ha in Quebec and 3.6 million ha in BC. Quebec however has a higher overall agro-climatic resource index–2 compared to BC's 1.4. (This index measures the number of frost free days, and moisture and heat supply: the values range from 1, representing the minimum requirements for cultivation of crops typical of higher latitudes, to 3, representing the most favourable conditions typical of southern Ontario). Dairying and livestock dominate both provinces' agricultural industries (85 per cent in Quebec and 63 in BC). A major difference is that in BC specialty crops represent about a fifth of the value of agricultural production, while they are of minor importance in Quebec (Smith, 1984).

The highest quality agricultural lands and the most dense population are to be found in the alluvial lowlands of the Fraser (BC) and St Lawrence (Quebec) Rivers. Vancouver had the second highest absolute population increase in Canada during the 1981–86 period with 112,500. Montreal was fourth with 60,900. Inevitably, large scale land conversion has been necessary to accommodate this. For the provinces as a whole, during the twenty year period beginning in 1966, BC converted 45,000 ha and Quebec 51,000 ha of which 21 per cent and 50 per cent respectively were rated as prime agricultural lands (class 1–3 of the Canada Land Inventory). Much of this land was converted at low densities–51 ha per 1000 population increase (PI) for BC urban-centred regions (UCRs) and 82 ha/1000 PI for Quebec UCRs between 1981–86. In the Fraser Valley, 4354 ha of rural land were converted to urban use between 1980–87, at an average intensity of 39 ha/1000 PI. For roughly the same period, the Montreal UCR converted rural land for new development at average an intensity of 55 ha/1000 PI (Environment Canada, 1989).

BC was the first province in Canada to enact exclusive agricultural zoning. True to its campaign promise of 1972, the New Democratic Government passed, in 1973, the Provincial Land Commission Act. This allowed for the establishment of an *Agricultural Land Reserve* (ALR) of approximately 4.7 million ha, administered by the Provincial Land Commission. Following a highly controversial freeze on all subdivision and non-farm use of land in 1973, through a Cabinet order in council, the ALR was created by means of a review of potential lands in conjunction with a lengthy consultation process with Regional Districts, the Ministry of Agriculture, municipalities and local farmers as shown in Figure 15.1. The selection of lands for the ALR was based upon physical not economic criteria. Although the primary mandate of the Commission was to protect the designated agricultural land base, including the family farm and community, the original Act empowered it to purchase land for urban green belts, land banks and recreational use (Wilson and Pierce, 1982). In 1977, shortly after the election of a Social Credit (right-of-centre) government, these latter powers were removed and the name of the act was changed to the Provincial Agricultural Land Commission Act.

Exclusion of lands from the ALR or a change of use of lands within the ALR had to come from one of the Provincial Agricultural Land Commission (PALC), Cabinet, or the Environment and Land Use Committee (ELUC) of Cabinet, depending on the source of the application. PALC approves private applications, Cabinet handles local government applications and ELUC deals with appeals.

Accompanying the passage of the Act was the Agricultural Credit Act, which provided for loans and loan guarantees for the purchase and/or improvement of land and the Farm Income Insurance Act, which allowed for income protection for farmers within the ALR. Farmers within the ALR also received differential tax assessment and qualified for a waiver of infrastructural assessment to offset the high costs of operating a farm within the vicinity of an urban area. They also became eligible for low interest loans for farm improvement under the *Agricultural Land Development Assistance Program* and assistance with processing and marketing of produce under federal-provincial *Agri Food Regional Development Subsidiary Agreements*. Right-to-farm legislation was passed in 1989.

The Municipal Act of 1968 authorised the creation of regional planning functions in 28 regional districts. Although these functions were changed in 1983 to exclude urban areas, the regional districts play an important role in land-use planning. The PALC is routinely involved in the review of local government plans, such as Community Plans, Rural Land Use By-laws and Zoning By-laws.

Five years following the inception of the BC program, Quebec introduced a similar initiative, under Law 90, entitled the Act To Preserve Agricultural Land. Administered by the Commission for the Protection of Agricultural Land, the Act first imposed an 'agricultural blanket' on all rural lands in over 615 municipalities of the province, stopping development until it was possible to identify and designate specific lands with potential for agriculture. The Commission, in consultation with the municipalities, determined within Designated Agricultural Regions (DARs) those lands over which the Commission would have powers with respect to exclusive agricultural zoning. In the 1980s there were approximately 6.8 million ha within the DARs. For each DAR an Agricultural Zone Plan was created which, once approved by Cabinet, required that any changes to the plan must be approved by the Commission. In the end, DARs contained lands divided into two zones, green and white: the former

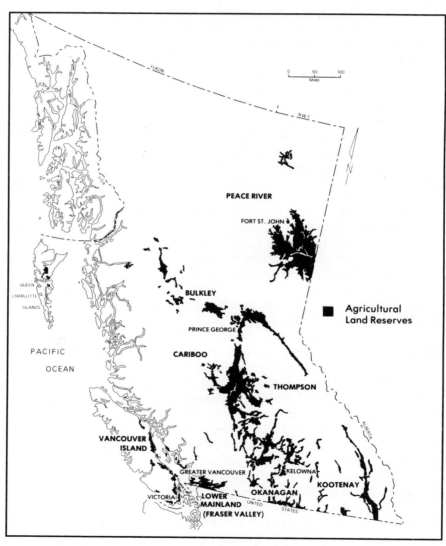

Figure 15.1 *Cities and regions within British Columbia's Agricultural Land Reserves*

representing agricultural lands, and the latter urban lands containing the potential for development.

In fulfilling its mandate to protect agricultural land the Commission is required, when reviewing applications for changes to land use within the DARs, to give due considerations to a set of minimum factors laid in Section 12. For example:

In rendering a decision or giving advice on a matter referred to it, the commission shall particularly take into consideration the biophysical conditions of the soil and of the environment, the possible uses of the lot for agricultural purposes and the economic consequences thereof, and the repercussions that the granting of the application would have on the preservation of agricultural land in the municipality and the region, and on the homogeneity of the farming community and the farming operations. (Quebec, 1988, Chapter P-41.1)

Although the Commission has prime responsibility over the management of the zone plan, Cabinet, under certain conditions, has the power to rezone portions of the DAR independent of the Commission. Moreover the Commission is unable to prevent development of agricultural land which is subject to 'acquired rights'. These rights apply to all owners of lands with permits for uses other than agriculture issued prior to the passage of the Act.

There is complementary legislation similar to that which exists in BC. Following the creation of the Act To Preserve Agricultural Land, the Quebec government moved to institute province-wide planning through Law 44, the Act Respecting Land Use Planning and Development. This comprehensive planning legislation created a system of regional governments organised on the basis of regional county municipalities (RCMs) with responsibilities to develop and implement land-use plans in their respective jurisdictions. In 1985, Law 44 enabled RCMs to negotiate with the Commission for the exclusion/inclusion of lands in a DAR. This was the first in a series of policy and legislative amendments following the election of the Liberal government which would shape a more lenient approach and interpretation of agricultural land preservation. The new approach was further formalised, in July 1989, by the passage of Law 100 which replaced Law 90 as the New Act to Preserve Agricultural Land. Among other things, it modified the criteria defining agricultural zones by creating dark and light green zones. The former applied to lands of high capability and the latter to lower capability in which greater lenience could be exercised by the Commission in making decisions on applications. A tribunal was also created for the appeal of Commission decisions. At the same time the new Act introduced a right to farm provision along with the availability of funds for the defense of farmers accused of nuisance and environmental contamination.

Trends and Issues

Sources

A number of different studies and data sources formed the basis for this assessment of the trends and issues in agricultural land preservation in BC and Quebec. Personal communications with staff in both Commissions, in conjunction with earlier studies, provided important information on prominent and emerging issues. Annual statistical reports and studies from the PALC in BC, combined with independent evaluations of the performance of the Commission by a number of researchers, allowed for identification of general trends in land-use change for the province and for specific pressure points such as the Vancouver Region and the Okanagan Valley. A more limited analysis of land-use trends was pursued in Quebec. Unlike BC, there is no annual published record of applications for exclusion nor of areas affected by the Commission's decisions. To provide information on the performance of the Commission, land-use changes in two municipalities on the south shore of Montreal were chosen for study. Both possess high capability agricultural land and are the scenes of land speculation and fairly intense urbanisation pressures. Population there doubled between 1971 and 1986. As well, a number of other recently completed agriculture and land-use studies were used.

British Columbia

The demand for agricultural land from built-up, recreational and other non-farm uses is closely tied to business cycles, housing starts, demographic trends and government policy. Figure 15.2 indicates the close correspondence between the number of applications for change of use/outright exclusion and housing starts from 1974 to 1989. Other studies have shown a strong association between the cumulative loss of agricultural land and population growth (Faber and Associates, 1987). A key factor affecting the growth of that population is inter-provincial and international migration. For the Lower Mainland Region of BC, approximately 75 per cent of the population growth in recent years has been due to this phenomenon. Over 50 per cent of the immigrants to BC are between the ages of 15 to 34 (Central Statistics Bureau, 1989).

The exclusion of land from the ALR is the outcome of two major types of applications. In one, the provincial government, regional districts and municipalities may apply to cabinet directly to exclude land. Under this section of the Act (section 11(1)) there were 264 applications between 1974 and 1989 to exclude a total of 87,406 ha, of which 76,537 ha were approved by Cabinet. The vast majority of the land excluded (72 per cent) was of secondary capability (i.e. class 4-7 of the Canadian Land Inventory). The

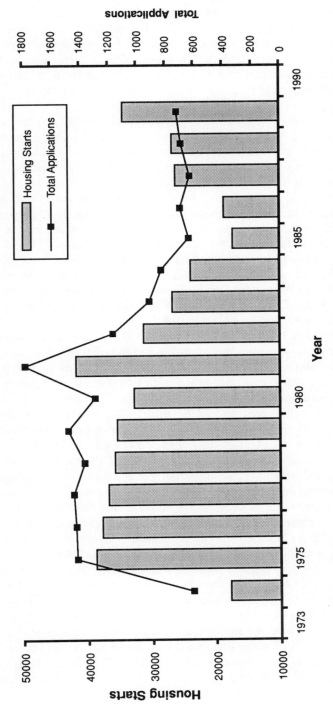

Figure 15.2   *Relationship between housing starts and applications to the British Columbia Agricultural Land Commission for change of use and exclusion of land*
Source: Central Mortgage and Housing Corporation (1990) and Provincial Agricultural Land Commission (1990a)

other category represents private applications to the Commission for permission to exclude land from the ALR (Section 12(1)). In this case, for the same period, 4,289 applications were received covering almost 76,000 ha. The Commission permitted the exclusion of 22,696 ha. The success rate for private applications was 45 per cent. Approximately 60 per cent of the land excluded in the period 1979–89 was land of secondary capability (PALC, 1990a).

Together these two categories of applications, along with the exclusion of a relatively small quantity of land from appeals to ELUC, accounted for the exclusion of almost 103,000 ha from 1974 to 1989. Offsetting these losses was the inclusion of over 82,000 ha from 1975 to 1989; although 86 per cent of this was classed as secondary land. While the majority of the land excluded was of poor quality, some high capability land, with good climatic resources and in close proximity to markets, was lost. However, had the Commission not rejected the number of applications that it did, the record of farmland loss would have been much worse.

Using past exclusion trends, one study predicted the future net loss to the ALR of 20,000 ha by the end of the century in the Lower Mainland Region (Faber and Associates, 1987). Ironically a study conducted by the Commission itself, of potential supplies of developable non-ALR land in the Lower Mainland, indicated a total of 22–40,000 ha (PALC, 1990b). This is equivalent to two to four times the size of the City of Vancouver.

The Commission was genuinely resolved to rely on physical and not short-term economic criteria in assessing the validity of applications. However, the locational and economic reality of agricultural operations in municipalities such as Richmond, Delta and Surrey (within Greater Vancouver) and the willingness of ELUC, during the regime of the Social Credit party in the 1980s, to exclude land under appeal, combined to undermine these goals. Generally, whenever ELUC involved itself in overturning a decision of the PALC, it weakened the credibility of the Commission and the fairness and impartiality of the whole decision-making process. Numerous examples exist where ELUC has overturned a decision of the Commission without providing a rationale for its decision. It must be emphasised, however, that ELUC approvals represented only a small proportion of the ALR which was excluded and, in recent years, individual large block appeals have been rejected. For example in 1990, 167 Okanagan Valley landholders made a block application to PALC for the exclusion of 1,500 ha of land from the ALR. The Commission rejected the application. It was subsequently appealed to ELUC but it too rejected the application. With the election of the New Democratic Party to government in 1991, legislative plans are under way to depoliticise the appeal process.

Less directly harmful to the agricultural environment, but an issue which may emerge as a major source of conflict in the not too distant future, are the provisions in the Act for the subdivision of land and/or non-agricultural use of land, while still remaining in the ALR (Sections 11(2), government to government applications, and 20(1), private applications to the Commission). From 1974 to 1989 there were 12,600 applications under these two sections (half of all applications). Of the 7,524 private applications considered between 1981 and 1989, 4,508 were approved by the Commission covering an area of over 109,000 ha. While no longitudinal data were available for the quality and size of parcels affected throughout the 1980s, in 1988–9 about one-third of the lands affected were prime agricultural land and over half of the new lots approved were less than 3 ha (PALC, 1990a).

Non-farm uses are one of the major sources of externalities in rural-urban fringe areas. Their impact on agriculture is frequently directly related to the degree of land fragmentation and the population density of the non-farm population. As one might expect, a disproportionate share of these applications came from those regional districts containing fast growing and sizeable urban centres such as Greater Vancouver, Victoria, and Kelowna which are shown on Figure 15.1. The Central Fraser Valley Regional District to the east of Vancouver recorded the single largest number of this type of application—over 1,300 for 1974–89. The Okanagan Valley, in the south central area of the province, has a rapidly expanding population, due in part to its attractiveness as a retirement and recreational centre. Combined with the changing economic fortunes of the fruit industry, this has made the area another pressure point in the demand for non-farm uses within the ALR (Environment Canada, 1985).

While privately Commission staff have expressed concern over the potential agricultural impact of these trends, there was considerable official concern over the proliferation of golf courses. Prior to 1978, golf courses were outright uses. From 1978 to 1988 they were conditional or special uses within the ALR, giving the Commission power over their development. In June 1988 Cabinet passed an order-in-council (#1141/88) changing the status of golf courses from conditional back to outright uses, subject to certain terms and conditions set by the Commission, and subject to any necessary approvals by local government. From 1988–91, the rush of applications was dramatic, with more than 181 received by the Commission. In light of the burgeoning demand, the Greater Vancouver Regional District commissioned a study on the subject with special reference to be paid to locational impacts (W. Grahm Argyle and Associates, 1991). The study concluded that at least 24 additional golf courses would be required by 2000. Much of the demand could be accommodated in existing parks and lower quality agricultural land.

Accompanying these proposals for golf courses were major physical developments for clubhouses and convention centres. One proposal in Pitt Meadows included three 20-storey condominiums. Aside from the irreversible loss of land from developments related to golf courses, the application for development has escalated agricultural land values in neighbouring farms from their ALR value of $10,000/ha to values ranging from $20,000 to $80,000/ha.

Until 1983, regional districts had zoning controls over land within municipalities but, with changes to the Municipal Act in that year, municipalities regained control over rezoning of land. Should municipalities issue development permits for these projects, it will introduce a number of (pecuniary and technical) externalities: competition for water; drainage problems; traffic congestion; pesticide poisoning of estuarine environments; and a decline in the available land for agricultural expansion. These issues have come to the forefront in Delta, a municipality to the south of Vancouver, which alone has received at least twelve applications for golf course developments. In one proposal, bordering the important migratory bird habitat of Boundary Bay, a coalition of environmental groups successfully challenged the municipality of Delta in BC Supreme Court with a breach of the Municipal Act. In Surrey, a bordering municipality to the east, $1.5 million of taxpayers' money has gone into the drainage of 170 ha of agricultural land which is now the scene of a proposed golf course.

Just after the election of the New Democratic Party to head a majority government, quick action was taken to rescind the 1988 'outright use' order-in-council (#1141–88) and replace it with a new one (#1392–91) which prohibited any further development on the 181 golf course applications until the Commission could evaluate their status and impact. By January 1992 the Cabinet, acting on recommendations from the Commission, exempted 67 applications from the moratorium on the grounds that they either would have been approved anyway or development had already proceeded to an irreversible extent.

Changes in agricultural policy must also be considered as influencing the long-term viability of the agricultural sector. The extension of the Canada-US free-trade agreement to include Mexico and proposed deregulation of trade in agricultural commodities under negotiations of the Uruguay round of GATT will increase competition and affect the profitability of agriculture. In the Okanagan, in anticipation of the loss of protection from free trade, vineyard owners wishing to eliminate grape production received $9,500/ha from the provincial government. This was a very generous settlement since it exceeded the capitalised loss in earnings that could be expected from free competition in the wine industry. In fact, the buyout represented close to the entire value of the land. No restrictions or covenants were attached to the future use of the land.

Tree fruit growers have been arguing for similar treatment. In fall 1991 tree fruit farmers were promised $38 million in direct aid. This support followed on the heels of a recent commission of inquiry into the tree fruit industry which argued that 'with some perhaps painful changes, in combination with carefully packaged short-term government support, a reasonable proportion of British Columbia's orchardists can compete and survive'

(Lusztig, 1990, p. 146). These conclusions (and support) have done little to stem the rising tide of applications for exclusion of land from the ALR. The BC Tree Fruit Association and the Land Owners Rights Association have argued that, given the declining profit margins of the industry, growers should have the right to opt out of the ALR. Further evidence of the dissatisfaction with the *status quo* is to be found in the Regional District of Central Okanagan, which has the highest cumulative total appeals to ELUC of PALC decisions.

In the northern part of the province, the Peace River grain industry is dependent for its survival on subsidies from farm income assurance, credit provisions and producer support schemes. For Western Canadian grain producers in 1987, producer subsidy equivalents, which measure direct and indirect benefits to farmers, were 42 per cent for wheat and 54 per cent for barley (Meilke and Warley, 1990). Similarly, in the Fraser Valley the dairy industry, as it is presently structured, depends for its survival on the continuation in producer quotas and limitations on entry into the market. Clearly changes to these long-established interventions into the production and trade in agricultural commodities (as expected under GATT), combined with surplus capacity within the system, will influence the profitability of the industry and in turn the legitimate agricultural demand for land. Although no studies have been conducted of the sensitivity of BC agriculture to the elimination of agricultural support policies, a recent study for Canada indicated that exports would decline by 42.5 per cent, imports increase by 27.9 per cent and land rental would decline by 53 per cent (OECD, 1989b). These changes, coupled with the pressures for urban/industrial expansion, will be likely to raise questions about the amount of agricultural land needed to sustain the agricultural industry.

Quebec

Rates of population and economic growth in Quebec have generally been lower than in BC during the last twenty years. Fertility rates are the lowest in Canada and net migration is well below the levels recorded for BC. Redistribution of population, however, has played an important role in affecting the demand for land in the Montreal region. For example, between 1961 and 1976 population grew by 27 per cent, yet the housing sector expanded by 68 per cent (Divay and Gaudreau, 1984). The population of Montreal Island (Ile de Montréal) actually declined from 1.98 million to 1.76 million between 1971 and 1981, with the south shore region of Montreal, containing some 500,000 ha of prime agricultural land, receiving much of the decentralised growth. As a consequence some 30,000 ha were converted to urban use between 1971 and 1982 (Thibodeau *et al.*, 1986). Montreal is unique in this regard. A recent comparative study of the dynamics of population redistribution in nine metropolitan regions of

Canada revealed that Montreal was the only centre whose urban fringe grew at a consistently higher rate than the core between 1971 and 1986 (Ellenwood, 1992).

The pressures on agricultural land in the urban fringe of Montreal have contributed to a process of destructuration (Thibodeau *et al.*, 1986). Like the impermanence syndrome, a term coined by Berry (1978) to describe a process of increasing uncertainty regarding the future of agricultural operations, destructuration refers to a decline in investment, and an increase in farm fragmentation and increase in the average age of farmers. But, as Bryant *et al.* (1991) observe for the south shore region of Montreal, destructuration (or as they refer to it as degeneration) is neither universal nor necessarily tied to urban growth pressures. They suggest that the great variation in the viability and health of the agricultural sector 'is partly linked to differences in production activities which immediately ties different farms into different systems of exchange, subjects them to different forces and is therefore likely to give rise to different response patterns' (Bryant *et al.*, 1991, p. 8).

The implementation of Law 90 was meant to address the decline in the environment for agriculture by reducing the uncertainty in the land market through the introduction of exclusive agricultural zoning. To test the effectiveness of the legislation Séguin (1990) chose two municipalities undergoing strong urbanisation pressures on the south shore of Montreal: Saint-Constant and Saint-Philippe which are shown on Figure 15.3. Since the early 1970s population growth has hovered around 5 to 6 per cent in both municipalities—two to three times the regional average.

The evaluation was in two parts. First, there was an analysis of all subdivision activity within the borders of the DAR (agricultural and urban zones) before (1970–8) and after (1979–87) the introduction of Law 90. For this part two evaluative criteria were used, namely the rate of development and the location of development. The second evaluation involved an analysis of the administrative record of the Commission. In this part, for the period 1979–87, 328 applications were reviewed involving proposals for changes of use and exclusion of land from the agricultural zone of the DAR. Since there were no outright exclusions (or changes to the agricultural zoning) the study focused upon authorisation for change of use. To judge the performance of the Commission in these authorisations, four evaluative criteria were chosen: number of applications received, average success rates, land area affected and intended use.

Regarding the analysis of subdivision activity throughout the DAR, Saint-Constant experienced a 30 per cent increase in lots subdivided over the preceding period following the introduction of Law 90, whereas Saint-Philippe experienced a 69 per cent decline. In both cases the pattern and extent of subdivision activity changed after 1979. Generally, subdivision activity favoured the urban zones, or those areas of the agricultural zone which had non-agricultural uses with moderate to high degree of former development activity. There was therefore a focusing and greater containment of urban development. Where subdivision activity did occur in the agricultural zone, it was at a very low density. Because Saint-Constant had greater reserves of undeveloped land within its urban zone than did Saint-Philippe (the urban zone in the former represented 13 per cent of the DAR compared to 2 per cent in the latter), it was able to continue the subdivision of land without consuming protected farmland. In the first few years after the passage of the Act, some of the subdivision activity was beyond the

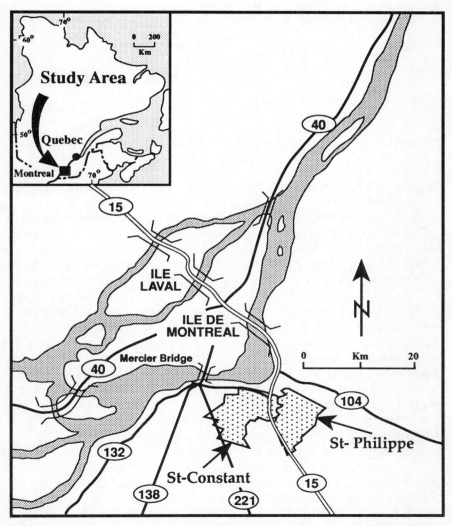

Figure 15.3   *The location of Saint-Constant and Saint-Philippe within the Montreal urban region*

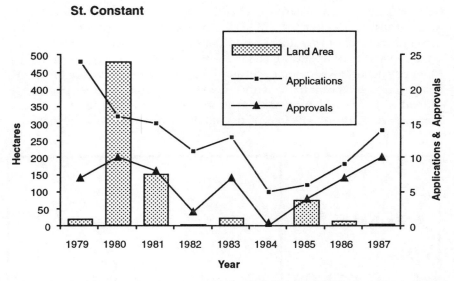

Figure 15.4   *Change of use applications in agricultural zones for Saint-Constant*

control of the Commission because it was based on the acquired rights provision of the Act.

In the second analysis, it was revealed that Saint-Constant, between 1979–87, received 117 applications for change of use, 48 per cent of which were approved as shown in Figure 15.4. In contrast, Saint-Philippe received 211 applications, of which 60 per cent were approved as shown in Figure 15.5. The area affected in the former, however, was over two and one-half times that of the latter. As in BC there was a general decrease in the number of applications with the age of the program, although there was variability in line with changes in the rate of economic growth. For example, as the economy began to increase its rate of growth after 1985 so did the number of applications. Moreover, success rates for both municipalities tended to increase with time. Similar trends in success rates were noted in an earlier study on BC's agricultural land preservation program. In that study it was suggested that 'individuals like their municipal counterparts have developed a greater expertise in the art of applying for exclusion of land from ALRs' (Pierce, 1981, p. 53).

The differences in the land area affected and in the number and success rate of applications between the two municipalities can be explained in part by their respective differences in intended use of the land and, as previously mentioned, in the land available for development in the urban or white zone. Historically Saint-Constant has been the scene of more commercial/industrial development involving larger tracts of land than Saint-Philippe. The quantity of undeveloped land within the urban zone

St. Philippe

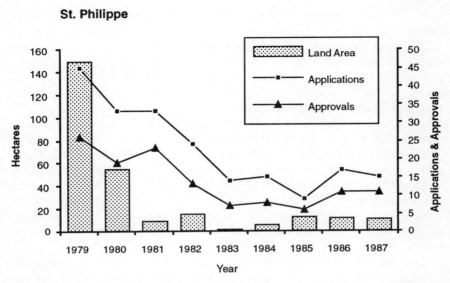

Figure 15.5 *Change of use applications in agricultural zones for Saint-Philippe*

of Saint-Constant in combination with the scale of the proposed developments in the agricultural zone provided justifications for limiting approvals
per application. In Saint-Philippe, on the other hand, development has
expressed itself most commonly in the demand for residential space. With
the large number of applications for low-density residential development,
the Commission compensated for the lack of developable land in its urban
zone by permitting a higher rate of approval, particularly for single family
residences, in the agricultural zone. As a result, average consumption of
agricultural land for residential use in Saint-Philippe was considerably
higher (1.25 ha per approved application) than Saint-Constant (0.35 ha per
approved application).

In general the study found that the Commission, in conjunction with the
Act Respecting Land Use Planning and Development, had been successful
at restricting the rate and spatial extent of urban development in the two
municipalities under study. The configuration of the agricultural zones
remained intact by preventing any outright exclusions of land. Subdivision
and non-farm use of agricultural land took place because of the acquired-
rights provision of the Act and the willingness of the Commission to relax
some of its controls over the use of the land. That willingness reflected
certain exigencies with respect to the supply-demand imbalances for land
for built-up purposes. Like BC, a relatively large number of non-
conforming uses occurred. The long-term effects of these non-conforming
uses are likely to be adverse for agriculture, although the exact threshold
is an unknown.

While this study did not extend into non-metropolitan regions, evaluations of the effects of Law 90 in more remote and unproductive regions suggest that it has impeded economic diversification (Vachon, 1988). Not only were there limits on the exclusion of land for non-agricultural purposes in these areas, but because agricultural support programs in Quebec are based on productivity and return on investment criteria, owners of marginal land were further penalised.

It should be emphasised that at the time of the study major revisions were under way to the Quebec agricultural protection program. The increase in both subdivision rates and Commission decisions authorising non-conforming uses for 1985–6, reflected a new philosophy of the government towards the protection of agricultural land through Law 44. And, as previously stated, the passage into law of Bill 100 allowed for greater flexibility in the management of lands—especially those of lower capability—through the application of two green areas within agricultural zones.

External factors, such as changes to agricultural policy, may threaten the integrity of the designated regions and ultimately the efficacy of the legislation far more than urban-based forces for change. A very significant share of the agricultural industry of Quebec is dependent upon farm support and quota schemes which are likely to be challenged, in whole or in part, through GATT if not through other free trade agreements. For example, the dairy industry, a corner-stone of Quebec agriculture representing 40 per cent of Canadian dairy production, is heavily protected, with estimates of producer subsidy equivalents ranging from 50 to 80 per cent. A recent study of the implications for Quebec of a liberalisation of international trade suggested that it would be likely lead to greater concentration in the industry although some farmers may be able to survive if they adopt novel forms of marketing to change consumer preferences regarding the benefits of locally produced goods (Bryant and Marois, 1992). In the absence of these novel strategies and/or mitigating measures, the removal of supply management programs will mean a decline in land rents and land values. Depending on proximity to urban areas the opportunity cost of holding land in agriculture will most likely rise, creating further imbalances in the land markets between the city and the countryside.

General comparisons

The fate of agricultural land protection policies is tied, on the one hand to the quality and consistency of the legislation, its administration and complementary legislation. On the other, it is influenced by a host of external factors which influence the price, demand and value attached to rural land for farm and non-farm uses. Although it has been difficult to be precise about the exact role of these factors, there is sufficient information to permit general comparisons regarding the performance of the respective programs and the dominant trends and issues in their operation.

The large number of applications for exclusion and change of use in the ALR in BC and DAR in Quebec, in relation to approvals, indicates that the rate of land conversion was slower in both provinces than it would have been without these programs. Overall, BC was more successful than Quebec at steering development onto lower quality lands. In the vicinity of both Montreal and Vancouver the laws encouraged more concentrated development. While both programs allow for outright exclusions from the reserves, BC has exercised this option more often than Quebec. It might be argued that this strategy allows Quebec a greater degree of control over the end uses of agricultural land.

In both cases there was evidence of political interference over the rezoning of agricultural land. Both Acts gave Cabinet or a Cabinet committee final say over the rezoning of land. Although the exclusions arising from this provision were not large, the fairness and impartiality of the decision-making process is open to question whenever Cabinets over-rule their respective Commissions. To this must be added the potential change of government every five years and its attendant change in political philosophies and attitudes towards the desirability of exclusive agricultural zoning.

Uncertainty about the decision-making process also extends to the individual rulings made by the Commissions. Although their decisions are based upon specific criteria, these criteria are often not understood by the applicants nor the public at large. The problem is often one of distinguishing 'what is' from 'what should be'. For example, biophysical and not economic criteria govern most decisions. Yet, from an applicant's perspective, the lack of economic viability is one of the principal reasons for seeking a change of use or exclusion from agricultural zoning. Members of both Commissions would counter that since economic viability is so closely tied to managerial skill and adaptive behaviour, physical criteria should remain as the paramount consideration in decision-making.

The growing number of non-conforming uses in the ALR and DAR may over the long term be seen as a threat to the viability of agricultural operations. This is not to suggest that agriculture cannot survive within a more diverse and complex land use system as Bryant et al. (1991) have amply demonstrated. It does underline the potential vulnerability of those operations which require additional supplies of land and/or large fixed capital investment and also the need for innovative strategies which recognise the diversity and complexity of farming under these conditions.

During the initial years of the implementation of each Act, attempts were made to incorporate exclusive agricultural zoning into regional planning decisions. Recent legislation in Quebec, however, gives additional powers to regional governments in their quest for more developable land.

In BC, changes to the Municipal Act in 1983 have eliminated the ability of regional governments to interfere in the rezoning of land within municipal boundaries. As a result, municipalities can rezone land once it is excluded from the ALR without reference to a larger regional plan. With municipalities capable of acting independently, in some cases to improve their tax bases, the bigger picture within which agriculture operates can be forgotten. While the bigger picture is important, so is the recognition of the legitimate needs and aspirations of the local community. In both provinces, the decision-making apparatus is, in general, highly centralised. An important challenge is how to modify this framework to create a better balance between local priorities, such as the need to create a more diversified industrial base, and regional and provincial priorities relating to the provision of food.

Beyond these internal issues, the fact remains that both Commissions still must respond to situations over which they have little or no control. Changes in the size, distribution and wealth of the populations and labour forces are the driving forces behind suburbanisation. An important factor influencing the calculus of demographic change is migration. The federal government plays the determining role in deciding the levels of immigration to Canada (approximately 130,000 annually). Quebec has the right to select its own immigrants through the Cullen-Couture Agreement. Vancouver's growth in the last twenty years has been directly tied to migration and it is expected to continue to play an important role especially as the 'repatriation' of Hong Kong approaches. In this situation the Commission, like all land-use planning agencies in the province, is relegated to reactive planning strategies. Proactive planning is a distant goal.

But perhaps the single most important factor affecting the integrity of the agricultural land reserves, which neither Commission controls, is the economic health of the industry—a product of terms of trade, growth in markets and agricultural policy. Should current trends continue, the demand for agricultural land for farm use will decline and with this decline will come increased pressures to exclude land if not to abandon farmland preservation altogether.

Looking ahead

Many of the major conditions which precipitated the use of exclusive agricultural zoning in Canada have changed during the last decade. The current surplus of agricultural land combined with the strong demand for land for urban and recreational uses raises the question—why continue to protect the resource base for agriculture? The land resource base seems to be valued merely for its commodity-producing value. Society continues to rely on present yield—increasing technology, production methods and imports, to secure an adequate supply of food. Over the short term, then, a strong argument can be made for the relaxation, if not abandonment, of these land-protection strategies. Further, as has been previously argued, zoning is no panacea for an ailing agricultural industry.

Clearly societies have long-term interests which need to be protected just as farmers require a degree of stability against the vagaries of the market and of food imports. Within these traditional justifications for public intervention into the rural land-use market can be found more compelling reasons for novel and adaptive approaches, which to date have received relatively little research attention. If society embraces the notion of sustainable development and is dedicated to its implementation, consideration will have to be given to changes, in some cases dramatic, in current modes of agricultural production. These are highly specialised, rely on depletable resources such as fossil fuels, and are often environmentally harmful in both on and off-site terms. A decline in direct farm support programs, and a shift to less intensive agriculture more compatible with the environment, is most likely to lead to farm diversification and extensification strategies (OECD, 1989a). There already is evidence in both provinces of a variety of diversification strategies and adaptive behaviour, responding above all to uncertainty and poor markets for traditional crops. While these strategies are market driven, there are many other alternative production approaches for which there are weak institutional incentives (e.g. research) as well as important services provided by the rural land base for which there are poor or non-existent markets and therefore no protection. In short, not only is there great potential for alternative food production schemes but in the future the land resource base will increasingly be valued for more than its commodity functions. Ecological, wildlife and amenity values require recognition and protection (Manning, 1986). Together these changes could very well lead to a reappraisal of the value and importance society attaches to production strategies and non-agricultural uses of the rural land base. By extension more, not less, land may be needed in the future to maintain food supplies—using lower-input agriculture—and to meet society's non-urban and non-commodity demands on the land.

There are other factors favouring the protection of agricultural land. While no one has attempted to calculate the economic cost of farmland loss or the associated loss in productive capacity in the two provinces, a strong argument can be made that agriculture, unlike forestry or mining, plays a critical role in stabilising regional economies during recessions. This was certainly the case in the Lower Fraser Valley during the severe recession of the early 1980s.

If there is merit to these arguments, how can the function and operation of these current programs be redesigned and improved to be more responsive to the changing environment for agriculture and land-use needs of society? Externally, as has been previously stressed, the agricultural sector requires not only a secure land base but a suitable economic environment for food production. Clearly farmland preservation programs will require support through changes to agricultural policy (such as decoupling income from production) which recognise the ecological, social and economic requisites for a healthy agricultural sector without at the same time being trade distorting. Most farmers would be supportive of programs that create options for alternative forms of agricultural development while preserving amenity values of the countryside

From an internal perspective, the programs themselves will have to shift their emphases away from single sector planning and a preoccupation with the commodity functions of the land base to a far broader mandate which attempts to balance the numerous and often conflicting values associated with rural land. This will be a challenging exercise for those jurisdictions which have right-to-farm legislation and for those provinces which place greater emphasis on individual rather than collective rights in the land. Naturally, such a change will require more comprehensive legislation that has, as its fundamental purpose, the better integration of these diverse values and functions. While no models of such a land-use organisation exist in Canada, consideration could be given to resurrecting a version of the original Land Commission Act in BC. Its mandate extended beyond agriculture to include green space, amenity value and land for urban development. Along with regional planning powers, then held by regional districts, these were potent pieces of legislation which, perhaps, were just ahead of their times—and which now could serve as a basis for future legislation.

Note

Jacinthe Séguin is an employee of Environment Canada. However, the research for this paper was completed while she was a graduate student at Simon Fraser University, and the opinions herein do not necessarily reflect those of Environment Canada.

References

Berry, D., 1978, 'Effects of urbanization on agricultural activities', *Growth and Change*, July: 2–8

Brklacich, M., Bryant, C.R. and Smit, B., 1991, 'Review and appraisal of the concept of sustainable food production systems', *Environmental Management*, **15**(1): 1–14

Bryant, C.R., 1986, 'Agriculture and urban development' in M. Pacione (ed.), *Progress in agricultural geography*, Croom Helm, Beckenham, UK, pp. 167–94

Bryant, C.R. and Marois, C., 1992, 'The Canada-US free-trade agreement as a factor of actual and potential agricultural change; the case of the Montreal

Region', a paper presented at the annual meeting of the Canadian Association of Geographers, May, Vancouver, BC

Bryant, C.R., Marois, C., Laurendeau, S., Deslauriers, P. and Nadeau, D., 1991, 'Changing agriculture and land-use policy implications south of Montréal', a paper presented at the annual meeting of the Association of American Geographers, April, Miami, Florida

Bryant, C.R. and Russwurm, L.H. 1982, 'North American farmland protection strategies in retrospect', *GeoJournal*, **6**(6): 501–12

Central Statistics Bureau, 1989, *British Columbia population forecast 1988–2011*, Central Statistics Bureau, Victoria

Crosson, P.R., 1990, 'Supplying the environmental values of agriculture', *Resources*, **98**: 4–8

Divay, G. and Gaudreau, M., 1984, *La formation des espaces residentiels*, INRS-Urbanisation et Presses de l'Université du Québec, Québec City

Ellenwood, D.S., 1992, *Population redistribution and 'counterurbanization': a study of nine urban regions in Canada*, MA, Thesis, Department of Geography, Simon Fraser University, Burnaby, BC

Environment Canada, 1985, *Okanagan fruitlands: land-use change dynamics and the impact of federal programs*, Lands Directorate, Land Use in Canada Series, No. 26, Ottawa

Environment Canada, 1989, *Urbanization of rural land in Canada, 1981–86, a state of the environment fact sheet*, Environment Canada, No. 89–1, Ottawa

Faber and Associates, 1987, *Provincial Agricultural Land Commission, strategic business plan*, Provincial Agricultural Land Commission, Burnaby

Furuseth, O.J. and Pierce, J.T., 1982, *Agricultural land in an urban society*, Association of American Geographers, Washington, DC

Lockeretz, W., 1987, *Sustaining agriculture near cities*, Soil and Water Conservation Society, Ankeny, Iowa

Lusztig, P.A., 1990, *Report of the Commission of Enquiry—British Columbia Tree Fruit Industry*, Ministry of Agriculture and Fisheries, Victoria

Manning, E.W., 1986, *Towards sustainable land use: a strategy*, Environment Canada, Ottawa

Meilke, K.D. and Warley, T.K., 1990, 'Canada' in F.H. Sanderson (ed.), *Agricultural protectionism in the industrialized world*, Resources for the Future, Washington, DC, pp. 133–80

OECD, 1989a, *Agricultural and environmental policies*, Organisation for Economic Co-operation and Development, Paris

OECD, 1989b, *Economy wide effects of agricultural policies in OECD countries*, Organisation for Economic Co-operation and Development, Paris

Pierce, J.T., 1981, 'The BC Agricultural Land Commission: a review and evaluation', *Plan Canada*, **21**(2): 48–56

Provincial Agricultural Land Commission (PALC), 1990a, *Agricultural land reserve statistics*, 1 January 1990, Provincial Agricultural Land Commission, Burnaby

Provincial Agricultural Land Commission (PALC), 1990b, *Non-farmland with long-term urban potential in the lower mainland*, Ministry of Agriculture and Fisheries, Victoria

Quebec, 1988, *An Act to Preserve Agricultural Land*, Revised Statutes of Quebec, Editeur Officiel du Québec, Quebec

Séguin, J., 1990, *An evaluation of the Quebec agricultural land protection legislation*, Natural Resources Management Program, Report No. 78, Simon Fraser University, Burnaby, BC

Smith, W. 1984, 'The changing geography of Québec agriculture', in M. Bunce and M. Troughton (eds.), *The pressures of change in rural Canada*, Department of Geography, York University, Toronto, pp. 54–72

Thibodeau, J.C., Gaudreau, M. and Bergeron, J., 1986, *Le zone agricole, un bilan positif—Les effets de la Loi 90 dans la région sud de Montréal*, INRS-Urbanisation, Montreal

Troughton, M.J., 1981, 'The policy and legislative response to loss of agricultural land in Canada', *Ontario Geography*, **18**: 79–109

Vachon, B. 1988, 'Quelques aspects géographiques, financial and politiques du zonage agricole au Québec', *Récherches Sociographiques*, **29**(2–3): 417–30

Wilson, J.W. and Pierce, J.T., 1982, 'The Agricultural Land Commission of British Columbia', *Environments*, **14**(3): 11–20

W. Grahm Argyle and Associates, 1991, *Golf course development in lower mainland*, Greater Vancouver Regional District, Vancouver

16 Providing post-secondary education in a remote rural area: the example of Northwestern Ontario

E.R. Zimmermann and D.R. Pakulak

Introduction

Northwestern Ontario covers nearly 60 per cent of the area of the province. In this region, which is larger than all of France, there are only about 250,000 people. Over half of them live in and around the only city, Thunder Bay. The balance is scattered in pockets along the Canadian Pacific and Canadian National Railway lines, along the two branches of the Trans-Canada Highway (Highways 11 and 17) and in remote settlements of native Indian (First Nations) peoples as shown in Figure 16.1).

Outside the city of Thunder Bay, the economy of Northwestern Ontario is based on the extraction or development of natural resources: mining, forestry and the generation of hydroelectric power. There are also significant centres of paper manufacturing. Agriculture, trapping and the fur trade are of only local importance, though tourism is growing. This limited, resource-based economy provides an insecure economic foundation for the region's small communities. As a result, an important part of the regional economy is made up of federal and provincial transfers of funds: welfare, unemployment payments, forgivable loans and municipal grants.

The City of Thunder Bay (formed in 1970 from the adjoining communities of Port Arthur and Fort William) is centrally located in the southern part of Northwestern Ontario, on the shore of Lake Superior. It is the most isolated metropolitan centre in mainland Canada: 1,400 km from the provincial capital, Toronto, and 700 km from Winnipeg, Manitoba. Because of its relative size and its location, it has become the principal service centre for the mines, forest operations, paper mills and small town and rural population of most of the vast Northwestern Ontario region.

Institute and college

At the end of World War II business and political leaders in Northwestern Ontario concluded that returning soldiers would need to complete and

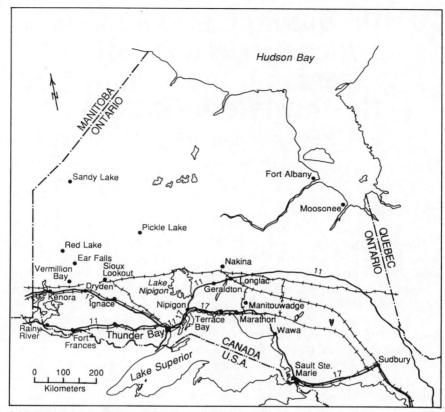

● Lakehead University Off-Campus Centres

Figure 16.1   *Lakehead University off-campus centres*

extend their secondary education, a task likely to be beyond the local high school system. They also anticipated a demand for skilled technicians and technologists. Both these needs, it was believed, would best be met by the establishment of a post-secondary institution in the regional centre, Thunder Bay. The result was the founding of the Lakehead Technical Institute, which took its first students (in mining technology) in 1948. Over time it became evident that there was less enthusiasm than had been anticipated for courses and programs in agriculture, forestry, mining and industrial arts. Instead, prospective students wanted regular university courses in the arts and sciences. In response, in 1957 the institution became the Lakehead College of Arts, Science and Technology (Braun and Tamblyn, 1987).

As early as the first post-war discussions, it was felt that an important role for any post-secondary institution in Northwestern Ontario would be to provide some kind of continuing education. Continuing education in this context is defined as the provision of post-secondary courses, primarily though not exclusively for adults, outside the regular schedule. Until then the only way students in Northwestern Ontario could pursue part-time studies was by enrolling in the Queen's University (Kingston) Summer School or by taking the correspondence courses offered by the University of Western Ontario (London). Neither of these was popular.

There were three types or categories of students who needed continuing education. There were residents of Thunder Bay and neighbourhood whose daytime employment prevented them from attending regular classes. Their needs could be met by courses timetabled for the evening, after regular classes had finished. There were many others who lived too far away to commute into Thunder Bay even once a week for an evening lecture. Some of these, notably teachers, were able to take time off in the summer. They could come into the city for six weeks or so in July and August and complete one or two accelerated courses then. Finally, there were those with shorter summer breaks. Their only chance to get a post-secondary education was for the courses to be taken to them and for classes to be offered in their local community. Given the unreliable economic base of most of these communities, education can be one of the most valuable contributions that can be made. It is with this last group, the residents of rural and small-town Northwestern Ontario, that this chapter is principally concerned.

The Technical Institute began to help the local part-time market by giving evening classes in 1949–50. In 1959–60 the College offered several non-credit adult education courses. This was followed, in response to public demand (especially from school teachers anxious to upgrade their qualifications) by the first Summer School which offered two Arts courses in 1960 (Ballantyne, 1966). From then on Summer School has been given every year. In 1963–4 the third category of students began to be assisted, with college courses offered in Atikokan and Dryden. In 1965 this service expanded to include Kenora, Nipigon and Geraldton (Braun and Tamblyn, 1987). A network of local representatives was organised based on an individual in each centre who acted as liaison with the College administration, who helped to determine which courses should be offered locally and tried to get at least the minimum number to register. These representatives are not salaried, but do get an honorarium in the form of free tuition.

Lakehead University

As the post-war 'baby boom' generation passed through high school the numbers applying to and being admitted into university climbed rapidly. Parents objected to their children having to go 1,400 km to southern Ontario to obtain a full university education, so in 1965 the College became Lakehead University (LU). Continuing education was growing, along with regular enrolment. By 1970 LU was teaching classes in ten communities across the region and offering over 50 Summer School courses. A faculty member had been appointed the first, part-time, 'Director of Summer School and Extension' in 1964, and this was made a full-time position in 1966.

However, despite vague government encouragement (education in Canada is a provincial matter) LU was running into difficulties with continuing education, particularly the off-campus component. There were sufficient faculty to offer a wide range of courses, but the nature of government funding meant that there had to be a minimum enrolment (which has varied over time from eight to 20). If that minimum was not attained, the course had to be cancelled. This was one of the principal reasons why LU has never been able to meet off-campus demand for Science degrees: there were never enough students in one centre willing to enrol. There were also problems with providing adequate laboratory experience. In the mid-70s LU tried to obtain some used truck trailers and equip them as mobile laboratories, but this imaginative scheme failed for lack of government funding. In addition, there was concern about the lack of continuing education for native people: there were neither courses about Indian cultures nor programs offered where Indians could most easily enrol. It was pointed out that native people participated in regular programs, and that there were too few qualified students to warrant taking courses to remote reserves (for example, the Sandy Lake reserve is 600 km from Thunder Bay).

In the early 70s, the Director of Continuing Education (as the position had become titled) tried to persuade departments to guarantee the provision of a certain number and sequence of courses at various communities around the region, so students could plan a complete degree program. This proposal was not taken seriously. Departments were facing declining on-campus enrolments and faculty cuts, and were unwilling to make long-term commitments. Moreover, the rapid expansion of the late 60s and early 70s saw the hiring of many foreign faculty nurtured in old-world style universities where scholarship was equated with research, publication and the advising of graduate students. Few had much enthusiasm for undergraduate instruction even on campus in regular hours, still less evenings and summer, and least of all in a remote centre hundreds of miles from the University.

Objections to off-campus teaching were and are not entirely unreasonable. In the regular academic year (September to April) faculty teach the equivalent of three hours a week per course for two twelve-week terms. If the off-campus centre is not too far from Thunder Bay—within about 150 km—the instructor drives out in the afternoon, teaches for three hours in the evening, and returns home late that night. For more distant locations (Kenora, for example, is nearly 500 km west) the practice is to drive or fly every second Friday; teach three hours Friday evening and three more

Saturday morning: returning, weather permitting, Saturday afternoon. In the really remote communities, such as Indian reserves accessible only by air, there is a once-a-month intense meeting from Friday night to Sunday morning. This involves a lot of travel time, disrupts family life and—especially in winter—can offer unwonted excitements on icy roads and snow-blocked runways. In summer there is no need for regular commuting, but the instructor has to relocate him/herself for at least six weeks. While there is an 'inconvenience allowance' this can pose problems, especially for married faculty.

Meanwhile, enrolment off-campus was declining. From an average of over 22 per course in 1970–1 numbers dropped to under 13 in 1974–5: largely because of a decline in the number of teachers seeking upgrading (newer teachers were getting their degrees before entering the profession). Despite these problems, LU continued in the later 70s to provide some kind of university education around Northwestern Ontario. To counter the unwillingness of many regular faculty to commit themselves to travelling off-campus, a number of instructors were hired specifically for that duty. Some shared teaching on-campus with a contractual obligation to teach one or two courses elsewhere; a few were actually stationed in the more populated centres as resident instructors. An exciting innovation at this time was the Lake of the Woods Centre for the Arts, in Kenora. This was a six-week summer program offering a mixture of university and college courses in Fine Arts and Dancing, as well as several workshops. Unfortunately it was never repeated: presumably it was deemed too risky for the University's rather sparse resources. Into the mid-80s the continuing education, on and off-campus, struggled on as well as it could, with no major changes.

The current situation

In the mid-80s LU went through a long-drawn-out process of re-evaluating its purpose and its goals. In a report to a commission on the future development of Ontario's universities, LU stated, among other things, that 'to fulfil our role as a regional access point we must project ourselves into the region by maintaining as effective an off-campus program as possible'. Eventually this was translated into the current 'motto' of the University: 'in the North and for the North'. This was a time of concern about the future for several of the province's smaller institutions, and LU was hoping to project a unique image of itself as taking an active role in a huge region that comprises well over half the province.

There have been a number of innovations in the late-80s in response to this new mandate. The University has established satellite campuses in Kenora and Atikokan. These modest facilities consist of two medium-sized classrooms and an office staffed on a part-time basis by the local representative. With funding from the government, LU has been able to enhance the role of the regional representatives, by offering specially designed workshops and orientation sessions on campus. Off-campus students now have access to books in LU's library. Library holdings are listed on microfiche in each centre. Students can call the Library toll-free and the required book will be sent out.

Currently an average of 85 courses is being taught on a regular basis in over 20 communities across an area in excess of 600,000 km^2 as shown in Figure 16.1. Both the Honours Bachelor of Nursing Science and the Honours Bachelor of Social Work are offered as complete degrees in Kenora. The Master of Education program has been made available off-campus. Responding to a much earlier concern, courses in native language, literature and anthropology are given in the larger communities. A significant breakthrough occurred in 1988 following a meeting in Sandy Lake between the President of LU, the Director of Continuing Education and the Elders of that community. The result was a multi-year bachelor's program to be delivered on-site. Other reserves have requested similar programs. This success has led to the development of a Native Teacher Education program for Sandy Lake, scheduled to begin in the fall of 1992. This innovative program combines on-site instruction with an on-campus component and is designed to assist the native population in meeting its educational, cultural and political aspirations.

The most ambitious strategy adopted and developed in recent years to provide wider access to university education in Northwestern Ontario is the distance education program. Distance education is defined by the physical separation of the student and the instructor. Unlike the traditional correspondence course, modern distance education makes use of the latest in multimedia programming and communications linkages. Much material is presented in video or audio format, supported by printed material. Regular meetings are held with the instructor, utilising the teleconference facilities of Contact North (a distance education network funded by the provincial government). The instructor uses a microphone and loud-speaker, while students in off-campus centres meet around similar equipment—sometimes with someone acting as on-site monitor—which allows them to speak to the instructor and to students in other centres without having to hold a telephone to their ears for two hours (those unable to make it to one of LU's centres can still participate, if less comfortably, by telephone).

The market for this format includes individuals requiring training or retraining due to career changes or job dislocation; native groups with special needs, mature students, and high school graduates unable to relocate near a university. This market is increasing with changing demographics and changes in the economy. Regular offerings range over the Humanities and the Social Sciences, in most cases adapted to make them more appropriate to the region. Through collaborative efforts with other institutions LU has also developed distinctive programs such as Environmental Assessment, Tourism and Recreation Resource Management, Education (additional basic qualification courses) and Nursing (post-RN program). Not all lead to degrees (the programs in Environmental Assessment and in Tourism grant certificates) but all are at degree level and may be applied to other degree programs. Although designed for the needs of the region, several of the programs have established a wider market. The Certificate in Environmental Assessment in particular has enrolment from every province and both territories, and limits have had to be imposed to keep numbers to something manageable (currently 50 students per class).

Experience elsewhere has shown that students studying on their own in remote communities suffer a high rate of attrition, largely because they lack the support found in an institutional environment. LU has faced this by designing a student support system specifically for the distance learner. As well as access to the University library, students can obtain study skills sessions, academic advice, and personal and career counselling. Students can call distance education and their instructor at LU's expense. This personalised approach has played a large role in the development of the program and its high retention rate. Numbers are growing rapidly. There were 89 full-course equivalent enrolments in 1987–8, the first year of operation, and 757 in 1991–2. This trend is expected to continue as more students become aware that access to university education is possible without the usual constraints of location and time.

Conclusion

In the period since World War II there has been an irregular but significant increase in the provision of post-secondary education throughout Northwestern Ontario. Bringing the University to a vast rural area is not a unique problem for LU. However, there are aspects of the situation that make for particular difficulties. The central institution is itself quite small (fewer than 300 full-time faculty) and very much on the periphery of the provincial higher educational scene (the nearest Ontario university—equally small—is 1,000 km away). The physical environment is hostile: immense areas of uninhabited bush interspersed with boggy lakes. Settlements are far apart, and instructors driving to distant classrooms in schools, libraries and churches (and, in one instance, a closed-down hospital operating theatre) have to cope with moose and bears on the road, deep snow everywhere and temperatures down to forty below zero.

Apart from the obvious educational and cultural impact, and the long-term benefits of a better-qualified population, continuing education makes a minor direct contribution to the economies of the small communities of Northwestern Ontario. Each visit of an instructor from Thunder Bay involves overnight hotel expenses, meals, drinks (more or less, depending on the driving/flying conditions), room rentals for classes and other incidental costs. Moreover, instructors often buy local handicrafts, and there is an increased local demand for notebooks and other study aids. These inputs may be small, but in centres where unemployment may be 40 per cent or higher, they are not insignificant.

Lakehead University has had, and will doubtless continue to have, its problems in dealing with the rural communities and small towns of its vast region. However, it is clear that LU has been and will continue to be the driving force introducing, expanding and enhancing higher education in Northwestern Ontario: a University 'in the North and for the North'.

Acknowledgements

This chapter is largely based on interviews and conversations with people who have been and are involved in the delivery and administration of continuing education at Lakehead University. The authors are especially grateful to Dr T.B. Miller and Mr K.L. Morrison; and to Ms S. Burton and other staff of the Office of Continuing Education. Any opinions expressed in this paper are those of the authors. The original version of this chapter was prepared for the second Circumpolar Conference, Tyumen, USSR in 1991. The authors acknowledge with thanks the efforts of the Canadian editor in rewriting the chapter to make it suitable for this publication.

References

Ballantyne, P.M., 1966, *A history of Lakehead University*, the Friends of Lakehead University Library, Thunder Bay
Braun, H.S. and Tamblyn, W.G., 1987, *A northern vision. The development of Lakehead University*, Lakehead University, Thunder Bay

17 Canada: the rural scene
Robert S Dilley

Introduction

The year 1992 was the Year of the Constitution in Canada: every other item of news seemed to be swept aside as federal and provincial politicians tried to persuade a sceptical public that the best possible blueprint for the nation's future had been achieved. It was strange to pick up a foreign newspaper, or to tune into an outside news program, and discover that other things were happening. In October the subject suddenly disappeared as the electorate firmly rejected the deal, and other concerns began to resurface.

Agriculture continued to be a headache: along with the concerns about negotiations for the General Agreement on Tariffs and Trades (GATT) mentioned below there was also a revival of fears about the long-term effects of free trade as the agreement between Canada and the United States, discussed by Troughton in PIRPAP I, was about to be extended to Mexico.

Aspects of the environment occupied many people's attention throughout the year, with much new legislation introduced or planned. Meanwhile, controversy over the Oldman River dam in southern Alberta continued. This project was subject to a federal environmental assessment (see MacCallum's paper in PIRPAP II). To the surprise of even most opponents of the dam, the panel recommended in May 1992 that the 76-metre-high dam should be left open to allow the Oldman River to run its course; thus negating the purpose of the construction. Both Ottawa, which ordered the assessment, and the Alberta government, which refused to participate in it, immediately rejected this solution. The Alberta Public Works Minister stated 'There is no way that the dam is going to be shut down'. The panel had made other suggestions, should their preferred one be turned down, and the federal government says that it is among these that an answer will be sought. By late November 1992 Ottawa had not acted on even one of the report's 23 recommendations and would give no guarantee of when anything would be done about any of them. This outcome must cast doubts on the value of federally-ordered environmental assessments.

As the recession bit deeper, as unemployment reached the highest point in nine years and as governments at all levels faced growing deficits, efforts were made across the nation to alleviate some of the problems of rural areas, and to try to safeguard at least some aspects of the rural environment.

Farming

The first part of last year's report on farming in Canada could be repeated almost word-for-word. Farmers are still suffering from low prices and from continuing problems with world trade. The protests described in PIRPAP II (p. 212) continued in 1992: 40,000 farmers braved the February cold to demonstrate against the failure to reach a settlement with GATT and the perceived threat to Canada's supply management system for dairy and poultry products. Federal politicians are in a dilemma over GATT negotiations. For the sake of the Canadian grain trade, they want an end to European and US government subsidies and price controls; for the sake of the domestic dairy and poultry industries they want to be able to keep government subsidies and price controls. An already unpopular government does not want to have to choose publicly between western grain farmers and eastern dairymen. Canada has been pushing for exemption for its dairy and poultry industries, but without much hope of success.

Meanwhile, farmers continue to rely on various forms of relief. Although grain production in 1991 reached yet another record high, any profit was coming from government programs. In fact, the federal Gross Revenue Insurance Plan (GRIP) encouraged farmers to plant and harvest more wheat than ever. The program sets a price for grain based on prices during the previous 15 years and guarantees farmers, based on their previous production record, a minimum revenue per seeded acre. Once farmers found out how much support they would get, the area planted with wheat increased nearly seven per cent. GRIP will pay out an estimated $1.5 billion on the 1991 harvest. Non-grain farmers had a more difficult time, and in the fall of 1991 the Ontario government announced a winter relief program for farmers, added to the $50 million offered in April. The new package includes an extra $11 million to help farmers offset the cost of borrowing money; $15 million for grain and oilseed farmers to cover their premiums in the province's income stabilisation program; $5 million to fruit and vegetable farmers, $1 million to other specialised producers and $3.5 million for farmers whose crops had been destroyed by drought. The Ontario Federation of Agriculture said that this was only a quarter of what would be needed to get farmers back on their feet. Certainly farm equipment sales in 1991 were well down: tractor sales were at the lowest level since the Canadian Farm and Industrial Equipment Institute started keeping records in 1966. The 1992 harvest will bring its own problems: the cold, wet summer in the eastern half of the country brought yields down significantly.

In an attempt to alleviate some of the farm problems, the federal government introduced a Bill in November 1992 to encourage farmers to diversify into other industries. This Farm Credit Corporation (FCC) Act will allow the FCC to lend money to farmers who want to expand off the farm and set up related or value-added industries. The federal Minister of Agriculture explained that 'The continued viability of family farm businesses, the agri-food sector and rural communities depend on the ability of farmers to develop new markets'.

Individual provinces continue to struggle with their own farming headaches. In Nova Scotia an Agricultural Planning Committee has been established, consisting of the provincial Department of Agriculture and Marketing Branch Directors together with the Executive of the Nova Scotia Federation of Agriculture. The primary goal of this group is to establish long-term economic and social objectives for the agricultural industry in the province and to provide a mechanism for discussion and direction in the establishment of policies and programs that will benefit the industry.

In Nova Scotia farmers are able to obtain financial assistance for selected capital expenditures related to the development of their farms and for the use of new technology within their particular sector of the agricultural industry. Provincially-funded programs include capital grants on barns, storage buildings and safety equipment (such as roll bars and safety cabs on tractors), beef development, sheep, limestone and fertiliser. Funds are also available to assist the Farm and Cottage Winery program, the Farm and Cottage Vacation program and Rural Beautification.

A number of specific programs have been developed in Nova Scotia to address environmental concerns related to farming. For example, guidelines have been established for the storage and handling of animal manures. The guidelines are a joint effort of livestock producers, professional agrologists and professional environmentalists.

Saskatchewan is continuing to assist farmers by changes in policies towards Crown lands (see PIRPAP II, pp. 212–3). Rural Development lease contracts are aimed at the smaller farmer. They provide long-term tenure and a stable farm base by offering 33-year lease renewals to lessees in good standing. Competitive rental rates allow farmers and ranchers to expand and diversify. A purchase program enables lessees to acquire eligible land. During 1991–2 there were 11,310 farmers holding Crown Land leases. Multiple land use is encouraged. The unrestricted tender sale program allows the use of vacant Crown Land for recreation and commercial uses, not just farming. Crown Land is made available, where possible, to rural communities for landfills, sewage treatment or commercial purposes. For example, the Hudson Bay Rural Development Corporation (see Rural development, below) leased 11,750 acres for a community forest project.

In a Report (August 1992) to the Ontario Minister of Agriculture and Food, the provincial Conservation Easement Committee addressed the question of *Agricultural Easements and the Niagara Fruit Belt: sustaining a unique resource*. The small area of the Niagara Peninsula between Lakes Erie and Ontario is one of only two significant soft-fruit-growing areas in Canada (along with British Columbia's Okanagan Valley). Among other fruits, it produces 70 per cent of the country's peaches. As well, the orchards and vineyards of the area constitute a significant tourist attraction. However, fruit growers are facing difficult economic conditions and continuous pressure from urban development. The Report recommends the implementation of an Agricultural Easement Program not later than 1993. It is proposed that growers of tender fruits would receive a one-time payment of between $20,000 and $30,000 per hectare (ha) for an agricultural easement. Applications would be ranked according to factors such as farm size and degree of threat of conversion. The easement would be perpetual, and apply to the whole parcel save for 0.4 ha for any farm residences. In the short term, the Program would be administered by a Niagara Easement Committee, as part of the Ontario Heritage Foundation (a non-profit agency of the Ministry of Culture and Communications). In the long term, a Niagara Trust would be established as a locally-based non-profit agency. The cost of the Program is estimated at $60–70 million, to be shared on a 15 to 1 ratio between the governments of Ontario and the Niagara Region.

Rural reorganisation

A *Task Force on Local Government* was the title of a report to the Government of Nova Scotia April 1992. It was established by the minister of Municipal Affairs to develop a strategy leading to an appropriate form of government for the province. 'Appropriate' was defined as being in accord with existing settlement patterns and balancing the concepts of economic and service-delivery efficiency with those of accountability and accessibility. The Task Force arose from a number of recent concerns about local government in Nova Scotia. Bodies studying economic strategy and education both reported that there were too many municipal units in the province, a viewpoint that also appeared frequently in the Minister of Finance's pre-budget consultations. In 1989, 1990 and again in 1991 the Union of Nova Scotia Municipalities approved a statement calling for the rationalisation of boundaries and a reallocation of service responsibilities.

The realignment of service responsibilities has been based on the concept of the province taking over all 'people' services, while the municipalities concentrate on property services. One of the more interesting proposals is that the costs of education should be removed from the municipalities, on the grounds that 'Municipalities should not be required to contribute towards the cost of any service over which they have no control, and the cost of which they cannot decide'. This principle, if adopted widely, could revolutionise rural taxes, which are usually heavily weighted towards education costs [in the reviewer's rural Ontario municipality, just over 75 per cent of the property tax levy is for School Board costs]. Restructuring is aimed principally at five areas, including Cape Breton County, where there are deemed to be too many local governments trying to deliver similar services to similar populations. Amalgamation of some of the smaller rural municipalities elsewhere is also considered. Throughout the province the unitary, one-tier, form of government is preferred in any restructuring.

The Manitoba Department of Rural Development has undergone an organisational review which has resulted in a major restructuring. Resources have been grouped into two major divisions. The Local Government Services Division will provide the services performed by the former Department of Municipal Affairs. The Rural Economic Development Division has been created to work in partnership with communities, community business organisations and individual entrepreneurs in meeting the challenge of economic growth and diversification in rural Manitoba. To help staff this new and expanding area, resources from the traditional land-use planning service have been redirected into a 'community economic development' role, which focuses more broadly on local sustainability.

The Manitoba Department of Rural Development is currently examining ways in which to involve the public and affected interest groups in its wholesale review of the Municipal Act. It is also finalising the process for a review and potential amalgamation of Manitoba's current Planning and Conservation Acts. A discussion paper has been prepared on ways to integrate more fully the development, management, conservation and planning of land and water use. The objective is to streamline the process and to reorient the legislation to make it more supportive of sustainable economic development. The Department recently initiated a review of provincial land-use policies adopted in 1980 under the Planning Act. This review will ensure that these policies reflect Manitoba's current economic, social and environmental objectives; incorporate the principals of sustainable development; and provide local authorities with better direction regarding the sustainable use of land. The proposed revisions have been forwarded to local municipalities, conservation and planning districts, and other interest groups for comments and suggestions. After a review of these submissions, the policies will be put forward for adoption.

In Alberta, the report *Partners in Stewardship* was prepared by the Minister's Council on Local Development within the provincial Ministry of Municipal Affairs. The report suggests a number of principles to stimulate local development. The basic philosophy of the report is that government departments, in pursuing local development, should act in such a way that they effectively meet the expectations of the people. The provincial government is implementing this philosophy by supporting local community initiatives that improve leadership, entrepreneurship and access to business information; and which increase local private investment in local private projects. A second thrust is to improve co-ordination of government services and to improve accessibility to these services. Options being considered include one-window access, regional service delivery and service delivery by local organisations.

Alberta has also been expending a substantial effort implementing the transition of Improvement Districts to Rural districts under the 1991 Rural District Act (PIRPAP II, p. 213). Eight Improvement Districts have commenced this transition, and the first Rural District may be formed by 1993.

Rural planning

In July 1992 the British Columbia legislature adopted the Commissioner on Resources and Environment (CORE). CORE was created as a permanent body independent of the various provincial ministries. It has been asked by the government to develop and help implement a strategy for land-use planning and management. The strategy will deal with land use and related resource and environmental management. This involves, among other things: developing a province-wide strategy; developing, implementing and monitoring regional planning processes, community-based participatory planning processes and a dispute-resolution system; and encouraging the participation of native peoples in all processes affecting them that relate to CORE's mandate. The design of a land-use strategy for British Columbia is under way. A set of fundamental principles (a draft Land Use Charter) has been compiled, intended to guide regional and community-based planning processes. Initially, CORE has been asked to focus on the Vancouver Island, Cariboo-Chilcotin and Kootenay regions, because of land-use conflicts in these areas. In addition, the government has requested recommendations on the complex land-use and related resource and environmental issues in the Tatshenshini-Alsek area of northwestern British Columbia. The concept of 'shared decision-making' is being employed by CORE, in response to the perceived need for significant public involvement in decision-making. Negotiating teams include government representatives together with representatives of those interests most directly affected by the decisions.

In September 1992 the Ontario Ministry of Municipal Affairs released the province's *Growth and Settlement Policy Guidelines*, following the inquiry outlined in PIRPAP II (p. 214). These Guidelines outline current thinking and existing practices on land-use planning issues, and integrate economic, environmental and social principles in one document. The intention is, by providing a framework for decision-making, to speed up the land-use planning process. The government sees this as a key component in its overall strategy to support economic renewal. The Policy addresses the processes for the development or redevelopment of land for new housing, businesses, industries, recreation areas, and the necessary infrastructure and services. As such, it is not confined to rural planning, but covers the entire province. The aim is to promote growth that will 'result in communities which are economically and environmentally sound and which meet the full range of needs of their current and future residents'. This is to be achieved by directing urban growth to the already built-up areas of the province and away from sensitive or significant environmental areas. It is intended to protect the integrity of the environment, of agricultural lands and of natural resources. The Policy Guidelines are to apply to all land-use decisions that are covered by the provincial Planning Act.

In a similar move, the province of New Brunswick has issued a Discussion Paper on *Land Use and the Rural Environment*. The Introduction notes that there is significant pressure on the province's resources and natural environment, especially in the rural areas. In 1971 rural New Brunswick accounted for 45 per cent of the province's population; by 1991 this had risen to over 52 per cent. New Brunswick now has the highest and fastest-growing rural non-farm population in Canada. This rapid growth has been mainly residential, though there has been some significant industrial and commercial development. Unplanned growth is resulting in conflicts with traditional rural activities such as farming and forestry. It is causing contamination of streams and wells with sewage from homes and with industrial and commercial pollutants. Sprawling settlement is infringing on fragile coastal shorelines. Urban sprawl and ribbon development are increasing the costs of community services such as fire, police and ambulance and of utilities such as water, sewage and power. Therefore, the province established a Commission on Land Use and the Rural Environment 'to recommend policies to protect and enhance the quality of our rural environment while fostering sustainable economic development and responsible uses of our natural resources'. The resultant Discussion Paper presents a series of problems and possible solutions, and asks for input. Topics covered include the following: under *settlement* urban sprawl and the location of commercial and industrial activities are discussed; under *Resources* are grouped such matters as protection of agricultural land; getting access to shorelines; protecting groundwater supplies; parks and recreation areas; mineral development; and forestry on private land; under *Natural Environment* protection of shorelines, environmentally sensitive areas, air quality and flood plains, and managing garbage and sewage are covered; and finally, under *Rural Planning Process and Structure* are considered the present planning structure; methods for regional service delivery; building and development approval; and financial incentives to encourage or discourage development.

Land Use and the Rural Environment is an especially well-produced and 'user-friendly' publication, which might well serve as an exemplar for other provinces contemplating similar planning exercises. Like Ontario's document, it is produced in both English and French (New Brunswick is the only officially bilingual province in Canada). It is not too long (51 pages in English) and is written in short sentences and clear language. Each of the 18 sections begins with a definition of a specific rural planning problem, with two small black-and-white illustrations (mostly showing a good and a bad example of the practice in question). There is then an explanation why this is a problem, and a list of possible ways of dealing with it. Each section ends with space for written suggestions. It is an admirable example of a document intended to be read and understood by the general public, not just by planning specialists, and clearly specifies what kind of input is needed and how to go about it.

Rural development

A number of new initiatives have been introduced in Manitoba to encourage economic diversification and economic stability in rural areas. Most notable is the *Rural Economic Development Initiative* (REDI), funded entirely from revenue from video lottery terminals located in rural Manitoba. REDI was introduced in April 1992 as one means for communities to implement the development strategies identified through *Community Choices* (PIRPAP II, pp. 215–1). The focus of funding under REDI is on commercially viable development with the potential for long-term economic benefits for communities in such things as business development, conservation projects and tourism. At this time, REDI has six programs. *Infrastructure Development* assists municipalities to develop infrastructure specifically designed to expand existing businesses or attract new businesses. *MBA Student Consulting for Rural Businesses* is conducted in partnership with the University of Manitoba. *Feasibility Studies* assists financially with the cost of hiring an independent consultant to help develop a feasibility study or business plan. *Development Support* provides a one-time contribution to fund innovative proposals in non-traditional areas to create business development opportunities. *Partners with Youth* provides matching funds for the hiring of youth by local government, rural businesses and non-profit organisations for activities that will provide lasting benefits to the community. *Green Team* provides one-time student employment opportunities in the upgrading of tourism destination points such as provincial parks.

Manitoba's *Rural Development Bond Program* (PIRPAP II, p. 215) is flourishing. The province has committed $10 million to guarantee the principal invested in eligible businesses for a period of up to ten years. Two communities have recently sold these *Grow Bonds* for the development or expansion of new industries, while a number of other rural communities are putting together their own Grow Bond Corporations to begin their investment process.

Manitoba is continuing its decentralisation initiative, to promote better access to government services while creating job opportunities in rural areas. To date, more than 500 jobs have been moved to rural locations, and more moves are planned for the near future. For the Department of Rural Development itself, services are now provided from 21 regional offices throughout rural Manitoba.

British Columbia takes a mixed approach to rural development, combining an emphasis on local initiative with provincial facilitation. The emphasis on local initiative is seen most strongly in programs such as *Strong Communities*, designed to increase local employment by fostering diversification and investment. Provincial facilitation is emphasised through a *Community Adjustment Program* designed to deal with the effects of resource industry closure or downsizing; through the new *Natural Resources Community Fund* which will co-ordinate the response to a crisis due to closure of a resource-based business; and through *Revenue Sharing*, which is the most important source of financial assistance to smaller communities in rural areas.

Saskatchewan Rural Development is working to try to enhance the economic and social well-being of rural residents. The Extension Service provides support for agricultural producers, entrepreneurs and rural organisations. It is intended to broaden and strengthen the economic base of the province by providing knowledge and skills which foster and develop ideas for diversification. Extension agrologists help develop programs that address the long and short-term needs of agricultural businesses and rural communities. District or regional conferences are organised to generate and spread ideas. Staff assist potential entrepreneurs by examining development and diversification opportunities and by participating in trade fairs, tours and field days. For example, the La Ronge office has provided leadership in a number of diversification projects in northern Saskatchewan. These include market gardens, mushroom and blueberry cultivation and testing of northern vigour in potatoes and strawberries. The Rural Development Corporation (RDC) and Community Economic Development programs provide assistance in developing community structures that promote local economic and social development in Saskatchewan. Programs include assistance in organising and maintaining community development groups, while help is provided in education and training, information and co-ordination, promotion and marketing, and project identification, management and funding. In 1991–2 seven new RDCs were established: there are now 38 RDCs representing 111 rural municipalities.

A new approach to community development is occurring in the town of Summerside, Prince Edward Island. Summerside (population 15,000) looked to be in for a bleak future with the closure in mid-1991 of the local

Canadian Forces Base. However, Slemon Park Corporation has been created as a for-profit development company to develop and manage the assets of the former base. The main activity so far has been the establishment of Summerside Aerospace Centre, and two other companies have begun operations. The Slemon Park Corporation has two other redevelopment thrusts. One is to seek tenants involved in training and retraining: on offer are classrooms, lecture halls and shop space. The other is to make Slemon Park a centre for athletic and recreation events and programs. With redevelopment of the downtown waterfront and the establishment of a federal tax processing centre, the town of Summerside has turned the corner to recovery.

As a result of federal budget cuts, the Canadian Environmental Advisory Council closed down at the end of April 1992. Before so doing it produced three volumes concerning *Indicators of Ecologically Sustainable Development*, arising out of a July 1990 workshop held in Ottawa. *Economic, ecological, and decision theories* contains three background papers on economic and decision-making theory prepared for the workshop, *Synthesised workshop proceedings* summarises discussions of economic, ecological and decision theories from the conceptual and the applied points of view; *Towards new fundamentals* identifies five principles that should be reflected in the next generation of decision-support indicators. These principles should: reflect a broader scope; reflect distributive elements which are important from a social equity viewpoint; have applications as a forward-looking projective tool; reflect explicit linkages between human economic behaviour and the degree of vigour and productivity of the broader ecosystem; and recognise the inherent uncertainty in ecosystem behaviour and responses. The language of these volumes is not easily accessible to those without a formal training in economics.

An innovative community enterprise letter has appeared entitled *Making Waves* which is aimed at people interested in resource development, strategic planning, venture development, human resource development and community-based business development. The April 1992 issue, for instance, contains several articles on the use of Community Land Trusts to add flexibility to the housing market. The newsletter is available from Westcoast Development Group, 163 West Hastings, Suite 337, Vancouver, BC, V6B 1H5.

National Parks

Environment Canada's two-volume *State of the Parks Report* is the first ever systematic, comprehensive review of every National Park and National Historic Site in Canada. The Report is a requirement of 1988 amendments to the National Parks Act which intended that regular information would enable better decision-making and provide a rational basis for the actions on National Parks and National Historic Sites promised in the Green Plan (PIRPAP-II, pp. 217–18). The first volume highlights the Systems Plans for National Parks, National Marine Parks and National Historic Sites. By giving examples of applications over the last few years and of ongoing work to create new parks and sites, it is hoped to show how government will meet some of the commitments in the Green Plan. The second volume contains profiles of every National Park, National Historic Site and Historic Canal. The special attractions of each site are listed, along with the services and facilities offered. These profiles are a first step towards cataloguing the national heritage. The sections on internal and external threats lay out some of the dilemmas facing park managers. Internal threats such as the need for better fire management seem to be more readily under the control of park managers. External threats, such as habitat losses outside park boundaries, may affect eco-systems within the parks themselves. Human activities—agriculture, logging, urban sprawl—encroach on the boundaries of parks, while threats such as acid rain and global warming are beyond the control of any park manager.

Support for parks is at a high level in Canada. More than 400,000 individuals and 230 organisations have joined the Endangered Spaces Campaign, organised by World Wildlife Fund Canada. New parks are being promised at an unprecedented rate. The federal government has accepted the 1987 Brundtland Commission's target of protecting 12 per cent of the national area, from the current 7.4 per cent, and towards that end has pledged to create 18 more National Parks by the year 2000. In May 1992 British Columbia promised to double the area of its parks and wilderness areas. A new bird sanctuary has been announced for Prince Leopold Island in the Arctic. Agreements may be completed in 1992 for two more National Parks in the Arctic: one with large muskox herds, on Banks Island, and one part of Yukon's Old Crow Flats, rich in waterfowl habitat. Six more National Marine Parks are in the planning stage and three more additions are being considered for the Canadian Heritage Rivers System. At the same time, there is a good deal of disagreement between governments and environmentalists on the definition of 'protection'. Logging, mining and other industrial activity is still permitted in many 'wilderness' areas: in 1992 the Canadian Parks and Wilderness Society sued Ottawa to stop logging in Wood Buffalo National Park. The World Conservation Union has put Wood Buffalo on its list of world heritage sites that have suffered serious degradation, and in May the federal government conceded that logging in the park violates the National Parks Act. Altogether, the World Wildlife Fund disputes the official figure of 7.4 per cent protection for Canada, claiming real protection is afforded to only 3.4 per cent.

The environment

Environment Canada's report, *The State of Canada's Environment*, released early in 1992, is selling well and has received positive reviews from newspapers and from Friends of the Earth. It is the most thorough summary of environmental conditions in Canada yet undertaken. It reviews the major environmental components—air, water, land, wildlife—and the effects of industry, agriculture and other human activities on environmental health. There are extensive chapters on issues of concern such as toxic chemicals, ozone depletion and habitat change. *The State of Canada's Environment* not only surveys environmental conditions; it also provides a thorough explanation of the scientific background and documents what is being done to respond to environmental conditions. In places it is strongly critical of the current situation: 'It is clear that our pressure on the ecosystem must be reduced dramatically, and that this will entail fundamental changes in our attitudes, lifestyles and ways of doing business'. However (not surprisingly) it contains no critical analysis of government policies on the environment, and does not detail the types of changes required. The volume (price $29.95) is available from Canada Communication Group Publishing, Ottawa, Ontario K1A OS9.

Ontario has produced a *Wetlands Policy Statement* with the goals of ensuring that wetlands are identified and adequately protected through the land-use planning process and that there is no loss of provincially significant wetlands. Wetlands provide a whole series of biological, hydrological and socio-economic benefits. Among other things: they are important for the control and storage of surface water and the recharge and discharge of groundwater; they trap sediments which would otherwise fill watercourses; they provide an important habitat for a wide variety of plant and animal species; they provide valuable resource products such as timber, fish and wild rice on a sustainable basis; and they provide active and passive recreational opportunities in green space settings. Wetlands are plentiful in Northern Ontario, but over three-quarters of the original wetlands in the province south of the Canadian Shield have been lost. The Policy therefore requires all planning jurisdictions to protect provincially significant wetlands (defined, subject to later revision, in *An evaluation system for wetlands of Ontario south of the Precambrian Shield*, second edition, 1984) in their official plans and zoning by-laws, and encourages them to protect all other wetlands. The stress is especially on the southern part of the province. The Policy Statement is to be administered jointly by the Ministry of Natural Resources and the Ministry of Municipal Affairs.

In July 1992 Ontario unveiled a proposed environmental bill of rights. It would give members of the public the right to demand that the government undertake investigations of alleged instances of pollution and, for the first time, the right to sue polluters. It would create an environmental ombudsman—to be called the Office of the Environmental Commissioner—and would lead to the creation of an electronic registry where all environmental laws and regulations planned by the government would be open to public scrutiny. Not long after, the Ontario Round Table on the Environment recommended that the province should appoint by 1994 a Commissioner of Sustainability—with an authority comparable to that of the Provincial Auditor—to report on Ontario's efforts to become more environmentally friendly. Other recommendations of the Round Table include moving to full-cost pricing for water and energy to provide incentives for conservation; totally banning the release of toxic substances that accumulate in the environment by the end of the century; and that all proposals requiring Cabinet approval be reviewed for their environmental as well as their fiscal impact.

In December 1989 a significant book was published in Quebec. Entitled *Pour que demain soit, Une région fait le point sur son environnement* (Ensuring the future, A region takes care of its environment) it provides an overview of the Saguenay-Lac-St-Jean area (Sagamie). Written by Michel Savard and published jointly by the Conseil régional de l'environnement and the Conseil régional de concertation et de développement, the book describes, analyses, maps out and summarises all human activities with an environmental impact. The book will be a valuable aid in Sagamie's long quest for sustainable development, and offers a model to the rest of the country for regional environmental analysis.

Acknowledgements

I am grateful to the following individuals for providing information used in preparing this report: Lowell Boyle, Assistant Deputy Minister, Municipalities, Culture and Housing, New Brunswick; E.G. Cramm, Acting Deputy Minister, Municipal Affairs, Nova Scotia; Bob Grodzik, Rural Development, Manitoba; Curt Halen, Ministry of Municipal Affairs, Ontario; Calvin Holden, Ministry of Agriculture and Food, Ontario; Tom Hong, Municipal Affairs, Alberta; R.J. Huggard, Department of Agriculture and Marketing, Nova Scotia; Adrian A. Seaborne, University of Regina, Saskatchewan; and Brian Walisser, Municipal Affairs, Recreation and Housing, British Columbia. Other items were taken from *State of the Environment Reporting*, newsletter of Environment Canada, Ottawa; from *Community Horizons*, newsletter of the Rural and Small Towns Research and Study Program, Mount Allison University; from *Canadian Geographic*; from the Thunder Bay *Chronicle-Journal* and *Times-News* and from the Toronto *Globe and Mail*.

Section V
Australasia

edited by

Geoff McDonald

Introduction
Geoff McDonald

Australasia is defined for this Journal to be Australia, New Zealand and the island nations of the South-west Pacific. Despite continuing hopes that a correspondent could be found for Melanesia and Polynesia, to report on recent events in countries such as Fiji, Tonga, Papua New Guinea, Noumea, Vanuatu and the Solomons, regrettably this has not yet happened. The Australasian section includes then only material from Australia and New Zealand.

There are very significant differences between the planning systems and planning experiences of Australia and New Zealand, the main one driving force for this being that Australia is a federation whereas New Zealand is a unitary nation-state. In structuring this section, it is necessary to cover developments in planning and policy at the federal (Commonwealth) level as well as for each state. Similar economic, social and political factors produce a family resemblance between the planning priorities and planning systems of the separate states of Australia. For political reasons, especially the ebb and flow of progressive and conservative governments and also different resources and economic growth patterns, states are often at different stages in their development of policies or use different approaches to implementation. The existence of the six independent states in Australia (or if the Northern Territory is counted as a state) allows for experimentation and learning, the transfer of planning technology and experience from state to state.

Dominating the rural planning priorities of both Australia and New Zealand are matters of economic policy and trade. Both countries continue to struggle economically after being forced to restructure their economies in recognition of trade barriers in traditional markets. Both have resolved to remove regulatory restraints on their industries, including rural industries and to promote free trade wherever anyone will listen. Each would benefit greatly from trade liberalisation and from the reduction in export restrictions and price damaging export subsidies in agricultural markets. Economic hardship and high levels of unemployment are prevalent in both countries and limit rural policy choices.

In this volume there is a review of recent developments in rural policy, economic, social and environmental at the increasingly important national level in Australia. This is followed by a review of developments in each Australian state.

The major article in the Australasian section is a contribution to the Australian debate on population resources and the environment by Doug Cocks. Population growth in Australia, basically synonymous with immigration, is an important issue for rural planning as the domestic population competes with rural industries for land and water resources and influences the relative importance of export markets for local industries. Doug Cocks is a principal research scientist at the Commonwealth Scientific and Industrial Organisation's Division of Wildlife and Ecology in Canberra. He is author of the recent provocative book *Use with Care* (Cocks, 1992) and author of many papers on rural land-use planning in Australia.

Reference

Cocks, K.D., 1992, *Use with care. Managing Australia's natural resources in the twenty-first century*, Sydney. University of New South Wales Press

18 Population, resources and environment: contributions to the Australian debate

K.D. Cocks

Introduction: the immigration debate in Australia

At over 1.2 per cent per annum (1985–90), Australia has one of the highest population growth rates in the developed world. To estimate future population size and composition, i.e. to project present population into the future, requires assumptions about the three main components of population change: fertility, mortality and immigration. As these components are difficult to anticipate and can change significantly over short periods, population projections, especially those estimating population size and composition in a more distant future, must be treated with a great deal of reservation. One way of drawing attention to the fragility of such long-term projections is to use high and low projections and to set out the assumptions used to produce them as shown in Table 18.1. One of the key variables is migration. For example, the present Australian population of around 17 million is estimated to increase to 26 million by 2031 if one recently recommended minimum gross migrant intake, 150,000 per annum, is adopted, or to 30 million if the migrant intake is raised to 220,000 per annum of AD 2000 (Committee, 1988). With zero net migration and replacement-level fertility (2.11 children per woman) the population would stabilise at around 20 million by the 2070s. Immigration is thus Australia's major source of population growth for the foreseeable future.

Immigration levels have been a contentious issue in Australia for many decades. Initially, the debate centred on the effect on the economy, i.e. does immigration increase Gross Domestic Product (GDP) or, more pointedly, GDP per capita? More recently, most concern has been about the size and significance of impacts on the environment (Mohideen, 1992) and this is the focus of the present chapter, and more particularly, the non-urban environment. To provide context, however, the chapter briefly recounts current economic and social arguments for and against a much higher population. To round out discussion of environmental impacts of population growth, it also comments on recent Australian government initiatives in resource and environmental management, recognising that

Table 18.1 *Two projections of Australia's population*

	Low projection	High projection
Assumptions		
Children/woman	1.93	2.11
Net immigration p.a	75,000	100,000
Life expectancy at birth	80.2	80.2
Total population (1984) (m)	15.6	15.6
Results		
Total population (2021) (mill)	22.0	23.8
Total population (2031) (mill)	23.5	26.2
Total population (2051) (mill)	27.0	31.6
Annual growth rate (% p.a.)	0.69	0.95

Source: Kane and Ruzicka, 1987

population growth is only one of many socio-economic processes standing to generate a need for such management. Although the author is on record (Cocks, 1992) as favouring minimal population growth in Australia, the present chapter attempts to be disinterested.

Economics of immigration

A series of studies and inquiries in recent years has been unable to identify more than minimal economic benefits from immigration. Indeed there may be economic factors which have not been fully considered in these studies which could make the economic case for immigration even weaker, perhaps to the point of reversing it, e.g.:

1. the diversion of foreign-currency-earning food exports into feeding a larger Australian population and the trade balance implications of this;
2. the 'financial crowding out' effect of investment in infrastructure to service migrants. Current infrastructure budgets are rapidly becoming inadequate even to maintain existing infrastructure (roads, sewerage, public buildings etc.), let alone provide new infrastructure for new populations. An associated argument (environmental rather than economic) is that servicing the infrastructure needs of growing populations tends to leave fewer funds for protecting natural environments;
3. population-induced loss of natural capital in the primary or resource-based industries including tourism, mining, farming, forestry and fishing (see below).

Two of the most influential recent studies addressing the economics of immigration have been the so-called 'FitzGerald Report' and the 'Report of the National Population Council'.

The FitzGerald Report (1988) The FitzGerald inquiry into Australia's immigration policies (Committee, 1988) concludes that, at any practical level and over time-spans of a generation or so, immigration's contribution to gross domestic product per head would be just a few percentage points. Even with a politically infeasible annual net intake of 300,000 young highly skilled immigrants a year, the estimated gain in gross domestic product per head by 2030 might perhaps reach 12 per cent above the present level. This is not high.

At this point cognitive dissonance sets in. The Committee does not come out and say that the immigration debate therefore needs to be conducted largely in terms of humanitarian, social and environmental issues. Instead they continue to emphasise that selecting immigrants for their potential economic contribution will have economically beneficial results; true, but no longer the 'most central issue in immigration reform'.

Further doubt on the positive economic aspects of immigration has been provided by Joske (1989) in his analysis of the report of the economic consultant to the FitzGerald Committee (Centre for International Economics, 1988) along with the earlier *The economic effects of immigration on Australia* (Norman and Meikle, 1985). The main conclusion from his review of these two studies was 'that immigration cannot be justified on economic grounds alone, and there may be negative effects of immigration, such as less training, distortion of investment and, in particular, balance of payments problems, which, although difficult to quantify, suggest that lower immigration may be desirable for economic reasons'. Joske's paper was attacked by the Minister for Immigration but it did lead to the setting up of a Bureau of Immigration Research to look at economic, environmental and social aspects of immigration.

Report of the National Population Council (1992) The National Population Council (NPC), an independent advisory body to the Australian government, has recently reported on 'major issues which could arise from the increase in Australia's population, in order to contribute to development of a national population strategy' (National Population Council, 1992).

On the relationship between population growth and economic growth, the report says:

In the absence of economies and diseconomies of scale, population growth *per se* has only marginal long-run impacts on per capita GDP.

Because of our limited present knowledge of economies and diseconomies of scale, it is not possible to state on this basis that population growth *per se* enhances or reduces the productivity basis for economic progress.

However, indirect analysis of population growth and growth in output per head
. . . not dependent on direct estimation of scale effects, has usually found a positive
effect.

Social-humanitarian arguments for significant immigration

If Australia took in 50 million immigrants, the number that might be
locally fed by forgoing food exports, the rest of the world would have zero
population growth for 215 days and many of the people formerly fed by
Australian exports would be less well nourished. Clearly, Australia cannot
solve the world's over-population problem. Nevertheless, there are good
humanitarian, political and social arguments for allowing refugees and
family-reunion immigrants into Australia, and it is widely agreed such
entry should be non-discriminatory as regards nationality, race, sex, political beliefs and religion.

Indeed, it is terribly important to decouple questions of immigrant
numbers from the demographics of those immigrants. The Australian
immigration debate has become confounded with the racial mix debate.
Too many people concerned about population growth are unwilling to
speak up for fear of being branded racist. In any case, the argument that
high immigration will lead to greater cultural diversity has weakened with
the realisation that Australia is already one of the most culturally diverse
countries in the world. Conversely, given an increasingly high proportion
of Asian immigrants, proponents of a 'white' Australia (the racists) or a
less multicultural Australia (not necessarily racists) have found cause to
join the 'anti-immigration lobby'.

It is legitimate, of course, to have selection criteria for immigrants based
on such things as age, language and other skills. Arguments for and against
choosing immigrants on the basis of race, religion, or nationality boil down
to the perceived benefits of multiculturalism versus 'social cohesiveness'.
Possibly, there may also be some geopolitical benefits in favouring Asian
immigrants.

Refugees   There are 15–20 million people around the world meeting the
United Nations criteria for refugees, and it is for Australia to be the most
generous refuge country in the world by taking in more refugees as a
percentage of population than any other country. This would still amount
to only a few tens of thousands of immigrants a year. Given that some
20,000–30,000 people leave Australia permanently each year, this would
result in a net migration rate close to zero.

Advocates of low (absolute) levels of humanitarian immigration offer
several answers to charges that they are selfish: (a) such behaviour would
still be *relatively* generous; (b) Australian food can only feed people

once—either locally or overseas; and (c) Australia tends to take the very migrants Third World countries can least afford to lose.

If the greenhouse effect eventuates in a major way, millions of coastal-dwelling people could be forced into the biggest mass migration the Pacific region has ever experienced and Australia could have to resettle hundreds of thousands of people. Precautionary thinking might suggest that current population growth rates should be conditioned by that contingency.

The precautionary argument against population growth

The essential argument here is that population growth cannot be readily reversed and therefore it is important to be confident that significantly higher population levels are desirable before embarking on such a path.

An onus principle is sometimes coupled with the precautionary principle namely that when any change from a status quo is being advocated, *proof of benefit* is normally the responsibility of the protagonists, in this case the advocates of higher population.

Arguing by analogy, proponents of the precautionary argument ask why Australia is different from the many other countries widely perceived to be already over-populated. In terms of energy and materials use, Australians already have the same impact on amenity and industrial resources as a Third World population of over 600 million., i.e. by Third World living standards, Australia already has a population equivalent to 500–600 million plus, mostly living in an area comprising about one-seventh of Australia (the damper parts). This is equivalent to about 400 Third World people per sq km in the settled parts of Australia. For comparison, Bangladesh has a population density of 760 people per sq km.

A particular version of the precautionary argument is that there are good geopolitical reasons for keeping the Australian population at a level compatible with food self-sufficiency. On the 1975 calculations of Gifford *et al.* (1975), Australia could feed about 60 million people. This would involve doubling the present area of irrigated agriculture, largely in northern Australia where uncommitted water supplies remain. It is time to repeat this exercise, since as some of the original authors themselves point out, many of their assumptions would be different today (Millington and Kalma, 1982). None the less, it is unlikely that reworking would boost the 1975 estimates.

Political and other considerations

Until several years ago, the main political parties in Australia were more-or-less agreed that net immigration of around 100,000 annually was desirable, partly for economic growth reasons and partly to attract the ethnic vote. This was despite the regular appearance of opinion polls showing around 70 per cent of Australians in favour of low or zero gross immigration (Goot, 1988).

A severe recession since the late eighties has sparked a perception of migrants taking the jobs of Australians and has led the main political parties to (less than explicitly) favour net immigration levels of around 50,000 annually. Indications are that this tacit target may fall further yet.

The military defence argument for a high population is rarely raised in these days when sophisticated weaponry rather than bodies is seen as the basis for national security.

Environmental quality and immigration

Turning to the paper's focal concern, will a much larger Australian population, via its impact on various determinants of environmental quality and rates of natural resource depletion, have a significantly increased impact on the quality of life of the Australian domestic population? Does the foreseeable impact stand to make the prospect of a significantly higher population politically unacceptable?

What is environmental quality?

In Australia, as elsewhere, the word *environment* has acquired many meanings. Comprehensively, an entity's environment is the set of exogenously mediated variables to which its behaviour is responsive. Most discussions of environment also focus on an open-ended subset of a total environment. Thus human communities are perceived to live simultaneously in many environments including, at the broadest level, the socioeconomic, the informational, the built and the biophysical.

The *biophysical environment* of a human community is usually regarded as those portions of the more-or-less natural (nature-given) and human-scale biological and physical worlds within which the activities of community members take place. It is normally the biophysical environment, particularly measures of change in the status of water, air, biodiversity and earth materials (WABEM) resources, which is being referenced in discussions of the impact of population on the environment or on *environmental quality*.

Measures of the functionality and availability of these resources are response-triggering *environmental indicators*. To assert that population growth reduces environmental quality is to claim a clear causal link between population growth and (adverse) movement in the values of WABEM indicators towards response-triggering values. Current Australian thinking on and initiatives to identify and monitor a useful national set of indicators of environmental quality are described in Appendix 1, *State of environment reporting*.

Population growth is, however, only one in a long list of societal processes/activities customarily seen as contributing to loss of environmental quality. Others on the list are population redistribution, increasing consumption of material goods, waste and residue disposal practices, intensification and extensification of primary and secondary industries, urban expansion, income redistribution, resource allocation procedures, etc.

Collectively, these processes, along with the generation of benefits, (a) consume, (b) ration, (c) degrade and (d) pollute natural resources. These impact descriptors, each with a negative connotation, imply adverse movement in environmental indicators. Degradation and pollution both imply loss of functional capacity, the difference being that pollution is a consequence of residue accumulation and degradation is a consequence of 'over-use'. Consumption and rationing imply reduced availability.

More concretely, concern over the impacts of human activity (not just population growth) on WABEM variables takes three main forms:

a. Decline in the availability and functionality (productivity) of natural resources valued for their role in primary or resource-based industries. These are tourism, mining, farming, forestry and fishing and the natural resources they depend on. Industrial natural resources, for example, include soils, water supplies, landscapes, forests, rangeland and fish stocks.

  The concern here is essentially economic—for the viability or sustainability of those primary industries which are depleting their natural capital. Current Australian responses to the related challenge of 'ecologically sustainable development' are discussed in Appendix 2.

b. Decline in the availability and functionality of natural resources valued for their direct contribution to people's physical and spiritual health, i.e. amenity resources. Lists of amenity resources include air for breathing, water for drinking, biodiversity for marvelling at and landscapes for playing in.

c. Decline in the availability and functionality of natural resources valued for their capacity to provide environmental services, that is, to improve the functioning of natural resources with productive and/or amenity values. Most environmental services can be viewed as recycling of some sort (de Groot, 1992). Lists of service resources include vegetation for maintaining atmospheric oxygen levels, wetlands for removing pollutants from water supplies, ecosystems for recycling nutrients through the food chain.

The phrase 'decline in the availability and functionality of natural resources' is an accurate but cumbersome description for the type of environmental quality loss of interest here. Shorthand alternatives which will be used are 'environmental impacts', 'environmental costs' and natural resource depletion'.

Some postulated environmental impacts of population growth

The impact of population growth on environmental quality is compounded by the impact of changing patterns and levels of economic and other activity, much of which, in itself, appears to have little direct linkage to changes in total population. However, there does seem to be one simple link between population change and environmental quality, supported by everybody in the sense that there has been no suggestion, either to official inquiries or in public debate, that continuing high immigration stands to *improve* environmental quality in Australia in any significant way. *Prima facie*, the issue simplifies then to the extent to which continuing high immigration stands to *reduce* environmental quality, and the political significance of this reduction.

As a device for organising discussion of the possible environmental impacts of markedly high populations (say a doubling by the mid-twenty-first century), a series of postulates are now presented and commented on. Following the classification already given, these selectively cover (i) availability and (ii) functionality of (a) industrial natural resources (b) amenity natural resources and (c) service (recycling) natural resources as shown in Figure 18.1.

The problem encountered in discussing the plausibility of quite general postulates about the impacts of population growth is that 'It all depends . . .'. It depends, for example, on where the population growth occurs, how that population behaves and what planning/market adjustment measures are taken to ameliorate pending impacts. This problem is quite separate from that of disentangling the impacts of population growth *per se* from the impacts of processes such as noted above.

A full discussion would develop population impact scenarios around combinations of these contingencies (*laissez-faire* vs, active planning and management; declining vs. non-declining consumption levels; dispersed vs. concentrated settlement, etc.), but space here permits only a few comments on each postulate, basically under the assumption of current or social realities. Perhaps that is fortunate to the extent that the data to support extended discussion are patchy at best.

The comments that follow reflect the materials used and issues raised in two major recent enquiries which, *inter alia*, have addressed aspects of the environmental impact of population growth. Further selected points from and comment on these inquiries are included as appendices. Appendix 3 discusses 'environment' aspects of the report of the National Population Council (National, 1992). Appendix 4 discusses a recent parliamentary report on patterns of urban settlement (Commonwealth of Australia,

CHANGE IN POPULATION

CHANGE IN DEMAND FOR LAND FOR:

* housing
* food production
* urban and extra-urban infrastructure
* waste disposal
* recreation and tourism

CHANGE IN:

* pollution
* degradation
* consumption
* rationing

OF BIO-PHYSICAL RESOURCES

* air
* water
* biodiversity
* earth materials

CHANGE IN INDICATORS OF ENVIRONMENTAL QUALITY FOR:

* industrial resources
* amenity resources
* service resources

Figure 18.1   *Schematic of the linkage between population growth and environmental quality*

1992). The latter makes the point convincingly that despite efforts to consolidate urban areas, most foreseeable population growth will result in expansion on the fringes of a small number of large cities and urban regions. This provides an anchor point for scenario construction.

As a generalisation, the process by which extra population stands to impact on the availability and functionality of industrial, amenity and service resources is via the demand for land (defined broadly) for:

—housing
—food production
—urban and extra-urban infrastructure
—waste disposal
—recreation and tourism.

Postulate: Population growth will have a modest impact on (a) the availability of land for primary production and (b) the area of land supporting amenity and service resources.

The growth of cities frequently increases the cost of supplying fresh produce (milk, fruit, vegetables, etc.) to city residents. Housing and farming both have a preference for level, well-drained soils but developers can pay more for land than farmers. Farmers thus can be forced out into areas where transport and other costs are higher. Australians have a liking for living on large urban lots and this imposes external costs on near-city farming.

While the areal fraction of Australia's existing agricultural land lost to urbanisation by the 2050s in this way stands to be small, any effect will be magnified simply because much of the best arable land (about five per cent of the country) is in the ecumene, the 20 per cent of Australia where over 90 per cent of the population lives and will continue to live (basic data on the detailed location of urbanised land is lacking).

Additional to the direct loss of farmland to urbanisation, growing cities make irresistible demands on a range of peri-urban sites for (e.g.) reservoirs, transport, power and communication links, construction materials. Some of these will take land from agriculture and, less commonly, mining or forestry.

Urbanisation, to a greater or lesser extent, always consumes (and degrades) amenity and service resources. Reclaiming mangrove mudflats in Cairns for building sites is a recent clear-cut example. However, as with primary production, these losses will normally be a small proportion of the totality of amenity and service resources Australia-wide. Conversely, they stand to be a high proportion of such resources within the urban field, the range of commuting and day-tripping recreation activity. This is the type of effect which should be detected by a state of environment reporting system.

Postulate: Population growth is likely to increase the daily pollution and congestion problems which most Australians experience

A high proportion of immigrants settle in the Sydney and Melbourne regions which already contain about half the Australian population. These centres are rapidly approaching threshold levels at which congestion costs, travel costs and pollution costs will escalate (Birrell and Tonkin, 1992).

Pollution problems emerge, basically because the limited assimilative capacities of regional airsheds and watersheds get 'overloaded'. Service resources can only remove entering pollutants up to some maximum rate beyond which these accumulate in ways which rapidly reduce air, water and soil quality. Additionally, existing methods of waste disposal, particularly of sewage and industrial effluents, poses a major threat to the functioning and existence of estuarine and marine ecosystems.

Given effective mechanisms for carefully decentralising population and/ or controlling emissions/residues, these problems may not arise. The natural northerly drift of population to Queensland will take some of the pressure off Sydney-Melbourne, but not much.

Postulate: Population growth will lead to more consumption, rationing, pollution and degradation of service and amenity resources in the coastal zone than elsewhere

The Australian coastal zone provides sites for a wider range of uses and functions than any other part of the continent. These include: residential and commercial use; recreational use; commercial fishing, ports (about 120 in all) and sea transport; waste disposal; tourism; conservation of natural environments; and industrial uses such as cooling, salt production, pulp production, mining and agriculture. Not only do Australians want to live (and hence work) near the coast, it is a major focus for outdoor recreation and local and international tourism.

For some decades now, about a quarter of the Australian population has chosen to live within 3 km of the coast (McDonald *et al.*, in press). If this proportion holds as total population grows towards a projected level of 27 million by 2051, there plausibly could be another three million people living in the coastal fringe by then. McDonald *et al.* (in press) conclude that three urban regions (based on Sydney, Brisbane and Perth) will not be able to accommodate their projected coastal fringe populations without resorting to some combination of (a) high population density, (b) building on depositional terrain which has considerable service value, or (c) urbanising currently unpopulated open space and rare vegetation associations, both of which have high amenity value.

Pollution and waste disposal are already widespread, although generally localised, issues in coastal zone management. Examples include runoff of agricultural chemicals, pulp mill effluents, sediment loads, offshore sewage disposal, heavy metal pollution, eutrophication from urban runoff and fertiliser leachates, oil spills, depletion of seagrass fish nursery areas, overdevelopment of biologially important estuaries and coastal water-bodies (Cocks, 1992). Unless much greater efforts are made to manage such problems, they can only get worse as population growth leads to the growth of coastal cities.

Appendix 5 outlines recent governmental responses to the perception that the 20 per cent of coastal Australia which is currently inhabited will be the area which will continue to experience most of the loss in environmental quality due to population growth and redistribution.

Postulate: Population growth will have little direct effect on the in situ *productivity of natural resources valued for primary production*

The major degradation of agricultural and pastoral land which has occurred in Australia has resulted from the activities of a small number of primary producers producing for export markets. Growing populations and domestic markets have had proportionately little effect, in area terms, on the pattern of agricultural land use and even less on the production technologies used. Population-induced changes in the product mix from the farm sector are and will be concentrated around cities or in higher rainfall areas where land degradation has always been less of a problem than in pastoral and extensive cropping areas.

Air and water pollution generated in new urban areas is unlikely to feed back in any major way on agricultural production, basically because most population growth is likely to be coastal and downwind and downstream from agricultural areas. Mariculture and inshore fisheries may be the exception.

Postulate: Population growth will reduce per capita shares of/access to those unique natural goods, like snow-fields, beaches and recreational rivers, which not even the most prosperous economy can create

Extensive recreation activities depend on natural landscapes which are *positional goods*, meaning unique goods that the market cannot produce in increased quantities. This means that under population growth they have to be rationed. For example, Australia's recreational snow-fields are extremely limited and already being rationed by price.

Proper management of landscape resources can improve access up to a point but is in itself 'defensive expenditure' to be subtracted from rather than added to GDP. Crowding and/or rationing of landscape resources is one of the few environmental impacts unequivocally flowing from population growth.

Postulate: Population growth is likely to lead to unacceptable degradation of natural resources used for tourism and extensive recreation

Larger populations lead to amenity resources being used more intensively in order to allow more people to enjoy them. Even with active management, heavily used amenity resources 'wear out', just as boat anchors are wearing out many of Queensland's coral reefs and feet are wearing out the approaches to Ayers Rock. Once degraded, such positional goods cannot be replaced.

Australia's landscape-based tourist industry is increasingly being seen as central to the country's economic health in the twenty-first century. By 2000 international tourism could generate demands for amenity and service resources equivalent to a permanent population with a high-impact lifestyle of perhaps 200,000 people, depending on assumptions. Alternatively, local tourists visit many of the areas popular with international tourists. Even with careful management, international tourists are likely to be degrading the amenity resources of the domestic population at the same time as local tourist numbers, swollen by population growth, are degrading the industrial resources (same resources, different label) of the international tourist industry.

Postulate: Population growth will increase Australia's difficulty in meeting its share of global environmental targets (the 'Toronto' argument)

The Australian government has accepted, although with escape clauses, the 'Toronto' target of a 20 per cent reduction of CO_2 emissions over 1988 levels by 2005. CO_2, production increases roughly in line with population (McGlynn, 1992) but this target will not be relaxed because of higher population. A higher population will simply make the Toronto target and similar future international obligations harder to reach.

The present paper concentrates on environmental effects of population growth on the Australian domestic population. However, what is fairly obvious, accepting that Australian GDP per head will not collapse under a larger population, is that population growth in Australia places much larger demands on the world's environment than population growth in most other countries.

Postulate: Population growth has little impact on the rate of exhaustion of non-renewable (mineral) resources

Australia is extremely well endowed with metalliferous minerals and energy minerals. Apart from oil and base grade construction materials, domestic consumption of most minerals is a small fraction of total production and even significant population growth will not alter this. The activities of the mining sector are, if anything, slightly constrained by population growth in so far as this increases demands for recreational land which may be mineralised (e.g. mineralised beach sands) and increases the interest which the environmental movement takes in mining operations.

Postulate: The impact of population growth on environmental quality will depend on the vigour with which social technologies for environmental planning and management are developed and applied

In discussing preceding postulates, effective resource mangement has been identified a number of times as an ameliorating response to the impacts of population growth on the availability and functionality of industrial, amenity and service resources.

At the broadest level, components of the community's resource management task are overseeing (a) the allocation of resources between competing functions and (b) the choosing of technologies for implementing these allocated functions. Respectively, the established social technologies for undertaking these tasks in ways which allow the balancing of environmental against economic values are *land-use (or environmental) planning* and *environmental (or project) impact assessment*.

Land-use (or environmental) planning can protect environmental quality by guiding land uses to sites where they have minimal impact on environmental values consistent with the achievement of efficient resource use. *Environmental (or project) impact assessment* can guide land users towards technologies which have low environmental impact. The extent to which environmental values are in practice protected by these social technologies depends on the community's implicit trade-off rate between these and economic values. The Great Barrier Reef Marine Park is Australia's brightest example of what can be achieved in balancing production and protection through use of environmental planning and management technologies.

Social technologies for environmental planning and management protect against loss of environmental quality irrespective of cause. Promising new social technologies for resource management include new forms of resource use rights, such as transferable water rights for irrigators. New types of taxes and charges on polluters, degraders and destroyers are also being developed for adjusting opportunities and cost-price signals for entrepreneurs in the public interest. Natural resource accounting is the developing art of working out what to charge (Cocks, 1992).

Discussion and conclusions

This chapter has discussed if the foreseeable impact of population growth on environmental quality stands to make the prospect of a significantly higher population politically unacceptable. This question is an abstraction from the more general question of the net benefits of population growth taking account of economic and social as well as environmental values.

The device of exploring the question through the evaluation of a series of postulates relating dimensions of environmental quality to population could only be applied in a minimal way here due to lack of space; nevertheless, the framework may be useful for organising future research.

However, even from this first brief examination it is hard to avoid the conclusion that while population growth can hardly improve environmental quality, it is difficult to identify potential impacts on environmental quality convincing enough to tip the immigration debate. Just as the economic benefits of immigration remain 'not proven', the significance of the environmental costs of immigration remain to be established.

In part, this is because none of the chapter's postulated impacts of population growth has been the subject of serious research. For example, there are no data on even such a basic issue as just where land has been converted to urban use (Commonwealth of Australia, 1992). For the future, active development of national state of environment reporting (Commonwealth Environment Protection Agency, 1992) offers the possibility of monitoring environmental indicator values to get a comprehensive view of changing environmental quality. The concept of environmental quality used in this chapter has been one of something measurable by appropriate indicators of the availability and functionality of industrial, amenity and service natural resources. It is only when the aggregate environmental impact of a spectrum of social processes on a working set of these is documented that it may become possible to tease out the specific impact of population growth.

Impacts will, however, ostensibly vary with the type (sensitivity? resilience?) of region acquiring the extra population. Here, what can be flagged is what impacts of future population growth on environmental quality will probably be concentrated in 'fragile' coastal regions, particularly the 20 per cent of coastal Australia which is urbanised or urbanising. This, however, ignores the question of to what extent and under what conditions there is interdependency between impacts in different regions. There is thus a need to study the spatial distribution of the land-use demands associated with an increment of population growth at different locations; and the pattern of intensification of land use associated with marginal population growth at different locations.

Accordingly, another debate which needs to be running in parallel with the immigration debate is one about settlement strategy. What is needed here are studies showing the impact on environmental indicators of various scenarios of (a) population increase and (b) settlement pattern combinations. Even with zero net immigration, some active redirection of settlement may be part of the cheapest way of coping with existing pollution, overcrowding and over-use.

One question which has not so far been raised is the environmental benefits and disbenefits, if any, of a stable population (irrespective of size). The associated widely-discussed concept of the steady state economy has had little public airing in Australia (Daly, 1982).

While waiting for the work which will isolate, quantify and proportion the contribution of population growth to Australia's self-evident losses of environmental quality, the symptoms of the complex of causal processes in the mean time still have to be treated. The environmental impacts of population growth should be subsumed, managed and traded off (against other values) as part of this complex by using established and evolving social technologies such as land-use planning and environmental impact assessment. Elaborated property rights and other economic instruments, however, have an increasing part to play.

Finally, while it may well be possible to argue convincingly for minimal population growth on grounds other than environmental, this has not been the task of the present chapter.

Appendix I: State of the environment reporting

The Australian government established a Commonwealth Environment Protection Agency (CEPA) in 1991 with responsibility, *inter alia*, for undertaking national monitoring and reporting of the state of the Australian environment. Within a year the Agency released (Commonwealth Environment, 1992) a discussion paper on how this responsibility was to be discharged. The relevance of this initiative here is that a state of the environment reporting system offers the best foreseeable prospect of generating data of value for understanding the relationship between population and environmental quality.

The currently fashionable practice of state of the environment reporting offers a practicable way into the concept of environmental quality. It is based on the premise that a community can manage its *quality of life* by managing, amongst other tasks, environmental quality, i.e., the dimensions of its biophysical environment which trigger adaptive or corrective action when they move outside definable limits.

While state of the environment reporting conventionally focuses on the biophysical environment, the built environment associated with human settlements is also considered on occasions. Whichever milieu is considered, the role of the state of the environment report itself is to identify environmental variables requiring active management or standing to require active management at some future date. Such management is necessarily through the management of social and economic activities, e.g. immigration.

A community attempting to manage environmental quality in an ideal fashion would need to have a model of the relationship between (i) causal social and economic activities, (ii) the resulting values of environmental variables, and (iii) a (multi-dimensional) measure of the quality of life. The model would then be used to identify where the costs of modifying values of environmental variables matched the quality of life benefits from maintaining or improving environmental quality. In practice, however, this is not possible, since there is no strict causal relationship between (most) environmental values and quality of life. At best, such a relationship would be both probabilistic and contingent on other factors such as the socio-economic environment.

In the absence of any possibility of such complete modelling, one pragmatic alternative is to attempt to identify by partial models or intuitive means, those *primary environmental variables or indicators* which are believed to be strongly correlated with strong determinants of quality of life as well as being strong determinants themselves. Such primary environmental variables or indicators are those for which small changes are asserted to lead regularly to significant changes in primary indicators of quality of life. A pragmatic approval would also try to manage these variables/indicators.

The next step is to define a *core set* of quality of life indicators as a set such that all significant changes in quality of life would be associated with changes in one or more indicators in that set. Hence, a core set of environmental variables can be defined as a set such that all significant changes in quality of life would be strongly associated with changes in one or more variables in that set.

A comprehensive state of the environment report would thus be a report which identified the current status of a core set of environmental variables and a core set of quality of life indicators and, minimally, judged whether these (both sets) were at acceptable levels. Beyond this such reports might identify trends in values of core environmental variables and core quality of life indicators; could predict future values; and could identify threshold values or standards beyond which change in an environmental variable would have a rapidly increasing effect on quality of life. This could be called a *comprehensive indicators approach* to the state of the environment reporting.

The setting of acceptable levels or standards for core environmental and quality of life indicators must be recognised as essentially arbitrary. Commonly such setting is done by taking the standards of another country respected for its environmental management. Another approach is to compare local levels of core indicators with comparable figures from a number of other regions, states or countries and flag local values which are 'outliers' in such company. More rarely, experimental or survey research is undertaken to identify the process relationship between an environmental indicator's values and quality of life indicator values. Even this does not avoid the fact that judgement is the source of environmental standards.

A less-than-comprehensive indicators approach to state of environment reporting would identify the current status of selected members of the core set of environment variables and the core set of quality of life indicators. Such a *selected indicators approach* is probably the best that can be hoped for in any attempt at state of environment reporting for Australia.

Appendix 2: ecologically sustainable development (ESD) and the intergovernmental agreement on the environment

A major Australian response to the Brundtland Report (World Commission on Environment and Development, 1987) was the initiation by the Australian government of the so-called ESD process recommendations on guidelines for achieving 'ecologically sustainable development' within sectors such as agriculture, fishing, mining, forestry and tourism. Additionally, groups looked at major intersectoral issues including population, urban issues and the future of the coastal zone where so many Australians live and recreate. Implementation of recommendations from the generally excellent reports from ESD working groups is currently stalled in negotiations between state and Australian governments as they struggle to agree on a *National strategy for ecologically sustainable development*.

Along with a 1992 Commonwealth-States *Inter-governmental agreement on the environment* (IGAE), ecologically sustainable development is seen by the Australian government as an 'umbrella' initiative under which a range of more specific new and existing environmental strategies can function as shown in List 18.1. The more general purpose of the IGAE is 'to improve intergovernmental co-ordination of environmental management and enhance consistency and certainty in government and business decision-making, while providing for better environmental protection' (Ecologically, 1992). Schedules to the IGAE spell out co-operative arrangements between governments in a range of specific environmental areas: data collection and handling; resource assessment; national environmental protection measures; climate change; biological diversity; national estate; world heritage; and nature conservation.

List 18.1: *Finalised and draft national environment/sustainability strategies*

National bicycling strategy
National biodiversity strategy
National building better cities strategy
National coastal zone management strategy
National conservation strategy
National drought policy
National endangered species strategy

National energy rating strategy
National environmental choice program
National fisheries management strategy
National forest strategy
National greenhouse response strategy
National guidelines for contaminated sites
National kangaroo management strategy
National landcare evaluation and monitoring strategy
National ocean rescue 2000 strategy
National regulations for intractable waste
National soil conservation strategy
National strategy for state of environment reporting
National strategy on land information management
National vegetation management strategy
National vertebrate pest management strategy
National waste minimisation strategy
National water quality strategy
National weeds strategy

Source: Australian Local Government Association

The ESD report on population highlighted the fact that the impact of population on the environment is a result not only of absolute numbers of people competing for available resources, but also of the socio-demographic characteristics of the population, such as its age structure, health status and geographic distribution. Per capita levels of consumption of goods and services, and of the production and recycling of wastes, are also significant and are influenced by, amongst other things, technology and cultural values (Ecologically, 1992).

The report recommended that: an ongoing program of studies be undertaken into the relation between population and the environment, both natural and urban; and, in the development of a national population strategy, attempts should be made to balance the elements of economic progress, ecological integrity, social justice and international responsibility.

The report introduces the idea of a *sustainable population*, where sustainability is assessed in terms of 'net economic, social and environmental outcomes'. However, 'further work needs to be done to develop reliable techniques to enable this sustainable population to be assessed'. This latter is the escape clause which has allowed the taking of a firmer position to be delayed. None the less, this is quite an interesting development. *Sustainable population* appears to be the intellectual successor to *optimum population* and *maximum carrying capacity*, two ideas which have been judged illuminating but non-operational (e.g., Cocks, 1992).

Appendix 3: Report of the National Population Council

This Committee (NPC, 1992) came to several conclusions in examining the impact of population growth on something they called *ecological integrity:*

1. the way (cf. extent) in which natural resources are used in primary industries is largely independent of population size. Certainly for mining, forestry, fishing and agriculture, there seems no reason why a larger population should induce different technologies, e.g., more labour-intensive;
2. landscape-based tourism could be different. It is still largely (c. 80 per cent) an industry servicing the domestic market and greater visitor numbers might lead to more intensive use of existing tourist destinations;
3. under population growth, industries producing for the domestic market (e.g. fresh food, housing, tourism) will expand, replacing comparable export industries to a greater or lesser extent. This changed production mix may change the rate at which natural resources such as soil and minerals will be consumed; and
4. consumption of the output from expanded domestic industries will increase residue production and hence, potentially, increase pollution of air, land and water residue-sinks. Population (growth) adds a significant component to growth of greenhouse gas emissions and other related demands on natural capital.

In much of its discussion however, the Committee has difficulty in separating the environmental and resource use effects of the production and consumption patterns of the existing population from those of a larger population.

The Committee's consultant in this area (McGlynn, 1992) says:

One of the primary determinants of the level of stress placed on the environment is, naturally enough, the size and structure of the population. All other things being equal, a larger population will demand more resources and create more waste and pollution. In reality, all other things are never equal, and the relationships between population change and resource use are complex.

McGlynn defines resource use as any decrease in the quantity or quality of resources which are available for use in the foreseeable future:

'As long as economies rely on consumption as the measure of welfare, there seems no alternative to the conclusion that increasing welfare will eventually run up against absolute resource limitations. Slower population growth now increases the amount of time until this point is reached, as do increases in resource efficiency. These are only postponements, not cancellations, of a terminal point. This suggests that it will indeed be necessary to eventually stabilise GDP. Without a stable or declining population, this would necessitate reduction in GDP per capita. The adoption of broader measures of welfare, including environmental integrity, means that stable or even declining GDP per capita is not inconsistent with improved standard of living.'

Appendix 4: Parliamentary report on patterns of urban settlement

The House of Representatives of the Commonwealth Parliament has a Standing Committee for Long-Term Strategies, which produced a report, in August 1992, on a desirable pattern for human settlement in Australia. It concluded, somewhat blandly, that a desirable pattern 'would be a matter of balance between population impact and environmental quality; between lifestyle needs and productive efficiency and between population distribution and employment opportunities'.

The report found that urban consolidation, the currently favoured strategy for managing urbanisation, will be nowhere able to contain projected urban growth. Thus, the first impact of urbanisation is the direct loss of natural areas and prime agricultural land. The second impact is the indirect loss and conversion of such areas to service urban growth (e.g. to reservoirs). The third impact, both inside and outside the urban fence, is increased pollution and degradation of natural areas, the beginning of a further cascade of impacts. Water pollution, both fresh and marine, is a particular problem for a dry country where most people live near the sea (equals sewer) or near a modest inland waterway (equals sewer).

There is no discussion in the report of the extent to which expansion of urban areas is differentially a function of (a) population growth or (b) population redistribution in response to economic and life-style opportunities. Given a strong northward and westward drift in population from south-east Australia where a majority of migrants settle, the new-housing needs of migrants are perhaps not as land-demanding as they could be.

The rapidly growing Australian tourist industry is largely landscape-based and is another source of urbanisation, commonly in places selected only for proximity to the resource. This raises the more general question of 'spotty' urbanisation, a commonplace in Australia, particularly coastal Australia. Despite *prima facie* evidence that many small urban areas will have a greater environmental impact than one large area, the report does not attempt this comparison.

Like the report of the National Population Council, this report avoids taking a position on immigration levels, saying that population growth is only one factor contributing to environmental problems. It does not ask whether the contribution is large or small.

National settlement strategy

The question of where up to 16 million additional Australians will live in the middle of the next century is one which must be answered either by market forces or by public policy or a mixture of both. Almost certainly most of them will live in one of a score of high population regions centred on existing metropolises and large cities.

It is widely perceived that the Sydney and Melbourne regions, collectively containing about half the country's population, are already too big; for example, the effectiveness of dispersing air pollutants decreases more than proportionately with city size. At the other extreme the loss of small rural service centres is seen as socially traumatic. It is of course difficult to do a convincing benefit-cost analysis to show that the social costs of enlarging the existing metropolises outweigh the individual, personal benefits which obviously draw people to these places.

Even if this were possible, the anti-planning atmosphere of Australian politics would not allow any significant effort to be made to direct the location of additional people. Not since the 'growth centre' days of the Whitlam Government (1972–5) has there been any serious attempt to guide the location of additional population.

None the less, the Committee recommends that the Australian Government develop a national settlement strategy which takes account of the: relocation of national activity; increasing regional differences; and environmental concerns associated with further coastal development and urban expansion. The report's only indication of the scope of this strategy is that it should include the development of mechanisms which facilitate: better regional planning between levels of government; and a more strategic approach to implementing long-term key infrastructure projects.

The Committee further recommends that governments work together to identify the most environmentally sensitive sites in urban growth areas with a view to determining those to be protected from development, those that may be developed at a later date and those available for immediate development.

Appendix 5: National Coastal Strategy

There is currently considerable concern in Australia over the consequences of the rapid coastal urbanisation which has been occurring in recent decades. Water pollution and ecosystem destruction/landscape degradation are amongst the most commonly cited consequences. The most recent expression of this concern is the report, 'The injured coastline', produced by the Commonwealth House of Representatives Standing Committee on Environment, Recreation and the Arts (Crawford, 1992). It concludes, *inter alia*.

As the pace of development and population growth along the coastline accelerates, so do concerns about the consequences of such development and the effects of increased human activities upon one of our greatest resources and assets, the beautiful Australian coast.

The Committee recommended that the Australian government develop a national coastal zone management strategy in co-operation with state and local governments. As a preliminary to this, the Australian government at the time of writing (October 1992) was developing a policy framework to guide and focus the actions and activities of Commonwealth agencies in the coastal zone.

Two Commonwealth initiatives already in place for addressing conservation-development issues in the coastal zone are the Resource Assessment Commission and the Ocean Rescue 2000 program.

The Resource Assessment Commission (RAC) is a statutory authority established in 1989 to provide advice to the Australian government on options for the use of Australia's natural resources, taking into account both conservation and development values. Its current reference is to inquire into the future use of the coastal zone with particular reference to the integrated management of building, tourism, mariculture and associated development.

Ocean Rescue 2000 (OR 2000) is a 10-year Australian government initiative that has as its objective the conservation and sustainable use of the marine environment of Australia and its territories. Key elements of OR 2000 include the production of a *State of the marine environment* report, a national marine conservation strategy and a national system of marine protected areas.

References

Birrell, R. and Tonkin, S., 1992, *Constraints and opportunities for urban growth: Sydney and Perth compared*, Consultants' reports to the Population Issues Committee, Australian Government Publishing Service, Canberra

Centre for International Economics, 1988, 'The relationship between immigration and economic performance', in *Immigration: a commitment to Australia*, Consultants' reports to the Committee to Advise on Australia's Immigration Policies, Australian Government Publishing Service, Canberra

Cocks, K.D., 1992, *Use with care: managing Australia's natural resources in the 21st century*, New South Wales University Press, Sydney

Committee to Advise on Australia's Immigration Policies, 1988, *Immigration: a commitment to Australia*, Report of the Committee to Advise on Australia's Immigration Policies, Australian Government Publishing Service, Canberra

Commonwealth Environment Protection Agency, 1992, *Development of a national state of the environment reporting system*, Discussion paper, Australian Government Publishing Service, Canberra

Commonwealth of Australia, 1992, *Patterns of urban settlement: consolidating the future?* Report of the House of Representatives Standing Committee for Long-Term Strategies, Australian Government Publishing Service, Canberra

Crawford, D., 1992, ' "The injured coastline"—a parliamentary report on coastal protection in Australia', *Coastal Management*, **20**, 189–98

Daly, H., 1982, 'The steady-state economy: what, why, and how?' in R. Birrell, D. Hill and J. Stanley, (eds), *Quarry Australia?* Oxford University Press, Melbourne

de Groot, R.S., 1992, *Functions of nature: evaluation of nature in environmental planning, management and decision-making*, Wolters-Noordhoff, Groningen

Ecologically Sustainable Development Steering Committee, 1992, *Draft national strategy for ecologically sustainable development*, Australian Government Publishing Service, Canberra

Gifford, R.M., Kalma, J.D., Aston, A.R., and Millington, R.J., 1975, 'Biophysical constraints in Australian food production: implications for population policy', *Search* **6**(6): 212–23

Goot, M. 1988, *Immigrants and immigration: evidence and argument from the poll 1943–1987*, Consultant's report to Committee to Advise on Australia's Immigration Policies, Australian Government Publishing Service, Canberra

Joske, S., 1989, *The economics of immgration: who benefits?* Legislative Research Service, Commonwealth Parliament, Canberra

Kane, P., and Ruzicka, L.T., 1987, *Australian population trends and their social consequences*, Commission for the Future, Melbourne

McDonald, W.S., Cocks, K.D., Wood, N.H., Ive, J.R., and Yapp, G.A., (in press), 'The future population of Australia's coastal lands', *Australian Geographical Studies*

McGlynn, G., 1992, 'Population and Australia's resource endowment' in National Population Council, *Population issues and Australia's future: environment, economy and society*, Consultants' reports to the Population Issues Committee, Australian Government Publishing Service, Canberra

Millington, R.J., and Kalma, J.D., 1982, 'Biophysical resource constraints: an overview', in L. Birrell, D. Hill and Stanley (eds), *Quarry Australia?*, Oxford University Press, Melbourne

Mohideen, R., 1992, 'Immigration and the environment: is Australia overpopulated?, *Green Left Weekly*, No.72

National Population Council (NPC), 1992, *Population issues and Australia's future: environment, economy and society*, Final report of the Population Issues Committee, Australian Government Publishing Service, Canberra

Norman, N., and Meikle, K., 1985, *The economic effects of immigration on Australia*, Department of Immigration and Committee for Economic Development of Australia, Melbourne

World Commission on Environment and Development, 1987, *Our common future*, Oxford University Press, Oxford

19 Recent developments in rural policy and planning in Australasia

Geoff McDonald

National rural policy in Australia

Times are bad in the Australian bush at present. Very bad. But this is not unusual. Farm net incomes in 1991 were down 75 per cent from the previous year and the net value of rural production was virtually zero. Some of the present hardship results from long-term trends in the terms of trade, but 1991 was an especially bad year due to a combination of widespread drought and continued low world prices for agricultural commodities. The GATT 'Uruguay Round' of trade liberalisation talks, on which Australia placed so much hope, were stalled and the EEC and the United State continued to export subsidised commodities into traditional Australian export markets.

Conditions were especially poor for Australia's rural export mainstays, wool and wheat. A combination of poor seasons and low prices made 1991 one of the worst years for Australia's farmers ever. This came at a time when the whole economy was in recession and farm indebtedness was at an all-time high (see Table 19.1). The net value of rural production was approaching zero, not a great return on so much capital, land and human resources used to produce it. In a very lean year most cash income was needed to support farm families and very little was available for maintenance and even less for investment. There were some bright spots for rural industries, notably cotton and wine production, and farmers producing predominantly for the domestic market, horticulturalists and dairy farmers were not so affected.

The national policy response has been to campaign strongly on international trade liberalisation, to promote the value of microeconomic reform in industries serving the rural sector, to build a more competitive Australia by lowering tariffs for all sectors (which benefits rural exporters), to rely on structural adjustment programs especially for rural industries and to provide general welfare to families through the social security system. Most importantly, the policy response is to wait out the drought and market problems in the hope of improvements. This has always worked in the past.

Table 19.1 *Indicators of rural economic conditions in Australia, 1980–92*

Year	Gross farm income $m	Net farm income $m	Total farm debt $m	Net farm income as a % of debt	Terms of trade	Wheat price $/t	Wheat value of production $m	Wool price $/kg	Wool value of production $m
1980	11,788	3,143	3,769	28	106	153	16,188	393	713
1981	11,550	2,764	4,361	24	100	155	10,856	411	701
1982	12,644	575	4,721	5	88	159	16,360	432	717
1983	11,627	3,508	5,497	29	84	173	8,876	443	702
1984	15,435	2,882	6,017	17	84	164	22,016	485	728
1985	15,533	1,681	7,224	10	80	172	18,666	505	814
1986	15,515	2,513	7,950	15	73	168	16,167	533	830
1987	17,373	3,850	9,894	18	74	151	16,778	626	887
1988	20,143	4,200	10,741	15	82	164	12,442	1,003	919
1989	23,152	4,928	12,317	13	85	179	13,253	1,050	952
1990	23,744	3,580	13,585	10	77	195	14,214	739	1,102
1991	21,126	976	14,264	3	66	129	15,068	560	1,066
1992	20,257	1,247	n/a	n/a	67	189	10,602	610	880

Source: ABARE, 1992

The policy response to drought warrants special mention since it has returned to centre stage again with widespread drought in eastern Australia. Since European colonisation of Australia, farmers have struggled to come to terms with an erratic climate and to accept that most of the country is either desert or at least very dry. Now meteorologists and farmers understand why this is so. 'El Nino', a pattern of Pacific ocean currents that periodically deprives Australia of moist airflows, is understood in most circles where weather is a critical factor. But adjustment on the ground to these realities seems no closer. Rural policy concerned with natural disasters and especially drought is still a dominant issue and in 1991 and early 1992 El Nino was operating.

The Australian Parliament's Senate established a Standing Committee on Rural and Regional Affairs, consisting of members from the National Party (farmer party), Liberal Party (conservative urban) and Labor Party (right socialist), the first all-party committee to address rural and regional affairs since 1942. One of the terms of reference for the Standing Committee in 1991/92 was to prepare a national policy on drought. The outcome was the *First Report on a National Drought Policy: Appropriate Government Responses to the Recommendations of the Drought Policy Review Task Force* (Australia, Standing Committee). The report, tabled in July 1992, was controversial, (Australia. Parliament, 1992) since it focused on measures to be taken by the Commonwealth Government based on the principle that primary producers should take a self-reliant, risk management approach to drought. This was in contrast to past policy which considered drought as a natural disaster and routinely provided emergency relief to deal with each specific event.

The Commonwealth announced the new policy in August 1992:

The objectives of the Drought Policy are to:

—encourage primary producers and other sections of rural Australia to adopt self-reliant approaches to managing for climatic variability;
—maintain and protect Australia's agricultural and environmental resource base during periods of extreme climate stress; and
—ensure early recovery of agricultural and rural industries, consistent with long term sustainable levels. (Minister for Primary Industries, 1992, p. 1)

A key feature of the new drought policy is the provision of incentives to encourage primary producers to be better prepared for drought by storing a 'haystack of funds', fodder and water. The main instruments to achieve this include income equalisation from year to year under the tax act and the extension of full tax deductibility and tax credits for expenditures on drought proofing measures. The Income Equalisation Deposit Scheme allows primary producers to deposit up to $300,000 for use during periods of hardship with concessional tax provisions. The associated Farm Management Bond allows farmers to invest up to $80,000 also for use during periods of hardship (Minister for Primary Industries, 1992).

The policy also recognises that, in the limit and despite definitional difficulties, there are severe droughts which are beyond the capacities of self-reliant farmers and will require disaster relief. In extreme events, the nation's livestock breeding capacity and land resources are thus threatened, and recovery would be limited unless specific payments are available. Accordingly the Commonwealth Government allocated $166 million for rural adjustment including drought assistance for farmers in NSW and Queensland during 1991/2.

None the less a National (farmer) Party Senator from Queensland disatisfied with this response moved:

That the Senate
a. recognises the tragedy and devastation afflicting 21 drought declared shires, 3 drought declared part shires and 1,026 drought declared holdings throughout Queensland;
b. calls on the Government to provide urgent funding to meet immediate fodder and adjustment costs;
c. urges the Government to adopt long-term strategies to combat drought, including workable Income Equalisation Deposits Scheme and the re-instatement of 'severe drought' to the National Disaster Relief Scheme; and
d. recognises the magnificent fortitude and resilience displayed by the people of rural Queensland, particularly in the St. George, Dirranbandi and Balonne areas, in their fight against drought. (O'Chee, 1992)

The debate thus goes on as to what constitutes a severe drought and what is an appropriate national response. At least now the Commonwealth Government is focusing on the requirements of farmers who are forced to deal with erratic production and economic conditions as being the heart of the problem and that while disaster relief will always be needed, structural adjustment is long since overdue. Governments at all levels must set appropriate economic incentives to encourage such adjustments.

Separately from drought policies the Commonwealth Government is implementing a new Rural Adjustment Scheme (RAS) to help farmers become more efficient and productive. In normal circumstances, farmers will be able to obtain incentives through interest subsidies on commercial finance or grants to finance farm improvement and development, and support services such as training, farm appraisal and planning. Eligibility for these forms of assistance will be based on proven sustainable long-term profitability of their farms. Funding will be on a shared Commonwealth-State basis. There are also funds to assist some farmers to leave farming altogether, including training programs and financial assessment. While most programs are based on individual farms, the RAS provides for regional adjustment and development where the necessary investments involve all farmers in a district, as for example in a Landcare project. The scheme provides for 'carry-on' finance, funds for struggling farmers who are viable in the longer term but need low-cost finance to buy fodder, stock or to meet the costs of crop planting for example.

The Standing Committee on Rural and Regional Affairs also addressed a seemingly minor policy issue, labour relations in the Australian shearing industry. At issue are the working conditions and solidarity of the country's oldest union, the shearers: a symbol of the union movement. Immigrant shearers from New Zealand are working for different wages and conditions, creating tension in the bush between the union and the graziers. The issue is simmering along and raising questions about the free flow of people between Australia and New Zealand and the industrial relations system generally.

The major economic debate in Federal politics at this time concerns trade policy, with both major parties resolved to reduce tariffs, and in the case of the Liberal Party, to zero by the year 2000. Free trade may in the long term benefit farmers by making the cost of manufactured inputs lower (for example vehicles and machinery) and reducing living costs (for example lower clothing prices). But farmers are in a dilemma: many rural industries are suffering from subsidised competition from the EEC and other countries. Industries such as the wheat and sugar industries have been most affected by distorted world markets and have pressed strongly, if unsuccessfully, for policy assistance. The sugar industry has argued for the retention of the $76 per tonne tariff on sugar imports and the wheat industry has campaigned for the reintroduction of a guaranteed minimum price scheme.

Forest policy

There were two major events at the national level affecting forest policy: first, the release of the Final Report of the Forest and Timber Inquiry by the Resources Assessment Commission (RAC) and second, the release of the Forest Conservation and Development Bill (resource security) by the Commonwealth. A coherent national forest policy is thus slowly taking shape.

The RAC report (1992b), under the chair of Justice Stewart (accompanied by two special commissioners, David James, an economist, and Ian Noble, an ecologist) required two years and cost an estimated $25 million. The Inquiry was charged with the responsibility of reporting in an objective manner on forest policy which had become a serious division in the community about the use of public native forests in particular. The Commission had a twelve-person secretariat in Canberra devoted to the Inquiry, and received expert advice from 33 consultancy reports, 550 submissions and 423 witnesses as the Commission travelled around the country.

The Report dealt with many controversial questions and reached conclusions including: (a) that forest overcutting is a greater cause of timber shortages than conservation restrictions, since the timber harvesting rate in native forests is not sustainable in many districts; (b) that tree clearing on agricultural land is a significant threat to the survival of some forest types; (c) that there is a need for timber mills to be restructured to process wood from sources other than old growth forests; (d) that the extraordinary expansion of the plantation sector will be the dominant source of supply of wood products in Australia in the future; and (e) that there is a need to take a national approach to conservation so that priorities for reservation can be identified rationally and nationally rather than site by site.

Following the release of the RAC report a Draft National Forest Policy Statement was prepared by state and territory officials, responding to many of the recommendations. The key elements of the proposed National Forest policy are summarised in Table. 19.2.

One of the most controversial issues facing the Inquiry was the question of resource security—the long-term guarantee of wood supply to industry. The Commonwealth Government drafted the Forest Conservation and Development Bill 1991 to provide resource security under conditions prescribed in the Bill (Australia, Parliament, 1991);

—where the investment is larger than $100 million and the project is directed at import replacement or export to encourage capital investment in wood processing industries.
—on the completion of an appropriate assessment process.

The process was to involve three parties, the Commonwealth, state and the forest products enterprise. Agreement between all three is required.

The Bill was introduced to the Commonwealth Parliament in June 1991. Progress in the refinement of this Bill was slow because of the tension it created between industry and conservationists and within both Labour Government and opposition ranks. The Bill was defeated in this parliament with the concurrence of the government and the Bill lapsed. The heart of this debate was industry claims that lack of reliable long-term access to wood resources is discouraging investment. Conservationists on the other hand are concerned that such legislation would commit governments to the logging of previously unlogged forest and the more intensive use of current wood production forests. In effect, this proposal has opened the whole forestry debate up again. It is clear that the conservationists want logging of all unlogged native forests in Australia to stop and future emphasis placed on plantation forests, especially increasing the area of native species plantations rather than pines.

Table 19.2 *The draft National Forest Policy—key elements*

1. Conservation	• Adequate nature conservation reserves • Protection of old growth forest and wilderness through a transition strategy • Ecologically sustainable forest management • Adequate forest protection
2. Wood production and industry development	• Promotion of efficient use and value-adding industries • Structural assistance and improving international competitiveness • Improving employment opportunities and labour productivity • Better wood pricing and end-use allocation
3. Integrated decision-making and management	• Decision-making processes as set out in the Inter-Governmental Agreement on the Environment • Integrated conservation and commercial management • Development of regional management plans
4. Private native forests	• Development of Codes of Practice • Provision of incentives to encourage conservation • Promotion of Landcare groups • Land clearing controls
5. Plantations	• Reviewing taxation treatment of plantations • Tree breeding and research program • Simplified approvals processes
6. Tourism and recreation	• Developing an eco-tourism strategy • Improving marketing and visitor facilities

Source: Standing Committee for Forestry of the Australian and New Zealand Environment Council, 1992

The frontier for native forest use in Australia is gradually closing as the key decisions about the future use of most of the forests are made: for example, some have been listed on the World Heritage List; others are protected in national parks; and yet other lands are set aside for future multiple use including timber production. This is not to say that society's attitudes to conservation and development, multiple use and other issues will not change again and reopen the debate about the use of the main forest regions of Tasmania, SE NSW, Fraser Island, North Queensland and the Southern west of Western Australia.

The new Commonwealth Environmental Protection Agency which administers the Commonwealth Environmental Protection (Impact of Proposals) Act (CEPIP Act) is now involved in the forest use decision-making process. So under the lapsed Bill, an EIA in compliance with the CEPIP Act would have been required on every major project requiring resource guarantees. The main thrust of the EIA proposal was to ensure that conservation values were taken into account in forest decisions; values that are or would be established by the Australian Heritage Commission, in consultation with a wide network of other organisations and with other Acts making the process very complex.

Ecologically Sustainable Development

Australia has responded very actively to the international call for sustainable development. In 1984 the Commonwealth Government prepared a 'National Conservation Strategy' in response to the first World Conservation Strategy. Unfortunately, the National Conservation Strategy was never implemented in any meaningful way, although it focused the country's attention on the new commitment of the national government to address environmental issues. Some states also produced state conservation strategies with a greater chance of implementation, although there was still a general feeling that these strategies were only exhortations without any great policy or statutory significance.

Subsequently, in 1989 Prime Minister Hawke released a major statement entitled *Our Country Our Future* (Hawke, 1989) in response to the Brundtland Report *Our Common Future* (World Commission on Environment and Development, 1987). This report again was mainly an issues document but it did identify priorities, especially land degradation, and led directly to the establishment of the Landcare Programme of co-operative soil conservation throughout the country. It also commenced a process of determining the long-term requirements of 'ecologically sustainable development'. It established a process because (in typical Hawke fashion) it was based on a 'summit' of industry, union and conservation organisations to formulate strategies for achieving sustainable development and for integrating environmental considerations into the decision-making process. This was known as the 'ESD process'.

The ESD process commenced with the publication of a background paper which defined the issues and initiated the detailed investigations (Australia, 1990). The Discussion Paper defined and elaborated the five major principles of ESD to be:

—integrating economic and environmental goals in policies and activities
—ensuring that environmental assets are appropriately valued
—providing for equity within and between generations
—dealing cautiously with risk and irreversibility
—recognising the global dimension (Australia, 1990, p. 7)

Following a period of comment on the Discussion Paper, nine Working Groups were established to consider the implementation of ESD in those sectors of the economy with major impacts on the environment: agriculture, energy production, land use, fisheries, forest use, manufacturing, mining, tourism and transport.

Each of the nine Working Groups prepared a very substantial draft report which was 'to identify the most important problem areas, set some priorities for achieving changes desired, develop solutions that meet both environmental and economic goals, and to propose time frames for change that take account of the Government's social justice policies and role in the world economy,' (Australia, 1992, p. vi). Cross-sectoral issues such as competition for land between sectors, land management, marine problems, waste management, biodiversity, global change and others were included in additional reports.

Approximately 2,500 pages of final reports summarise this major exercise in community consultation in policy formulation. It is not possible to convey the breadth of these reports, each of which adopted a very broad framework for each sector, touching on both economic and environmental issues and then problems of management. For the rural sector, the agriculture, forest-use and cross-sectoral reports are most important.

The agriculture report identifies a very wide range of actions necessary to achieve ESD from the perspective of that sector alone as shown in Table 19.3. A similar breadth and diversity of recommendations came from each of the other eight sectoral groups and then additional ones from the cross-sectoral reports. Attention is given in each report to the timing, direct financial costs and responsibilities for implementation of each of the recommendations.

The ESD process was a comprehensive effort to come to terms with the most complex and long-term issues of rural policy. Now it is the task for rural policy-makers to accept the recommendations and implement them. The implementation step will be difficult. There are enough issues there to give any government indigestion, especially given the problems surrounding two relatively simple pieces of policy in the same year, Resource Security and Drought Policy. The progress of rural policy may be slow. One can only hope that now it is heading in the right direction.

Blue-green algae

As if by some divine intervention to reinforce the importance of ESD, in late 1991, some of Australia's largest and most important rivers, notably the Murray-Darling system and its tributaries, had severe outbreaks of blue-green algae (*Nodularia, Anabaena, Oscillatoria* and *Microcystis* spp). Blamed on increasing nutrient content in farm runoff and to a lesser extent on urban sewerage effluents, both of which stimulate the toxic blue-green

Table 19.3 *ESD priorities for agriculture*

Group Approaches
2. * Extend Landcare
    To resources management in
    general
    Additional resources for technical
    support
    Seek alternative sources of funds
  * Revise delivery programs

Planning
3. Strengthen Integrated Catchment
   Management Plans
4. Support whole-farm approach to
   planning
   Promote benefits of planning
  * Assistance to meet 50% of the
    cost of plans
  * Ready availability of resources to
    assist planning
5. Government Review Project
   Approval Procedures

Crown Lease Land
6. Review lease terms and conditions

Management of Pests
7. * Allocation of resources for pest
    management, control and research
    Development of management
    plans for kangaroos

**Vegetation Removal and Nature
Conservation**
8. Vegetation Conservation
  * States review regulatory
    procedures and provide
    appropriate sanctions
9. Support for use of privately
   owned land for multiple purposes

Direct Incentives
10.* Extended assistance for farm
    improvements

Water Use and Quality
11. Education, management,
    development of guidelines
  * Water pricing
  * Transferability of entitlements
    Review allocation and supply
    system
    Review of public funding
    Development of quality guidelines

Chemicals
12. * Government to act on Senate
    report
13. Testing
    Review NRS and MBS
14. Monitoring and Research
    More information on toxicology
    Information on effects on human
    health
    Assess effects of minimum tillage
    herbicides
    Integrated Pest Management
    Develop methods for field testing
    residues
15. Setting of Targets

Education
16. ESD to be incorporated into
    curricula
  * Review of national standards
  * Provision of funding for course
    development

Extension
17. * Training of group facilitators
18. * Financial support for group
    organisers
19. Support for the development of
    decision support packages

Research
20. Research organisation to adopt
    ESD in their strategic planning
21. Integrated approach to research
    R&D Corps to adopt ESD
    principles
    Interdisciplinary research which
    is user driven
    Include interdisciplinary research
    in funding guidelines

Institutional Arrangements
22. Government and Semi-
    Government Agencies
    Review programs to ensure they
    meet ESD guide-lines
    Incorporate ESD criteria in
    corporate goals
23. * Integration of resources
    management responsibilities of
    Ministerial councils
24. * Review project approval
    procedures

Table 19.3

Global Warming
25. Assessment of policy measures to limit Australian agricultures contribution to greenhouse gases
26. Identification of possible agricultural management responses to lessen emissions
Reporting and Review
27. Introduce 5-year review to monitor progress in achieving ESD

Note: *Very high priority recommendations

Source: Australia, 1992, pp 35–41

phytoplankton, the blooms expanded alarmingly, depleting oxygen levels and even causing eutrophication in streams and producing toxic levels of waste which threatened water supplies and aquatic life. Water consumers can treat the problem in the short term with copper sulphate but no easy policy solutions are evident, other than long-term changes in land management practices and in waste disposal as suggested in the ESD process. Periods of higher rainfall and river flows will diminish the problems temporarily only for it to reoccur, perhaps more extensively next time unless long-term land management changes are made (Anon, 1992, Hart, 1992).

This highly visible evidence of land and water mismanagement in rural Australia served to underline the importance of Commonwealth programs such as Landcare and its sibling, Integrated Catchment Management. The Commonwealth will continue to provide substantial funds to these programs, although their implementation is largely in the hands of the states.

Conclusion

Despite the rapidly changing distribution of powers in Australia, the states still have a dominant influence over rural planning matters and the remainder of this review discusses each state in turn.

Geoff McDonald

New South Wales

With New South Wales in the grip of recession, rural policy and planning has become something of a battlefield for the various interests involved with the physical environment of rural regions. In particular, lines have become firmly drawn between the 'development' and 'conservation' lobbies. For example, powerful lobby groups such as the Coalition for Economic Advancement representing timber and mining interests have confronted conservation organisations which have become increasingly effective in exploiting legal processes. At the state governmental level both the Labour opposition and the minority conservative government have grown increasingly uncertain as to how far they should go in supporting job creation at the expense of environmental values.

The state government has given little leadership to the parties involved, for while it has preached the ideals of ecologically sustainable development, regional economic growth and increased community participation, it has at the same time given active policy support to private sector logging of old growth native forests and mining developments in reserved Crown Lands. In its 1991 budget it also foreshadowed a further reduction of 18,500 public jobs by 1996 mainly in State Rail and community services to rural regions; and increasingly intervened in the planning decisions of local councils, generally in the interests of 'fast tracking' new developments.

Developments in the planning system

Notwithstanding that its motives for this may be uncertain, the state government has certainly demonstrated a commitment to reviewing much of what constitutes the 'planning system'. First, during the latter half of 1991 the government issued a 'draft exposure' Bill which, as well as widening the scope of local government, also sought more efficient management of and public accountability for the operations of local government. For physical planning the Bill offered the prospect of integrating planning, building, subdivision and environmental approvals (many local councils have already restructured their building and development control departments into 'environmental services' departments) as well as more effective ways of recouping the external costs of development from developers. Second, the state also commenced a public review of planning as it operates under the Environmental Planning and Assessment Act 1979 (EPA Act). Third, the discussion paper *Modernising the Planning System in NSW* foreshadows a simplification of development control and a clearer definition of the roles and powers of local and state government departments. Fourth, the state began an internal review of the National Parks and Wildlife Service (NPWS) and its 1974 Act to resolve some of the conflicts which have arisen in the Service between the roles of protecting wildlife/aboriginal artefacts and of managing various kinds of nature conservation reserve and recreation areas.

It is interesting that in all these reviews the government has said much about a greater role for local governments and yet at the same time has increased its level of intervention by Ministers (of Agriculture and Public Works as well as of Planning) to overturn or take over planning decisions at local level, for example:(a) a 1992 policy announcement that the Minister of Planning will take over determining applications for large and/ or 'environmentally sensitive' developments; (b) establishment of an Environmental Protection Authority with sweeping powers to override local councils on matters to do with air, water and land quality (one of the EPA's first actions was to prevent local use of algicides to destroy toxic algae blooms in inland and coastal rivers but at the same time relaxing the licensing of effluent; and (c) a new Mining Act which, although it does streamline the approvals process for mining and exploration and strengthens provisions for environmental protection, keeps the approvals process in the hands of central government.

In addition to these reviews the State government has also restructured most of its Crown Land management agencies into one Department of Conservation and Land Management (which incorporates a downscaled Soil Conservation Service, much to the anger of farmers), with the possibilities of other such agencies being brought into this Department.

As might be expected, the planning profession has reacted with suspicion towards these reviews, acknowledging the need for review and reform but questioning the government's motives and indeed its responsibility for creating many of the needs. At the same time Parliament's own Committee on State Development continues to question the effectiveness of the government's approach to development control in coastal areas.

Other Procedural Developments

From the observer's viewpoint the most interesting procedural developments have been those which arose out of a decision by the Land and Environment Court which castigated the Forestry Commission for failing to observe obligations under (a) the National Parks and Wildlife Act (NPW Act) to protect endangered species; and (b) under the Heritage Act to care for natural heritage (the Commission had relied on an interpretation by the Minister of Planning, deemed to be wrong, that the Heritage Act applied only to cultural heritage) when it decided to allow logging in an old growth native forest (the Chaelundi State Forest).

The government's response to the Court's decision was to draw up a regulation to exempt government agencies from the requirements of the NPW Act. This regulation was however disallowed by Parliament which instead passed a Private Member's Bill as the Fauna Protection (Endangered Species) Act. This Act, with its related regulations, has *inter alia*: empowered the NPWS temporarily to stop activities which may endanger endangered species; required a Fauna Impact Statement in cases where a species may be subject to *significant* endangerment but this possibility is not adequately dealt with by an EIS; and led to amendments of the EPA Act which require in the determination of a development application a consideration of whether the development may endanger fauna, habitat or species of flora.

These developments have led to a flurry of activity particularly in instrumentalities such as the Forest Commission and Electricity Commission (both of which have been taken to task by the Courts for flouting responsibilities under planning legislation) to develop rigorous methodologies for assessing 'endangerment' and the planning 'significance' of same. They have been followed by actions by the Director of NPWS to stop logging in several forests, and by the Heritage Council to impose an interim conservation order on parts of the Chaelundi Forest, both against the wishes of the Minister of Planning! But—illustrating the nature of relationships between planning, policies and politics—they have also led to the opposition Labor Party backing off from moves for further legislative protection of old growth State forests, and the creation of new National Parks because of the perceived threats to timber industry jobs.

Another important development has been the government's requirement that local councils detail procedures under which they intend to exact contributions from developers (in respect of new or improved services and amenities which are related to new developments) under s.94 of the EPA Act. The Department of Planning has produced a draft Guide on this and local councils are expected to have their procedures embodied in development control plans by the end of 1992.

A number of other developments are interesting because they reflect issues which have arisen out of the recessionary environment. For example, the Department of Planning: (a) has relaxed requirements relating to dual and multiple occupancies to allow more affordable alternatives to conventional housing and also flexibility in developments such as for tourism: (b) now requires development consent for relocatable dwellings in caravan parks which are to be used for long-term occupancy (this reflects significant increases in caravan dwelling, and the greater security of occupancy which caravan dwellers now have: (c) has advised councils to be sparing in defining special Environmental Protection zones because of the restrictions which these are seen (by some) to impose on agriculture, forestry and mining: (d) has urged councils to use mediation procedures so as to hasten the approval of developments and reduce a growing use of the Land and Environment Court as the final arbiter of controversial development applications: and (e) has allowed a particular council (Bathurst City) to institute a local Environmental Planning instrument which gives an illegal development (a transport depot) legal status for five years to gain time for it to relocate.

Conclusion

It is apparent that the policy and planning instruments which have been developed over the last fifteen years in NSW are affording much of the protection to environmental resources and qualities which was intended and that this is not always to the pleasure of government or private entrepreneurs who are currently rather hamstrung in curbing the effects of this regulation in rural areas in a time of recession.

Nevertheless, the regulatory emphasis in policy and planning continues to deprive rural areas of the strategic guidance which they require. For instance, first, there is still no public discussion of options being studied to deal with implications of the Sydney region literally running out of developable land about 2006; second, the state government procrastinates about proposals for an upgraded Sydney-Melbourne and a new inland Brisbane-Melbourne rail link; and third, a search for a rural location for the disposal of intractable waste which has taken 4 years and cost $2m, has now been restarted from scratch because the earlier studies arrived at no politically acceptable conclusions.

In the absence of strategic guidance much substantive planning at local and regional levels has become based on little more than the expectation that present trends will continue. This planning is reflected in recent studies of settlement strategies for the pressured Lower Hunter and North Coast regions as well as, locally, in a review being conducted by Bathurst City of a 1974 structure plan.

Rural policy and planning in NSW in 1991/92 seems to have exhibited much activity and little direction!

Ian Bowie

Victoria

Undoubtedly, the most significant development in planning in Victoria over the past twelve months was the release in April, 1992 of *A Place to Live*, the state's urban development strategy to the year 2031. The strategy has major implications for both metropolitan Melbourne and the rural parts of the state. Otherwise it has been a year of consolidation and review, although two new pieces of legislation, the Heritage Rivers Act, and the National Parks (Wilderness) Act, were introduced.

As noted in last year's report, it is forecast that more than 1.5 million additional people will have to be accommodated by the year 2031, which will require an estimated 845,000 new dwellings. Four possible options were put forward for discussion: a compact, more densely populated Melbourne; twin cities, with a second city being developed on the south-eastern fringe of Melbourne; a series of 'new towns' surrounding Melbourne; and the growth of eight country towns.

The development of 'new towns' was rejected, but elements of the other options appear in the strategy, together with an advocacy for higher densities in existing urban areas, which it is estimated would absorb up to one-third of the projected population increase.

Four underlying objectives guided the formulation of the strategy:

—the need to curb the outward sprawl of Melbourne;
—the need to make better use of the state's regional assets;
—the need to make development ecologically sustainable; and
—the need to improve the planning and design of urban centres to integrate employment opportunities and transport more effectively.

It is stated in the strategy that two metropolitan activity centres will be developed, one centred on Dandenong on the south-eastern edge of Melbourne and the other in the north-western suburbs, with both offering opportunities and services similar to those available in central Melbourne. The development of these centres will have implications for the nearby rural areas.

Urban growth in the short term will continue to be focused in the three designated metropolitan growth corridors—Plenty, Werribee, Southeastern—but once these have been developed, growth will be directed to a 'Central Crescent' embracing Melbourne's northern and western fringes and the regional centres of Geelong, Bendigo and Ballarat. It is recognised that the regional centres will not prosper unless there are good job opportunities and good transport and communication links. Export-oriented industries (e.g. computer hardware, food processing) will be encouraged and mass rapid transport links will be developed between the centres and with Melbourne.

Unlike the urban strategy, an anticipated rural land-use strategy has yet to appear. However, in response to concerns expressed in submissions to *The Review of Rural Land Use in Victoria*, tighter controls will be introduced to prevent development in remote unserviceable urban fringe areas, and new rural subdivision policies will be introduced. A state of the environment report, *Agriculture and Victoria's Environment*, due to be released by the Office of the Commission for the Environment before the end of 1992, may raise other concerns and issues.

There have been a number of statutory developments over the past twelve months. The new Mineral Resources Development Act, which streamlines administrative and planning procedures, was proclaimed in November, 1991. The vegetation clearing controls, which were described in last year's report, were finally passed by both Houses of Parliament with only minor modifications, and a number of additions have been made to the lists of threatened tax and plant communities contained in the schedules to the Flora and Fauna Conservation Act. The lists now contain 165 entries and action statements have been prepared for 31 of these. Under the Act, the Director-General of the Department of Conservation and Environment can enter into co-operative agreements with other agencies. The first such agreement relating to the conservation of the Yarra gum (*Eucalyptus yarraensis*) was recently signed with the Shire of Morwell. It is hoped that this will be the first of many such agreements. Rural cemeteries, for example, fifty of which are known to have significant conservation values, could be protected by future agreements with shire councils.

In addition, two new acts of parliament were proclaimed in mid 1992: the National Parks (Wilderness) Act and the Heritage Rivers Act. The former adds significant areas to the existing Big Desert Wilderness Park in the north-west of the state, creates a new Wabba Wilderness Park in Gippsland and introduces 19 wilderness zones to existing national parks. The wilderness parks and zones will remain undeveloped and there will be no vehicular access, a point of contention with a number of recreation groups. In addition, 21 'remote and natural' areas are identified on public land throughout the state where managers will be required to prevent the degradation of the 'natural condition or appearance' of the land.

The Heritage Rivers Act lists 18 rivers or sections of rivers and 26 natural catchments which are to be managed for the protection of their intrinsic values, for recreation and for education. Management plans for each river and catchment must be prepared within five years.

Other initiatives by the government include a review of Melbourne's water supply needs, and the preparation of a Landcare plan. If Melbourne's increasing demand for water continues, the existing storage system will be inadequate by the early years of the next century. A review panel has advised the government that a range of water conservation measures can extend the life of the existing supply to the year 2020, after which additional supplies will probably be required. With this in mind, the panel recommended that a number of 'cross-divide' diversions be investigated, a recommendation that will probably be opposed by the rural communities downstream of the potential intakes. With respect to Landcare, the government released in February 1992 its *Decade of the Landcare Plan* which sets the framework for the rehabilitation of degraded areas and the continuing development of sustainable land management systems. Its goal, in keeping with the nation-wide program, is to achieve ecologically sustainable land use by the year 2000.

Administratively, there have been no changes of any significance over the past twelve months, but if, as widely predicted, the Opposition wins the state election in October, an extensive rearrangement of portfolios can be expected.

Colin Leigh

South Australia

The major event in the South Australian rural planning arena during the last year has been the release of the third and presumably final consultation draft of the Mount Lofty Ranges Management Plan. The long-running policy review for this important region, which forms the bulk of the rural-urban fringe around metropolitan Adelaide (shown in Figure 19.1 by the thick black line), was mentioned briefly in Volume II. p. 258, which described something of the nature of the interests which characterise the Mount Lofty Ranges namely an established horticulture industry in an isolated high rainfall area; rapidly expanding country townships; rural living/hobby farm development in the commuter belt around Adelaide; commercial softwood forestry and quarrying activities; areas of landscape, nature conservation, tourism and recreation significance; and a high bush-fire hazard; all set within the main water catchment of Adelaide Entren-ched 'development rights' expectations (Foyel and Houston, 1992) to add a further level of complexity.

The review process sought to mediate a balanced outcome from this situation by instigating an integrated and consultative approach involving all major players from state and local government, industry and community groups. This has resulted in a strategy-oriented plan which emphasises: enhancement and protection of natural and cultural characteristics; management of water resources on an ecologically sustainable basis; and protection and enhancement of commercial primary production (Department of Environment and Planning, 1992). Key features of the plan are:

—Regional Management Authority to perform an overview role, assuming some of the development control functions of local government (21 councils) and providing advice and co-ordination for regional planning and natural resources management policy;
—redesignation of a Water Supply Protection Zone (WSPZ) and a Primary Production Zone (PPZ) which are intended to provide a policy context more conducive to water quality and agriculture respectively;
—heavily curtailed opportunities for residential development in townships as well as rural areas, particularly in the WSPZ and to a lesser extent in the PPZ;
—integration of novel measures into the planning scheme, with resource management mechanisms such as land capability analysis, peer-based codes of practice for water and effluent management, and farm/property plans now having a role in development control considerations; and
—a local variation on a transferable development rights scheme to shift development potential away from sensitive water resource areas and to compensate affected landowners.

Despite the time taken to develop this plan, the proposals represent, at

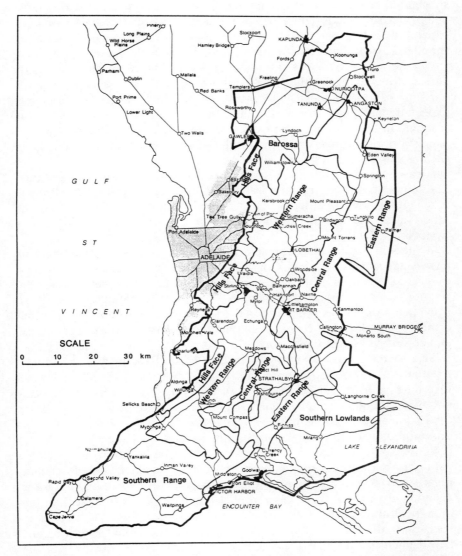

Figure 19.1   *Area subject to the Mount Lofty Ranges Management Plan showing proximity to the metropolitan area and major bio-physical character units*
Source: Mount Lofty Ranges Review, Government of South Australia

least symbolically, a significant and progressive departure both in philosophy and process from the current arrangements. However, a number of substantial problems have already been identified (Bunker and Houston, 1992). These include concerns over the method of application of land capability analysis and transferable development rights, concepts which in the South Australian context are new and untried; the failure of the plan to set out a convincing strategy to secure or improve the position of agriculture and agricultural land resources; and the generally clumsy handling of a major policy shift which has radically altered development expectations. Given the institutional and professional neglect of rural planning in this state until now and the consequent lack of expertise and sophistication of analysis where rural matters are concerned, difficulties such as this were perhaps to be expected.

Away from the specific issues of the rural-urban fringe, other significant developments include the proposals to establish an Environmental Protection Authority (EPA), mirroring the trend towards this type of body in other states and at the Commonwealth level, and a Natural Resources Council (NRC).

While still in the formative stages, the EPA proposal seems likely to have significant consequences for water resources management throughout the state. In particular, those functions concerned with water quality that require licences (i.e. establishment of water quality standards, issuing of licences to point-source polluting activities, monitoring/auditing and enforcement) seem likely to be subsumed by the EPA in an effort to centralise and co-ordinate most of the state's environmental protection laws.

This seems a curious move after the Water Resources Act brought together water quality (pollution) and quantity (use) considerations for the first time in a formal sense only two years ago, and appears to be a potential hindrance to integrated management of the resource. It will leave the Engineering and Water Supply Department to deal with issues of water diversion and use, along with those quality matters linked to non-point pollution sources, which by their nature cannot be licensed.

Furthermore, although standards and policies are not likely to change greatly with this shift in administrative responsibility, it will be interesting to follow the impact that a high profile, regulatory body like an EPA has on agricultural activities and practices in a number of key water resource districts. Critical here will be the balance between remote monitoring and enforcement on the one hand and active, consultation and involvement with land-user groups on the other, as has been emphasized by the EWS in recent years.

The Natural Resources Council, a high-level advisory body on resource management policy matters that includes representation of government departments, industry and community groups, is already operating. Its essential role is to overview resource management generally, with particular emphasis on cross-sectoral issues that arise on a regional or state-wide basis. It was felt that existing policy advisory councils and committees for specific natural resource areas (e.g. soil conservation, native vegetation, water resources) have not been able to address properly cross-sectoral matters in the past.

The NRC is likely to have a central, if not instigating, role in a variety of rural planning and resource management matters such as: management and allocation of Crown Lands; preparation of regional management plans; assessment and restructuring of marginal agricultural areas, rising groundwater levels and associated salinisation problems; alienation of agricultural land; and outback tourism management. Against the background of difficulties encountered in the Mount Lofty Ranges Management Plan, the formation of this body may be an important development in raising the status of rural planning in South Australia.

In the other key resource management areas of soil conservation and native vegetation, legislation and policy remains essentially as reported in Volume I; however brief progress reports are appropriate. On the soil conservation front, there are now 26 soil conservation district boards in place providing almost complete coverage of the state's pastoral and agricultural areas: a rapid growth from the 7 that existed only 5 years ago and no doubt due in part to the Department of Agriculture's 'Decade of Landcare' program. These boards are all charged with producing a district-wide soil conservation plan which embraces land capability principles and articulates land management guidelines for various rural activities by 1995.

While this approach to soil conservation and Landcare was greeted enthusiastically at its inception in 1989, based as it is on a positive and active role for landholders, recent times have seen a slowing in progress towards the new regime. In particular, the complex process involved in preparing these plans, given that there is no proven model to follow, appears to have become a significant hurdle in some districts. It would seem that some focused R&D effort is necessary to clarify, in conceptual and operational terms, the process of developing soil conservation district plans. In this context, the relative lack of resources available to boards has proved a frustration.

Additionally, some boards are being requested to play a proxy community consultation role in a number of contexts besides that of the soil conservation district (eg. regarding native vegetation and water resources management and in comprehensive planning exercises like the Mount Lofty Ranges Review).

'All of this is apparently testing the goodwill of board members in their voluntary capacity and overwhelming others with the complexity of demands being placed on them. It suggests attention needs to be given to clarifying the nature of the district boards' role and, depending on this outcome, corresponding commitments made to their funding and support staff needs' (Department of Environment and Planning, 1992).

Regarding native vegetation management, a minor legislative change recently heralded what is effectively the end of broadscale clearance of native vegetation in this state and with it the era of agricultural expansion that has prevailed since European settlement began. Although this follows a period of almost a decade during which clearance required approval of the Native Vegetation Management Authority, symbolically it will demand a new attitude to rural development amongst the farming community.

An interesting development in the northern arid pastoral areas is the move to restrict tourists to designated public roads. Previously all parts of pastoral leases (approx. 50 per cent of the state) were theoretically accessible to the public by virtue of being Crown Land. This situation has long been contested by lessees who have argued that visitors and campers place an undue onus of responsibility on them, invade their privacy, disturb stock and damage property. The local environmental lobby also suggest that with increasing ownership of four-wheel drive recreational vehicles, this degree of freedom has had significant wilderness, nature conservation and land degradation impacts. Whether the new restriction on movement will cause these concerns to be alleviated remains to be seen. Indeed concentrating the tourist presence may serve to increase locally some environmental impacts. The consequences for the tourism sector of the outback economy are also unclear.

Peter Houston

Western Australia

Three particularly significant developments in 'policy and rural planning' in Western Australia over the past 12 months have been: the presentation of the State Parliamentary Select Committee into Land Conservation's *Final Report* (Select Committee, 1991); the release of the Department of Conservation and Land Management's controversial draft nature and forestry conservation strategies; and the review of the state's 1986 Environmental Protection Act.

The Select Committee's *Final Report* is based on two years' work and three major discussion papers totalling 1,200 pages. In their Executive Summary, the Committee states that it

has been shocked to learn of the extent and severity of the deterioration of Western Australia's environment ... The primary cause ... is the development and use of the land for primary production. (Select Committee, 1991, p. 7)

Figure 19.2 graphically summarises their findings. Further, the estimated annual loss of production from the area likely to be affected by secondary salinity 30–50 years from now is $952 million—an order of magnitude greater than any of the other estimated costs. Of the more than 7,000 vascular plant species recorded in the state, 1,024 are rare or threatened,

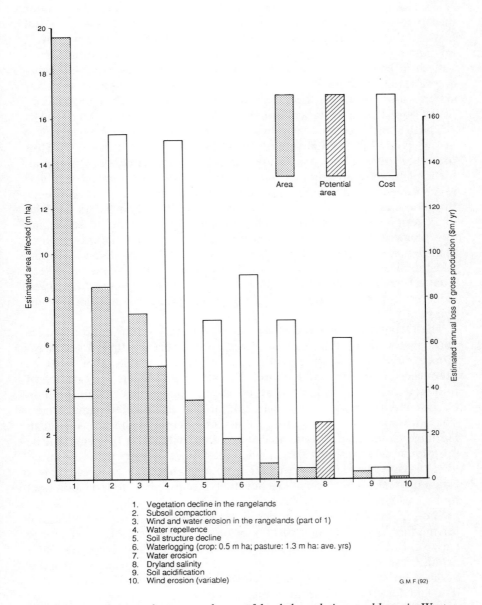

Legend:
- Area
- Potential area
- Cost

1. Vegetation decline in the rangelands
2. Subsoil compaction
3. Wind and water erosion in the rangelands (part of 1)
4. Water repellence
5. Soil structure decline
6. Waterlogging (crop: 0.5 m ha; pasture: 1.3 m ha: ave. yrs)
7. Water erosion
8. Dryland salinity
9. Soil acidification
10. Wind erosion (variable)

G.M.F. (92)

Figure 19.2   *Estimated extent and cost of land degradation problems in Western Australia*
Source: Select Committee, 1991, Table 1

with 83 per cent of those from the south-west. The area of forest is estimated to have been reduced by half, and fungal diseases pose major threats to the remaining indigenous flora. More than two-thirds of coastal plain wetlands have been damaged or destroyed. Some 60 per cent of medium-sized mammal species have disappeared from the central wheat-belt since European settlement commenced in 1829. Finally, 'the highly deteriorated condition of the majority of the State's waterways and river systems south of the Pastoral Region provides graphically visible evidence of the poor health of the environment' (Select Committee, 1991, p. 11).

The Report's recommendations are in three Parts: (I) 'What needs to be achieved?'; (II) 'What support measures are needed?'; and (III) 'How to implement the land conservation strategy?'. Part I contains proposals for implementing sustainable land-use systems, managing for drought as a regular event, undertaking reforestation and revegetation, and improving the economic performance of rural enterprises. Part II considers the roles of government and the community in land conservation, research and development, the provision of education and extension in natural resource management, a scheme for purchasing and rehabilitating degraded lands, and the necessary financial and legislative support. It remains to be seen what actions will be taken by the state government to implement the Select Committee's recommendations. To date the indications are not encouraging.

The Department of Land Management's (CALM) draft nature forestry and conservation strategies were released in February 1992 for a three-month public discussion period, after which a ten-year plan is to be produced for their implementation. The strategies include the creation of four new National Parks, setting up an endangered species unit within CALM and increasing the protection of rare and endangered plant species. The forestry strategy, determined in conjunction with the Australian Heritage Commission, states that more than 100,000 ha of forest will be set aside in new National Parks, while the timber industry will be allowed to take its existing quota of timber from a smaller area of forest. It was claimed by the government agency that research had found additional timber resources within existing areas.

The forestry strategy was criticised by the Forest Industries Federation for missing an opportunity to harvest an extra 200,000 tonnes of timber each year at sustainable levels (*West Australian*, 6/2/92). Later, Dr Beth Schultz, for the Western Australian Conservation Council, launched a detailed criticism of the strategy (*West Australian*, 24/2/92), claiming that it would lock the woodchip industry into old growth, virgin forest for another decade, that much of the increased areas to be set aside as reserves are not forested and that additional areas of forest had in fact been made available to timber interests. As was indicated in last year's review, CALM's dual responsibilities of catering to timber interests *and* managing state-owned forests for flora and fauna conservation place it in an impossible position.

The third development is the current review of the state's Environmental Protection Act. A panel has been appointed, comprising an out-of-state environmental professional, a local industrialist and a local conservationist, and was due to report at the end of August 1992. Early in the review process, representatives of various interests, including the Environmental Protection Authority (EPA) itself, presented their views for discussion at a well-attended seminar. A spokesman for the mining industry wanted the EPA to be restricted to be dealing solely with what was quaintly termed 'technical matters', meaning the biophysical environment only and not human aspects of the environment. Similar, if somewhat less extreme views were presented by a spokesman for the Chamber of Commerce. Both wanted the EPA's powers to be severely curtailed.

Predictably, the EPA considered that it was doing an excellent job and brought an obligatory 'overseas expert' (an environmental lawyer from Manchester, England) to say so, albeit based on very flimsy evidence. Equally predictably, a conservation representative was less enthusiastic. The Act may well have excellent provisions and procedures for developing environmental policies, carrying out environmental impact assessments and controlling pollution. But the claim that Western Australia is leading Australia—if not the world—in these respects is exaggerated. For example, a recent paper by Harvey (1992) on the relationship between ecologically sustainable development and environmental impact assessment (EIA) in Australia, in the context of the proposed national approach to EIA, barely mentions the Western Australian legislation. More to the point, reference to the above discussion concerning the Select Committee's (1991) report, and to Figure 19.2, refutes any possible claim that the environment of Western Australia is being protected at all adequately. Worthy though many of the EPA's actions undoubtedly have been, there can be little doubt that much of the environmental protection effort in this state has been too narrowly focused on EIA and pollution control in relation to urban and industrial problems. Even so, at the same seminar the Minister for the Environment stated that in 1991 Perth had exceeded Sydney's air pollution levels. Moreover, the EPA's miserly budget of $8.6 million for a state of 2.5 million square kilometres is manifestly inadequate for the task of maintaining and improving, the state's environmental quality. There simply is little scope for the agency to deal with the complexity of problems relating to cumulative impact assessment and regional environmental planning and management over such a vast area.

The problem does not pertain solely to the EPA. Amongst other requirements, there is an urgent need to integrate environmental protection practices with soil conservation, forestry, catchment management, and regional planning and management processes, within the various Acts pertaining to the activities of the relevant agencies. The state's new planning legislation, in particular, continues to be stalled several years after drafting.

Numerous other issues have emerged during the past year, some important and others of purely local significance. They have included: an initiative by the EPA to encourage local governments to produce their own conservation plans after consulting community groups and developers; a proposal for World Heritage listing of 7 million ha of the Nullarbor Plain on the Western Australian side of the border, fiercely resisted by some 60 local pastoralists and local business operators; and a proposed multimillion dollar resort complex at 'Port' Kennedy, south of Perth. Conservationists have strongly opposed the latter proposal, which includes an international hotel, low cost holiday units, two golf courses, a marina and shopping centre in an area which is provisionally listed on the Register of the National Estate. But in the long run, the outcomes of the three developments outlined at the beginning of this report are likely to be of greater significance for the environmental future of the state.

Arthur Conacher

Queensland

The reporting period July 1991 to June 1992 essentially represents the mid-term period of the new state Labor government. Since this new government replaced the previous long-serving conservative government in late 1989, a significant number of planning and management issues have been raised for discussion along with a number of options for change.

The most important legislative action in the year was the passage into law of the Nature Conservation Act 1991. The Act is a long overdue consolidation and streamlining of nature conservation in the state, bringing together the nature conservation provisions of a range of older Acts concerning National Parks, environmental parks, flora and fauna conservation, and fisheries and habitat conservation into one Act. In so doing, some functions were moved from other Departments to the Conservation Division of the Department of Environment and Heritage. The most innovative feature of the Act is that it sets up the mechanism for voluntary conservation agreements between private land holders on the one hand and state and local governments on the other. While such agreements assist the achievement of conservation objectives on private land at low cost, their popularity and effectiveness remains to be proven.

The most recent period is characterised by a large number of initiatives which have or will result in policy changes with major consequences for the state's rural environment. Some of the more important initiatives relevant to rural areas are shown in Table 19.4.

Table 19.4 *Some recent policy initiatives relevant to rural areas in Queensland*

Department of Housing Local Government and Planning	• 'Planning. Is it too complex?' Discussion Paper • 'Planning provisions for heritage conservation', Guidelines • 'Towards a planning framework for government', Concept paper • 'Local authority bonding and other security arrangements for developments in Queensland', Discussion Paper • 'Preservation of Good Quality Agricultural Land', State Planning Policy Number 1 • 'Systems Review', Report and guidelines
Department of Environment and Heritage	• 'Environment Protection Legislation', Public consultation paper • 'Wet Tropics World Heritage Area—Strategic Directions', Draft strategic plan • 'Nature Conservation Act—section by section guide', explanation of legislation • 'Moreton Bay Strategic Plan—Proposals for Management', Draft plan and administrative structure • 'Brisbane River Management', Discussion paper • 'Management planning for National, Environment and Marine Parks of Bribie Island and Pumicestone Passage'
Department of Primary Industries	• 'Integrated Catchment Management', Draft strategy • 'Guidelines for the identification of good quality agricultural land', Guidelines
Department of Lands	• 'Land for the Future', New administrative processes
Queensland Treasury	• 'Private sector involvement in infrastructure development in Queensland', Policy and guidelines
Queensland Premier's Department	• 'Trinity Inlet Management Plan', joint State-Local management plan • 'Leading State', Key economic policy paper • 'Planning and construction approvals in Queensland—The Guide', Guidelines

There has been a shower of paper emanating from the bureaucracy which has new-found vigour, purpose and latitude. It remains to be seen how much of this new material, breathlessly released, will result in changes on the ground. An interesting observation concerning this flurry of publicly disseminated documents is the blurring of the conventional distinction between discussion papers, green papers and white papers as well confusion as to whether papers are issued by the bureaucracy as opposed to those of ministerial initiative.

The most far-reaching planning initiatives during the period were the commitment to regional planning and an amendment to the Local Government Planning and Environment Act 1990, which allow the state government to make statements of policy specifically binding on local government planning. During 1991 the first such policy statement was released, requiring that local governments assess Good Quality Agricultural Land in their plans and take it into account in consenting to new development. This state-planning policy is administered by the Department of Housing Local Government and Planning which changed its name in accordance with this new-found function. The adoption of this additional form of planning brings Queensland into line with the other mainland states in having clear state policies over land use and planning issues at the local level. There are many more policy statements to be added to this first one.

Regional planning

The state government is committed to regional planning with the SEQ2001 project (South East Queensland), the flagship for formal regional planning. This regional planning process, if it completes its tasks successfully, will provide a framework for future development of this rapidly expanding conurbation. Issues addressed include *inter alia* Agricultural Land, Nature Conservation, Rural Residential Development, Rivers and Coastal Management. Planning in Queensland has a very high level of community consultation and the process adopted in SEQ2001 includes an elaborate program of public consultation and involvement. The primary board advising the state Cabinet is the Regional Planning Advisory Group to which a secretariat and a whole range of committees and public meetings report directly or indirectly as set out below:

Regional Planning Advisory Group
   —State Ministers (4)
   —Local Government representatives (3)
   —Public interest group members (business, unions, environmental, professional, social welfare) (6)
Reference Groups
   —For public interest groups (4)

Working Groups
—For technical input into environment, urban design, transport issues
(4)

In addition to all these committees and representatives, the preparation of all planning papers results from public meetings in the community and submissions made to working parties and the SEQ2001 secretariat. Some people are now confused that the year 2001 will be the study completion date rather than the target planning date. This regional planning process has begun in the other major urban growth region of the state, the Far North Region centred on Cairns.

A further major rural planning initiative was initiated during the period, the Cape York Peninsula Land Use Study (CYPLUS). This joint Commonwealth-state initiative deals with one of the country's least developed regions and is concerned with significant planning issues such as: mining; Aboriginal Land claims; conservation; tourism; and the future of the cattle grazing industry so heavily affected by disease eradication programs. A potential commercial space-launching centre was the catalyst for this study.

Darryl Low Choy and Geoff McDonald

New Zealand

In the last review of rural planning in New Zealand (Willis, 1991), rural areas had been forced to cope with massive changes in the levels of government assistance due to removal of all agricultural subsidies, huge planning changes arising from the complete reorganisation of local government and a new planning act, the Resource Management Bill, which came into effect on 1 October 1991. In this review it is possible to report on the effects of these major changes further down the track.

Farmers appear to be coping tolerably well with the removal of subsidies and the creation of a level playing-field. Dairy farming especially is going through a boom period with most major dairy areas experiencing significant conversion to dairying from other land uses, mainly due to increased payments because of more favourable international prices and financial efficiencies at home. Dairy farm prices have returned to, and in some cases exceeded, their pre-1984 price levels, with an average farm now costing about half a million dollars. The average size of milking herd in New Zealand is now over 160 cows. Because of these high land values, a rather unusual migration south has been occurring, with at least 30 dairy farmers shifting to potential dairying areas in the South Island, such as Southland, in order to buy larger farms at cheaper prices. Unfortunately for them, the shift has coincided with one of the coldest, wettest winters on record, with

Christchurch, for example, receiving the heaviest snowfall it has experienced since 1945.

These adverse weather conditions have hit the sheep industry badly, at a time when at last prices for sheepmeat were beginning to rise. Initial estimates indicate the loss of around 50 per cent of the lamb flock for 1992, and this will prove very difficult for many debt-ridden South Island sheep producers already in a precarious financial situation as a result of the removal of subsidies, several years of drought and low returns for meat and wool products. The bad winter will also exacerbate the trend towards a fall in sheep numbers.

Total sheep numbers stood at over 67 million in 1986 but had dropped to 57 million by 1990 and will fall further (Ministry, 1991). While the total number of stock units has fallen, the drop in sheep numbers has been partly offset by an increase in beef cattle numbers, especially in the North Island, and a huge percentage increase in non-traditional livestock, for example, deer numbers increased by 150 per cent between 1986 and 1990 (Ministry, 1991).

These trends in the economic fortunes in New Zealand's main branches of farming have also been reflected in changes in the financial viability and numbers of traditional rural industries. On the one hand the trend in the dairy manufacturing industry has been rationalisation, increase in scale and greater output per worker. The classic case study is the region of Taranaki, where in the 1960s there were over 50 co-operative dairy factories, but in the 1992/93 season all the milk will be processed in one massive complex near Hawera.

In the meat freezing industry almost the opposite trend has occurred. While some meat freezing works have closed in urban areas there has been a significant increase of smaller specialised smaller export works in rural areas. The result has been more companies competing for fewer stock meaning many rationalisations, mergers and take-overs have arisen, and some closures have eventuated with more likely in future. Table 19.5 which is based on 1989 figures, illustrates these points.

The issue of indigenous rights to land and resources has also figured prominently in rural areas. Under the previous Labour Government, the Treaty of Waitangi was partially 'resurrected' as a kind of founding document guaranteeing Maori rights to land and fisheries, this being especially significant in the absence of any formal constitution in New Zealand. Consideration of Maori rights and culture was given further prominence in the Resource Management Act 1991, with one practical outcome being that Regional Councils are increasingly employing planners who have a knowledge of Maori language and culture. But the political realities of land and resource claims were well illustrated by the recent claim by the Ngai Tahu tribe to virtually all the fishing resources of New Zealand's South Island, not the mere 10 per cent guaranteed in the Maori Bill 1989. In an attempt to settle such claims, the government recently

Table 19.5   *Comparison of New Zealand's meat and dairy industries*

	Meat	Dairy
No. of factories	321	151
Persons employed	30,847	7,983
Tonnes of product	1,218,900	836,700
Value of exports	$2,421,000	$1,877,000
Exports per worker	$78,500	$235,120

offered the Maori a half share in New Zealand's largest fishing company, which was up for sale, on the understanding that this share would remove the need for any further compensation. Predictably enough, some tribes were not happy with this arrangement, firstly because they did not benefit as much as the major players, and also because they did not wish to jeopardise the treaty rights of future generations. Elements of the arrangement appear a good compromise, especially the possibilities of employment for young rural Maoris, whose rate of unemployment is over 25 per cent in some regions.

The major elements of the reorganised local government structure now appear to be in place, comprising regional councils and their constituent district councils. Certain government members still appear unhappy about the power of regional councils, especially the Minister of Local Government, Warren Cooper who continues his attacks on the unnecessary cost of the extra level of government as he sees it. He has actually succeeded in abolishing the Nelson Marlborough Regional Council, but most commentators see this as an isolated and special case.

The Resource Management Act is now firmly in place and Regional Councils are on a major learning curve as to how to implement its provisions. The Act replaces more than 20 major planning statutes, including the Town and Country Planning Act, Water and Soil Regulation, and laws covering minerals, geothermal resources, air and noise pollution and coasts. It is the first environmental regulation of its kind in the world and the main principle and purpose of the Act is to provide the sustainable management of natural and physical resources. The integration of statutes means that the environment as a whole must be looked at when authorities are planning and making decisions.

At present rural planning authorities are preparing management plans under the provisions of the Act in such areas as coasts, land use, water use, esplanade reserves and waste management. Critics of the Act say it places insufficient emphasis on social and economic issues and that the broad principles are too diffuse, difficult to define in practice and as yet untested by case law. A good example is hill country land use on much of New Zealand's broken tertiary hill country in the Central North Island.

What, farmers ask, is sustainable land use? The Act defines this very much in physical terms, for example one regional planning council deeming that all land greater than 48° in slope is too steep for grassland farming, too subject to erosion, and should therefore be planted in exotic forestry or left to reserves of natural vegetation. Most farmers, on the other hand, argue that sustainability is very much an 'economic' concept—that this steep land can be farmed profitably without severe degradation if prices are high enough.

No doubt these and other difficulties will occupy the energies of New Zealand's rural planners for many years to come.

Richard Willis

References

ABARE, 1992, *Resources Quarterly*, Australian Bureau of Agricultural and Resources Economics, Canberra

Anon, 1992, 'What can be done about blue-green algae?', *Ecos*, **14**: 14–19

Australia, 1990, *Ecologically sustainable development a Commonwealth Government discussion paper*, Australian Government Publishing Service, Canberra

Australia, Ecologically Sustainable Development Working Groups, 1992, *Final Report—executive summaries*, Australian Government Publishing Service, Canberra

Australia, Parliament, 1991, *Forest Conservation and Development Bill*, Canberra

Australia, Parliament, 1992, *Hansard*, Debate on Report of the Standing Committee on Rural and Regional Affairs, 'A national drought policy appropriate government responses to the recommendations of the Drought Policy Review Task Force', Canberra

Australia, Standing Committee on Rural and Regional Affairs, 1992, *A national drought policy: appropriate government responses to the recommendations of the Drought Policy Review Task Force*, Canberra

Bunker, R. and Houston, P., 1992, 'At and Beyond the Fringe: Planning Around Australian Cities', *Urban Policy Research* (in press)

Department of Environment and Planning, 1992, *Mount Lofty Ranges management plan: consultation draft*, Department of Environment and Planning, Adelaide

Foyel, J. and Houston, P, 1992, 'Planning in the rural-urban fringe: the challenge of perceived development rights and the significance of land-use systems', *Australian Planner*, **30**(1): 45–51

Hart, B.T., 1992, 'Ecological conditions of Australia's rivers', *Search*, **23**(1): 33–4

Harvey, N., 1992, 'The relationship between ecologically sustainable development and environmental impact assessment in Australia: a critique of recent national reports', *Environmental and Planning Law Journal*, **9**(4): 265–73

Standing Committee of the Australian and New Zealand Environment and Conservation Council, 1992, *A new focus for Australia's forests. Draft national forest policy statement*, Canberra